TRADESMEN and TRADERS

The World of the Guilds in Venice and Europe, *c.*1250 – *c.*1650

Richard Mackenney

CROOM HELM
London & Sydney

Croom Helm Ltd, Provident House, Burrell Row,
Beckenham, Kent BR3 1AT

Croom Helm Australia, 44-50 Waterloo Road,
North Ryde, 2113, New South Wales

British Library Cataloguing in Publication Data

Mackenney, Richard
Tradesmen and traders: the world of the guilds in Venice and Europe, c1250–c1650.
1. Guilds—Europe—History
I. Title
338.6'32'094 HD6456

ISBN 0–7099–1763–5

Printed and bound in Great Britain
by Billing & Sons Limited, Worcester.

Contents

Tables and Figures

Tables

Figures

For Mum and Dad and Linda

Preface

This book is based on some ten years of study and research in Venice, Cambridge and Edinburgh. Parts of it were used in a PhD thesis examined in Cambridge in 1982. I am deeply grateful to the Rotary Foundation for giving me the chance to study Venice in Venice, to the Hardings Educational Foundation of Aylesbury and to the SSRC for funding my research at Queens' College. Subsequent visits to London and Italy were made possible by a very generous grant from the British Academy at a time when further research would otherwise have been impossible. The University of Edinburgh funded a final excursion to check references. I am pleased to have the opportunity to thank all these bodies for their support for the project.

The personal influences which have shaped the production of the book have been equally important. In Cambridge itself the most significant were those of Professor G. R. Elton and Dr (now Professor) Jonathan Riley-Smith. The architecture of the book owes much to the helpful and searching examination of the dissertation carried out by Professor Charles Wilson and Dr David Chambers. I would like to thank all members of the Edinburgh History Department for their friendship and encouragement: especially Terry Cole, Ken Fowler, Rosemary and Hugh Gentleman, Maurice Larkin and Nick Phillipson. Angus MacKay and John Stephens have been most generous with their time and energy in commenting on drafts of the different chapters. Rob Bartlett laboured through the entire typescript and gave invaluable advice. In Venice, the staff of the Archivio di Stato have been consistently helpful, as have many other Venetians. For their kindness I thank Siegfriedo and Bruna Arguzzoni, Bruno and Carla Borsato, Paolo and Daniela Catapan,

Edoardo and Giuseppina Menegazzo Pipa and Loredana Potz, Massimo and Nadia Schiavon, Giuliano and Sandra Soldani, Gianni and Daniela Vignati, and above all Fortunato and Sandra Selandari. Some influences have transcended geographical distances. I am especially aware of what my work owes to Nick and Sarah Davidson, to Peter Laven and to Stephen Lees. I must also thank Bruce Hunter, Richard Stoneman and Mark Barragry for their patience during the protracted process of production, Geoffrey Parker for some wise words as the book neared completion, and Alison Munro for her work on large parts of the typescript. Most especially, I must thank Brian and Janet Pullan for their friendship, hospitality and countless helpful suggestions. The book could not have been written without Brian's work and anything of worth it may contain owes much to his influence. My family have lent untiring support in often difficult times, especially Rob and Lyn, Roger and Jane, and George and Thelma. The dedication to my wife and parents is intended as recognition of what they have had to put up with.

The kindness and encouragement of all these have saved me from innumerable errors. Many others no doubt remain, and for those I alone am responsible.

RICHARD MACKENNEY
Edinburgh

Introduction

This study of guilds over a period of four centuries is an attempt to reassess the importance of a generally neglected institution in the context of a city which is particularly attractive to historians. The book was conceived — or rather misconceived — as an investigation of three forces whose varying relationship had a formative influence on the civilisation of Western Europe: capitalism, absolutism and popular culture. When applied to the documentary evidence of a single city, these great concepts dissolved into a much more amorphous reality. One of the decisive solvents was religion, which constantly impinged on economic activity and exerted a significant influence on a guildsman's political and cultural outlook. Such at least is the impression left by the Venetian evidence, which is dominated by two institutions, the *arte* or trade guild and the *scuola*, a devotional confraternity which was often associated with an occupational group, but which frequently transcended the boundaries of craft or parish.

From this evidence, the book attemprations. The title *Tradesmen and Traders* identifies the most significant impression left by the documents: that the gulf between craftsmen and merchants, workers and businessmen, production and investment, was once hard to distinguish, partly because of the peculiarly dynamic relationship of mind and hand which characterises the civilisation of the Renaissance.

The study of guilds

Guild associations have obscure origins.[1] In this book the term is used to describe the organisations which began to crystallise in the towns of Europe from the thirteenth century: free associations of laymen who acknowledged a common identity as townsmen, as practitioners of the same trade, as spiritual brothers. Such groupings were especially prominent in the communities which formed on the great urban axis of medieval Europe from Flanders through Germany and into northern Italy. Guilds were the component parts of the medieval city-state, regulating markets, electing councillors, offering aid — some material, some spiritual — to members. By the sixteenth century, they were apparently in decline. In an age of expansion, the concentration on a fixed membership had emphasised their exclusiveness, the protection of professional secrets denied them access to an expanding labour market, and they were thus outflanked by merchant capitalists. In political life, guilds decayed with urban liberties, surviving, if at all, for their fiscal utility, not their effectiveness as a form of economic organisation.

It is the misfortune of guilds to have been studied too often as abstractions rather than as groups of people, and too often in the narrow context of craft manufacture. Little is known about the role of guilds in commercial economies, and little has been done to explain why guilds could help foster economic growth in the Middle Ages, fail to be part of another phase of expansion in the sixteenth century and then be responsible for the decline of certain economies, especially in Italy, in the seventeenth. Nor have historians paid much attention to the economic life of guilds in its political and cultural context. The chapters which follow try to broaden the setting of guild-based economies to take in a wider milieu. This can be achieved only in the case of a city whose political and cultural history is relatively well known.

The study of Venice

In contrast to guilds, the city of Venice has exercised a consistent attraction on historians. In the last ten years or so, however, historical study of the city has widened and intensified. The distinctive features of the Venetian Republic were its commercial economy and its strong sense of state sovereignty.[2] It used to be thought that the unique stability of the city was to be explained by a perfect constitution, and, from the sixteenth century onwards, this myth captivated Europeans seeking permanence in a world of alarming change. Nowadays, scholars are more occupied with the reality: the machinery of government, the social institutions which looked to the needs of the poor.[3] Even so, relatively little has been done to assess the human foundations of the city's stability. In this one area the city of Venice is neglected — partly, one suspects, because it involves the unfashionable subject of guilds. In the census of 1563, some 120,000 souls in a population of about 170,000 were described as artisans and their families.[4] Not all of them were members of guilds in the sense of being formally enrolled, but the openness of Venetian corporations meant that they touched the lives of a vast number of ordinary people in a variety of significant ways. This, then, is the world of the guilds, the world of three-quarters of the people of Venice. This book is about the balance of human forces on which the Republic's unique stability was founded, though the limitations of the evidence prevent us from weighing those forces as precisely as we would like.

The Venetian evidence

The documents used in this study were found in the State Archive in Venice. Most of the data were assembled from the systematic exploitation of the records of the trade guilds (*arti*) and devotional confraternities (*scuole*). These have been related to the published statutes of the guilds, originally drawn up in the thirteenth century. Those records give some idea of the structures of guild life and the deeds of guildsmen. Two other bodies of evidence relate to their words: their depositions before the tribunal of the Holy Office, their protests to the government over the supply of oarsmen for the fleet in the early seventeenth century. The sources are described in full in the bibliography. For the sake of brevity I have kept references in the footnotes as concise as possible. In addition, the book draws heavily on the work of Frederic Lane and Fernand Braudel, and it reads back to the Middle Ages some of the conclusions reached by Richard Rapp for the seventeenth century. As will be clear throughout, the book owes a great debt to the work of Brian Pullan: the tradesmen and traders encountered here had their place between the rich and the poor whom he himself has described so vividly. The basis of what is said about cities other than Venice is altogether more general.

The choice of comparisons

The comparative essays which follow each chapter are designed to offer general ideas about the uniqueness of Venice and the role of guilds in European urban life from the thirteenth century to the seventeenth. The vast bulk of material used is drawn from secondary sources, the comments and conclusions are often speculative and impressionistic. This may result in a discrepancy between the Venetian detail and generalisations about other cities. However, it is easy to treat Venice as a special case without explaining precisely why, and it seemed worthwhile trying to set the city in a European context. A balance is attempted between traditional centres like Florence and the great boom towns of the sixteenth and seventeenth centuries like Lyons, London and Amsterdam, and the selection is based on the available work of historians who have studied major commercial and financial centres.

The symmetry of the first five chapters is abandoned in the last which avoids the problems of comparing the city of Venice and the experience of centralised territorial states: this is a measure of how much of the history of the Venetian state remains unwritten. A good deal of the comparative work also shows how little detail is generally available on guilds in virtually any European city. Though this book is influenced by ideas of 'total history', there are significant gaps in the coverage — demography, the family, women, the neighbourhood — which one justifies because the evidence consulted — mostly compiled by guildsmen themselves — did not say anything significant about them. The absence of a general conclusion is intentional: this book does not set out to say the last word about guilds, Venice, or even the guilds of Venice. On the positive side, the different perspectives on economic, cultural and political history opened up by a study of guild materials in Venice allow room for the hope that the historical fraternity may exploit such documents in the record offices of other cities.

Notes

1. See in general A. Black, *Guilds and Civil Society in European Political Thought from the 12th Century to the Present* (London, 1984); F. Braudel, *Civilisation and Capitalism, 15th–18th Centuries*, trans. S. Reynolds, 3 vols. (London, 1982), vol. 3 *The Perspective of the World*, pp. 92–110; and in particular E. Coornaert, 'Des confrèries carolingiens aux gildes marchandes', *Mélanges d'Histoire Sociale*, vol. 2 (1942), pp. 5–21; idem, 'Les gildes mediévales (5e–13e siècles): définition–évolution', *Revue Historique*, vol. 199 (1947), pp. 22–55, 208–43.

2. B. S. Pullan, 'The Significance of Venice', *Bulletin of the John Rylands University Library of Manchester*, vol. 56 (1974), pp. 433–62; Braudel, *The Perspective of the World*, pp. 116–37.

3. On the Middle Ages, see in particular S. Chojnacki, 'Crime, Punishment and the '300 Venetian State', in L. Martines (ed.), *Violence and Civil Disorder in Italian Cities, 1200–1500* (Berkeley and Los Angeles, 1972), pp. 184–228; D. Queller, 'The Civic Irresponsibility of the Venetian Nobility', *Explorations in Economic History*, vol. 7 (1969–70), pp. 223–35. On the Renaissance, see J. C. Davis, *The Decline of the Venetian Nobility as a Ruling Class* (Baltimore, Md., 1962); B. S. Pullan, *Rich and Poor in Renaissance Venice: The Social Institutions of a Catholic State* (Oxford, 1971); idem, 'Service to the Venetian State: Aspects of Myth and Reality in the Early 17th Century', *Studi Seicenteschi*, vol. 5 (1964), pp. 110–47; G. Cozzi, 'Authority and the Law in Renaissance Venice', in J. R. Hale (ed.), *Renaissance Venice* (London, 1974), pp. 293–345.

4. K. J. Beloch, 'La popolazione di Venezia nei sec. 16 e 17', *NAV*, new ser., vol. 3, pt. i (1902), p. 14; A. Contento, 'Il censimento della popolazione sotto la Repubblica veneta', *NAV*, vol. 19, pt. ii (1900), p. 180; D. Beltrami, *Storia della popolazione di Venezia dalla fine del sec, 16 alla caduta della Repubblica* (Padua, 1954), pp. 80–2.

THE MAGISTRATES OF THE MILIZIA DA MAR

A. del Moro

The magistrates pay money for the maintenance of the fleet to Mars (right) while St Mark (left) looks on

1

Guilds and the Medieval Polity, *c.*1250–*c.*1400

Introduction

The importance of guilds in the history of medieval towns has long been established and can scarcely be exaggerated. By the thirteenth century, the economic and political life of most European cities revolved around these corporations and the principles of association and mutual aid which separated them from the feudal world. Guilds organised the production of the goods which could be sold in exchange for food; they organised the production of clothing and the building of houses; they regulated the markets around which urban communities had grown up; they often gave shape to political life through the merchants, and later the craftsmen, who sat on city councils. In short, guilds organised supply, regulated manufacture and installed the principle of corporate association at the centre of urban politics. Moreover, they established mutual aid schemes for members — conviviality at an annual banquet, modest financial support in the event of illness or accident, commemoration of the dead — and frequently played a distinctive part in a city's cultural life through their participation in festivals and processions.[1]

The different strands which make up the thread of guild history are impossible to distinguish: economic, political and religious life constantly interacted and were probably not perceived as different by members themselves. This chapter is essentially concerned with the place occupied by guilds in economic life and city politics in the thirteenth and fourteenth centuries, but in Venice in particular it will be seen that the religious fraternity played a central part in defining the place of guilds in the constitution and in society.

The discussion, then, is about foundations and the structures built upon them. But the process of development, the work of building, did not take place in a constant climate and did not always proceed smoothly. The period with which we are dealing divides roughly into two: a phase of general expansion in the thirteenth and early fourteenth centuries, a phase of contraction and recession in the aftermath of the Black Death of 1348. Both were accompanied by turbulence.

The first wave broke most violently in the towns which were in the vanguard of economic advance, especially Flanders and northern Italy. There was violence in Douai in 1245, Arras in 1253, Genoa in 1258 and 1276, Siena in 1257, Viterbo in 1281, Bologna in 1289, Florence in 1293–95.[2] The later fourteenth century saw more general discontent in the aftermath of demographic collapse. Paradoxically, the ravages of plague increased the prosperity of many of the survivors by raising the price of wage-labour. But the social and political implications of prosperity among the common people produced a fierce reaction among the great. In England under a feudal monarchy or in Florence under capitalist oligarchs, the authorities sought to check the ascent of newly prosperous groups. The clash of the urge to climb and the impulse to trash for overtopping produced violent unrest. Such was the background to the guild revolts in German towns, the 'peasant' rebellion in England (which had a strong urban dimension), the *Ciompi* revolution in Florence.[3] Guildsmen and artisans, especially in the textile trades, were prominent in both phases of violence. However, despite evidence of tension in the thirteenth century and despite sharp points of crisis in the ruling class in 1310 and 1355 there were no popular rebellions in Venice. Indeed, until 1797, Venice stood aloof from the turmoil which disrupted the ordering of other European states. In 1380, Venetians united to crush the Genoese fleet which threatened to take the city, all social groups harnessed to a common goal, whilst around them the traditional order in both feudal monarchies and city-states seemed to be about to collapse.

The exclusion of the common people from Venetian politics was virtually complete by 1300. How then had the Venetian *popolo* come to terms with a political system which gave them no part to play in the life of the state? Why did economic problems and political uncertainties leave Venice unscathed? Can a detailed study of guilds in a single city shed light on the more general problems of economic and political life in the later Middle Ages?

The Venetian experience

The guilds of Venice are usually cited as an exception to the pattern of corporate life in medieval cities. The guilds, known as *arti*, had no place in Venetian overseas trade, and after 1297 their members were denied even the prospect of involvement in the government of the city. Venetian merchants engaged in the buying and selling of goods, and the wealth they gained overseas was the basis of political power.[4] There were no merchant guilds in Venice, but the city's economic life revolved around what merchant guilds elsewhere sought to promote and protect: the staple.[5] From the thirteenth century, the association of commercial and political dominion in the Adriatic drew to the Rialto market goods from both East and West and the exchange was regulated by Venetian merchants who profited from the process of buying and selling.[6] The assertion of one scholar that Venetian merchants did not need a guild 'because they were living in one' is an exaggeration, as we shall see, but it nevertheless expresses an important truth about the Venetian economy.[7] Even in the thirteenth century, one discerns that Venetians — whether they were patrician merchants or ordinary shopkeepers — were essentially brokers engaged in the provision of services. There was no sharp division between merchants and producers, and at an early stage the guild system itself was based upon units which were not 'greater' and 'lesser' companies but which shared a similar status somewhere between the two. Put another way, in Venice the guilds helped shape an economic life where 'capital' and 'labour' did not clash, and this had vital implications for the city's political stability — something which constitutional arrangements alone could never have ensured.

The 'constitutional arrangements' were themselves a reflection of the Venetian economy. By the end of the thirteenth century, the merchant oligarchs were able to put the finishing touches to a constitution which gave an exclusive group of patricians a democracy amongst themselves and a collective sovereign power over the rest of society. All other Venetians, by contrast, were shut out of politics. As will be suggested in due course, the closing of the corridors of power to all non-patricians might be seen as part of a more comprehensive economic and political process, a design which involved the systematic subordination of the populace to the will of the city's merchant rulers in the years after 1260.[8]

What has to be explained, or at least investigated, is why,

despite the predominance of mercantile interests in politics, the common people never seriously challenged their authority. Whether this was because the Venetian government was in a strange way 'representative' of the interests of the community at large is an open question. This chapter is designed around the idea that the economic life of Venetian guilds needs to be set firmly in its political context: the elaboration of the Venetian state in the thirteenth century. In the medieval context, the crucial point is that although they were excluded from direct participation in political life, Venetian guildsmen enjoyed a clearly defined position before a generally recognised body of law. They enjoyed access to courts presided over by magistrates who, on the whole, did not represent interests within the guild structure itself. The Venetian artisan's rights of appeal contrast sharply with the situation in Florence. There, a large proportion of the workforce was excluded from the guilds altogether and any right of appeal against the authority of the guild tribunal was specifically denied. The historian of guilds stands before an institution which can look like the protector of members' interests, the medium of state control and the outlet for religious aspiration. The interaction of these characteristics made them of singular importance in the formation of the Venetian state.

Contrasts with the guilds of other cities will be pursued in the third part of the chapter. Before any comparisons can be made, however, we must try to define the precise character of Venetian guilds and the groups of the Venetian population which they embraced.

Guilds as social institutions

The guilds of Venice had two components, whose functions look separate to us, but which in the thirteenth century or even the sixteenth were inextricably linked.[9] The *arte* was a trade guild, an association of those practising the same occupation. Since exclusiveness through rigid demarcation is often seen as an essential characteristic of guilds, it is intriguing to note that in medieval Venice, guilds were often federations of related trades, a flexibility which was to prove crucial to the city's economy in the sixteenth century. The guilds themselves often subdivided. The hemp spinners split into the *ars grossa* and the *ars suptile*, the furriers into the *ars nova* and the *ars vetera*, the doctors into physicians and surgeons. The sawyers had their own statute but worked as part of the guild of house carpenters. The warden of the metalworkers was chosen by electors from the smiths, cauldron-makers and armourers. The fustian weavers formed a guild which included throwsters and beaters as well, and there were six branches of the painters' guild — *dipintori*, painters of shields, painters of saddles, painters of chests, painters of pictures and painters of furniture.[10]

The corporate organisation which could include members from different trades was a religious confraternity, a *scuola*. This institution must be examined in detail if the guilds of Venice are to be fully understood. The *scuola dell'arte*, that is the confraternity associated with a trade guild, was a species of social club which existed for banqueting, the distribution of alms and the provision of burial. In other towns, especially those of northern Europe, trade guilds and confraternities were usually coterminous. This assertion is much more difficult to make in the case of Venice where craftsmen were members of an *arte* and would go on to set up their own *scuola* as a distinct organisation. As we shall see in Chapter 2, the *scuola* existed as a purely religious organisation, its members linked by ties of religious brotherhood grouped round the cult of a saint, a particular 'nation' and, by the mid-sixteenth century, the cult of the eucharist.[11] The difference between the *scuola* and the *arte* is perhaps best summed up by the fact that a craft guild could institute its own confraternity, but the reverse was unlikely to occur.

The interaction of the confraternity and the guild took a variety of forms and the closeness of the relationship needs to be stressed. There is some evidence, for instance, that not all members of a *scuola* engaged in the trade identified with the *arte*. The fustian weavers, who formed an *arte* in about 1275, did not expel those who did not practise the trade until 1289.[12] The confraternity usually fulfilled a financial function: one-third of the fines imposed on the tradesman were generally payable to his *scuola*. On the acceptance of an apprentice's masterpiece, his qualification for the status of master in the trade or craft, two-thirds of the fee were given to the confraternity. Immigrant workers were expected to join the confraternity appropriate to their trade.[13]

As an extract from the skeiners' statute illustrates, the confraternity helped define the social and legal role of the guilds in Venetian life. The authors of the statute were

> anxious to reform the guild of skeiners and to ensure that no-one may be deceived by any members of the guild through dishonest work, by binding the guild together as a true confraternity of brothers under a set of rules as the other guilds are bound by oath.

The oath gave the *arte* its politcal identity and defined its constitutional position, the confraternity was the forum for its social activities. Various dues were paid by members 'to sustain the poor and infirm of the guild'. Money from subscriptions and fines was spent on the annual banquet, visiting the sick and burying the dead. All such activities were a vital source of support when the need for clothes or the loss of earning capacity through sickness could raise the cost of living which on the whole seems to have been modest.[14]

Funds were collected at the annual banquet or *pastum*. The close relationship of conviviality and philanthropy in the confraternity is indicated by the occasional reference to a *pastum sive caritas*. The cappers used to dine, give alms and elect officers on the same day. And it is essential to point out that the guilds' social functions were not confined to an élite of masters, at least prior to the fifteenth century.[15]

It was the masters, however, who were expected to be present at the banquet unless they had a good excuse and they made their contribution to costs beforehand, whether or not they attended. Master turners paid 10 soldi and journeymen 6 'for the feast and for the candles'. If some members were too poor to pay, the fee could be waived at the discretion of the guild's officers.[16] Amongst the barbers, even apprentices were expected to make a contribution to the cost of candles 'on the day of the feast', though we cannot be sure that they actually joined the masters to dine.[17]

In a fundamental sense, then, the *scuola* was a charitable institution, in that its members were joined together by the principle of *caritas*. This term usually described love between equals, while philanthropy practised by the better-off towards the disadvantaged was known as *misericordia*.[18] The *scuola* encouraged the suspension of everyday divisions of status and members enjoyed a certain equality as Christians and Venetians. Certainly, 'the poor' referred to in the statutes were not all masters. The doublet-makers celebrated a feast 'inter se et inter pauperibus pro anima fratrum' and a similar practice obtained amongst the fishmongers. The glassworkers held a banquet 'with a group of poor men'. The skeiners gave their leftovers to the poor and the carpenters sold anything that remained from the meal and returned the money to their *scuola* to be distributed as alms.[19]

Most members, it would seem, were eligible for some form of relief. The potters' guild gave sickness benefits to journeymen.[20] All guild officers were obliged to visit sick members or delegate others to do so. Failure or refusal was punishable with a fine.[21]

The solidarity inherent in *caritas* extended to the dead as well as the living. Attendance at the funeral of a departed brother guildsman was one of the most solemn expressions of fraternity. It was compulsory in any guild that all members be present.[22] Masters might be expected to pay their last respects 'at the house where the body lies'. A member who died outside the city might still be commemorated by his comrades in the city.[23] The skeiners were quite specific in their delineation of what was required. Members were expected to stay for the whole service and to carry a candle worth at least fourpence. The importance of candles in Venetian devotional life and of wax in the economy are subjects to which we shall often return.[24] Workshops closed on the day of a funeral — which could be that of a journeyman doublet-maker, commemorated with five 'our fathers', or the wife of an oil vendor, whose funeral stopped work in the guild as would that of a master.[25]

The setting of these activities is more easily discussed for the fifteenth century when we can trace the number of *scuole* and the altars they maintained and embellished. In the earlier period, it looks as though Santa Maria dell'Ascensione, a monastery of the Knights Templar which once stood at San Marco, was something of a centre for guild devotion. There the doublet-makers had a burial place for members and they and the carpenters kept candles burning at altars in the church. Here too the ironmongers met for their banquet.[26]

The character and functions of the *scuola* mean that the life of Venetian guilds must be viewed historically in a context larger than that of workshop or market place. What is distinctively Venetian about Venetian guilds must be investigated in terms of the relationship of occupational group and devotional confraternity to each other, to the state and to the Church. Having defined what a guild was in the thirteenth century, we must now turn to what those who belonged to guilds did and how marketplace and workshop fitted into the pattern of the city's economic life.

The relation of guilds and government

In economic terms, it is easier to define what Venetian guilds were not than what they were. To talk of 'middling guilds' somewhere between the division of 'greater' and 'lesser' which obtained in Florence or London, still leaves the parameters of the subject imprecise. In medieval Venice, the guild system did *not* divide between merchant capitalists and dependent producers, or even, before the fifteenth century, between masters and men. This was most likely to happen in the textile industries and the absence of large-scale cloth manufacture may well have helped Venetians to avoid the clash of interests which characterises the histories of other medieval towns. In Venice, it is impossible to discern clear 'class' lines from occupational titles. In records relating to the trades of the city, *fabbro* could refer to an ironmonger or a blacksmith while a 'mercer' might be a merchant or a street pedlar.

How can we establish a more positive framework for the discussion? Perhaps the starting point should be that the Venetian economy depended on commerce rather than manufacture. Where industrial handicrafts were important, as in shipbuilding, specific aspects of the organisation of work help to explain the absence of tensions between employers and workforce. The balance of economic interests which the guild statutes sought to establish was embodied in a clear legal framework supervised by magistrates whose own interests did not threaten that balance.

The city's merchant patricians were engaged in overseas trade which distanced them, geographically, economically and politically, from the world of craftsmen and producers in the city itself. The most valuable commodities were thus monopolised by a merchant nobility who invested in and profited from Venice's position 'astride a river of gold'.[27] Venetian merchants did not form guilds. Their companies might be based on family interests and these were protected by a staple which gave local merchants exclusive handling rights in certain commodities. Professor Lane sums up the position when he states that 'all the merchant nobles of Venice operated as one large regulated company of which the board of directors was the Senate'.[28]

In the guild system itself, no great textile industry dominated the economy. The guilds of Venice did not stand apart from or over a mass of *sottoposti* instrumental in making profits for merchant capitalists yet denied a voice in the running of the guild and forbidden to form their own. The guilds fulfilled a dual function as administrative units for the government, and as associations of craftsmen.[29]

The danger inherent in this cosy characterisation is that one idealises the vision of a united polity. The absence of contending economic interests may have contributed to Venice's political stability in turbulent times: so too did government policy — and policing. One should avoid any notion that members of the government occupied themselves with the interests of international commerce and left the guilds to themselves. There were numerous bodies which sought to control the life of the populace directly or indirectly through the guilds. It is worth cataloguing the most important of them.

The *Giustizia Vecchia* was responsible for the supervision of the *arti*, approving and imposing statutes on the city's trades throughout the thirteenth and fourteenth centuries. Established in 1173 to standardise weights and measures, the magistrates sanctioned the guilds' regulations and quality controls and used these regulations to protect the consumer by making them a sort of Trade Descriptions Act. One of its offices became a separate magistracy in 1261, as the *Giustizia Nova*, mainly concerned with foodstuffs and the supervision of taverns and the wine trade. Oil vending was subject to the office of the *Ternaria* (1225), though the guild itself remained subject to the *Giustizia Vecchia*.

It is significant that the textile industries were recognised as having special characteristics and problems best dealt with by separate officials. In the thirteenth century the silk industry remained under the control of the *Giustizia Vecchia*, while woollen cloth manufacture, such as it was, became the responsibility of the *Provveditori di Comun*. They continued to supervise the industry, though somewhat remotely, even after the establishment of the *Camera del Purgo* in the sixteenth century, unusual in Venice in that it was an association of employers.[30]

We cannot be sure how many Venetians belonged to guilds in the Middle Ages, nor can we relate disturbances or the lack of them to movements of wage rates and bread prices: the evidence has yet to be unearthed. Such evidence as survives takes the form of statutes, regarded with suspicion because the pronouncements they embody may not have been reflected in enforcement.[31] For the later period, the relation of rulebook to reality may be investigated more rigorously. For the thirteenth and fourteenth centuries, guild statutes can still tell us a good deal about the underlying structure of the Venetian state and what it was supposed to mean to the ruled.

This raises the problem of how far guilds represented 'the ruled'. Venetian *arti* may, as elsewhere, be seen as organisations for people of the middling sort. The width and diversity of that social stratum raises some doubts as to whether the guilds excluded poor masses who simmered between penury and revolt. The Venetians recognised many more trades as being worthy of organisation into separate guilds, and opted for careful division of labour. This had the additional effect of fragmenting the working population and inhibiting anything resembling class conflict. The *Giustizia Vecchia* itself registered the statutes of 52 guilds between 1218 and 1330. Over a similar timespan Florence never had more than 21 guilds, Bologna 13.[32] The period of most intense activity comes at an intriguing moment in Venetian history. Between October and December 1271, twelve new and revised statutes were presented for the magistrates' approval. The great religious confraternities, the *Scuole Grandi*, had been given formal recognition in the 1260s. Doge Lorenzo Tiepolo's election of 1268 had been greeted with extraordinary enthusiasm by the populace. The *Serrata* of 1297 set an end to the political ambitions of those whom it excluded from eligibility for office. Do these events represent the struggle — or at least the changing balance — between an 'ambitious element of unrest' in the *popolo* and an oligarchy of *grandi* which eventually triumphed? Whatever one may think of the idea of great subcutaneous tension, the magistrates of 1271 were among the most prominent to hold office at the *Giustizia Vecchia* and were likely to have sought to restrain the political aspirations of the *popolo* by any means at their disposal, as we shall see in due course.[33] But before we can assess the guilds' place in the city's constitution, we must survey those areas of the economy in which the *arti* were involved.

The organisation of guild economic life in the thirteenth and fourteenth centuries

The guilds represented in the statutes presented to the *Giustizia Vecchia* fall into three major categories: shipbuilding in the Arsenal; handicraft and manufacture in the city itself (a category which requires further subdivision); and — an intriguing insight into the government's urge to control — guilds of officials who supervised the other two groups. The guilds were, in other words, vital links between the commercial, industrial and administrative life of the city physically represented by the Rialto markets, the Arsenal and the government offices at San Marco.[34]

The Arsenal

When speaking of Venice's fundamentally commercial character, it is easy to overlook the fact that even in the thirteenth century the Arsenal was the biggest industrial concentration in pre-industrial Europe.[35] Dante's often quoted lines from the *Inferno* bear repetition, for to the poet the noise and horror of the place were fiercely evocative of hell:

As in the Venetian Arsenal
In winter, pitch boils like glue
To seal unsound ships
Which are not fit for sea, then
Someone refits his ship, another plugs
The ribs of a much voyaged vessel
Someone hammers at the prow, another the poop
Someone works to mend the mizzen, another the mainsail
So, not by fire, but by art divine
Boiled a thick mass which smeared the bank at every turn.
(*Inferno*, canto xxi, ll. 7–18)

The image of heat and dark seems closer to Coalbrookdale than Castello and it is only proper to emphasise how much Venetian commerce depended on foundries, factories and yards which seem precursors of the industrial age.

The Arsenal trades were organised into guilds, studied with vast authority by Professor Lane. Ropemakers registered their statute as early as 1233, the sawyers and oarmakers in 1262, carpenters, caulkers and smiths in 1271. By the fifteenth century, the ropemakers worked in a group 100-strong in a factory, by the sixteenth the production-line in the shipyards could fit out a galley in less than a day. Arms manufacturers such as bowyers and smiths produced weapons in quantities which amazed visitors.[36]

Yet Arsenal workers were no proletariat. They were a highly skilled labour aristocracy who formed the Doge's bodyguard and who could expect donatives from visitors to the city.[37] The picture is clear: high wages, high productivity in a highly complicated site which housed a vast number of workers engaged in many different trades. Yet they were still grouped in guilds. The demarcation inherent in any craft organisation did not prevent gang bosses from hiring tradesmen with different skills for building a ship: few could argue that guilds stood in the way of eocnomic advance in the Arsenal of medieval Venice.

The city

There were private boatyards (*squeri*) in the city itself but no separate guild was organised until 1589.[38] Even in the thirteenth century, the city trades were notable for their diversity, though we can make some sense of this by organising them round the general categories of food, clothing, household items and building.

Corn chandlers formed a guild, buying, presumably, from the aristocratic merchants who imported wheat from Sicily, Egypt, Greece and the Balkans. The government allowed anyone to bring grain into the city, presumably to keep full the public granaries depicted in the mosaics of San Marco. Oddly, the statute of the bakers was not registered until 1333. Perhaps before then Venetians ground their own corn and baked their own bread.[39] The fishmongers registered their statute in 1227 and were certainly selling wholesale at the Rialto by the fourteenth century. The oil measurers' statute was confirmed in 1227, that of the oil vendors in 1263: they too rubbed shoulders with bankers at the Rialto. Fresh water was also ensured. A guild of sand suppliers was established in 1280 and much of their statute is concerned with the provision of fine quality sand for use in the filtration process in the city's wells.[40]

Despite the absence of a major woollen industry the *Giustizia Vecchia* itself supervised many trades associated with textiles and clothing. The dyers had a statute as early as 1243, but they probably finished cloth which came from outside the city. Silk throwsters registered their statute in 1265, well before the arrival of the Lucchese who helped the industry to flourish in the fourteenth century. Makers of linen and fustian formed a guild in 1275, perhaps in response to the thriving cotton trade, and the skeiners were recognised through a statute of 1289. Spare parts for the industry were provided by the comb makers (1279) and spindle makers (1282). Clothes-makers and sellers were also prominent: tailors and doublet-makers had the earliest statutes (1218 and 1219, respectively) and there were two guilds of secondhand dealers (1233 and 1278) as well as hatters (1279) and cappers (1281). Tanning and bleaching were carried on at the Giudecca and statutes were registered for the appropriate guilds in 1271 and 1276. Cobblers' and furriers' work made less of a smell and they practised in the city itself (both trades were recognised in 1271).[41]

As in the Arsenal, economic life in the city was not inhibited by guild demarcation. The work of distributing and retailing a wide variety of wares was carried on by the mercers, whose statute was confirmed in 1271 and who, by the mid-fifteenth century, were becoming the commercial powerhouse of the guild network. They sold textiles — usually of high quality — which groups them with luxury traders. They provided churches with rich fabrics, altar cloths and vestments. Gold thread in such items would have been supplied by goldsmiths (statute 1233), whose stalls stood at Rialto, then as now. The painters' statute dates from 1271, and two guilds dealt in glassware (1271 and 1319).[42]

More mundane household items and packaging for the wares which poured into the city were supplied by the ironmongers (1271). There were guilds of coopers (1259) and turners (1300) and earthenware was provided by the potters (1301). The bell-founders had a statute registered in 1282.

Statutes connected with the building trades were registered at an early stage — kilnmen (1221) and brick porters (1222) pre-date by half a century the house carpenters and wallers (both 1271) and the stonemasons (1307). As early as the fourteenth century, the cooperation of workmen from different trades in loosely organised workgangs parallels the organisation we have already observed at the Arsenal and indicates the flexibility with which the guild system met the city's economic needs. By the early fifteenth century, as many as 64 workmen from different trades could be engaged on site at the Ca' d'Oro.

Medicines, and no doubt medical advice, were available from barbers (1270). Physicians and apothecaries (both 1258) did not have their own officers and were kept under the direct control of the magistrates.[43] In other cases, state invervention was less overt.

Government regulation

The activities of the various trades were often supervised by government officials also organised into *arti*. These guilds operated in the Arsenal where they checked that imported naval hardware was made to specification (a statute of 1289) and inspected the composition of pitch (1301). In the city itself, weights and measures were supervised by other inspectors (1262). Another such organisation was set up to check the quality of precious metals (1278) and they also made a twice-yearly inspection of the goldsmiths' weights and measures.[44]

Control is evident in other ways. The use of trademarks made it easier to trace counterfeit goods. The mark was not transferable. This was specified in the rules of the bowyers and cappers. The bellmakers had to stamp their work and required a further seal of approval from the magistrates. The seal of the commune was also attached to fustians and wine jars, and vessels used to measure oil and corn were also standardised. Crossbows and shoe soles were subject to standard specifications. There were regulations which governed the size of a sandbarge and a limit on how far it could be immersed in water when loaded. The government even took a hand in fixing prices — those of wood and stone for the brickmakers, of oil for the pork butchers, and the price of gold was related to the market value of the ducat.[45]

These regulations are important in a variety of ways. They show the dual utility of guilds: to artisans as units which protected trade standards, to the state as administrative units which were convenient regulatory mechanisms. The statutes aimed at least to use the guilds as a means of balancing public and private interests in everyday economic life. This concern for the mundane seems to be part of the more general process of definition which the Venetian polity was undergoing in the later thirteenth century.[46]

Such were the trades supervised by the *Giustizia Vecchia*. The survey of the city remains only partial for it omits wool and silk which were less important in Venice than in other medieval cities, but which were to grow into significant industries in a later period.

Woollen cloth

The Venetian woollen industry started 'virtually from scratch' in the sixteenth century. However, there is evidence of some activity in this sphere in the earlier period; clearly the contrast with Florence can be overdrawn.[47] Professor Cracco has asserted that the industry was strangled at birth as a threat to the commercial interests which dominated the city. This seems altogether too crude, for three reasons. First, if the absence of a cloth industry was the result of government policy then it may reflect a desire to avoid social conflict rather than enter into it. Moreover, in an era before Venice had acquired a territorial state on the mainland, a major textile industry in the city itself would have faced severe problems in terms of the supply of fresh water and the possibility of putting out work to the subject Terraferma would not have presented itself.[48] Most important of all however was the competition which woollen cloth faced from cotton and silk goods. The textile sector was significant enough to be represented by a number of guilds, but it was not over-dependent on a single type of cloth.

That said, the early records of the woollen industry show that it shared important features with other Venetian guilds. In 1269, the guild's officers were empowered to fine members up to a maximum sum of 100 soldi. Built into the same regulations however, was the members' right of appeal to an external tribunal, the *Consoli dei Mercanti.* Three years later, the guild was put under the overall authority of the *Provveditori di Comun.*[49] The woollen industry of medieval Venice was never large enough to become the amphitheatre of struggle: but what of silk?

Silk manufacture

The guild of silk throwsters was certainly active in Venice by the middle of the thirteenth century. The main stimulus to expansion came with Lucchese exiles in the early fourteenth century. Some 300 dyers, throwsters, weavers and merchants are said to have arrived in 1309, the merchants settling in Calle della Bisa and others near San Zuan Grisostomo, San Cancian and Santi Apostoli. Many joined the *scuola* of that name, but by 1360 the Lucchese had their own confraternity at Santa Maria dei Servi, which claimed to have 600 members. There were disputes between merchants and journeymen in the 1370s, and the masters were anxious to preserve their own independence between the two. The evidence suggests that merchant capital was reducing the status of masters to that of dependent workers. Even so, there is no evidence of serious conflict.[50]

The explanation for this is unclear but the following may have reduced the volatility which accompanied the clash of capital and labour in other cities. First, the records show that silk-workers were permitted to organise in a guild which included wage labourers and therefore gave them a negotiating body. The general solidarity of the Lucchese 'nation' may also have had a cooling effect. Most important, the arrival of the Lucchese appears to have given the Venetians a commodity which could integrate smoothly into an economy based on high-quality, high-priced goods. Silk was not dependent on a huge popular market: its expanding manufacture in the fourteenth century gave the Venetians a head start over their rivals in the period of adaptation which followed the Black Death, a process of adjustment which proved acutely painful elsewhere.[51] These ideas remain highly speculative, but even in the fifteenth century the tensions of merchants and producers seem still to have been contained within a political framework established in the thirteenth and fourteenth centuries. What does this say about guilds? Do the textile industries merely typify a guild structure submerged by the tidal waves of merchant capital and the oligarchic state? The picture is more complicated. The statutes of Venice's guilds suggest a network of social institutions which protected the interests of their members under the eyes of a state which sought to ensure high standards in the interests of the consumer. There was also a shared concern to maintain the productive and distributive capacities of the various trades.

Raw materials, production and marketing

Venetian statutes give a clear idea of how supply, production and marketing were supposed to fit together. The purpose of these regulations was to protect guildsmen from dependence on merchant interests outside or inside the corporation. Raw materials were usually bought in bulk by guild officers or by members appointed by them. In this way the pork butchers obtained their meat, the blacksmiths their charcoal, the tanners bleach, the potters lead oxide, the bell-makers copper, the hatters wool. Wood was essential as a raw material to the Arsenal in general and to turners, oarmakers and coopers. The glassmakers also used it as fuel and bought crystal and emery in much the same way.[52]

The clearest explanation of how the system worked is found in the statute of the ironmongers. Large quantities of charcoal were offered in shares (*partes*) to members. These shares were given out in order of asking and payment had to be made within four days. In 1295, the smiths elected three buyers to supply the guild and 'anyone [else] who buys charcoal in Venice'. This was a genuine monopoly. The Mint had first claim on the charcoal, then the smiths themselves, and only then other users.[53]

The hatters' regulations discouraged speculative buying with a view to profitable 'putting out'. All purchases of wool were to be offered in shares to members at cost price. Purchases of crystal had to be offered to any guild members who wished to buy a share; but no one was allowed to buy merely to resell. The oarmakers obliged non-members who imported wood to offer at least some of it for sale to guildsmen.[54]

In the strict provision against buying for resale, the statutes show a deep suspicion of anything approaching a modern cartel within the guild — such organisations were classed as conspiracies. If there was to be a cartel then it was to be coterminous with the guild, which seems to bear striking resemblance to the organisation of merchant companies operating in distant markets and which suggests that 'guilds' and 'businesses' were by no means mutually exclusive.[55]

Raw materials were turned into finished products and marketed in the course of a working year restricted by at least 90 holidays. Exceptions were made for barbers, who were permitted to bleed customers on Sundays, and for builders' apprentices, who were allowed to work on feast days 'in limited spells and without any kind of payment'.[56] Other trades were further restricted. Brickmakers and glassmakers only worked during certain months and the potters had to cease their activities in December and January: one wonders whether this helped prevent fuel shortages in the city in winter, and fears of fire were presumably heightened in the hot summer months.[57]

The working day was regulated by the city's bells: the *Marangona* summoned workers to the Arsenal, the *Trottiera* urged members of the Great Council to hurry to the council chamber.[58]

The city's marketplaces had their main artery at Rialto from which wholesale merchandise was pushed to retail outlets, the most important at San Marco and San Polo.[59] In the marketplace, stalls were allocated by guild officers. Each stall-holder was given a numbered docket to indicate where he could set up. The arrangement was changed every month by the turners, every six months by the mercers. Sales without a stall were forbidden amongst the goldsmiths; the shoemakers clearly squabbled about allocations.[60] As in the case of supplying raw materials, so in the marketing of wares, the statutes reflect a fear of any individual or group who might seek to corner the market.

The guild did however acknowledge the existence of *societates* within it. In keeping with the idea of 'middling guilds' which stood between 'merchants' and 'workers', these units were probably equivalent to something between 'workshop' and 'business'. Each was restricted to a single stall which could not be sub-let or used by a relation of the titular holder.[61]

Production and sale were to be carried on 'bona fide and without fraud', and there was a universal prohibition on the sale or handling of stolen goods.[62] And in other ways, the guilds' concern for the maintenance of standards of production could be translated into rules designed to protect the consumer.

The legislators assumed that the customer would be cheated unless proper provision was made. The statute of the dyers (1243) begins: 'since almost the whole world seems to have lapsed into deceit . . . the innocent buyer, pure in heart, may scarcely evade the frauds of the guild's workers.'[63] This rather chaste view of the exploited purchaser had some grounding in a number of artful dodges. In this area, statutory prohibitions are probably less important for what they achieved than for what they say about sharp practice, but the catalogue of frauds, detected or not, makes interesting reading.

All goods were to be sold under their exact name and any mixture of types — oil from Puglia with that from the Marche, sheep hide with goatskin in shoes, or the use of less durable hides such as horse or donkey — was strictly forbidden. Even sand from fresh and salt shores had to be kept separate. Old material was not to be incorporated into a supposedly new item. Fishmongers were not to use seaweed to freshen old stock, ragmen were not to brighten old clothes with sulphate to make them look new. Builders had to report the use of inferior materials by workmates.[64]

There were restraints, too, on the geographical liberty of the workforce to ensure that trade secrets were kept in Venice. While the Venetians benefited from the immigration of skilled workers (like the Lucchese) they guarded jealously their own 'mysteries'. Neither glassmakers nor dormouse skinners were permitted to work outside Venice. Indeed, as early as 1356, the Lucchese themselves were forbidden to take their skills elsewhere.[65]

Perhaps by way of recompense, foreign imports were sometimes discouraged. Glassmakers, tanners, furriers and turners could not handle non-Venetian wares. Spindles made outside Venice were taxed on arrival in the city.[66] Significantly, at this early date, there were fewer restrictions on retailing than on buying raw materials or on manufactures. Ironmongers and painters could relax their standards on goods for the overseas market. No trademark was necessary on some metalware *de caravana*, leather-covered shields were not given so long to dry.[67] Quality controls which provided for the accurate description of goods did not apply to mercery priced at less than 12 soldi — and the unwitting tourist was fair game, even in the thirteenth century. The mercers were permitted to make sales to pilgrims from Rome even on Sundays, probably equipping them for their voyage to the Holy Land.[68]

From this, one might conclude that neither Venice's great merchants nor its shopkeepers were suspicious of *commercial* enterprise, but that guilds were more circumspect about mercantile capital in *manufactures*. Guilds like the leather bleachers, tanners, painters, combmakers and potters excluded anyone who did not know how to work the trade with his own hands. The coopers could not buy staves from a middleman or lids from a merchant: both were to be bought direct from manufacturers. To maintain the equal distribution of opportunities within the craft, the coopers also swore not to help salesmen and forbade the taking of more than one share in a purchase of raw materials by any one member even in the name of another.[69]

There were other insurances against the formation of dominant groups and therefore against ties of dependence which might subject masters to merchants. Once again — and this is a theme which will be developed more fully in Chapter 3 — guilds did not oppose 'capitalism', they merely sought to foster prosperity within the guild system to the benefit of members rather than that of a few outsiders.

As we have already seen, the guilds, like mercantile companies, tolerated no threats to their own monopolies from rival organisations. There were other limitations on enterprise. Units of production were kept small and the putting out of work by a sedentary capitalist was strictly controlled. More important still, those who worked within the guild system were subject to a carefully formulated law of contract.

The coopers allowed each master only one apprentice. A painter could employ a single apprentice and up to two other masters but he was liable to a tax of 5 soldi on each of the latter. No carpenter could employ other masters in his boatyard. Silk weavers opposed the degradation of any master to the status of wage labourer.[70]

A workshop with a staff of 20 was not unknown in the building trade in the fourteenth century, but a number of them were members of the master's family. Moreover, it was extremely difficult to extend one's business interests by gaining control of more than one shop. All master tanners had to be over 15 years of age, so a shopowner could not set up premises in the name of young children. The son of a master could not contract with apprentices unless he was independent of his father's business and could provide evidence of the fact.[71]

The activities of 'middlemen' were also regarded with caution. All hides distributed for finishing by mercers had to belong to the putter-out, meaning that he could not be the dependent agent or representative of more powerful merchants. Glassworkers could only take on work on their own behalf 'and not to give out to others'.[72]

On the other hand, much guild economic activity depended on a 'boss' figure, referred to in the statutes as a *patronus*. He supplied work by virtue of his ownership of fixed capital assets — a house or ship which needed repairs, a furnace for making glass or bricks. In shipbuilding, the *patronus* gave work to a *proto* or foreman who organised masters from different trades into a gang which completed the job. The owner of a furnace was tied by the same regulations as other masters and since he was disqualified from office in the guild had no chance to change the rules to his own advantage. Non-members could also be covered by regulation of this type. No mercer could engage in tanning or bleaching without the express permission of the tanners' guild. The intrusion of the mercers in the activities of a variety of guilds made their enterprise part of the guild system, not a threat to it.[73]

Statutes, it must be reiterated, are not ideal sources for instances of class hatred. However, there is no evidence of serious conflict between merchants and producers in thirteenth- and fourteenth-century Venice. And whatever statutes do *not* reveal, there is a clear concern within them to regulate economic relations through the law of contract.

Conditions had to be agreed before work started and guildsmen were not to take on a second contract before completion of the one in hand. The agreed materials had to be handed over within a week of the contract's acceptance and the work completed in the time stipulated. Builders were to be paid within three days of finishing the job. If goods were not paid for or work unfinished, neither could be the subject of a new contract between the *patronus* and other members of the guild. Fellow members could not take work from an employer in dispute with another craftsman. It was part of a guild warden's responsibility to ensure that his members honoured agreements.[74]

Some of these mechanisms applied in other parts of Italy. In Venice, built into the law of contract and helping to obviate another potential source of tension were provisions against indebtedness. In other cities, especially those with significant textile industries, indebtedness was an explosive problem often linked to failure to pay wages.[75] In Venice, interestingly, the laws against indebtedness are most clearly articulated in the statute of the fustian weavers. In their case, as in that of the pewterers, such laws could be used by masters against journeymen. *Lavoranti* in these trades could not be party to a new contract before clearing their debts with a previous master. A new employer was not allowed to make the payment on the journeyman's behalf. Materials and work could be exchanged only to the tiny value of 2 denarii at a time and had to be finished before any further payment could be made. No more than 5 soldi at a time could be given to a journeyman under any conditions. This limitation applied to glassmakers as well but referred to 5 soldi over and above a wage payment, perhaps to limit the bonuses which an entrepreneur might offer to concentrate journeymen in dependence on himself. The corresponding figure for bleachers, coopers and weavers was only 2 soldi.[76]

Do these statutes represent prevalent abuses or effective correction? In Venice, responsibility for enforcement lay with the guilds' officers. When discussing the gulf between what the statutes laid down and what actually happened, careful attention must be paid to the role of the warden and his assistants. Is it possible that they ushered at least part of the law from pronouncement to enforcement? The post of *gastaldo* and the administrative structure of the guild in relation to the state give the guilds of Venice some of their most characteristic features.

Officers and members

Officers, their election, duties and perquisites, occupy a large proportion of the statutes, reflecting the importance of the guild as a means of political control and as a social institution. In both guises, the guild had to be administered. The chief officer was the warden (*gastaldo*). He was elected every year, sometimes on the same day as the banquet, and he was usually expected to have resided in Venice for a minimum of 20 years. He was paid, if at all, by members' contributions. A committee was elected with him and he was not at liberty to interfere with their decisions, though he carried general responsibilities in matters of contract law and guild finances. The *gastaldo* was responsible to the magistrates rather than to members. In the tanners' guild, the warden held his office 'on behalf of the justices' and he might be expected to present new regulations to the magistrates for their approval. The bell-founders' statute reveals that the magistrates actually chose the guild's officers themselves. Perhaps because of his responsibility to the state, rudeness towards the warden was universally banned. At the head of each guild, therefore, stood a figure whose task was to enforce the government's will in political and administrative matters and in technical regulation.[77] The rest of the committee was referred to as *iudices*, *decani* or *suprastantes*. Their duties involved the adjudication of minor disputes and the supervision of the *gastaldo*.[78]

At the annual election, the outgoing officials elected five guildsmen to choose their successors.[79] There were variations on this pattern. The fustian weavers were more directly democratic, nine electors being chosen by lot. This unusual degree of representation should be seen in relation to their regulation of debt and putting out but only the turners had a straight majority vote.[80] There were fines for refusing office and a former committee member normally faced a period of between two and five years' disqualification before he could be re-elected, thus ensuring the rotation of office.[81]

The committee's work revolved around inspections and fines. There were twice-yearly visits of workshops among the shoemakers, twice-weekly among rope-makers. Sometimes the officials were responsible for petty cash — and members could demand to inspect the guild's accounts at any time. Perhaps this level of record-keeping expertise points forward to the business skills which aided commercial growth in the sixteenth century.[82]

With regard to members themselves, the same general categories of masters, journeymen and apprentices were present in Venice as in the rest of Europe. Participation in elections was usually confined to masters though the mastership could be attained at the early age of 15.[83] Generally speaking, apprentices played little or no part in administrative life. This was probably because they were tied by contract to individual masters and only on submission of the masterpiece did the guild as a whole open up to them.[84] There were no more than two apprentices attached to a master at one time and the length of training ranged from a year and a half for a fustian weaver to eight for a glassmaker or a non-Venetian seeking to become a master goldsmith. Most lasted between four and seven years.[85]

The living and working conditions of journeymen are not easy to establish. The statutes show a general suspicion of workers' reliability: the glassmakers demanded a deposit, the fustian weavers an oath. But there were some safeguards for the *lavoranti*. Journeymen bleachers had to be given two months' notice of dismissal and a mercer's assistant was to be compensated by the master who terminated his contract. These fragments of evidence gain importance in a comparative context when one sees that in other cities lack of representation and indebtedness amongst wage labourers were often the sparks to the tinder of *furor populi*.[86]

One group likely to have been prominent among journeymen was that composed of immigrants. The early statutes suggest that they were absorbed with relative ease, perhaps indicating that the status groups did not become too rigid — vital to a city which depended on the influx of outsiders both for expansion and recovery. Like native Venetians, foreign workers were obliged to enter the *scuola* in order to practise the trade — usually within a week of arriving in the city. Those qualified as masters had, in the case of a hatter, to serve a probationary year before being recognised as a full master in Venice.[87]

The guild structure also found room for women, and not just as wives. Predictably they were to be found in the textile and clothing trades — fustian weavers, comb-makers, cappers, tailors, doublet-makers and secondhand dealers. They engaged too in petty retail such as ironmongery and haberdashery.[88] Their role can be more fully discussed in the context of the sixteenth and seventeenth centuries, but even in the years around 1300 their presence suggests yet again that status groups within a guild were by no means rigidly defined.

The pattern of control

The foregoing survey has examined guilds as social or devotional institutions and as a means of organising and regulating production and sale. We have already glanced at the presence of the government in guild life but the political context of the late thirteenth century needs further elaboration, since it coincides with the formative period in the history of the Venetian constitution. What was the nature and purpose of the government's role in guild life? The guilds had no access to political power after 1297, but they never sought to storm the citadel of patrician power. Why? Had they been successfully subordinated to the will of the mercantile oligarchy? Was the registration of statutes in the late thirteenth century a question of administrative formality or was it part of a grander design? Should we look for a political programme beyond that of sensible decisions taken by a tough-minded ruling class? There is a simpler question more directly relevant. Did subordination have its compensations?

The prism through which we can observe some aspects of this shadowy process is the *Giustizia Vecchia*, whose nature and competence were explained earlier. Originally responsible for the food trades, the magistracy acquired important police functions and initiated change of a non-technical character within the guilds. The central thrust of policy was to extend traditions of state service and elaborate them into a set of laws which bound the guilds to the will of the state. This may have helped to prepare the way for the *Serrata* of 1297, ensuring the guilds' compliance before their exclusion.

The first craftsman we know anything about in Venice — and we shall return to him — was Giovanni Sagorino, a blacksmith called upon in about 1030 to work at the ducal palace in the service of the state.[89] The smiths were still obliged to work in the ducal palace in the thirteenth century and the coopers' warden was paid a salary for his work there. Carpenters were responsible for all ships belonging to the state and could be put to work on feast days. Each carpenter was liable for three days' unpaid work on the Doge's ceremonial barge, the *Bucintoro*. The *gastaldo* of the oarmakers was to assemble the guild whenever the state required, and the same claim could be made upon caulkers and carpenters. Service to the state was not confined to the Arsenal trades. The house carpenters had to supply 15 masters whenever necessary and could expect no more than their food as payment. Some guilds — cobblers, pork butchers, fustian weavers — were obliged to make gifts of goods and money to the Doge. These obligations were at their most burdensome in the early seventeenth century when the government's requirements took the form of demands for oarsmen and money for the fleet. As a foretaste of the petitions through which the guilds were to register their protests, the combmakers were complaining as early as the fourteenth century that the guild's poverty was due to the state's needs for galley crews.[90]

State intervention in guild life brought other more permanent obligations. Guildsmen were bound together by an oath to uphold their statutes, the content of which was controlled by the government. By the 1270s, the oath to abide by guild regulations had become an oath of allegiance to the state. How did this come about? We can offer an answer of some sort by examining the statutes themselves and the magistrates who implemented the change.

An oath to uphold the regulations of the guild appears for the first time in the statute of the goldsmiths of 1233. A similar moral obligation to deal fairly appeared in the statutes of the dyers, the coopers and the sawyers. By the 1270s, no one was to engage in a trade unless he had taken the oath nor work with partners not under oath. While this may reflect a desire to strengthen each trade's separateness, it can only be fully understood in a political context. By 1265, the significance of the phrase *iurare artem* had changed. On 30 November in that year, four laws were passed to harness the guilds to the will of the state and fix their position in the constitution down to the fall of the Republic.[91] And some evidence suggests that these changes were not effected easily.

One of the laws of 1265 seems routine — the restriction of a warden's term of office to one year. On the other hand, it would clearly be difficult thenceforward for any popular leader to organise opposition to the patrician state from within the guilds. That objective would certainly be in line with the more overt purpose of the other laws — a purpose on which two historians as different as Professor Lane and Professor Cracco seem largely in agreement.[92] These laws imposed the immovable authority of the state on the political freedom of the guilds. An oath was taken to accept not only the regulation of the craft but also the orders transmitted by the government, an oath to the state 'which the magistrates shall give them'. No guildsman was to engage in anti-state activities and had to swear not to form any 'organisation, company, armed band or conspiracy by oath, bond or any other sworn commitment against the honour of the Doge and his council, the commune of the Venetians or against any other person'. The guild was allowed to assemble twice a year and at one of these meetings the statutes had to be read. Other assemblies required the formal permission of the magistrates.[93]

As in the case of labour service, these measures were an extension of traditions rather than a break with them. The oath had always bound the guildsman to inform on the frauds of his fellows.[94] But in 1265, the emphasis of the obligation *manifestare* shifts from 'report' to 'denounce'. By 1271, the coopers even had sworn agents who were to seek out contraventions of the statutes. In other guilds members were to inform on any irregularities. The combmakers specifically undertook to denounce any conspiracy, or even an unauthorised confraternity. In the fifteenth century when their statute was rewritten in the vernacular, the command is succinctly translated as an obligation 'to inform the government of anyone who speaks or acts against the honourable state of Venice'.[95]

These oaths were administered not by guild officers but by the magistrates. This meant that the artisan took his oath as an individual rather than as part of a corporation which mediated between him and the state. Such action enabled the government to deny guildsmen the possibility of organising political opposition, but there were compensations for the individual. Any benefits may not have been apparent in the late 1260s, as is suggested by the political circumstances in which the laws were passed and by the magistrates charged with their enforcement.

For Venice, the 1260s were a difficult decade. Despite a succession of costly war fleets sent to supplant them, the Genoese had firmly established themselves in the eastern Mediterranean. The burden of taxation to pay for the campaigns produced a riot in 1265 — the year of the new guild laws. According to the fourteenth-century chronicle of Doge Andrea Dandolo, it had been rumoured that the price of grinding corn was to double. This resulted in a riot at San Marco: the ducal palace was pelted with stones and some noble homes were ransacked.[96]

Tension continued in the 1270s. Professor Cracco has seen in this a trial of strength between oligarchs and common people, with artisans subject to particular repression as a result of their support for Doge Lorenzo Tiepolo. Can we see an association of non-nobles seeking to wrest privilege from their patrician masters?[97] In the final part of the chapter, it will be argued that such a view is inappropriate to late medieval Venice. We can begin to approach the problem by looking at who did what among the magistrates and how their activities affected the life of the guilds.

Who were the men who implemented and perhaps formulated

government policy towards the city's trade corporations? Those who held office in the magistracy were often men who had been close to the centres of power. Some of them may have been among the architects of the Venetian state.

Amongst the justices of the later thirteenth century are found electors of Doge Lorenzo Tiepolo and members of the rival Dandolo clan, experienced ambassadors and members of the ducal council.[98] This book is not concerned with the intricacies of division amongst the patricians, but the career of one of the magistrates can be pieced together. Marco Badoer was a magistrate in 1271, the most hectic period of the registration of statutes, and held office again in 1276 and 1288. He came to office with vast experience of public affairs. In 1256 he led Venice's crusading army against Ezzelino. Three years later he was *podestà* of Treviso and organised the confiscation of the tyrant's property and the grisly destruction of Alberico and his family. In 1264 he served as ambassador to Pope Urban IV and led another Venetian army, this time against Bologna, in 1269. He is identified by Cracco as standing in the vanguard of hardliners whose aim was to crush communal movements on the mainland and the *popolo* in Venice itself. He was perhaps the richest man in Venice and a fierce opponent of Lorenzo Tiepolo whose election as Doge in 1268 was joyously celebrated by the guilds. It has recently been suggested that political irregularities in the late 1260s put him into the political wilderness in the 1270s and that his tenure of office at the *Giustizia Vecchia* was insignificant.[99] There is an alternative interpretation.

In 1271, Badoer and his colleagues registered 13 statutes — a quarter of the total — excising what they deemed '*irrita et inane*'. Moreover, he was at the same post in 1276, the year after the death of Lorenzo Tiepolo and therefore when hardline oligarchs could be rehabilitated.[100] As far as the guilds were concerned, his career may have been a decisive influence. Here is a figure who might have engineered the political repression of the guilds before the *Serrata* delivered a *coup de grâce* in 1297. It seems possible — though only further research can decide the matter — that this troubleshooting oligarch was entrusted with the tough business of subordinating the guilds to the state. The 1270s saw the major sectors of the guild economy — the Arsenal, the building trades and the textile industries — subjected to statutes which display considerable uniformity, especially in terms of the conspiracy laws we have already examined. Badoer could have been one of the driving forces behind the government's action in this period. It is even possible that his second period of office in 1276 was a response to anti-state activities amongst artisans the previous year, when a silk worker and a goldsmith were among those exiled.[101]

The turbulence of the later thirteenth century can be seen as part of a process of state formation beginning with the establishment of the *Scuole Grandi*, the extension of the corporate principle to the trade guilds and culminating in the *Serrata*. But the statutes were more than a tool of oligarchy and offered concrete benefits for guildsmen themselves. Whatever his aims and the background to them, even the rule of Marco Badoer was the rule of law. The statutes which sought to crush conspiracy also offered the individual guildsman protection against injustice. Giovanni Sagorino, the eleventh-century blacksmith, is mentioned in a chronicle precisely because he objected to the burdens of service, took his case to court and won: effectively gaining the verdict against the Doge himself.

Seen in a perspective which looks beyond the 1260s and 1270s for another four centuries, the *Giustizia Vecchia* emerges as a legal authority independent of guild officers, a court to which artisans could appeal against the guild tribunal. Guild officers could only impose fines up to a certain sum. Beyond that, appeal was always available. If the plaintiff lost, then he was liable for costs, so it is unlikely that guild administration was hamstrung by complaints against every tiny decision.[102] Nor were guild officers allowed to interfere with the appeal procedure. In the case of the shoemakers, they were obliged to present to the appeal court a formal record of earlier proceedings. An apprentice potter could appeal against the rejection of his masterpiece, if dissatisfied with both guild officers and the magistrates, a sand digger was encouraged to take his case to the State Advocates.[103]

It is impossible to be certain about the efficiency of Venetian justice without more detailed evidence. What is important is that the tradition of appeal was a remarkably resilient one and eventually served the corporate interests of the guilds rather than the interests of individual members.[104] In other words, the position of the guilds before the law not only exposed the individual artisan to the wiles of Marco Badoer, it also made the state's justice, even in a limited sense, accessible to him. It is this which made the guilds of Venice different from those of other medieval cities and it is in a comparative context that the point is best illustrated.

Comparisons and contrasts

The distinctive feature of Venetian history — the absence of *furor populi* — may be explained in part by the close administrative relationship and separate economic interests of the guilds and the government. Put more positively, it was in the interests of the rulers of Venice to permit, even to promote, the formation of guilds. The *arti* fulfilled important functions in economic and social life without threatening the interests of the ruling class. Their political quiescence, however, should not be seen purely as the result of Machiavellian policies. There were important compensations for guildsmen in terms of the legal principles which the statutes embodied, especially the accessibility of courts of appeal. The solidity of these principles and the institutions which protected them help to explain the stability and durability of the guild system for seven centuries.

In comparison with other European cities, Venice's good fortune in avoiding social and political upheaval might be attributed to geographical and economic accident. The city was well placed to take advantage of maritime commercial opportunities, but before the sixteenth century did not develop a major textile industry, so often the arena of conflict elsewhere in the thirteenth and fourteenth centuries.[105]

The confrontation of capital and labour in textile trades was in evidence in Flanders by the mid-thirteenth century. The earliest strike (called a *takehan* because of the principles of association and solidarity it embodied) took place in Douai in 1245. Three decades later, strikes were punishable by death, but a communal uprising broke patrician power in the town in 1296. A series of *takehans* was organised in Ypres in 1280 when weavers took on merchant aldermen. Pirenne estimated that the weavers of Ghent numbered 4000 in a town of 50,000 and the city's dependence on the market for textiles made it vulnerable to social unrest, especially given the unbending interests of exploitative capitalism embodied in men like Boinebroke and Lanstier. So modern do such conflicts appear that they seem like precursors of the struggles of 1848.[106]

Similarly, in Florence, it has been suggested that the concentration of capital resources in the hands of a few rich merchants enabled them to organise production through a proletariat of wage-labourers who were sometimes employed under one roof in embryonic factories.[107]

However, closer examination of the organisation of production in the textile industries and of the political context of these struggles raises doubts that late medieval uprisings were clashes of employers and wage-labourers in capitalist industry.

In Flanders, political instability should be seen in terms of the relationship of urban and rural production, of the different interests of large towns and smaller centres, and of the relations of all these to the legal and personal authority of the Count. The textile industry was not exclusively urban in the thirteenth century, still less was it organised around mass production. The 50 or so different types of cloth in production were hardly the standardised products of large-scale enterprises. Boinebroke's 'exploited' workers enjoyed the kind of independence in relation to the means of production which makes it hazardous to classify them as proletarians.[108]

The course of Florentine political development remains the subject of great controversy. There was a conflict of political principle — corporatism against oligarchy — within a guild structure which excluded many workers from the textile industry, and it seems that the contending political interests of different factions (which went back to the twelfth century) were based on the interests of different families rather than different social classes.[109]

With regard to labour conditions, a far more complicated picture than that of rapid expansion before 1340 and sudden collapse thereafter — a picture painted by the chronicler Villani and taken as accurate by modern historians — has now emerged. Among the *Ciompi* were many independent masters such as dyers — scarcely the ragged proletarians conjured up by Doren and Rodolico — and the majority of them may have been from the building trades rather than the textile industries.[110] Indeed, Hidetoshi Hoshino's painstaking research on the Florentine woollen guild tends to lessen rather than heighten the importance of his subject. Villani's much-quoted figures are no longer usable. Without them there is not much to suggest that Florence had a high quality cloth industry before 1320. Its period of prosperity seems to have been the late 1350s and decline set in after 1367. Hoshino argues from late fourteenth-century evidence that units of production were small: 283 premises produced a maximum of 28,000 pieces of cloth in 1382: not one of them produced more than 300 pieces, and the majority between 50 and 150 pieces. These businesses were a safe haven for small investors rather than over-extended enterprises which tied workers to capitalist bosses. Villani's 75,000 pieces a year would have required nearly 4500 weavers working flat out throughout the year, which makes the absence of weavers from the *Ciompi*'s ranks inexplicable. The fundamentally commercial character of the Florentine economy means that contrasts with Venice can be overdrawn.[111]

As we have seen, textiles are certainly not to be ignored in the economy of medieval Venice.[112] By the early fifteenth century, Doge Mocenigo's *arringa* emphasised the vast numbers of textile workers which the city could now boast. Venice too had its *sottoposti* with no right to their own association, and they seem to have made a disproportionate contribution to violent crime in the fourteenth century. The building industry, (which flourished even in the aftermath of the Black Death), the leather, glass and shipbuilding trades all showed traces of capitalist organisation.[113]

To blur the distinction still further, there is plenty of evidence of savage conflict in towns *not* dominated by textile industries. The uprising in Siena in the early fourteenth century seems to have been inspired by the butchers, who were also active in Florentine violence. Despite the growth of textile manufacture in a commercial centre, the disturbances in Genoa in 1258 had little to do with discontented clothworkers. In the case of London, the growth of the crafts in the fourteenth century culminated in the triumph of twelve great companies, something like the *Arti Maggiori* in Florence. There was no great textile industry, but there were violent clashes of merchants and producers in many other trades: lorimers and saddlers, cordwainers and curriers, cutlers and chaplers.[114] The English cloth industry, on the other hand, was based on manufacture in rural areas, just as most Florentine wool was spun in the *contado*.[115] This does not sit at all easily with ideas of 'factory production'. Rather, it opens up the problem of rural influences on medieval towns, dependent on the countryside not only for immigrants and food, but also for the stages of wool processing which preceded weaving it into cloth.

The economic relations of town and countryside had crucial political implications and help to explain the exceptionally strong influence of the feudal world on the history of so-called 'city-states'. This helps one to understand why Venice was different. In most cities, the urban economy's links with the rural economy were paralleled by the political overlap of towns and seigneuries.[116] It is in Florence's failure to break out of a rural and seigneurial context and Venice's good fortune never to have been subordinate to one that the two cities differ. In a curious way, a study of guilds as a measure of what political structures meant to ordinary people helps to make this plain. In other areas of Europe discussed in this section, towns need to be set in a context of rural economic life and feudal politics. Marxists seem generally to have missed this by overrating the degree of 'capitalist' advance in medieval towns. American historians are wont to be bewitched by the spell of 'republicanism' when very few *res publicae* really existed. It is worth pursuing this in the case of London, part of a country where the roots of urban life were never very deep in the Middle Ages.[117]

Medieval London might acknowledge no king but its mayor, but only while the king himself was out of the country. The city itself was a tenant-in-chief. The violence of 1263 saw the genesis of a 'revolutionary commune', but it emerged 'under the aegis of Montfort', or in other words attached to the interests of a feudal baron. Thereafter the city was dominated by a 'siege mentality' within the feudal environment. London's society was divided into *potentiores*, *mediocres* and *populares*, which reflected the feudal origins of the leading groups.[118]

In Flanders, the guilds grew up in the vacuum left by the collapse of public power. The jurisdiction of the urban authorities beyond the city walls remained deeply confused throughout the fourteenth century, and much depended on the personal authority of the Count, who was no sovereign but who could interfere in the legal process within the towns themselves. He himself, of course, was the vassal of the King of France.[119] In France itself, in Toulouse, the guilds were administered in the first instance by the Count, not by the town consuls, the city's patriciate remained a landed rather than a commercial aristocracy. It has been said that even in the fifteenth century, Paris was the only town in France.[120] Spain's urban communities have been dubbed 'agro-towns' to give proper place to their dependence on the surrounding countryside.[121]

Only the towns of the Hansa provide something of an exception. The organisation itself never claimed to be a state, but the member towns were governed by a sovereign body of law. However, their very existence required seigneurial permission. Lübeck, which was to become the dominant town in the dominant commercial organisation in northern Europe, was brought into being by command of Henry the Lion.[122]

What of Florence? In the late thirteenth century, there were no signs of a precocious 'civic' world with highly developed 'capitalist' organisations. Political and economic life were largely shaped by feudal influences. In the 1290s political life was dominated not by guilds but by *consorterie*. Society was divided between the magnates, 'the fat people' and 'the little people', each group in turn criss-crossed with Guelph–Ghibelline squabbles. The 'fat' came to power with the Guelphs in the years around 1300, but it took repeated and concerted attacks on the *grandi* to break their political power, even after the Ordinances of Justice of 1293: the 'state' in the early fourteenth century was dominated by mercantile interests operating through the Greater Guilds rather than by the guilds themselves.[123]

There was little distinction between the great families and the commune. In a sense, this was true of Venice as well, but there, family power was successfully welded to political authority. Clan interests were subordinated to the public weal, at the centre of which lay a rational system of justice rather than a series of untidily overlapping jurisdictions. In Florence, the guilds were much less important than powerful figures *within* the guilds. The corporations themselves did not represent the workforce, and those that existed were not equal before the law. The priorate represented 'an aristocracy at the height of artisan society', not artisan society itself.[124] Thus, the contrast between the guilds of Venice and those of Florence is that Venetian artisans were excluded from government, Florentine artisans from factional struggles at the centre of city politics. When the *Ciompi* enjoyed their brief moment of power it was in guilds 'born of political revolution with the favour of a faction' and, of necessity, 'they ran the risk of other revolutions of other factions which would have threatened their very existence'.[125]

The consuls of the guilds of Florence enjoyed inappellate jursidiction. As in Bologna, there was no independent tribunal to cut what it thought *irrita et inane* from the statutes. The pledge to observe the 'precepts and orders' of the guilds' rectors had little of the force of the oath sworn by Venetian artisans. The statutes were not framed according to the will of the magistrates. The pork butchers of Florence were to obey 'all the just commands which shall be made to me by the rectors and consuls of this guild'. There was no right of appeal, no court which could decide what constituted a 'just command'.[126]

In Florence, too, whatever the scale of the woollen industry, the historian faces the problem of the large numbers of people excluded from guilds. The *sottoposti*, by no means all textile workers, were at the mercy of guild consuls, but had no protection from a guild of their own and, in effect, no political existence at all. Many of them were specifically denied wage payments in ready money — something specifically assured to Venetian textile workers.[127]

The wool guild's power was buttressed by its own prison and its own police, headed by the detested *ufficio forestiere*. He had the right of inspection and search, the power to mutilate those he deemed to be offenders. Clothworkers could not work with only one hand.[128] This inappellate jurisdiction and the lack of representation for craftsmen in the legal process did not escape Machiavelli who saw it as the main source of conflict behind the *Ciompi* rebellion.

> those citizens who had formerly been Guelfs and under whose government the magistrate was always sworn had favoured the rich merchants of the greater guilds and oppressed the members of the lesser ones. . . . In addition to this, many industries in which only small traders or the lower classes laboured had no guild of their own but submitted to one of the guilds which happened to assimilate in some degree to their own industry. Hence it followed that when the people became dissatisfied with their wages, or oppressed by their masters they had no other course open to them but to appeal to the syndics of the guild to which they had submitted themselves and from which they rarely received that justice to which they believed themselves entitled.[129]

The source of the imbalance can be seen in the very ordinances which excluded the magnates from power in 1293, which narrowed the basis of political life rather than widening it. The political structures of Florence therefore served to protect the economic interests of the ruling oligarchy which had succeeded in excluding the magnates but refused to open to other groups. The organisation of the wool guild supports the idea that the Greater Guilds possessed absolute power in their own affairs. It was entirely in keeping with Florentine traditions of weak public power and strong private interests that when the Medici came to power, the family superseded the guild as the key to control. But whether we look at a commune dominated by powerful interests within the Greater Guilds in the fourteenth century, or dominated by powerful families in the fifteenth, public office is no more than a shield for the controlling influence of extra-legal interests which did not need to acknowledge the sovereignty of a commonly accepted body of law. The Medici did not even need to hold office to hold power.[130] The feudal ties of lord and vassal operated in the urban context as those between patron and client. In both cases we are looking at feudal politics — public power in private hands.[131]

Conclusion

Venice's enduring characteristics were wealth and stability. There were no *grandi* to eliminate in the thirteenth century. Guildsmen's possibilities of organising themselves, and the government's desire to organise them, provided some security and no single guild came to dominate the economic life of the Venetian people. The separateness of patrician commercial interests from those of the guilds meant that both could respect the rule of law.[132] When Venice acquired a territorial state and expanded its industries in the fifteenth century, they were apppended to a republican polity and to a commercial economy.

In the later fourteenth century, the differences between Florence and Venice are well summarised by contemporary chroniclers. Of Florence, Marchionne di Coppo Stefani wrote:

> Everything which has led to no good in the blessed city of Florence has been caused by greed for office and beyond that by everyone wanting them all for himself, trying to win them from his fellow like the hedgehog who flattered the snake out of its hole. Every outsider, gangs, lords, tyrants, despised and trampled on the city from without because of the divisions within.[133]

As the war of Chioggia reached its climax, Daniele di Chinazzo observed of Venice:

> In those brave days, Meser Vetor Pisani carried stones in his own hands as did Meser Giacomo Cavali, Meser Tadeo Giustinian, Lunardo Dandolo and all the other nobles and notables, stones and lime. The builders of Venice worked inside [the fort] some building up the wall and some mixing

> mortar, and all the soldiers and all the men from the ships helped carry stones to build up the towers.[134]

Venetian guildsmen enjoyed little in the way of *libertas*, but they could be sure they were part of a *res publica*.[135]

The interaction of economic and political life in medieval cities was overlain by religious influences. In the Florentine *contado*, the Church operated to reinforce mercantile authority by preaching at regular intervals that shoddy work was sinful.[136] There was another side to its activities: exalting the poor, which may have given a particularly keen ideological edge to events in 1378.[137] In the next chapter we shall examine the role of the institution which played the most important part in the religious life of Venetian guildsmen — the *scuola*.

Notes

1. A. B. Hibbert, 'The Towns', in *CEH*, vol. 3, pp. 158–228; S. L. Thrupp, 'The Guilds', ibid., pp. 230–81. On the idea of the guild, see A. Black, *Guilds and Civil Society in European Political Thought from the 12th Century to the Present* (London, 1984), pp. 44–85. On their social role, see J. Heers, 'Les métiers et les fêtes en France du nord et en Angleterre', *Revue du Nord*, vol. 55, no. 218 (1973), pp. 193–206. On contrasts between urban and rural society, see G. Duby, 'Medieval Society', in his collected essays, *The Chivalrous Society*, trans. C. Postan (London, 1977), p. 10. On Italy, see P. J. Jones, 'Economia e società nell'Italia medievale: la leggenda della borghesia', in *Storia d'Italia, Annali 1: dal feudalesimo al capitalismo*, (Turin, 1978), pp. 185–372; G. Fasoli, 'Gouvernants et gouvernés dans les communes italiennes du 11e au 13e siècle', *Recueils de la Société Jean Bodin*, vol. 25 (1965), pp. 47–56.

2. G. Lestocquoy, *Les villes de Flandre et d'Italie: aux origines de la bourgeoisie* (Paris, 1952), pp. 131, 147.

3. In general, see M. Mollat and Ph. Wolff, *The Popular Revolutions of the Late Middle Ages*, trans. A. L. Lytton-Sells (London, 1973); G. Fourquin, *The Anatomy of Popular Rebellion in the Late Middle Ages*, trans. A. Chesters (Amsterdam, 1979).

4. F. C. Lane, *Venice: A Maritime Republic* (Baltimore, Md., 1975), pp. 44–113; G. Luzzatto, *Storia economica di Venezia dall'11 al 16 secolo* (Venice, 1961), pp. 20–45; Y. Renouard, 'Mercati e mercanti veneziani alla fine del '200', in *La civiltà di Venezia del secolo di Marco Polo* (Florence, 1957), pp. 83–109.

5. Hibbert, 'Towns', pp. 158–69.

6. Lane, *Venice*, pp. 62–3; G. Luzzatto, *Studi di storia economica veneziana* (Padua, 1954), pp. 89–116.

7. B. Z. Kedar, *Merchants in Crisis: Genoese and Venetian Men of Affairs in the 14th-century Depression* (New Haven, Ct., 1976), p. 58.

8. F. C. Lane, 'The Enlargement of the Great Council of Venice', in J. G. Rowe and W. H. Stockdale (eds.), *'Florilegium Historiale': Essays presented to Wallace K. Ferguson* (Toronto, 1971), pp. 263–74; G. Cracco, *Società e stato nel medioevo veneziano* (Florence, 1967), pp. 209–350; B. Cecchetti, 'I nobili e il popolo di Venezia', *AV*, vol. 3 (1872), pp. 421–46.

9. F. C. Lane, *Venetian Ships and Shipbuilders of the Renaissance* (Baltimore, Md., 1934), pp. 72–3.

10. A. Sagredo, *Sulle consorterie delle arti edificative*, (Venice, 1856), p. 158; G. Monticolo (ed.), *I capitolari delle arti veneziane sottoposte alla Giustizia e poi alla Giustizia Vecchia dalle origini al 1330*, 3 vols. (Rome, 1896–1914) (henceforward *CAV*), vol. 1, pp. 102, 145; vol. 2, p. 7, n. 3, 113, 361, 389, n. 2. There was no separate guild for painters of pictures until 1682. See E. Favaro, *L'arte dei pittori a Venezia* (Florence, 1975), p. 119.

11. B. S. Pullan, 'Natura e carattere delle scuole', in T. Pignatti (ed.), *Le scuole di Venezia* (Milan, 1981), pp. 9–26.

12. *CAV*, vol. 2, p. 578.

13. Ibid., vol. 1, p. 46; vol. 2, p. 74.

14. On the skeiners, *CAV*, vol. 3, p. 283; on mutual aid, ibid., vol. 1, pp. 18, 46, 69; vol. 2, p. 355; vol. 3, pp. 56, 103, 126. On the cost of living in the fourteenth century, Luzzatto, *Studi*, pp. 285–97.

15. *CAV*, vol. 2, p. 294; vol. 3, pp. 47, 67, 79.

16. Ibid., vol. 2, pp. 16, 128, 192, 300; vol. 3, pp. 193–4.

17. Ibid., vol. 2, p. 55.

18. For a discussion of these concepts, and an illustration of how they became confused in the act of relieving poverty, see J. A. Ryan, 'Charity and Charities', in *The Catholic Encyclopedia*, 15 vols. (London, 1907–12), vol. 3, Brow-Clancy, pp. 592–604; J. F. Delany, 'Mercy', ibid., vol. 10, Mass-Newman, pp. 198–9; J. D. O'Neill, 'Alms and Almsgiving', ibid., vol. 1, Aachen-Assize, pp. 328–30.

19. *CAV*, vol. 1, pp. 52, 68; vol. 2, p. 219; vol. 3, pp. 127, 288–9.

20. Ibid., vol. 3, p. 199.

21. Ibid., vol. 1, p. 51; vol. 3, p. 255.

22. Ibid., vol. 1, p. 35; vol. 2, pp. 220, 296, 465; vol. 3, pp. 45, 90, 190, 199, 255–6, 277.

23. Ibid., vol. 2, pp. 189, 257, 260.

24. Ibid., vol. 3, p. 277.

25. Ibid., vol. 1, p. 50; vol. 3, p. 20.

26. P. Humfrey and R. Mackenney, 'The Venetian Trade Guilds as Patrons of Art in the Renaissance', *The Burlington Magazine* no. 998, vol. 128 (1986), pp.317–30; *CAV*, vol. 1, p. 50; vol. 2, pp. 177, 347.

27. H. A. Miskimin, *The Economy of Early Renaissance Europe, 1300–1460* (Cambridge, 1975), p. 157.

28. F. C. Lane, *Andrea Barbarigo, Merchant of Venice, 1418–1449* (Baltimore, Md., 1944), p. 94; Luzzatto, *Studi*, pp. 125–65, 195–200; F. C. Lane, *Venice and History: The Collected Papers of Frederic C. Lane* (Baltimore, Md., 1966), pp. 36–55, 128–42, 193–226.

29. Lane, *Ships and Shipbuilders*, p. 73.

30. On the magistracies see A. da Mosto, *L'Archivio di Stato di Venezia*, 2 vols. (Rome, 1937–40).

31. V. I. Rutenburg asserts that 40,000 Venetians were guildsmen in

the fourteenth century, but he cites no primary source for this figure, 'Arti e corporazioni', *Storia d'Italia vol. 5: Documenti* (Turin, 1973), p. 626; on the dangers of over-reliance on statutes, see R. de Roover, 'A Florentine Firm of Cloth Manufacturers: Management and Organisation of a 16th-century Business', in his collected essays, *Business, Banking and Economic Thought in Late Medieval and Early Modern Europe* (Chicago, Ill., 1974), pp. 110–11.

32. On Florence, *Fonti sulle corporazioni artigiane del medio evo* (*Deputazione Toscana di Stoira Patria*, Florence, 1940 onwards); on Bologna, A. Gaudenzi (ed.), *Gli statuti delle società del popolo di Bologna*, 2 vols. (Rome, 1899, 1896), vol. 2, *Società delle arti*.

33. On the *Scuole Grandi*, B. Pullan, *Rich and Poor in Renaissance Venice: The Social Institutions of a Catholic State* (Oxford, 1971), p. 38; on the *Serrata*, Lane, 'Closing of the Great Council'; on the struggle of *grandi* and *popolani*, Cracco, *Società e stato*, pp. 209–350; Lane, *Venice*, p. 106.

34. G. Perocco and A. Salvadori, *Civilità di Venezia*, 3 vols. (Venice, n.d.), vol. 1, pp. 215–99; vol. 2, pp. 495–544.

35. Lane, *Venice*, p. 163.

36. Lane, *Ships and Shipbuilders*; *CAV* vol. 1, pp. 95–114; vol. 2, pp. 3–8, 197–230, 231–82, 329–62; vol. 3, pp. 229–48; on the Tana, Lane, *Venice and History*, pp. 269–84; idem., *Venice*, pp. 361–4.

37. C. Yriarte, *La vie d'un patricien de Venise au 16e siècle* (Paris, 1874), pp. 299–308.

38. Lane, *Ships and Shipbuilders*, pp. 76–7, 84.

39. Lane, *Venice*, p. 59; Arti, b. 445 *pistori*, *mariegola*, *1333–1682*. The riot of 1265 was a response to an increase in the cost of grinding corn, not in the price of bread, see A. Dandolo, *Chronica per extensum descripta*, *RIS*, vol. 12, part i, (Bologna 1938–40), p. 314.

40. *CAV*, vol. 1, pp. 59–74, 75–7; vol. 2, pp. 10–26; vol. 3, pp. 41–54. On the filtration process, see Perocco and Salvadori, *Civiltà di Venezia*, vol. 1, p. 270.

41. On textile manufacture, *CAV*, vol. 1, pp. 139–44; vol. 2, pp. 27–38, 535–82; vol. 3, pp. 101–6, 157–86, 271–90; T. Bini, *I Lucchesi a Venezia: alcuni studi sopra i secoli 13 e 14* (Lucca, 1856); M. F. Mazzaoui, *The Italian Cotton Industry in the Late Middle Ages, 1100–1600* (Cambridge, 1981). On cloth and clothing, *CAV*, vol. 1, pp. 9–22, 23–54, 135–8; vol. 2, pp. 457–86; vol. 3, pp. 55–68, 69–84. On leather, *CAV*, vol. 2, pp. 99–114, 115–36, 137–68, 487–534.

42. *CAV*, vol. 1, pp. 115–34; vol. 2, pp. 61–98, 363–90; vol. 3, pp. 123–52.

43. On wood and metal, *CAV*, vol. 2, pp. 329–62, 397–456; vol. 3, pp. 107–22, 187–94, 195–214. On building trades see *CAV*, vol. 1, pp. 5–8, 79–94; vol. 2, pp. 169–96, 283–306; vol. 3, pp. 249–64, and A. Wirobisz, 'L'attività edilizia a Venezia', *SV*, vol. 7 (1965), pp. 307–43. On services, *CAV*, vol. 1, pp. 145–50, 159–70; vol. 2, pp. 39–60.

44. *CAV*, vol. 1, pp. 181–2; vol. 2, pp. 153–6; vol. 3, pp. 215–22, 291–324.

45. Ibid., vol. 1, pp. 84–90, 152, 172, 175; vol. 2, pp. 10, 13, 45 and n.7, 74, 357– 8, 392, 554–5, 559 and n. 5; vol. 3, pp. 45 and n. 7, 80, 109, 153–5, 320.

46. See the collection contained in *Biblioteca Marciana*, Venice, MS. It. cl. VII, 1571, 7642.

47. D. Sella, 'The Rise and Fall of the Venetian Woollen Industry', in B. S. Pullan (ed.), *Crisis and Change in the Venetian Economy* (London, 1968), pp. 88–105; N. Fano,' Richerche sull'arte della lana a Venezia nei secoli 13 e 14', *AV*, vol. 27 (1936), pp. 73–213. On the essentially commercial character of the Florentine economy, R. de Roover, 'Labour Conditions in Florence around 1400: Theory, Policy and Reality', in N. Rubinstein (ed.), *Florentine Studies: Politics and Society in Renaissance Florence* (London, 1968), pp. 298–9; and H. Hoshino, *L'arte della lana in Firenze nel basso medio evo* (Florence, 1980), pp. 36, 66, 72.

48. Cracco, *Società e stato*, pp. 198, 294 n. 1. See the review by B. S. Pullan in *Rivista Storica Italiana*, no. 81 (1969), pp. 184–5. On the organisation of putting out, see Lane, *Venice*, pp. 313–14.

49. PC, b. 57, *Lanifizio: terminazioni ecc. circa panni et università drappieri et processi*. The relevant documents are unfoliated and are headed with the dates 10 April 1269 and 3 August 1272.

50. *CAV*, vol. 2, pp. 27–38; Arte della Seta, b. 552, *Capitolare nuovo del'Officio e arte de testori de panni di seda e oro*, fols. 5r, 12v–15r.

51. Miskimin, *Early Renaissance Europe*, p. 104.

52. *CAV*, vol. 2, pp. 78, 334, 414, 511–12; vol. 3, pp. 9, 63, 111, 125, 188, 196, 232.

53. Ibid., vol. 2, pp. 334–5, 360.

54. Ibid., vol. 3, pp. 63, 125, 134–5, 236.

55. Ibid., vol. 1, pp. 10, 25, 141; vol. 2, pp. 18, 171, 350, 500. On cartels, Luzzatto, *Studi*, p. 196.

56. C. M. Cipolla, *Before the Industrial Revolution: European Society and Economy, 1000–1700* (London, 1976), p. 90; J. Larner, *Italy in the Age of Dante and Petrarch, 1216–1380* (London, 1980), p. 197; B. Geremek, *Salariati ed artigiani nella Parigi medievale*, trans. G. Pinto (Florence, 1975), p. 66; *CAV*, vol. 2, pp. 47, 299.

57. *CAV*, vol. 1, pp. 79–80; vol. 2, p. 91; vol. 3, p. 196. On technical aspects of production, see Lane, *Venice*, pp. 156–60.

58. G. Lorenzetti, *Venice and its Lagoon*, trans. J. Guthrie (Trieste, 1961), p. 145.

59. Perocco and Salvadori, *Civiltà di Venezia*, vol. 2, pp. 636–7.

60. *CAV*, vol. 1, p. 125; vol. 2, pp. 164, 321; vol. 3, p. 191.

61. Ibid., vol. 2, pp. 109–10, 144; vol. 3, p. 23.

62. For examples see ibid., vol. 1, p. 141; vol. 2, pp. 170, 499. On the prohibition against stolen goods, ibid., vol. 1, pp. 10, 40–1, 122, 137; vol. 2, pp. 67, 79, 124, 146, 181, 204, 233, 290, 313, 342, 380, 405, 458, 504; vol. 3, pp. 3, 35, 46, 59, 77, 104, 110, 125, 159.

63. Ibid., vol. 1, p. 139.

64. Ibid., vol. 1, pp. 28, 63–4, 96, 103, 157; vol. 2, pp. 10, 34, 105, 117, 142, 300, 321, 459, 501; vol. 3, pp. 42, 73, 159.

65. Ibid., vol. 3, pp. 129, 266; Arte della Seta, b. 552, *Capitolare nuovo*, fol. 8r.

66. *CAV*, vol. 2, pp. 86, 104, 106; vol. 3, pp. 125, 188.

67. Ibid., vol. 2, pp. 352, 373.

68. Ibid., vol. 2, pp. 308, 322.

69. Ibid., vol. 2, pp. 134, 386, 424, 429, 444, 528; vol. 3, pp. 168, 199.

70. Ibid., vol. 2, pp. 206–7, 370, 413; Arte della Seta, b. 552, *Capitolare nuovo*, fols. 14v–20v.

71. Wirobisz, 'L'attività edilizia', p. 325; *CAV*, vol. 2, p. 326; vol. 3, p. 134.

72. *CAV*, vol. 2, p. 326; vol. 3, p. 125.

73. On brick kilns, Wirobisz, 'L'attività edilizia', p. 326; on mercers and tanning, *CAV*, vol. 2, pp. 117–18, 135.

74. *CAV*, vol. 2, pp. 4, 83, 131, 132, 173, 189–91, 198, 295, 299, 335; vol. 3, pp. 47, 72, 91, 198, 234.

75. V. I. Rutenburg, *Popolo e movimenti popolari nell'Italia del '300 e '400*, trans. G. Borchini (Bologna, 1971), p. 42; idem, 'La vie et la lutte des Ciompi de Sienne', *Annales*, vol. 20, no. 1 (1965), p. 109; N. Rodolico, *I Ciompi* (Florence, 1945), p. 42.

76. *CAV*, vol. 2, pp. 29, 93, 134, 419, 545–6, 567, 574.

77. B. Cecchetti, 'Le industrie a Venezia nel sec. 13', *AV*, vol. 4. (1872), p. 214. On the residence requirement, see *CAV*, vol. 2, pp. 347, 436, 552. On payments and shares of fines, ibid., vol. 1, pp. 72, 110; vol. 2, pp. 129, 189, 528. On financial responsibility, ibid., vol. 2, pp. 15, 30, 44, 67, 101, 121, 140–1, 161, 179, 192, 203, 239, 247, 288, 314, 337, 367, 381, 402, 435, 566; vol. 3, pp. 74, 231, 252. On the ban on *rusticitas*, ibid., vol. 1, pp. 39, 68, 177; vol. 2, pp. 30, 82, 127, 141, 188, 211, 255, 295, 322, 344, 380–1, 494, 556; vol. 3, pp. 36, 45, 60, 89, 105, 154, 164, 191, 217, 231, 252–3.

78. *CAV*, vol. 1, pp. 105, 121–2; vol. 2, pp. 16, 36–7, 40, 67, 68–9, 102, 142, 148, 181, 204, 240, 289, 364, 402, 460; vol. 3, pp. 10, 135.

79. *CAV*, vol. 1, p. 18; vol. 2, pp. 17, 183, 206, 242, 364, 407; vol. 3, pp. 60, 130, 166, 230.

80. Ibid., vol. 1, pp. 70, 110; vol. 2, pp. 30, 541, 571; vol. 3, p. 189.

81. Ibid., vol. 1, p. 54; vol. 2, pp. 80, 163.

82. Ibid., vol. 1, pp. 37–8; vol. 2, pp. 15, 30, 44, 67, 79–80, 101, 121, 127, 140–1, 178–9, 192, 203, 239, 247, 288, 314, 337, 367, 402, 566; vol. 3, pp. 74, 231, 252.

83. E.g. ibid., vol. 3, p. 260 (stonemasons).

84. Ibid., vol. 3, p. 347 (skeiners).

85. Ibid., vol. 1, pp. 124–5; vol. 2, pp. 85, 259, 294, 312–13, 336, 439, 497, 546; vol. 3, pp. 78–9, 104, 132, 169, 189, 217.

86. Larner, *Age of Dante and Petrarch*, p. 198; L. Martines, *Power and Imagination: City-States in Renaissance Italy* (New York, 1980), p. 136.

87. Lane, *Venice*, p. 165; *CAV*, vol. 2, p. 496; vol. 3, p. 68.

88. *CAV*, vol. 1, pp. 18, 30; vol. 2, pp. 312, 354, 462, 557; vol. 3, pp. 78, 159.

89. On the *Giustizia Vecchia*, G. Monticolo, *L'ufficio della Giustizia Vecchia a Venezia* (Venice, 1892); On Sagorino, G. Monticolo (ed.), *Cronache veneziane antichissime* (Rome, 1890), pp. 175–6.

90. *CAV*, vol. 2, pp. 157–8, 329, 398, 525–6, 558; vol. 3, pp. 21, 181, 276.

91. On the oath, ibid., vol. 1, pp. 119, 142, 152; vol. 2, pp. 4, 101, 175, 180, 240, 314–15, 339–40, 367, 394, 468, 538, 559. On the laws of 1265, ibid., vol. 2, pp. 22–3, 75–6, 107, 126, 146–7, 185–6, 208–9, 247–8, 293–4, 318, 344, 377–8, 408, 418–20, 506–8.

92. Lane, *Venice*, pp. 106–7; Cracco, *Società e stato*, pp. 214–15, 262–3.

93. *CAV*, vol. 1, p. 67; vol. 2, pp. 70, 103, 183, 232, 292, 315–16, 342–3, 369, 408, 503; vol. 3, pp. 137, 162, 190, 200.

94. Ibid., vol. 1, pp. 56, 60, 119–20, 148, 152; vol. 2, pp. 16, 404.

95. Ibid., vol. 2, pp. 404, 461.
96. Dandolo, *Chronica*, p. 314.
97. Cracco, *Società e stato*, p. 262. On the rest of Italy, see Larner, *Age of Dante and Petrarch*, p. 113.
98. For the list of magistrates, *CAV*, vol. 1, pp. lxi–lxxx.
99. M. Pozza, *I Badoer: una famiglia veneziana dal 10 al 13 secolo* (Padua, 1982), pp. 52–60; Dandolo, *Chronica Breve*, pp. 318–19, 528; Cracco, *Società e stato*, pp. 183, 322–3; Lane, *Venice*, p. 107.
100. Pozza, *I Badoer*, p. 58 and n. 84.
101. Cracco, *Società e stato*, p. 262.
102. *CAV*, vol. 2, pp. 155, 433.
103. Ibid., vol. 2, p. 159; vol. 3, pp. 53, 200.
104. R. T. Rapp, *Industry and Economic Decline in 17th-century Venice*, (Cambridge, Mass., 1976), p. 15.
105. H. Pirenne, *Early Democracies in the Low Countries: Urban Society and Political Conflict in the Middle Ages and the Renaissance*, trans. J. V. Sanders, intro. by J. H. Mundy (New York, 1963), pp. 94–109; Lestocquoy, *Les villes*, p. 76; Pullan, Review of Cracco, *Società e Stato*, p. 187; R. S. Mackenney, 'Arti e stato a Venezia tra tardo medio evo e '600', *SV*, new ser., vol. 5 (1981), p. 123 and n. 26.
106. Pirenne, *Early Democracies*, p. 72; idem, *Economic and Social History of Medieval Europe*, trans. I. E. Clegg (London, 1936), pp. 189–90; Lestocquoy, *Les villes*, pp. 78, 131, 139, 141.
107. A. Doren, *Die Florentiner Wollentuchindustrie* (Stuttgart, 1901), pp. 353, 389, 400, 447; Rodolico, *I Ciompi*, pp. 2–10; idem, 'The Struggle for the Right of Association in 14th-century Florence', *History*, vol. 7 (1922–23), pp. 178–90; Rutenburg, *Popolo*, pp. 78, 104; S. Cohn, *The Labouring Classes in Renaissance Florence* (New York, 1980), p. 9.
108. D. M. Nicholas, *Town and Countryside: Social, Economic and Political Tensions in 14th-century Flanders* (Bruges, 1971), pp. 9, 69–70, 103, 177, 182; A. Derville, 'Les draperies flamandes et artésiennes, vers 1250–1350: quelques considérations critiques et problématiques', *Revue du Nord*, vol. 54, no. 215 (1972), pp. 355–62; E. Coornaert, 'Draperies rurales, draperies urbaines: l'évolution de l'industrie flamande au moyen age et au 16e siècle', *Revue Belge de Philologie et d'Histoire*, vol. 28, no. 1 (1950), pp. 59–96.
109. J. M. Najemy, *Corporatism and Consensus in Florentine Electoral Politics, 1280–1400* (Chapel Hill, N.Ca., 1982), pp. 17, 30, 43–78, 164.
110. G. A. Brucker, 'The Ciompi Revolution', in N. Rubinstein (ed.), *Florentine Studies: Politics and Society in Renaissance Florence*, (London, 1968), pp. 327–8, 333, 356; B. Stahl, *Adel und Volk im Florentiner Dugento* (Cologne, 1965), pp. 132–61.
111. G. Villani, *Cronica: Con le continuazioni di Matteo e Filippo*, ed. G. Aquilecchia (Turin, 1979), pp. 196, 206–9; de Roover, 'Labour Conditions'; C. M. de la Roncière, *Prix et salaires à Florence au 14e siècle* (Rome, 1982); Brucker, 'Ciompi Revolution', pp. 328, 336–7; A. Sapori, *Una compagnia di calimala ai primi del '300* (Florence, 1932), p. 127; Hoshino, *L'arte della lana*, pp. 38, 74, 131, 138, 160, 198, 199, 202.
112. Fano, 'Richerche', p. 96; Mazzaoui, *Cotton Industry*, pp. 108, 113, 164.
113. Quoted in Luzzatto, *Storia economica*, p. 166. See also ibid., pp.

90–6; G. Ruggiero, *Violence in Early Renaissance Venice*, (New Brunswick, N.J., 1980), p. 62.

114. W. M. Bowsky, *A Medieval Italian Commune: Siena under the Nine, 1287–1355* (Berkeley and Los Angeles, 1981), pp. 125–36; R. S. Lopez, *Studi sull'economia genovese nel medio evo* (Turin, 1936), pp. 65–206; G. A. Williams, *Medieval London: From Commune to Capital* (London, 1963), pp. 106–95. On Italy in general see L. Martines (ed.), *Violence and Civil Disorder in Italian Cities, 1200–1500* (Berkeley and Los Angeles, 1972).

115. A. R. Bridbury, *Medieval English Clothmaking: An Economic Survey*, (London, 1982); Doren, *Wollentuchindustrie*, pp. 248–9.

116. Jones, 'Economia e società', pp. 291–5, 303–4, 310.

117. S. L. Thrupp, *The Merchant Class of Medieval London*, (Chicago, Ill., 1948), p. 14.

118. Williams, *Medieval London*, pp. 1, 15, 21, 24, 74.

119. Pirenne, *Early Democracies*, p. 21; Nicholas, *Town and Countryside*, pp. 54–5, 69–70.

120. J. H. Mundy, *Liberty and Political Power in Toulouse, 1050–1230* (New York, 1954), pp. 63, 67; Ph. Wolff, *Commerce et marchands de Toulouse, vers 1350– vers 1450* (Paris, 1954), p. 622.

121. A. I. K. MacKay, 'Ciudad y campo en la Europa medieval', *Studia Historica*, vol. 2, no. 2 (1982), pp. 27–53. I am most grateful to Dr MacKay for drawing my attention to the Spanish examples he has studied.

122. Ph. Dollinger, *The German Hansa*, trans. D. S. Ault and S. H. Steinberg (London, 1970), pp. 3–84; and on Henry the Lion, pp. 379–80.

123. M. Tabarrini, 'Le consorterie nella storia fiorentina del medio evo', in *La vita italiana nel '300* (Milan, 1912), pp. 98–127; Jones, 'Economia e società', p. 307; D. P. Waley, *The Italian City-Republics* (London, 1969), pp. 170–82; G. Salvemini, *Magnati e popolani in Firenze dal 1280 al 1295*, (1899, reissued, ed. E. Sestan, Milan, 1966), pp. 61–3, 146; Stahl, *Adel und Volk*, p. 169; M. B. Becker, 'A Study in Political Failure: The Florentine Magnates, 1280–1433', *Medieval Studies*, vol. 27 (1965), p. 265; idem, 'La esecuzione della legislatura contro le pratiche monopolistiche delle arti fiorentine alla metà del sec. 14', *ASI*, no. 117, disp. 1 (1959), p. 20; Najemy, *Corporatism and Consensus*, pp. 9–17, 43, 164, 227, 299–300.

124. N. Ottokar, *Il comune di Firenze alla fine del '200* (Florence, 1962), p. 16.

125. Rodolico, *I Ciompi*, p. 79.

126. *Fonti sulle corporazioni*, vol. 4, p. 255; vol. 9, p. 7; vol. 5, p. 16; vol. 1, pp. 63, 69.

127. A. Doren, *Le arti fiorentine*, trans. G. B. Klein, 2 vols. (Florence, 1940), vol. 2, p. 69; N. Rodolico, *Il popolo minuto: note di storia fiorentina, 1343–78* (Florence, 1968), p. 17.

128. Larner, *Age of Dante and Petrarch*, p. 196; Doren, *Arti fiorentine*, vol. 1, p. 237.

129. N. Machiavelli, *Florentine History*, trans. W. K. Marriott (London, 1909), p. 116.

130. Ottokar, *Comune di Firenze*, p. 31; Doren, *Wollentuchindustrie*, pp. 242–3; F. W. Kent, *Household and Lineage in Renaissance Florence: The Family Life of the Capponi, Ginoti and Rucellai* (Princeton, N.J., 1977), pp. 226, 299;

R. A. Goldthwaite, *Private Wealth in Renaissance Florence: A Study of Four Families* (Princeton, N.J., 1968), p. 253; R. C. Trexler, *Public Life in Renaissance Florence* (New York, 1980), pp. 27–30. On Florentine statehood, see M. B. Becker, 'An Essay on the Quest for Identity in the Early Italian Renaissance', in Rowe and Stockdale (eds.), '*Florilegium Historiale*', pp. 294–312; N. Rubinstein, 'Notes on the Word "Stato" in Florence before Machiavelli', in the same volume, pp. 313–27; J. H. Hexter, '"Il Principe" and "Lo Stato"', *Studies in the Renaissance*, vol. 4 (1957), pp. 113–38. On the Medici, J. R. Hale, *Florence and the Medici: The Pattern of Control* (London, 1977), pp. 39–42.

131. Trexler, *Public Life*, p. 27; J. R. Strayer, *On the Medieval Origins of the Modern State* (Princeton, N.J., 1970), pp. 7–9; Jones, 'Economia e società', p. 349.

132. S. Chojnacki, 'Crime, Punishment and the '300 Venetian State', in Martines (ed.), *Violence and Civil Disorder*, pp. 222–8.

133. Marchionne di Coppo Stefani, *Cronaca fiorentina*, in *RIS*, vol. 30 (Città di Castello, 1903), p. 413, rubric 923 for 1382.

134. D. di Chinazzo, *Cronica de la guera da veniciani a zenovesi*, ed. V. Lazzarini (Venice, 1958), p. 61.

135. B. Cecchetti, 'Il vitto dei veneziani nel sec. 14', *AV*, vol. 29 (1885), p. 235; Jones, 'Economia e società', p. 340.

136. Doren, *Arti fiorentine*, vol. 1, p. 169; Rodolico, *Popolo minuto*, pp. 11, 16.

137. De la Roncière, *Prix et salaires*, p. 790; M. A. Gukowski, 'Chi fu a capo della sommossa dei Ciompi?', in *Studi in onore di Armando Sapori*, 2 vols. (Milan, 1957), vol. 1, pp. 707–14. For a suggestive interpretation of the link between the textile industries and heresy, see L. Zanoni, *Gli umiliati nei loro rapporti con l'eresia: l'industria della lana ed i comuni nei sec. 12 e 13 sulla scorta di documenti inediti* (Milan, 1911).

2

Guilds and Christian Brotherhood, *c.*1350–*c.*1520

Introduction

In the last chapter, guilds, especially those in Venice, were used as a way of examining the relationship between rulers and ruled in the medieval commune. The economic, administrative and political functions of guilds were, however, inseparable from their devotional activities. As has been said of Nuremberg, 'piety and devotional exercises had always been considered aspects of civic conduct and as such not so different from selling shoes or guarding moats and walls'.[1] We must understand the nature of the fraternal impulse which brought people together to form religious sodalities as well as trade guilds. The commitment of both types of guild to a religious routine, to piety and good works, was one of their most significant characteristics.

As we have seen, trade guilds were associations which united in Christian brotherhood the practitioners of a particular occupation. Some confraternities existed purely for devotional purposes and were not formed around the practice of a common trade. Religious sodalities of this type are best defined as 'voluntary groups of laymen who met together at regular intervals to do pious and charitable works in honour of a patron saint'.[2] This chapter explores further the religious life of late medieval guilds, first through pious confraternities and then through the charitable institutions attached to trade guilds.

From the thirteenth century onwards, under the guidance of the Mendicant Orders, brotherhoods were formed to carry out the works of corporal mercy enjoined in Matthew, XXV, 31–46: to feed the hungry, to give drink to the thirsty, to clothe the naked, to harbour the harbourless, to visit the sick, and to these were added the obligations to ransom the captive and to bury the dead.[3] The recipients of these mercies were not always found within the ranks of the confraternities themselves, but outsiders who were assisted were usually the permanently and obviously needy: widows, cripples, orphans, or those who, like Saint Francis, had renounced the world for a life of apostolic poverty. For members themselves, the provision of burial and the cult of the dead gained special emphasis.[4]

There are acute problems of method and conceptualisation attached to the study of urban confraternities before the Counter-Reformation. How do we measure the social foundations of Christian sentiment? Was there a connection between 'popular movements' and permanent brotherhoods? Did the Church seek to promote the formation of brotherhoods to enhance lay orthodoxy, or to restrain them as potential nests of heresy? Did confraternities develop out of a recognition by the merchant class and the Church of a common interest in preserving the status quo by convincing the poor of the spiritual worthiness of poverty and channelling their aspirations toward rewards in the hereafter rather than improvements in the here and now?[5]

Perhaps the most important traps to avoid are the stereotypes associated with 'popular' and 'institutional' religion or with 'élites' and 'masses' in society.[6] 'Popular' religious feeling could be stirred by Dominicans acting without the approval of higher authority.[7] As for the interests of the 'merchant class', this is an artificially precise term. One of the main arguments prompted by the Venetian evidence is that the status and interests of guildsmen, and indeed the relationship to the means of production of those engaged in business activity, were so diverse that to speak of a 'class' is misleadingly simple. Confraternities are perhaps to be understood as standing at the intersection of the religious and economic life of a wide range of different sorts of people. They sought to glorify God by exalting poverty, and their devotion and their philanthropy were inseparable.

The breadth of the social stratum with which we are concerned takes us into the world of guilds and guildsmen who did not figure amongst either the very rich or the permanently needy, but of people who may have given alms on one occasion and been in need of them on another. Some supplementary aid of a modest sort may well have been available to artisans through the mutual aid schemes of trade guilds, which appear to have proliferated in the course of the fifteenth century.[8] However, while the charity of confraternities was directed towards those in permanent need, to those in a state of apostolic poverty and to those who could afford to be guild members, there was no real recognition of poverty as a temporary problem produced by unfavourable economic circumstances which affected society as a whole. Put more simply, confraternities, whether or not they were attached to trade guilds, made scant provision for dependent wage-labourers. Late medieval associations dealt in palliatives and tended to promote charity as conscience money rather than developing schemes for the systematic relief of material want at times of economic hardship. The devotional character of charity was more prominent than the easing of material indigence. In some parts of Europe, by the late fourteenth century, commemorative masses attracted considerably greater bequests than alms.[9] Confraternities retained a connection with the traditions of apostolic poverty, but they also looked forward to the cult of the splendour of holiness associated with the Counter-Reformation.[10]

The Venetian experience

Given the precocity of Venice as a sovereign state, it is not surprising that the Church occupied a distinctive place in the constitutional and institutional life of the city. By about 1500, there were vast numbers of religious buildings in the city: 70 or so parish churches, 64 monasteries and convents.[11] The location of the cathedral is perhaps the most telling symbol of the place occupied by the Church in Venetian life. It stood at San Pietro di Castello in an isolated area of the city near the Arsenal. It is easy to overlook the fact that the centre of Venice's religious life, San Marco, was the Doge's private chapel, a constant reminder of the intimate relationship between religious and political power, a material manifestation of the divine favour attached to Venice's wealth and authority, both of which were unmistakably worldly.[12] Neither the Church nor churchmen ever became foci for discontented opposition to the patrician state. When, in the early seventeenth century, the Jesuits seemed to pose a threat to the sovereignty of the Venetian Republic, they were expelled from the city, which was then placed under the papal ban. The authorities could still ensure a staggering display of worldly riches, priestly obedience and popular loyalty at great festivals like Corpus Christi.[13]

At the parish level, the Church was tied to an unusually democratic way of life in that local residents elected their own priest.[14] Many of the altars in parish churches, however, were maintained by brotherhoods, the *scuole*, which often had nothing to do with the life of the parochial community.

The Venetian *scuola* was a devotional confraternity which existed for the conviviality of an annual feast, the celebration of saints as intercessors and the commemoration of dead brothers at mass where candles were burned in their memory. As we have already seen, virtually all the trade guilds or *arti* of Venice had a *scuola* attached to them, though these had a stronger emphasis on the provision of benefits in the event of accident or illness than was the case in sodalities which were not based on a particular profession. Confraternities of this latter type themselves took a variety of forms. The most prominent were the *Scuole Grandi* which had little to do with parochial life but established their own impressive halls in each of the city's six *sestieri*. The earliest of them were the great confraternities established in the 1260s, a time of acute religious uncertainty in Italy.[15] By the end of the thirteenth century, there were four of these institutions, San Giovanni Evangelista, Santa Maria della Misericordia, San Marco and Santa Maria della Carità. Another was established, probably in direct response to repeated bouts of pestilence, in the name of San Rocco in 1489. In 1554, the *scuola* of San Teodoro was given the status of *Scuola Grande*, a move which reflected the growing wealth and prestige of the mercers' guild to which the *scuola* was attached.[16] The Scuola Grande dei Carmini was added to the list in 1767.[17]

In the first instance, the *Scuole Grandi* were allowed a maximum membership of 550. They were brotherhoods of *disciplinati* who practised flagellation, regular confession and, periodically, sexual abstinence.[18] But they became great charitable institutions. The splendour of their processions, recorded in the masterpieces of Gentile Bellini and Carpaccio, should not distract attention from their extensive philanthropic activities. Membership was divided into clearly defined orders of rich and poor: people who gave alms and people who received them, both on a regular basis. As Professor Pullan has shown, the *Scuole Grandi* also exercised an important influence on the development and funding of other charitable institutions, particularly hospitals.[19]

The combination of devotion and philanthropy which was the central organising principle of the *Scuole Grandi* was passed on to the smaller confraternities with which this chapter is concerned. These existed as pious associations of devout layment from different parts of the city and often from different professions who met to promote the cult of a saint through regular liturgical exercises.

Other types of *scuole* included those which formed among the various foreign communities of 'nations' which had established themselves in the city. There was a *scuola* for Greeks, another for Albanians, and the Slavs established a confraternity at the old Hospital of Saint John in 1451. Other regions of Italy were represented by confraternities of Milanese, Florentines, Bergamascs and Lucchesi. There were even *scuole* amongst the Jews. Such institutions were formed by people engaged in professions, trades and crafts, and they usually offered some sort of scheme of spiritual and material benefits. There were also organisations which looked to groups on the margins of society. There was a confraternity whose business it was to accompany the condemned to execution, and another consisted of cripples.[20]

Like the trade guilds, the *scuole* were carefully regulated by the government. The smaller confraternities were under the control of the *Provveditori di Comun*, but from 1360 the statutes of new confraternities were referred to the Council of Ten for approval. Pious confraternities were perfectly acceptable to the Venetian government as long as they were legally recognised and therefore legally controllable. But the authorities had no time for spontaneous fervour. When the Bianchi organised a procession at San Zanipolo in 1399, the assembly was swiftly dispersed by order of the Ten.[21]

Formal application seems in the main to have resulted in formal approval. As can be seen from Appendix I, the confraternities maintained an ubiquitous presence in the city, though we cannot be entirely sure precisely how many *scuole* existed at any one time because the brotherhoods tended to form and reform in response to the enthusiasm — or lack of it — among members. Between 1360 and 1476, 45 new statutes were registered by the Ten.[22] In 1521, Marin Sanudo recorded in his diary that 119 *scuole* were in procession at the Doge's funeral.[23] An eighteenth-century survey listed no fewer than 357 confraternities; at least 80 have left some impression on the material fabric of modern Venice.[24] Our best guide may be the fifteenth-century poem written by a Florentine merchant, Jacopo d'Albizzotto Guidi, which mentions a figure of 200 confraternities — the author himself was a member of San Cristofalo dei Mercanti, a confraternity which bulks large in the rest of the chapter.[25]

All of them were more closely related to the Venetian state than to the universal Church. The close relationship which existed between the brotherhoods and the political structures of the state has drawn some commentators to suggest that the *scuole* provide another reason for the lack of unrest in the city of Venice. As early as the 1520s, Gasparo Contarini wrote that competition for office in the *Scuole Grandi* allowed people of the middling sort to channel their aspirations toward positions of prestige in a manner which imitated the aristocracy, but without threatening the patriciate's monopoly of power.[26] Much more recently, Professor Pullan's study of the *Scuole Grandi* presents the idea that the availability of a wide variety of forms of poor relief within a large number of charitable institutions may well have eased conditions of hardship which were otherwise politically and socially volatile.[27]

Dr Mueller has argued that the *Scuole Grandi* cannot have involved more than about 10 per cent of the population in their activities and that this inhibited their potential for the relief of poverty and the soothing of social tension.[28] It would appear that the *scuole piccole* extended the devotional activities of the *Scuole Grandi* but did not build up their charitable work in the way that the larger confraternities did, but there are three reasons for this. First, members of the *scuole* would not have regarded devotion and charity as separate principles, still less as competitive ones. The idea that devotional commitment might somehow reduce the capacity to relieve the poor would not have occurred to them before the sixteenth century. Moreover, confraternities were concerned with the welfare of members rather than outsiders, and members would not have viewed poverty as a problem in society at large. However, there may be other grounds for suggesting that the *scuole* helped to preserve social harmony in Venice. The principles of brotherhood embodied in the *scuole piccole* cut across lines of occupation, 'class' and parish, and before the sixteenth century the charitable activities of the *scuole* attached to trade guilds may have protected guildsmen from the worst effects of shortage.

'Devotional philanthropy'

The purpose of a *scuola* was made plain in the preamble of its statute. The scuola of Santa Maria della Celestia, one of the many established round the cult of the Virgin, reminded members that 'we do not have a lasting city here, but, as the Apostle says, we must seek the Eternal City and strive to go there'.[29] The merchants of the scuola di San Cristofalo advised each other, 'you must always have before the eyes of the mind the end of this transitory life and think upon it'. They continue:

> Let there be increase of the church and monastery where we are gathered and exaltation of this blessed scuola and comfort and utility for the poor, bearing in mind that the more we turn with praise, reverence and devotion to St Christopher, the more fervent will he be [on our behalf] before Our Creator.[30]

Santi Apostoli had statutes which lugubriously warned 'you know not the day or the hour of your death'. Salvation was to be sought through prayer and alms, and a reference to St James shows how closely linked were devotional activity and philanthropy:

> inspired with divine grace we have begun to ponder on how through brotherhood, prayer and alms we may acquire the salvation of our souls, recalling what St James says; 'Pray for each other that you may be saved, for the prayer of a just man is worth much.'[31]

On religious festivals and state occasions, the brethren took part in processions, often with the participation of clergy who in some cases were formally enrolled in the *scuola*. Members were encouraged to attend mass once a month and, in accordance with canon law, to confess once a year. There were also stern words about the need for mutual correction. Sometimes, as in the *Scuole Grandi*, this took the form of flagellation; more usually, members seen to be in a state of sin were reported, examined and told to reform or else leave the brotherhood. This was part of the Church's work in the world but since the state controlled the statutes, it was also the state's work amongst Venetians.[32]

While the statutes' emphasis on penitence, works and the cult of the dead is similar to those of the *Scuole Grandi*, there were no formal orders of rich and poor in the smaller confraternities. Some philanthropy was practised: a poor artisan's declaration of want could lead to a collection on his behalf, and sometimes members gave a meal to outsiders.[33]

The Carità was re-formed in 1350 as the scuola di Santi Apostoli and its statute enjoined members to watch over the sick.[34] But their philanthropy was overlain with devotion, and benefits often covered the next world rather than this one. A member of Sant'Orsola who lay ill would be visited by two friars who would 'give consolation as to the salvation of his soul'.[35] Members who died outside Venice were buried at the expense of the *scuola* and were assured of a memorial service. Candles were to burn at the Celestia's altar 'for the salvation of our souls and of all brethren and sisters of the *scuola* who have passed from this life'.[36]

The funding of these activities remains something of a mystery. The finances of the *scuole piccole* cannot be examined through surviving evidence. It may well be that they never needed regular funds for much more than bread, candles, the occasional object of devotion and 'one-off' collections for members who were hard up, though this remains speculation until more concrete evidence is found. The records do enable us to address the vital question of membership. Who joined the confraternities? Who could regard whom as brother?

The composition of membership

The preambles to the statutes of the *scuole piccole* suggest that the religious insecurity of the later Middle Ages drove people together to seek salvation through brotherhood. However transient earthly life might prove, there was some comfort in the knowledge that the bonds of brotherhood could last for ever. New members of the brotherhood kept alive the memory of those who had died. The impulse to join an association of Christians may have been especially strong in Venice where the individual found identity as part of a group — family, patriciate, guild, confraternity — rather than as an independent being. If Death was a great leveller, so was brotherhood, and brotherhood might triumph over Death itself. The way in which the *scuole* brought different sorts of people together as Christians and Venetians is the theme of the remainder of this chapter.

It is impossible to be more than impressionistic about how many Venetians belonged to confraternities in the fourteenth and fifteenth centuries. The *Scuole Grandi* were limited in theory to 550 members each, but in 1446 the Misericordia embraced almost three times that figure.[37] Professor Sbriziolo's research led her to suggest an average figure of about 60 or 70 members in a *scuola piccola* in the fifteenth century.[38] A list of members of Santa Maria della Carità for 1288 includes 21 names.[39] As early as 1325, the scuola di Sant'Agnese had set a maximum of 550 on its membership, probably in imitation of the *Scuole Grandi*.[40] Around 1350, the records of the Celestia speak of as many as 700 brothers.[41]

The statute or *mariegola* of the Celestia, drawn up in 1337, includes a list of members, and there are three similar lists from the *trecento*: from Santi Apostoli (1350), Sant'Anna di Castello (1351) and, most intriguing in terms of its designation, San Cristofalo dei Mercanti (1377), which met at Santa Maria dell'Orto.[42]

The four lists were drawn up in alphabetical order and provide name, parish of provenance and, in about half of all cases, occupation. This material enables us to gain some idea of the kinds of people who joined a particular *scuola* and the relationship of the confraternity to the parish in which it met.

The major drawback of the lists is that the exact period of time they cover is unclear: it is impossible to say how many members there were in a particular year. The concluding date used in the tables, 1520, is based on the inclusion in San Cristofalo of Giovanni Bellini and Alvise Vivarini. Bellini died in 1515, Vivarini in 1523 (by which time he was also a member of the Scuola Grande di San Marco).[43] The other lists do not include such famous names, but finish in the same style of handwriting. It may be that by the early sixteenth century the older confraternities were gradually being displaced or transformed by institutions associated with Catholic reform, a process speeded up by the plague of 1528–29 and by the Counter-Reformation.[44]

It is disconcerting that the lists represent only two of the six areas into which the city was divided and it is disappointing that there are no lists of women members, for some *scuole* included them in separate but parallel organisations within the sodality.[45]

Given problems of this type, conclusions drawn from the lists must be circumspect. But it is unusual in Venetian evidence of this period to find the names of nearly 5000 adult males identified in even this much detail. If one member of each nuclear family or household is represented only once, and if, as in Verona, the average Venetian family comprised about four persons, as many as 20,000 Venetians are in some way connected to these four *scuole*.[46] Much can be learned about the occupations and parishes of provenance of those who joined a *scuola*.

Occupation and status

The occupational composition of the four *scuole* is shown in Table 2.1. Professional title is not an entirely reliable guide to social status, especially in Venice, with its wide band of guildsmen not riven by the gulf which separated merchants and dependent wage earners. All members of the *scuole* were 'respectable', many of them 'well-to-do', but what needs to be emphasised is the breadth of the social stratum covered by such terms, even in a *scuola* supposed to be 'of the merchants', as San Cristofalo was.

Table 2.1: *Composition of the scuole piccole by occupation*

	S. Anna		Celestia		S. Cris.		Apostoli	
total no. of entrants	889		1269		1352		1284	
time span of lists	1351–1520		1337–1520		1377–1520		1350–1520	
	no.	%	no.	%	no.	%	no.	%
professions and civil service	12	1.35	11	0.86	27	1.99	15	1.16
luxury trades, books, art, music, jewellery	29	3.26	81	6.38	67	4.95	42	3.27
groceries and drugs	21	2.36	18	1.41	34	2.51	15	1.16
traders, brokers, merchants	17	1.91	41	3.23	90	6.65	31	2.41
Arsenal workers, boatmen	71	7.98	19	1.49	12	0.89	74	5.76
textiles and clothing	72	8.10	123	9.69	155	11.46	279	21.72
footwear and leather	17	1.91	40	3.15	11	0.81	34	2.64
victuals and wine	28	3.15	36	2.83	26	1.92	53	4.12
building	27	3.03	31	2.44	33	2.44	42	3.27
wood and metal	45	5.06	49	3.86	28	2.07	33	2.57
household utensils	6	0.67	18	1.41	4	0.30	44	3.43
barbers, surgeons, dentists	8	0.89	11	0.86	21	1.55	16	1.25
servants	—	—	1	0.07	—	—	6	0.47
porters	2	0.22	2	0.15	1	0.07	10	0.78
priests	79	8.88	6	0.47	—	—	15	1.17
nobles	73	8.21	132	10.40	65	4.81	9	0.70
total specified by occupation	507	56.98	619	48.70	574	42.42	718	55.88
unspecified	382	43.02	650	51.30	778	57.58	566	44.12
total	889	100	1269	100	1352	100	1284	100

source: See n. 42.

If we start at the bottom of the lists and the top of the social scale comprehended by 'the middling sort', we find a number of aristocratic members. However, despite the precision of the designation *nobile* in political life, in the confraternities it is ambiguous. Many — probably most — of those listed as nobles had simply bought the title from the *scuola* and held the status only within the confines of the confraternity. Nobles were not allowed to hold office in the confraternity, so those non-patricians who could afford to do so bought a 'title' from the *scuola* which made them ineligible to stand for election to the *scuola*'s committees. Those listed in the Tables as 'nobles', in other words, were not part of a legally defined status group outside the confraternity. At the Celestia, this category included a high-ranking civil servant, a builder, an engineer, a goldsmith, two notaries and a dealer in silk.

The category 'textiles and cothing' masks numerous gradations between weavers, stretchers, dyers, drapers and cloth merchants. The silk industry's base in Santi Apostoli may have led manual workers to join the local scuola, those involved in the textile trade as retailers and merchants were more likely to join San Cristofalo dei Mercanti. Spinners and dyers who were members were probably heads of shops and may have been as prosperous as lesser merchants. Carders do *not* figure in the lists, but the Venetian equivalent of the *Ciompi* (probably not a large group in any case) had their own organisation which maintained an altar at San Simeon Profeta.[47]

These points should be borne in mind as one considers the figures themselves, concentrating all the time on who joined a *scuola* rather than who was excluded.

Sant'Anna, located not far from the Arsenal, had a relatively high proportion of tradesmen engaged in the shipyards and related trades. Nearly 8 per cent were Arsenal workers and boatmen and some of the wood, metal and building workers may have been employed, at least spasmodically, in the shipyards. As in the other three *scuole*, the largest trade represented was textiles (8.1 per cent) though they were outnumbered by priests (9 per cent) and nobles (8.2 per cent). Why there were so many priests is unclear: perhaps the clergy of the Cathedral at San Pietro were encouraged to attach themselves to a specifically Venetian institution.

As can be seen from the map (Appendix I), Santa Maria della Celestia was the nearest of the *scuole* to San Marco. Here, nobles were the largest group represented, though nearly 10 per cent of members were involved in the textile trades, and this category may well overlap with some of the luxury trades (6.38 per cent) and the general merchants (3.23 per cent). The Arsenal work-force is poorly represented (1.49 per cent) but a total of nearly 10 per cent from trades such as leather (3.15), building (2.44), wood and metal (3.86), strongly underlines the tendency of the confraternities to involve all occupational groups from merchants to handicraft workers.

San Cristofalo was located near Santa Maria dell'Orto. Only about 40 per cent of members were identified by trade, suggesting that the *scuola* was dominated by businessmen (the *Mercanti* of the *scuola*'s title) and this is reinforced by the relatively high proportion of luxury traders (4.95 per cent) and general traders (6.65 per cent), which are more than double the figures in any one of the other *scuole*.

By contrast, Santi Apostoli seems to have included many more craft workers. There were few nobles and over one-fifth of the membership was in the textile trades. Arsenal workers (5.76 per cent), tanners (2.64), food-sellers (4.12), building (3.27), wood and metal (2.57) and household trades (3.43) make up nearly another quarter. It looks as though almost half the members could be identified as artisans.

Table 2.2: *Composition of the scuole piccole by occupation: an overall view, 1337–1520*

	number	% of entrants
professions and civil service	65	1.36
luxury trades, books, jewellery, art, music	219	4.57
groceries and drugs	88	1.83
traders, brokers, merchants	179	3.73
Arsenal workers, boatmen	176	3.68
textiles and clothing	629	13.12
footwear and leather	102	2.13
victuals and wine	143	2.98
building	133	2.77
wood and metal	155	3.23
household utensils	72	1.50
barbers, surgeons, dentists	56	1.17
servants	7	0.15
porters	15	0.31
priests	100	2.09
nobles	279	5.82
unspecified	2376	49.56
total	4794	100.00

This brief survey indicates that the sample includes two *scuole* for businessmen (the Celestia and San Cristofalo) and two which found more room for craftsmen (Sant'Anna, Santi Apostoli). But it is vital to stress that all four confraternities included a wide variety of occupational groups, a point made even more clearly when the same occupational categories are applied to the figures as a whole (Table 2.2).

The figures demonstrate that the differences between the *scuole* were of shade rather than colour (rather like the *arti medie* of the guild system). The *scuola* was not the preserve of a particular class and its all-embracing quality is emphasised by the fact that members could be drawn from all over the city. Little is known about the importance of the neighbourhood in Venetian life.[48] These membership lists seem to say that before the sixteenth century, the bonds of brotherhood transcended parish ties.

Membership and the parish

The point to be made here is a straightforward one. The *scuole* under examination were supra-parochial institutions and the lack of a parochial focus for the religious life of the Venetian laity is likely to have made the brotherhoods even more significant in the city's history. This is best demonstrated by reference to Appendix II which gives a breakdown of all four membership lists according to parish of provenance. Two other sets of figures are included to give a very rough idea of the relative size of the parishes themselves. They are late sixteenth-century estimates of numbers of parishioners made by Francesco Sansovino and by clerics involved in the Visitation of 1581.[49]

Over 70 churches are represented in each *scuola*, though it is clear that the two which seemed biased toward lower social groups had a tendency to express a certain neighbourhood solidarity. Nearly a third of the members of Santi Apostoli came from the parish of that name. Bearing in mind the occupational composition of this *scuola*, we might conclude that textile workers were permitted to be part of an association which expressed the ties of locality and trade, and in this sense the *scuola* could be seen as a microcosm of the Venetian polity itself. Sant'Anna drew 226 members (not all, of course, at the same time) from San Pietro di Castello, and significant numbers from other parishes near the Arsenal (San Zuan in Bragora, San Martino). The other two *scuole* with their 'businessmen' membership reveal no concentrations of this kind. However, while no one from San Pietro ever joined the 'businessmen's' scuola of San Cristofalo, only one from San Pietro, a 'worker's' parish joined the 'craftsman's' scuola at Santi Apostoli. Small parishes like San Bartolomeo and San Salvador, which were close to the commercial centre of Venice at Rialto, sent high numbers to San Cristofalo and to the Celestia. Few who resided near Rialto were attracted to the nearest *scuola*, Santi Apostoli.

The figures from Appendix II can be presented in a more digestible form. Venice was divided into six areas or *sestieri*. By arranging the parishes according to the sestier in which they were located, we can establish a general picture of the spread of membership through the city. The results are summarised in Table 2.3 and Figure 2.1.

Table 2.3: *The distribution of membership in the sestieri (%)*

	S. Anna	Celestia	S. Cris.	Apostoli
San Marco	21.49	25.30	12.94	4.36
Cannaregio	8.44	9.70	22.49	54.44
Castello	56.92	41.69	6.88	5.92
San Polo	3.82	7.41	10.43	2.65
Santa Croce	2.36	5.67	9.91	4.05
Dorsoduro	2.92	5.04	5.10	1.40
Unidentified by parish	4.05	5.19	32.25	27.18
total	100.00	100.00	100.00	100.00

The membership of Sant'Anna was concentrated in two contiguous areas (San Marco and Castello). Large numbers of members seem to have been local inhabitants. This local concentration was repeated in Santi Apostoli. Members of San Cristofalo were evenly spread, a further indication perhaps that the *scuola* was universally attractive to those who liked to think of themselves as *mercanti*. The membership of the Celestia tended to come from San Marco and Castello, but over a sixth of members had to cross the Grand Canal to attend an assembly of the brethren.

With the partial exception of the very small numbers who hailed from Dorsoduro and were members of Santi Apostoli, there is a signficant number of people from each sestier in each of the *scuole*. People who did different jobs mingled freely in the *scuole*. These same people generally came from different parishes.

The scuola and the Venetian social structure

By expanding the horizons of the parish to the limits of the sestieri, we can form a general idea of the geographical spread of different trades in the city, as shown at Table 2.4. Castello was dominated by the

Figure 2.1: *Percentage of total membership in each sestier*

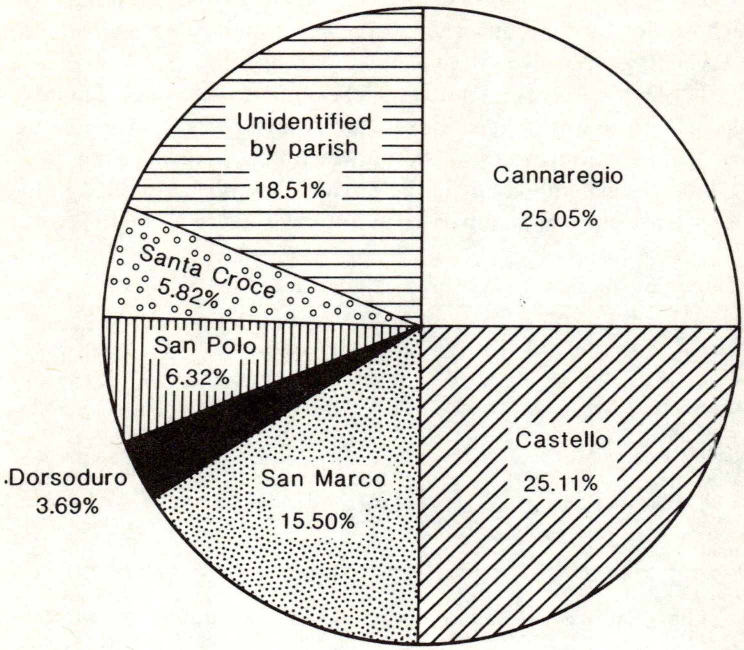

Arsenal, San Marco by the retail trades which lined the Merceria and by the ironmongers in Calle dei Fabbri which ran parallel to it, Cannaregio by the textile trades. For reasons of security (fire and theft were obvious hazards), independent craftsmen worked in or near their home parish and in many cases home and shop will have been one and the same place. The major exceptions to this were Arsenal and textile workers. Of those not identified by parish, about a quarter worked in these industries. There is some evidence, perhaps, that although the *scuole* were institutions for respectable Venetians, some of their members may have been on low incomes, some even dependent assistants. At one end of the spectrum, the world of the guilds shaded into that of merchant patricians, as the high proportion of those who liked to be called

Table 2.4: *Occupations in the sestieri*

	S. Marco		Cannaregio		Castello		S. Polo		S. Croce		Dorsoduro		unidentified by parish	
	No.	%	No.	%	No.	%	No.	%	No.	%	No.	%	No.	%
professions and civil service	8	1.08	16	1.33	8	0.67	5	1.65	3	1.08	1	0.57	24	2.71
luxury trades, books, jewellery, music, art	52	7.00	40	3.33	55	4.57	14	4.62	5	1.79	7	3.95	46	5.18
groceries and drugs	27	3.63	11	0.92	16	1.33	6	1.98	1	0.36	4	2.26	23	2.59
traders, brokers, merchants	45	6.05	24	2.00	37	3.07	13	4.29	10	3.58	7	3.95	43	4.85
Arsenal workers, boatmen	10	1.35	38	3.17	73	6.06	3	0.99	5	1.79	5	2.82	42	4.73
textiles and clothing	57	7.67	196	16.32	105	8.72	29	9.57	43	15.41	21	11.86	178	20.07
footwear and leather	20	2.69	31	2.58	30	2.49	6	1.98	4	1.43	—	—	11	1.24
victuals and wine	13	1.75	38	3.17	37	3.07	9	2.97	11	3.94	5	2.82	30	3.38
building	10	1.35	25	2.08	53	4.40	6	1.98	3	1.08	4	2.26	32	3.61
wood and metal	75	10.09	24	2.00	25	2.08	11	3.63	3	1.08	1	0.57	16	1.80
household utensils	4	0.54	32	2.66	12	1.00	4	1.32	1	0.36	1	0.57	18	2.03
barbers, surgeons, dentists	4	0.54	12	1.00	14	1.16	5	1.65	2	0.72	1	0.57	18	2.03
servants	—	—	7	0.58	—	—	—	—	—	—	—	—	—	—
porters	2	0.27	7	0.58	3	0.25	—	—	—	—	—	—	3	0.34
priests	34	4.58	19	1.58	41	3.41	1	0.33	2	0.72	—	—	3	0.34
nobles	62	8.34	65	5.41	69	5.73	20	6.60	11	3.94	12	6.78	40	4.51
unidentified by profession	320	43.07	616	51.29	626	51.99	171	56.44	175	62.72	108	61.02	360	40.59
total	743	100.00	1201	100.00	1204	100.00	303	100.00	279	100.00	177	100.00	887	100.00

'noble' shows. At the other it blended into the world of day labourers. More ideas on the middling stratum of guildsmen in Venetian society are presented in the next chapter. From the statistics presented in this one, Venetian society begins to look like the ducal palace; solidity and bulk at the top, filigree and subtlety of structure in the middle, the lower reaches spacious and airy.

Venetian confraternities encouraged among members a sense of solidarity as Christians and as Venetians. This owed something to medieval piety, which moved all social groups. The figures presented here suggest that even when piety was expressed on a regular institutional basis rather than spontaneously, the spiritual appeal remained comprehensive, at least within a wide and diverse middling group. In that group and within the confraternities, high and low rubbed shoulders. The *scuole* found room for merchants, textile-workers, Arsenalotti and perhaps cut across economic and social groups whose differences might have become clusters of discontent in time of hardship. The mingling of people from different trades and different neighbourhoods was in itself an expression of brotherhood, and the solidarity of members permeated a wide range of different sorts of people.

The confraternities of medieval Venice were 'floating' institutions. The religious life of Venetian laymen transcended parish ties. Pious confraternities expressed the spiritual aspirations of the laity, and those aspirations were not generated or guided by clerical influence. Their character was to change when the Counter-Reformation made the parish church the focus of lay devotion. Parish-based confraternities helped defend the sacraments. According to the Visitation of 1581, all but four Venetian churches housed an altar to the Santissimo Sacramento, and Sansovino said that each altar represented a separate *scuola*.[50]

Before then, the *scuole piccole* may have acted as another of the vaccines which immunised Venice against revolution, but not for predictable reasons. Their potential for the relief of poverty was limited by the constraints of 'devotional philanthropy'. The principle of brotherhood, however, was a binding force in Venetian society, all the stronger because it found a permanent institutional expression in the *scuole*. Venetian confraternities were more than instruments of policy or agencies of poor relief and before they were superseded by the more militant brotherhoods of the Counter-Reformation, they had exercised a considerable influence on the character of Venetian trade guilds.

The confraternities of the trade guilds

As is clear from the map at Appendix I, many of the altars and chapels in Venetian churches were maintained by the trade guilds. The religious brotherhoods of the *arti* shared a number of characteristics with the *scuole piccole*, and they can be set in the same general framework of 'devotional philanthropy'. In 1436, the linen sellers fixed a payment of 4 soldi for women members to buy candles 'for the souls of the dead and for the well-being of the living of the same guild and for the sustenance of the poor and infirm of the same'.[51] The boatmen distributed bread and candles on the feast of St John Lateran in whose church they established a *scuola* in 1451.[52] Some of the corporations elected *poveri* from among their members and those chosen could receive recurrent payments. In the fifteenth century, the painters elected five of their number as *poveri* after a species of means test. By 1529, the mercers were giving six poor members 31 soldi a month.[53] The potters' statute of 1593 reiterated a principle established in the fourteenth century: that the guild should provide relief 'for any master or journeyman who falls into poverty'.[54] Even so, devotion remained costly, material relief rather slight. By the mid-sixteenth century, the goldsmiths were spending a quarter of their outgoings on commemorative candles, a little less on alms (below pp. 171–3).

Like the *scuole piccole*, the *scuole delle arti* were only loosely tied to the parish in which they met. This was due in part to the supra-parochial bond of a common profession which brought members together. However, clear provision for a change of venue was often part of the agreement which the guild made with the local clergy. Thus the mercers held a monthly mass at San Daniele, but every Friday there was a service for members at San Zulian as well (this was much handier for the mercers' shops). The glass-sellers' confraternity met at San Polo, but by the mid-fifteenth century they were seeking a larger chapel. When they moved in 1580, it was from San Zuan Novo to Sant'Anzolo.[55] In 1516, the boatmen made a detailed agreement with the priests of San Silvestro for the performance of a mass on every fourth Sunday 'with organ music and a procession'. There was a mass for the dead every Friday and half a ducat in alms for the priests at any guild burial service. The boatmen were at liberty to improve and embellish their altar, though decorations were to be left behind if the guild transferred its meeting place to another church.[56]

The possibility that guilds would decorate the church in which they assembled may have made them welcome to local priests for reasons of prestige. The mercers commissioned a polyptich for 'one of the finest altars in Venice' at San Daniele and the painting is said to be by Gentile Bellini.[57] They also commissioned Palma Giovane to paint an *Assumption* at San Zulian. The tailors hired Bonifacio de' Pitati to paint a Madonna with their patron Sant'Omobono for their altar in San Giacomo di Rialto. The same artist worked for the poulterers at San Zuan Elemosinario. The considerable catalogue of works of art commissioned by the *scuole delle arti* perhaps reflects a desire to imitate the great cycles by Gentile Bellini and Carpaccio which brought fame and honour to the Scuola Grande di San Giovanni Evangelista.[58]

Guilds contributed things other than paintings to the material fabric of Venetian churches. The mercers kept a chest at San Daniele containing great candle sticks and chandeliers. The pewterers' statute records that they had crosses of copper, tin and wood, six gilt torches, six brass candlesticks and twelve of iron for their altar, and two gilded angels in wood.[59] An inventory in the ironmongers' records included a silver cross, a sword and scabbard decorated with purple and silver, five processional banners (with brass stands) and five painted crosses.[60] Some of these items may not have been commissioned as prestigious vanities: some of the objects carried in procession may well have served to advertise the excellence of the guild's wares.

The *Scuole Grandi*, the *scuole piccole* and the *scuole delle arti* shared common characteristics in their 'devotional philanthropy' and their patronage of the arts, but they did not form a coherent network of charitable institutions with the means of addressing poverty on any great scale. In this the weak links were probably the *scuole piccole* whose potential for the relief of material want seems to have been slight. The mutual aid schemes of the *scuole delle arti* may have been more effective but they were once again restricted to those who were members of the guild, even when membership was, as in the case of the bakers, interpreted fairly broadly.

The bakers' confraternity

There were two different guilds of bakers in Venice. Those who figure in the next few pages were the *forneri*, owners of ovens to whom people took dough to be baked. Those who both kneaded the dough and baked it formed a guild of confectioners (*pistori*).[61]

The records of the *forneri* are typical of the documents relating to guilds in the Venetian archive. There is a large and disorderly file marked 'Various Acts' with documents from the fifteenth century to the eighteenth. Some are bound into booklets but the vast majority are loosely arranged in chronological order. They relate to the original guild statute, afford insights into the supply of galleymen in the sixteenth century and include miscellaneous items relating to guild administration. There are no long series, no comprehensive membership lists, no detailed financial records. There is no searchlight on the Venetian past, no continuous beam on Venetian development. The bakers' records offer a variety of glimpses and insights into certain aspects of what guilds were for, which included the imposition of fines for swearing and the fixing of fees payable to the guild for the right to light up an oven. Most important of all, there are some unusual pieces of information about how a *scuola* was established, what it spent on an annual feast and how its members set up a hospital.[62]

In 1445, the bakers asked permission of the Council of Ten to form a *scuola*. 'All the mysteries and guilds . . . have a confraternity with its own statute . . . such as in our guild and mystery of bakers we have not had.' They wish 'to govern our trade with reason and order and avoid disorder and sources of trouble'. Any political purpose is expressly denied.[63]

The *scuola* held its banquet on the feast of the Magi. The meal, of bread, cheese and wine, cost L.28 in 1447, L.41 in 1453. The next year there were two gatherings, the first for masters only at a cost of L.19, 18 soldi. At the second, 30 members were present and L.51 was spent, over half of it on wine. Musicians were also hired but were kept sober: in 1458, 8 soldi was spent on 'milk for the players'.[64]

The fare was clearly very simple, but far from cheap. The meal for 30 in 1454 cost more than double the L.25 which a journeyman in the confectioners' guild could expect to earn in a year.[65] All the same, the *scuola* expressed the solidarity of members — and not just masters — through material benefits as well as through conviviality. In 1465, the guild petitioned the

Doge — Cristoforo Moro, who would have been familiar with the *scuole* through his membership of San Cristofalo — for permission to found a hospital. The petition emphasised the need to look after those affected by age, sickness or 'poverty through misfortune'.[66] A site about 70 feet square was found in 1471 near Santa Maria dell'Orto. The cost was 1000 ducats, 600 payable at once, the rest over twelve years. By 1477 the project was threatened due to lack of funds, and masters' fees were raised from 7 soldi a month to 8, those payable by assistants from 2 soldi to 4. The increase was approved by the masters and 'many *lavoranti*' which might imply that the latter were entitled to share the benefits of the hospital or could reasonably expect to attain the status of master at some stage in the foreseeable future.

It is worth reflecting on what this tells us about how the guild viewed poverty. The emphasis of the petition was on the need to provide for what historians now call the 'structural poor', or in the bakers' terms, those invalided out of work by age or illness ('*poveri, vecchi, indisponenti*'). They may not have been in this condition on joining the confraternity, but the guild would try to support them if they subsequently became so. However, the fact that the journeymen also contributed to the project suggests that there was some aid for the temporarily disadvantaged or 'crisis poor' as well. Indeed, this is specified in other documents. The guild's officers were allowed to use their discretion in offering shelter 'for a few days to those who in their judgement have not found work through no fault of their own (*non per suo difetto*)'.[67] The hospital was a place of shelter rather than an institution which offered medical treatment and it is striking that the guild could view being out of work not as the result of idleness but as a temporary condition to be treated sympathetically.

This still tells us very little about the scale of guild benefit schemes. It is unclear how many guilds had hospitals. The tailors, silk throwsters and painters certainly did.[68] And there may have been other places of shelter not necessarily called *ospedali*. In 1467, the carpenters bought a property which they renovated 'for the alms of piety and the poor', an illustration of the fluid boundary between devotion and practical help. By 1502, the building was being maintained by members chosen by lot to work on it, including those who were in debt to the guild: they were able to work off what they owed at a rate of 25 soldi a day; other members were welcome to work *amore Dei*. Shelter may also have been available in the *scuole* built by the furriers and shoemakers. In about 1500, the tailors' hospital at the Crosechieri harboured 17 members and their families. This made 'more than 50 mouths to feed . . . supported entirely by alms'.[69] We cannot measure how many people could be supported by the combined welfare structures of Venice's guilds but there is evidence that there was help for those experiencing temporary hardship as well as the permanently needy.

However, to receive guild charity it was essential to be a guild member. There is little to suggest that the *scuole* had the capacity to cope with the poverty of those who were not enrolled in guilds, even had they assumed that it might be their responsibility to do so. As social institutions, guilds may not have done much to reduce the level of poverty in Venice, but, as we have seen, their religious and charitable functions were bound up with their economic life. The business activities of guildsmen occupy the next two chapters, but we shall return to the religious context of economic life in Chapter 5.

Comparisons and contrasts

In the first chapter, great stress was laid on the rural and seigneurial context of urban politics in the late Middle Ages in most towns apart from Venice. The distinctiveness of popular religious life in Venice is more elusive of definition. For many of the features of pious confraternities and their members discussed in this chapter were formed by a religious atmosphere which also pervaded rural communities. Much of what follows is therefore couched in very general terms and the peculiarities of Venice emerge most clearly in a concluding comparison with Nuremberg and Florence.

One of the *scuola*'s preoccupations, praying for the souls of the dead, can be linked with a community as rural and remote as a Pyrenean village. In fourteenth-century Montaillou, the dead had an important role to play, perhaps because the living were 'preoccupied with salvation' and identified easily with life in the hereafter.[70] And one of the most important studies of late medieval religion covers an entire region, Champagne, rather than its towns or its rural areas in isolation. There, too, one can discern characteristics familiar from Venice. Confraternities were much concerned with the cult of the dead and devotion had no strong links with the life of the parish. Members came from a wide variety of occupational and social groups and they made the brotherhoods wealthy enough to embellish many churches. Alms might have been given to the permanently indigent, but, in return, paupers were expected to act as torch-bearers at the donor's funeral, an emphasis of his largesse and their lowliness. Wage labourers, the 'crisis poor', were generally excluded from the charitable works of the brotherhoods. The involvement of the institutional church seems to have been slight, and it often failed to restrain the restless energies of popular devotion, especially at Corpus Christi, a feast day frequently associated with social disturbance. All this was to change under the impact of the Counter-Reformation.[71]

In medieval England, even very small towns were honeycombed with confraternities — there were 40 in Bodmin in the fourteenth century.[72] In larger centres, the overlap with trade guilds was more pronounced even than that of *arti* and *scuole* in Venice. Devotional confraternities attached to trade guilds were almost invariably coterminous with them and the influence of the parish on the life of the brotherhoods was again slight.[73] Religious guilds of all types were regarded with suspicion by the authorities, especially in London, where, as in Florence, they were seen as potential nests of conspiracy. Nevertheless, in London in particular, the incentive to join a confraternity was strong, especially for the widely diversified 'merchant class'. Pious devotion trained the merchant for death — and training was essential for those engaged in a quest for profit, which was scarcely an appropriate preparation for salvation.[74] Again as in Venice, the merchant stratum was very wide and this may help to explain why the city's social institutions were grouped into greater and lesser companies rather like the *Scuole Grandi* and the *scuole piccole*.[75] Like the Venetian bakers, London confraternities held an annual banquet which was a significant event. Some of the confraternities were specifically concerned with members' material welfare — the weavers' brotherhood especially so — but in general the amount of help available was limited.[76] The sixteenth century saw considerable change and England's break with Rome is said to have brought about the destruction of 2374 guilds, chantries and free chapels.[77] However, as Professor Unwin urged long ago, one should be cautious in assessing the impact of 'the Reformation' on guilds since change could have been under way for centuries beforehand. Confraternities may have formed, fallen into disuse and re-formed like the Venetian *scuole*.[78]

If we turn to the more densely urbanised landscape of Flanders and Germany, similarities with Venice are more difficult to discern.

Popular religious energies in these regions in the late Middle Ages were often violently millenarian, but only in spasms at moments of crisis and they tended to generate little in terms of lasting organisations.[79]

Those confraternities which did form seem to have attracted merchants, apparently in the belief that alms extinguished sin and could therefore act as a kind of bill of exchange with heaven. Once again, however, charitable activity was a 'natural but secondary' part of a greater devotional activity.[80] Whether these generalisations hold up is hard to assess without a larger number of regional examples. They seem to apply to fourteenth-century Douai where the bourgeois were engaged in a number of charitable activities, perhaps reinforced by stronger parochial organisation than is obvious elsewhere. The objects of charity were once again the permanently poor or sick and clerics in a state of apostolic poverty. The devotional emphasis of alms-giving increased among merchants in the late 1300s. By then, a merchant might leave 20 times more money for commemorative masses than for gifts to the poor. This concentration on devotion may have resulted in a squeeze on the town's 20 hospitals.[81]

As in Venice, there is some evidence that such tendencies were slightly offset in the fifteenth century by new initiatives among the trade guilds. In Strasbourg some of the crafts built their own hospitals — though here too devotional philanthropy generally excluded wage labour.[82] Much the same can probably be said of Lille where 50 per cent of specialised workers in the fifteenth century were described in one survey as indigent. In Augsburg's population of 4700 in 1475, 3378 people were described as *nichil habentes* and this group included 2700 artisans, mainly from the textile trades.[83] There is little to suggest that guild philanthropy in any of these cities was equipped to deal with poverty on this scale.

As a city whose economy was based on high-quality craft production without a major textile industry, Nuremberg seems strangely similar to Venice.[84] After the middle of the fourteenth century, when associations of craftsmen sought to wrest power from the merchants, guilds were suppressed. The town's artisans were organised in authorised crafts (*Geschworene Handwerke*). Confraternities existed as drinking clubs (*Trinkstube*) which were viewed with suspicion by the authorities, less because they were a threat to oligarchic control than because their rowdiness was a civic nuisance.[85] Such associations had little to do with the city's highly developed array of social institutions. 'There was hardly an ill fortune not mitigated by some sort of charitable establishment.' Even so, the efficacy of hospitals was hindered by a concern to save souls rather than bodies.[86] Perhaps Nuremberg was a fortunate city in that its charities were not put under the kind of strains experienced in towns where poverty could be increased by unemployment in the textile trades.

That speculation can be more easily anchored to available evidence in Florence. Thanks to two recent studies, we know a great deal about the changing fortunes of Florentine confraternities in the fourteenth and fifteenth centuries.[87]

One of the obvious contrasts between the trade guilds of Florence and Venice in economic and political life was that the Florentine distinction between 'greater' and 'lesser' guilds did not exist in the Venetian Republic. When we turn to guilds as social institutions, the position is reversed. The formal difference between *Scuole Grandi* and *scuole piccole* in Venice is not found among Florentine confraternities. Nevertheless, the brotherhoods of Florence were by no means all of one type or size.

For the period 1240–1495, Dr Henderson has traced the foundation of 156 confraternities in Florence.[88] Their appeal was universal and may have included 'all Florentines above the poverty level'.[89] The most prominent of these institutions was at Orsanmichele, which may have had as many as 3000 members in 1324–5.[90] Its location next to the public grain market made a visible link between the city's devotions and its charity — the kind of link established in Venice by members of the *scuole* who carried bread and candles in procession.

The confraternities which formed in Florence in the thirteenth century often met to sing the praises of the Blessed Virgin and took their name, *laudesi* companies, from this activity.[91] As in Venice, the cult of the dead which these sodalities practised had repercussions for the relief of material want.[92] There were flagellant companies too, but their origins and functions were markedly different from those of the Venetian *Scuole Grandi dei Battuti*. They formed in the period after the Black Death rather than in the later thirteenth century and their consistent rejection of property in favour of austere piety meant that they had less impact on the material fabric of the city and the material conditions of its inhabitants than did the *Scuole Grandi* in Venice.[93]

There was apparently no equivalent of the Venetian *scuola dell'arte* in Florentine trade guilds before the fifteenth century when artisans from particular trades began to form devotional confraternities, as did the different 'nations' in the city.[94] This might suggest that the vitality of the *scuole* of bakers or tailors in the fifteenth century was not merely the product of a long tradition stretching back to the thirteenth century but owed something to ideas and initiatives stimulated by changing economic circumstances.

In Florence, however, the Church played a more forceful role in shaping the character of confraternities than in the case of the Venetian *scuole*, but once again the parish had little part to play. The Mendicant Orders were the crucial influence in the fourteenth century. The Franciscans oriented charitable activity in the confraternities towards those in a state of apostolic poverty, i.e. themselves, rather than towards lay indigence.[95] The Dominicans set up the confraternity of Santa Maria della Misericordia in the thirteenth century specifically to combat the Paterine heresy.[96] San Pier Martire was transformed in the 1440s 'from an independent lay association with a substantial capital of its own into an organisation which administered property on behalf of the Dominican friars'.[97]

The strength of ecclesiastical interests in the brotherhoods of Florence was also apparent in the heavy devotional burdens placed on members. They might be obliged to attend an evening service every day as well as a monthly meeting, frequent festivals and funerals. Attendance was registered and absence could be punished with expulsion.[98] One might have expected these obligations to encourage the formation of localised brotherhoods in particular parishes so that there was not far to go to be present at an assembly of the brethren. In the event, as in Venice, the confraternities drew members from all over the city. In the membership lists of San Zanobi in the 1330s, each *sesto* (Florence, like Venice, was divided into 'sixths' at this time) was represented, and so were 43 of the city's 57 parishes.[99]

One reason for attending a confraternity some distance from home was that it was part of the penitent's responsibility in identifying with Christ incarnate to withdraw from the family.[100] In this sense, confraternities may have had some potential for easing the political and social tensions which derived from family allegiances.[101] Such an interpretation works well in Venice where the *scuola*'s emphasis on the solidarity of Christians and Venetians may well help to explain the city's social and political stability. In Florence, however, in Nuremberg and in London, the secular authorities remained suspicious of fraternal organisations as potentially subversive. In the fifteenth century, Florentine confraternities were repeatedly banned altogether.[102]

Precisely this unofficial and secret character of many confraternities in the fifteenth century makes it very hard to measure their effectiveness in the relief of poverty. For the fourteenth century, we are rather better informed. Orsanmichele was unique in terms of membership and resources, but in 1324–5 the confraternity spent 85 per cent of its outgoings on alms and seems to have offered help to as many as 14,000 people. Of the recipients, who were systematically selected, 9500 may have been women and a high proportion of those given bread and alms were resident in the surrounding *contado*. The vast majority were 'respectable' and there is nothing to suggest that doles were given to those of no fixed abode.[103] This tendency was even stronger in the fifteenth century: in 1412–13, one-third of the alms distributed by the company went to 'small master craftsmen whose homes were scattered throughout the city'.[104]

Some of the money given to women could have reached wage-earning husbands, but the *sottoposti* and dependent workers were not generally catered for by guild-based charity. This obtained in Venice as well: the crucial difference is a question of scale. Since Venice was a commercial centre, many fewer Venetians were engaged in activities which might make them members of the 'crisis poor' during years of slump. The 'industrial' character of the Florentine economy must not be exaggerated, but the dependence of its prosperity on the successful management of huge capital resources by a small number of people is undeniable, and forcefully illustrated by the collapse of the Bardi and Peruzzi banking houses in 1346 and the consequent shock waves in Florence, Tuscany and Europe as a whole.[105] M. de la Roncière has argued that the material conditions of wage labourers in 1378 made their poverty a condition of bondage and subjection rather than of indigence. The *Ciompi* uprising, he suggests, owed much to the idea spread by people like Taddeo Dini that the poor were exploited or ignored but never looked after except in a haphazard way at moments of severe famine. In this ideology of the exploited poor has been seen the emergence of the notion of 'dangerous classes'.[106]

Florentine artisans were rather better catered for in the fifteenth century when there was an increase in the number of trade based confraternities. Intriguingly, eight of the twelve which Dr Henderson has traced were formed by textile workers. In 1451 the washers and carders founded the Compagnia di Sant'Andrea at the church of Santa Candida.[107] And at least some of the basic requirements of poor artisans were met by the hospitals which some trades were setting up in the same period.[108]

Conclusion

The chapter has been fundamentally concerned with the social composition of devotional confraternities and the places occupied by piety and charity in their activities in the late Middle Ages. Certain characteristics of these brotherhoods can be seen in terms of the general context of popular religion, though one must be wary of making the latter the main cause of the former.

What has to be stressed is that the restrictions which devotional commitments placed on the relief of material want were universal. The insoluble riddle is whether there would have been any charity at all without the devotional impulse. Such charity as was administered tended to look to the permanent or 'structural' poor — widows, orphans, cripples of those in a state of apostolic poverty. These categories cannot be too rigid since confraternities would have looked after members who became permanently needy even though they had not been in this condition when they joined. All the same, 'devotional philanthropy' seems on the whole not to have identified wage labourers as worthy recipients of alms. This had important consequences in towns where a large proportion of the population were workers of this status, especially in the fourteenth century. In the course of the fifteenth century material support systems may have been extended to a limited number of artisans who were temporarily needy.

A further point which can be made in general terms is that the study of confraternities and their administration of charity reinforces Professor Bossy's thesis that 'the Church of the late medieval centuries was not in actual fact a parochially grounded institution'.[109] This seems to have made supra-parochial institutions like confraternities particularly vulnerable during the Counter-Reformation. The cult of the eucharist in parish confraternities was one of the most significant roads along which reformed Catholicism was to 'reach the people'. In sixteenth-century Germany, confraternities were easy targets for reformers, perhaps because in a city like Nuremberg they existed as drinking clubs rather than mutual aid societies or charitable organisations.

Introducing the changes associated with Reformation and Counter-Reformation emphasises the importance of examining the religion of the laity in the late Middle Ages on its own terms and not as it was caricatured or condemned by sixteenth-century reformers. The role of the parish church in the religious life of the laity after the Counter-Reformation has obscured the strength of lay commitment to an involvement in the Christian life in both the spiritual and practical spheres of existence. Protestant attitudes to collective organisations which permitted people to 'go through the motions' of works should not hide the fact that in Italy, France and Spain confraternities required a positive commitment to identify as an individual with Christ incarnate and to do penance as a poor sinner. Criticisms of confraternities for ostentatious and self-indulgent art patronage at the expense of the poor were more valid but were just as strident in Catholic Venice as in the Protestant North.[110] Such criticisms apply generally after about 1520 when the growth of the European population, especially in towns, and the expansion of the economy put all sorts of strains on basic mechanisms of production and supply. For the fourteenth and fifteenth centuries, the terms of reference must be different, though the economic profile of a city was of vital importance in determining the capacity of its inhabitants to cope with the problem of poverty.

The distinctiveness of Venice's confraternities in the late Middle Ages was determined by the city's most striking features: a commercialised economy and secular statehood. The city's institutions never seem to have been threatened in the late Middle Ages by the mass poverty of the 'crisis poor' who were never an integral concern of 'devotional philanthropy'. In this, the city had more in common with Nuremberg than with Florence. On the other hand, Venice was at least as large as Florence and certainly much larger than Nuremberg. Bearing that in mind and looking at the vast number of institutions which developed under the twin influences of 'devotional philanthropy' and trade solidarity, Venetians seem to have contained the problem of poverty rather impressively by the standards of the time. Again as in Nuremberg, the guilds of Venice were denied the opportunity to unleash political energies, though, in contrast to the German city, they seem to have channelled their interests into the organisation of social institutions to meet members' needs. In Venice, the authorities recognised such organisations with the confidence born of state sovereignty: elsewhere they were looked upon with nervousness and suspicion. In religious life as in the economy or politics, the guilds of Venice formed a clearly defined link between state and society rather than being manipulated by the former or resisting manipulation on behalf of the latter.

In the sixteenth century the picture was to change. Population growth changed patterns of urban demand and menaced the guilds as economic entities; the accompanying growth of urban poverty threatened to undermine guilds as social institutions. The former is a question often dealt with in terms of the 'rise of capitalism', the latter a problem overlain by the further complications of Reformation and Counter-Reformation. The chapters that follow assess the response of guilds in Venice and elsewhere to the challenges of the new age.

Notes

1. G. Strauss, *Nuremberg in the 16th Century: City Politics and Life between Middle Ages and Modern Times* (Bloomington, Ind., 1976), p. 154. I. Origo, *The Merchant of Prato* (London 1963), pp. 9, 319–25 shows the interaction of religion and devotion in the life of Francesco Datini. Specifically on confraternities, see G. Le Bras, 'Les confréries chrétiennes. Problèmes et propositions', *Revue Historique du Droit Français et Etranger*, ser. 4, vols. 19–20 (1940–41), pp. 310–63.

2. J. Henderson, 'Piety and Charity in Late Medieval Florence: Religious Confraternities from the Middle of the 13th Century to the late 15th', Unpublished PhD thesis (Westfield College, University of London, 1983), p. 2. I am immensely grateful to Dr Henderson for many fruitful discussions on the nature of confraternities.

3. J. Ryan, 'Charity and Charities', in *The Catholic Encyclopedia*, 15 vols. (London, 1907–12), vol. 3, Brow-Clancy pp. 592–3. I am most grateful to Dr Robert Bartlett for his advice on this point.

4. J. Huizinga, *The Waning of the Middle Ages*, trans. F. Hopman (London, 1972), pp. 134–231; G. Leff, *The Dissolution of the Medieval Outlook* (New York, 1976), p. 134; M. Meiss, *Painting in Florence and Siena after the Black Death* (Princeton, N.J., 1978), pp. 59–131; E. Delaruelle, 'La pietà popolare alla fine del medio evo', in *10° Congresso Internazionale di Scienze Storiche*, vol. 3 (Rome, 1955), pp. 515–42; idem, 'La spiritualité aux 14e et 15e siècles', *Cahiers d'Histoire Mondiale*, vol. 5, no. 1 (1959), pp. 59–71.

5. For these various possibilities, see R. Manselli, 'L'anno 1260 fu

anno gioachimitico?', in *Movimento dei disciplinati nel settimo centenario dal suo inizio* (*Perugia, 1260*), *Appendice* 9 to *Bolletino della Deputazione di Storia Patria per L'Umbria* (Spoleto, 1962), p. 107; G. Alberigo, 'Contributi alla storia delle confraternite dei disciplinati', in the same volume, p. 165; G.-G. Meersseman, *Dossier de l'ordre de la pénitence au 13e siècle* (Fribourg, 1961), pp. 1–12, 25, 33; G. M. Monti, *Le corporazioni nell'evo antico e nell'alto medio evo* (Bari, 1934), p. 140; J. Henderson, 'The Flagellant Movement and Flagellant Confraternities in Central Italy, 1260–1400', *Studies in Church History*, vol. 15 (1978), pp. 147–60; A. Sapori, *The Italian Merchant in the Middle Ages*, trans. P. A. Kennen (New York, 1970), p. 32; J. T.Noonan, *The Scholastic Analysis of Usury* (Cambridge, Mass., 1957), pp. 79, 134, 407; L. K. Little, *Religious Poverty and the Profit Economy in Medieval Europe* (London, 1978), p. 195; R. C. Trexler, 'Charity and the Defense of Urban Elites in the Italian Communes', in F. C. Jaher (ed.), *The Rich, the Well-Born and the Powerful: Elites and Upper Classes in History* (Chicago, Ill., 1973), pp. 64–105.

6. N. Z. Davis, 'Some Themes in Popular Religion', in C. Trinkhaus and H. A. Oberman (eds.), *The Pursuit of Holiness in Late Medieval and Renaissance Religion* (Leyden, 1975), pp. 313–14.

7. C. M. de la Roncière, 'Pauvres et pauvreté a Florence au 14e siècle', in M. Mollat (ed.), *Etudes sur l'histoire de la pauvreté*, 2 vols. (Paris, 1974), vol. 2, p. 745.

8. See below, pp. 65, 67, 70.

9. See below, p. 67.

10. E. Panofsky, *The Life and Art of Albrecht Dürer* (Princeton, N. J., 1971), pp. 110–13.

11. M. Sanudo, *De origine, situ et magistratibus urbis Venetae: ovvero la città di Venetia, (1493–1530)*, ed. A. Caracciolo Aricò (Milan 1980), pp. 40–6. See also P. Prodi, 'The Structure and Organisation of the Church in Renaissance Venice: Suggestions for Future Research', in J. R. Hale (ed.), *Renaissance Venice* (London, 1974), pp. 409–30.

12. F. C. Lane, *Venice: A Maritime Republic* (Baltimore, Md., 1975), p. 12. On the sacred character of the Venetian state, see A. Pertusi, '"Quaedam regalia insignia"', *SV*, vol. 7 (1965), pp. 3–123.

13. On the Interdict, see W. J. Bouwsma, *Venice and the Defense of Republican Liberty: Renaissance Values in the Age of the Counter-Reformation*, (Berkeley and Los Angeles, 1968), pp. 293–482; G. Benzoni, *Venezia nell'età della Controriforma* (Milan, 1973), pp. 50–78; D. Wootton, *Paolo Sarpi: Between Renaissance and Enlightenment* (Cambridge, 1983). On the Corpus Domini procession of 1606, see B. S. Pullan, *Rich and Poor in Renaissance Venice: The Social Institutions of a Catholic State* (Oxford, 1971), pp. 58–61.

14. Pullan, *Rich and Poor*, p. 8; Prodi, 'Structure and Organisation', p. 419.

15. Pullan, *Rich and Poor*, pp. 33–62.

16. R. Gallo, 'La Scuola Grande di San Teodoro di Venezia', *Atti dell'Istituto Veneto di Scienze, Lettere ed Arti*, vol. 120 (*Classe di Scienze Morali e Lettere*) (1961–2), pp. 461–95.

17. S Gramigna and A. Perissa, *Scuole di arti mestieri e devozione a Venezia* (Venice, 1981), p. 70.

18. Pullan, *Rich and Poor*, pp. 45–6.

19. Ibid., pp. 197–215.

20. B. S. Pullan, 'Natura e carattere delle Scuole', in T. Pignatti (ed.), *Le Scuole di Venezia* (Milan, 1981), pp. 9–26.

21. B. Z. Kedar, *Merchants in Crisis: Genoese and Venetian Men of Affairs and the 14th-century Depression* (New Haven, Ct., 1976), p. 313. See also Origo, *Merchant of Prato*, pp. 319–25; E. Delaruelle, 'Les grandes processions de pénitents de 1349 et 1399', in the volume *Movimento dei disciplinati*, pp. 109–45.

22. L. Sbriziolo, 'Per la storia delle confraternite veneziane: dalle deliberazioni miste (1310–1476) del Consiglio dei Dieci: Scolae comunes, artigiane e nazionali', *Atti dell'Istituto Veneto di Scienze, Lettere ed Arti*, vol. 126 (*Classe di Scienze Morali e Lettere*) (1967–8), pp. 405–42.

23. M. Sanudo, *I diarii*, ed. R. Fulin *et al.*, 58 vols. (Venice, 1879–1903), vol. 30, cols, 399–401.

24. Pullan, *Rich and Poor*, p. 34, n. 7; Gramigna and Perissa, *Scuole* p. 34.

25. V. Rossi, 'Jacopo d'Albizzotto Guidi e il suo inedito poema su Venezia', *NAV*, vol. 5 (1893), p. 403 on his membership of San Cristofalo, p. 427 for the figure of 200 scuole.

26. G. Contareno, *The Commonwealth and Government of Venice*, trans. L. Lewkenor, (1599, facs. repr. Amsterdam, 1970), p. 146.

27. B. S. Pullan, 'Poverty, Charity and Reason of State: Some Venetian Examples', *SV*, vol. 2 (1960), pp. 17–60; idem, *Rich and Poor*, pp. 641–2.

28. R. C. Mueller, 'Charitable Institutions, the Jewish Community and Venetian Society: A Discussion of the Recent Volume by Brian Pullan', *SV*, vol. 14 (1972), pp. 38–78.

29. SP, b. 726, *Santa Maria della Celestia*, *mariegola*, *1337–1764*, preamble.

30. SP, b. 406, *Santa Maria e San Cristofalo*, *mariegola*, *1377–1545*, fol. 2r.

31. SP, b. 57 bis, *Santi Apostoli*, *mariegola*, *1350–1708*, fol. 2r.

32. Ibid., fols. 3r–v; SP, b. 597, *Sant'Orsola*, *mariegola*, *1300–1785*, fol. 14r; b. 726, *mariegola*, fol. 9r.

33. SP, b. 726, *mariegola*, fol. 9v.

34. SP, b. 57 bis, *mariegola*, fol. 11r.

35. SP, b. 597, *mariegola*, fol. 4r.

36. SP, b. 726, *mariegola*, fol. 6v.

37. L. Sbriziolo, 'Per la storia delle confraternite veneziane: dalle deliberazioni miste del Consiglio dei Dieci. Le Scuole dei Battuti', in *Miscellanea G.-G. Meersseman*, vol. 2 (Padua, 1970), p. 748.

38. Ibid., p. 727.

39. SP, b. 1 *bis*, *Santa Maria della Carità*, *mariegola*, *1288*, fly leaf.

40. SP, b. 1, *Sant'Agnese*, *catastico da 1325 in avanti*, fol. 20r.

41. SP, b. 726, *mariegola*, fol. 3r.

42. SP, b. 726, 57 *bis*, 24 and 406 respectively.

43. P. Zampetti, *A Dictionary of Venetian Painters*, 3 vols. (Leigh-on-sea, 1969), vol. 2.

44. B. Pullan, 'Le Scuole Grandi e la loro opera nel quadro della Controriforma', *SV*, vol. 14 (1972), pp. 83–109.

45. SP, b. 57 *bis*, *mariegola*, fol. 3r; b. 726, *mariegola*, fol. 13r.

46. D. Herlihy, 'The Population of Verona in the First Century of Venetian Rule' in Hale (ed.), *Renaissance Venice*, p. 104.

47. Gramigna and Perissa, *Scuole*, p. 125.

48. Now, however, see the important article by D. Romano, 'Charity and Community in Early Renaissance Venice', *Journal of Urban History*, vol. 11, no. 1 (1984), pp. 63–82.

49. F. Sansovino and G. Stringa, *Venetia: città nobilissima et singolare* (Venice, 1663, facs. repr. Farnborough, 1968), pp. 1–278; S. Tramontin, 'La Visita Apostolica del 1581 a Venezia', *SV*, vol. 9 (1967), pp. 500–33.

50. Sansovino, *Venetia*, p. 290.

51. Arti, b. 182, *linaroli, ordinazioni per l'arte, 1436, capitolo 16*, fol. Bv.

52. Arti, b. 7, *barcaruoli, mariegola, 1451–1767, capitoli 33–4.*

53. Arti, b. 103, *dipintori, mariegola, 1517–1682*, fol. 39r; b. 314, *marzeri, capitoli e parti, 1508–1608, libro di capitoli e parti*, entry of 13 August 1529.

54. Arti, b. 11, *boccaleri, mariegola, 1300–1804, capitolo* 5.

55. Arti, b. 725, *venditori di vetro, mariegola, 1436–1768*, fols. 6v, 72v.

56. Arti, b. 7, *mariegola*, agreement dated 6 January 1516.

57. Arti, b. 312, *marzeri, mariegola, 1471–1787*, fol. 14r; Gramigna and Perissa, *Scuole*, p. 46.

58. P. Humfrey and R. Mackenney, 'The Venetian Trade Guilds as Patrons of Art in the Renaissance', *The Burlington Magazine* no. 998 vol. 128 (1986), pp.317–30; G. Perocco and A. Salvadori, *Civiltà di Venezia*, 3 vols. (Venice, n.d.), vol. 2, pp. 737–70.

59. Arti, b. 312, *mariegola*, fol. 14r; b. 436, *peltreri e stagneri, mariegola, 1477–1803.* The inventory is dated 2 March 1504 and is found on p. 16.

60. Arti, b. 110, *fabbri, inventarii, 1595–1720*, fol. 1r.

61. Lane, *Venice*, p. 306.

62. What follows derives from Arti, b. 152, *forneri, atti diversi, 1447–1797.*

63. Ibid., doc. of 14 April 1445, '*tratta dalla matricula*'.

64. Ibid., booklet of 1447–1459.

65. Arti, b. 445, *pistori, mariegola, 1333–1691*, fol. 19v.

66. Arti, b. 152, *atti diversi*, doc. of 1465 beginning 'Christophorus Mauro . . .'

67. Ibid., *copia istrumento di aquisto*, fols. 2r, 6r.

68. Pullan, *Rich and Poor*, p. 208.

69. Arti, b. 308, *marangoni di casa, atti diversi 1446–1805*, docs. of 4 June 1467, 25 April 1484, 17 April 1502; Arti, b. 501, *sartori, capitoli e parti, 1492–1683*, fol. 3r.

70. E. Le Roy Ladurie, *Montaillou: Cathars and Catholics in a French Village, 1294–1324,* trans. B. Bray (London, 1980), pp. 312, 347–52.

71. A. N. Galpern, *The Religions of the People in 16th-century Champagne* (Cambridge, Mass., 1977), esp. pp. 52, 60–2, 70–7, 188.

72. H. F. Westlake, *The Parish Gilds of Medieval England* (London, 1919), p. 91.

73. Ibid., pp. 22, 50; G. Unwin, *The Gilds and Companies of London* (4th edn., London, 1963), pp. 52, 93–109.

74. S. L. Thrupp, *The Merchant Class of Medieval London* (Chicago, 1948), pp. 19, 314.

75. Ibid., pp. 28, 37.

76. Westlake, *Parish Gilds*, p. 42; Unwin, *Gilds*, pp. 139, 148.

77. Westlake, *Parish Gilds*, p. 135.

78. Unwin, *Gilds*, pp. 201–16.

79. In general see N. Cohn, *The Pursuit of the Millennium* (London, 1970), pp. 127–251; Huizinga, *Waning*, pp. 134–92.

80. M. Mollat, *Les pauvres au moyen age* (Paris, 1978), pp. 173, 313.

81. F. Leclère, 'Recherches sur la charité des bourgeois envers les pauvres au 14e siècle à Douai', *Revue du Nord*, vol. 48, no. 189 (1966), pp. 139–54.

82. Mollat, *Les pauvres*, pp. 91, 346.

83. Ibid., pp. 284, 295.

84. Strauss, *Nuremberg*, pp. 133–45.

85. Ibid., pp. 97, 99–100.

86. Ibid., p. 197.

87. Henderson, 'Piety and Charity'; R. F. E. Weissman, *Ritual Brotherhood in Renaissance Florence, 1200–1600* (New York, 1982).

88. Henderson, 'Piety and Charity', p. 26.

89. M. B. Becker, 'Aspects of Lay Piety in Early Renaissance Florence', in Trinkhaus and Oberman (eds.), *Pursuit of Holiness*, p. 188.

90. Henderson, 'Piety and Charity', p. 151.

91. R. Hatfield, 'The Compagnia dei Magi' *JWCI*, vol. 33, (1970), pp. 107–62.

92. Henderson, 'Piety and Charity', p. 126.

93. Ibid., pp. 77–97.

94. Ibid., p. 320.

95. Ibid., pp. 6–7, 173; Weissman, *Ritual Brotherhood*, p. 44.

96. P. Landini, *Istoria dell'Oratorio e della venerabile Arciconfraternita di Santa Maria della Misericordia della città di Firenze* (Florence, 1843), p. 2.

97. Henderson, 'Piety and Charity', p. 123.

98. Ibid., pp. 47–50.

99. Weissman, *Ritual Brotherhood*, pp. 10, 46, 67, 68.

100. Ibid., p. 44.

101. F. W. Kent, *Household and Lineage in Renaissance Florence: The Family Life of the Capponi, Ginoti and Ruccellai* (Princeton, N.J., 1977), p. 169.

102. Henderson, 'Piety and Charity', p. 36; Weissman, *Ritual Brotherhood*, p. 167.

103. Henderson, 'Piety and Charity', pp. 163–73.

104. Ibid., p. 284.

105. A. Sapori, *La crisi mercantile dei Bardi e dei Peruzzi* (Florence, 1926).

106. De la Roncière, 'Pauvres et pauvreté'; Mollat, *Les pauvres*, p. 271.

107. Henderson, 'Piety and Charity', p. 320.

108. Weissman, *Ritual Brotherhood*, p. 65.

109. J. Bossy, 'The Counter-Reformation and the People of Catholic Europe', *PP*, no. 47 (1970), p. 53.

110. On Italy, Pullan, *Rich and Poor*; on France, Galpern, *Champagne*; for a Spanish example, M.-C. Gerbet, 'Les confréries religieuses à Caceres de 1467 à 1523', *Mélanges de la Casa de Velasquez*, vol. 7 (1971), pp. 75–113. I owe this reference to Dr Angus MacKay.

3

Guildsmen and Enterprise, *c.*1450–*c.*1650

Introduction

The two previous chapters sought to describe the basic structures of guild life in the Middle Ages: their economic functions, legal and political status, religious life and charitable works. Those structures were formed in a period of general expansion in the thirteenth century and were adapted to meet the recession which followed the Black Death. By about the middle of the fifteenth century, a new cycle of growth had begun and it was to last into the seventeenth. This phase of expansion has been described by M. Braudel as 'the long sixteenth century'.[1] Its general characteristics and their impact on the guilds of Venice are the subject of this third chapter.

Perhaps the most useful starting point from which to begin an examination of patterns of economic change in the period is the growth of population. A figure in the order of 80–85 million people for Europe in about 1500 may have risen to 100 or even 110 million by about 1600.[2] Growth was at its most marked in the period 1500–70 and as such was 'the most striking fact about the sixteenth century'.[3] That comment was made in a book about peasant life, and Europe remained overwhelmingly rural in character, but even more striking than the demographic expansion itself is the fact that an increasing proportion of people lived in towns. Many of these — Seville, London, Lyons, Antwerp — grew as part of the great economic boom. Others — Naples, Madrid, Rome — emerged as political capitals which concentrated together the increasing numbers of the state's servants.[4]

The new urban centres placed greater demands on the

agrarian economy. Within the towns themselves, increased production was necessary to generate the wealth needed to buy food. This did not always occur. Crop failure generated high prices and terrible hardship, especially for the poor, and empty stomachs were all the more vulnerable to recurrent bouts of disease.[5] Moreover, the process of growth was distorted and distended by periods of fierce inflation. This was fuelled not just by the demands of the increasing population and by silver from the New World, but also by the military and bureaucratic requirements of great empires and national states, whose uncontrollable collisions gathered pace in the aftermath of the Reformation. For the historian, the violence of short-term fluctuations can seem as important as general tendencies: what each contributed to the other is hard to discern and complicates basic questions of cause and effect.[6]

What happened to guilds in such stormy times? The simple answer, long accepted as valid, is that they went to sleep. According to this view, guilds remained essentially 'medieval' institutions left behind by the new era. They did not open their ranks to the new and larger labour force which was instead exploited by capitalist entrepreneurs whose concentrations of resources enabled them to take advantage of the wider markets now available for their wares. Production, especially of textiles, was moved into rural areas to outflank urban workshops with their high costs and restrictive practices. Where guilds were to survive — in France for instance — they did so as docile tax units exploited by the fisc.[7]

Most historians would admit that it is dangerous to see the breaking-down of 'guild restrictiveness' as a sort of path-clearing operation which opened the way to the Industrial Revolution. However, the precise role of guilds in the 'long sixteenth century' remains ill-defined. There is no evidence at all to suggest that industrial capital had made much impact on traditional organisation before the eighteenth century: Jack of Newberry's textile 'factory', even if it existed, was the exception rather than the rule.[8]

M. Braudel has argued that capital was still invested in and generated by commerce, but we know very little about guilds in relation to commerce as opposed to manufacture. In the case of Italy, it might be more accurate to say that even by 1650 it is extremely difficult to define the difference between the commercial and industrial sectors, not just because the former was so much more important, but because of the close association of manufacture and marketing in the guild system. In northern Italy, as was argued in Chapter 1, there is evidence of a pervasive commercial ethic by the thirteenth century and this was compatible if not always comfortable with vigorous guild life.[9]

This is probably more apparent in Venice than anywhere else. The city was above all a commercial centre and its guilds stood between 'craft' and 'mercantile' organisations.[10] In Venice, guilds and enterprise traditionally overlapped. They continued to do so in the 'long sixteenth century' as part of a metropolitan economy dedicated to business.

What follows is an examination of some features of Venetian economic development which do not tie in with accepted ideas about guilds. First, Venice extended its industrial sector by extending its guild system. Second, guilds continued to flourish throughout the sixteenth century in commerce and manufacture. In short, they showed continued vitality as traditional institutions in an economy whose character became increasingly metropolitan. This raises important questions about the 'secular trend' and how historians see it forming. The general trend is itself a myriad of incidentals. The documents of Venetian guilds yield few long series of figures. What survive are fragments of day-to-day experience within the framework of an institution. Did these fragments and institutions merely float helplessly in the 'secular trend'? Were they merely shaped — and broken — by the forces of long-term change? Or is it possible to piece together evidence which shows guildsmen and guilds active as well as passive, capable of shaping and not just being shaped, making their own contribution to the direction and trajectory of the general trends which gave the early modern period some of its most distinctive features?

The Venetian experience

Venice's constitutional arrangements seemed changless, but the Venetian economy was constantly on the move, engaged in a ceaseless process of adjustment and diversification which enabled the city to sustain its prosperity.

As mentioned in Chapter 1, the maritime commerce so important to Venice in the Middle Ages was dominated by the patriciate, and their activities were far removed from the world of the guilds in the city itself. In the course of the fifteenth century, partly because of the threat posed by the Turkish advance to the security of traditional trade routes, there was greater investment in manufactures in the city itself. This sector of the economy, which depended on the city's handicraft organisations, continued to develop throughout the 'long sixteenth century' and adjusted to yet another set of new conditions in the seventeenth.[11]

The move from commerce to industry can easily be exaggerated for the two sectors were interdependent in certain important respects. One obvious point of contact was the Arsenal where craftsmen laboured to build the ships which carried or protected the traffic of merchandise. The industrial expansion itself depended on pre-existing guild structures, especially in the luxury trades. Moreover, the commercial mechanisms of the economy continued to develop as ligaments linking overseas trade and local production in small retail enterprises. Petty commerce continued to provide opportunities for employment in the seventeenth century when large-scale manufacturing, notably woollen textiles, had entered a period of decline.[12]

Thus, by the fifteenth century, rather than entering an 'industrial phase', Venetians had begun to develop new manufactures and new channels of distribution within the city itself. Rather than juxtaposing 'commerce' and 'industry', it is more helpful to see the Venetian economy of the Renaissance as 'metropolitan': increasing production of textiles, increasing production of luxury goods, linked by a distributive network in which — as in the Middle Ages — retail stood between wholesale and manufacture, but overlapped with both.

For much of the fifteenth century, Venice's traditional source of wealth — the handling of goods between East and West — continued to flourish. The major interests of a merchant like Andrea Barbarigo still involved dealing in a wide variety of goods in many markets: cotton from Syria, tin from Cornwall. 'While selling cloth at Venice, estimating the future of the cotton market and calculating the prices of grain in central Italy, Andrea was watching conditions in the western markets, and especially in Bruges.'[13] When in 1423 Doge Tomaso Mocenigo delivered his famous oration, Venetian wealth still seemed to him to derive from the handling of goods produced by somebody else — or even by allowing others to handle goods in Venice. The Florentines for instance were said to spend 150,000 ducats a year in the city 'and they buy French or Catalan wool, kermes grain, silk, wax, gold and silver thread, sugar, unrefined silver, spices in any quantity, alum, indigo, leather and jewels'. According to Mocenigo, Venice exported 2¼ million ducats' worth of goods to Lombardy — cotton, wool, silk, pepper, cinammon, ginger, sugar, dyestuffs.[14]

The expansion of manufactures

The Doge also speaks proudly of Venetian industries. While his figure of 16,000 weavers in the city is almost certainly an exaggeration, it is clear that the manufacture of fustian (a mix of wool and cotton) and silk was becoming increasingly important.[15] The growth of manufactures is reflected in the history of the guilds, in whose records there is evidence for the development of unfamiliar tensions between bosses and workers. In 1460, there was a serious disagreement between shipowners and caulkers over wage levels, though a settlement was reached through which available work was rotated amongst the matriculated masters.[16] More dangerous contentions developed in the textile trades.

. The records of the silk guild reveal the kind of tensions generated within the corporations by entrepreneurial expansion. However, it is equally noticeable that the balance between bosses and workforce was kept by the law and, for the most part, outright conflict seems to have been avoided.

It was established in 1421 that merchandise was not to be used to pay for work completed. The provision was repeated in 1429 and 1475 and was still being enforced in 1542. This may have done something to limit the problems of debt and dependence often associated with the textile trades. All the same, the guild records that 1543 saw 'tumult, scandal, confusion and bloodshed' and the carrying of weapons at guild meetings was prohibited.[17]

The main source of conflict was ownership of the means of production, the loom. Any loom sale had to be recorded with the magistrates. In 1457, the number any one producer was permitted to own was limited to six, despite an appeal from some members that they should set to work as many looms as they chose. The limitation was not effective, despite its reiteration in 1488. By 1493 the masters were increasingly nervous about 'eight or ten' merchants 'who have the means to control 20, 30 or even 40 looms'. The consequence of concentration of this sort was a reduction in the status of masters to dependent wage-earners — and the reduction of wages themselves.[18]

In silk manufacture, there was also a chance that such workers might depend directly on a merchant patrician. The list of those who registered as merchants in the guild in 1462 shows the aristocracy heavily involved in the silk business. In April alone, the names were Mocenigo, Pesaro, Dandolo, Loredan, Cabriel, Pisani, Giustinian, Tiepolo, Foscarini and Querini.[19] A situation in which former masters might be dependent on capital resources provided by the city's political élite was potentially explosive. The careful provision of appeal courts — Silk Office, Consuls of Merchandise and Commissioners of the Commune — may have helped to contain conflict within the rule of law. However, even in the fifteenth century, entrepreneurs and guildsmen were not of necessity destined to conflict, because entrepreneurs were sometimes guildsmen.

As early as 1422, some members of the *arte* went to the Silk Office requesting that they be allowed to do as they chose with their money despite a counter-proposal that a merchant could not be a weaver and vice versa. Something of a compromise was reached. Those who wished to combine the two roles had to register their names with the magistrates. Curiously, it was the *merchant* who was allowed only one loom. A master could have more but he in turn had to work for a merchant. This gave the master ownership of the means of production but not total independence from mercantile interests. The merchant could employ a master but could not infringe on his independence in terms of ownership of the loom.[20]

This strange settlement appears to have operated in practice. In 1529, a petition was presented to the Doge by those engaged in 'the manual labour of us poor citizens, silk merchants'. Even allowing for the rhetoric of hard luck inherent in petitions, the association of manual labour and merchant status is unusual. It suggests that the traditions of the *arti medie* were still very much alive despite increasingly strong entrepreneurial impulses amongst guildsmen. Merchants were still trying to register as weavers and weavers as merchants in 1617.[21] While some were suspicious of business enterprise, others welcomed it — all were guildsmen and all worked under the eye of magistrates who were pleased to encourage enterprise but careful to use guilds to ensure that enterprise was not entirely 'free'.

The expansion of the woollen industry in the sixteenth century was perhaps the most spectacular aspect of Venice's development as a manufacturing centre. Production rose from less than 2000 cloths shortly after 1500 to over 20,000 in 1569 and a peak of 28,000 in 1602, with an equally spectacular decline thereafter. The pattern reflects the artificiality of the industry's growth, which occurred by default. While the rest of Italy was disturbed by warfare, the coordination required for the complicated process of manufacture was difficult to maintain, and once a measure of stability returned to the peninsula, demand for the Venetian product faltered.[22]

Rather surprisingly, the records of the trades associated with cloth production are both sparse and dull as far as guilds are concerned. There were some basic similarities to the silk industry. Those who put out wool to spinners were expected to register at the *Camera del Purgo*.[23] Weavers were to be paid in cash, not in materials.[24] Disinterested officials were to give summary judgement on 'merchants, spinners, weavers and all other workers' (one notes the inclusion of the latter *within* the guild framework) and in 1450 the Commissioners of the Commune were given the role of a higher appeal court for disputes within the industry.[25]

This did not entirely prevent violent conflict. In 1517, the Council of Ten intervened in the guild's affairs to prevent weavers from going to the *Camera del Purgo* bearing arms. In 1556, the shearmen organised a strike: precisely the kind of *conspiracio* which the medieval statutes of other guilds had so carefully forbidden.[26]

There were areas other than textiles in which manufactures developed: larger-scale enterprises grew in glassmaking, printing, tanning and soap-making. Chandlers asked to form a guild but were forbidden to do so by the magistrates who, by a narrow majority, decided to give a free hand to the merchant employers, the apothecaries.[27] The repercussions of the decision on the trade are not clear, but there is a good deal of evidence in the records of other guilds that expansion generated a certain nervousness. Linen-sellers placed severe restrictions on the number of shops a member could own. So did the pork butchers, who took pains to ensure that meat could not be bought up for re-sale to members, protecting, in other words, the traditional mechanism of bulk purchases by the guild itself.[28]

There was increasing nervousness about possible violence at guild meetings. We have already looked at prohibitions against weapons in the silk and woollen industries, the tinsmiths imposed a similar ban in about 1490. German journeymen in the confectioners' guild worked, alleged the masters, with weapons at their sides. And they seem generally to have been an intimidating crew to have to employ. 'When a baker wants to find a journeyman, he has to go cap-in-hand to pick one up — well-oiled — from some tavern.' The journeymen's quarrelsome habits had resulted in murder at San Barnaba in 1543.[29]

Amongst the tinsmiths, the apprentices were content to accept fairly large-scale enterprises provided that the status of master were subsequently open to them. In 1489, they asked the magistrates to permit a master to take on as many assistants as he chose. As things stood, an eight- or nine-year apprenticeship might not hold any prospect of becoming a master.[30] Was this exclusiveness on the part of the masters or is it evidence of a general urge toward freer enterprise within a traditional guild framework?

The metropolitan economy

The interpretation just mentioned looks far-fetched until one considers the commercial mechanisms which the guilds developed to display and sell manufactured goods. Figure 3.1 gives a very rough idea of the economic geography of Venice in about 1550. At Rialto were concentrated warehouses and food wholesalers, bankers and goldsmiths. From this main artery were pumped round the goods which sold on market stalls at San Marco, Santa Maria Formosa, Santi Apostoli, San Giacomo dell'Orio and San Polo.[31] There were many permanent retail outlets as well which formed the veins of the system.

The city's shops exercised an increasing fascination for visitors. Though Commynes was most impressed by the Arsenal, William Wey was smitten by the Venetians' urge to do business. A pilgrim could buy a mattress for threepence with a guarantee from the trader that he would buy it back for half price after the return voyage.[32] Canon Pietro Casola's description of the city reads in parts like a holiday brochure. He noted that 'the special products for which other cities are famous are all to be found there' and went on:

> Who could count the many shops so well furnished that they also seem to be warehouses, with so many cloths of every design, tapestries of every sort, camlets of every colour and

Figure 3.1: *Metropolitan Venice, 1550*

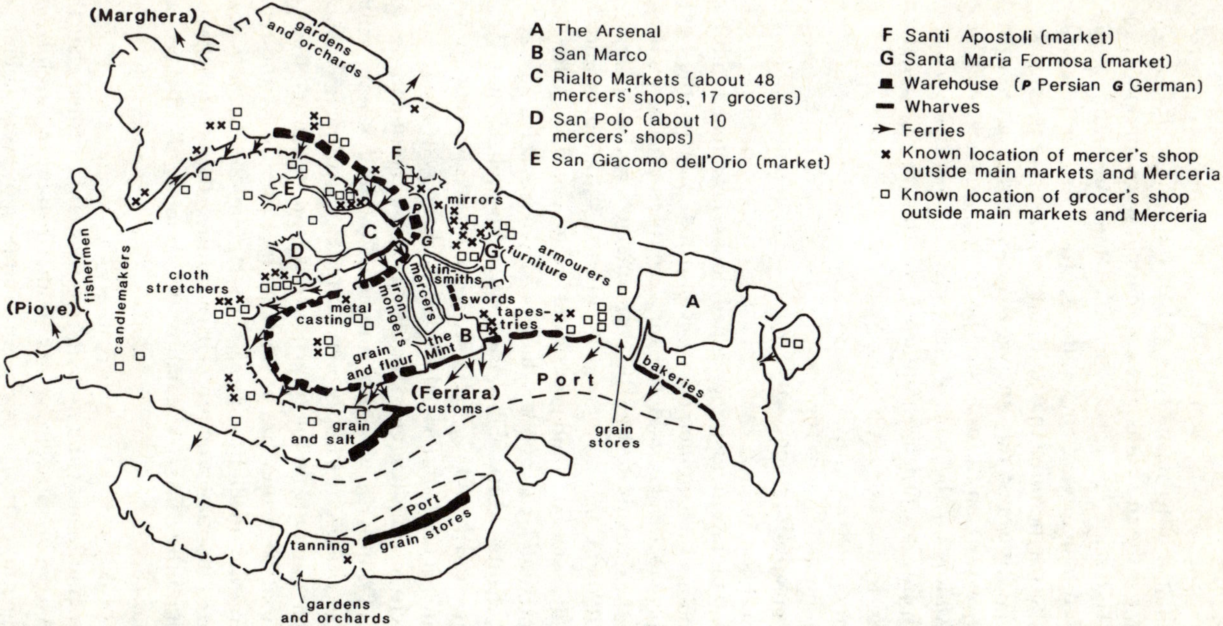

The Rialto market complex consisted of wharves for oil, wine , iron and charcoal, wholesale markets for fish, meat, cheese and vegetables, the shops of coopers, wool and silk merchants, grocers, goldsmiths, mercers, the Giro bank and insurance services. By 1660, retail outlets were countless: see Braudel, *The Mediterranean*, vol. 1, p. 314.
Sources: G. Perocco and A. Salvadori, *Civiltà di Venezia*, 3 vols., (Venice, no date), vol.1 p.291; vol. 2, pp.610–11, 614–15, 636–7; MM, b.446 (see below, n.39).

> texture, silks of every kind; so many warehouses full of spices, groceries and drugs, and so much beautiful white wax! These things stupefy the beholder — it cannot be fully described to those who have not seen it.

He even made a trip to see a glassworks on Murano where 'all the beautiful glass vases which are taken throughout the world are made'.[33]

His comment that the shops 'also seem warehouses' is especially pertinent to the commercial activities of Venice's *arti medie* whose retailing blended at one end into manufacture and at the other into wholesale. Retailing enjoyed more and more economic *Lebensraum.* Patricians began to invest on the mainland in the hope of higher returns than were available in overseas trade bedevilled first by Turks and then by pirates. Economic activity within the city itself quickened as more and more non-patricians turned to the production and marketing of luxury goods.[34] There were services as well as goods. In 1543, William Thomas heard tell that there were some 12,000 boats operating in the city. The *traghetti* which crossed the Grand Canal at the points indicated on the map were like taxi ranks. In 1572–73, 45 licences to use boats at the various stations were auctioned to a total value of over 3300 ducats with a price range of between 2 and 370. Occupations among the successful bidders — who included several nobles — were shoemaker, cordwainer, goldsmith and mason. There were 'leisure industries' too: plenty of inns, drinking houses and brothels.[35]

These were some of the structural changes which were beginning to take place in the middle of the fifteenth century and given extra momentum by the gathering pace of economic growth in the sixteenth. By 1563, the city's population stood at over 160,000. In 1569, woollen cloth production touched 26,000 pieces, a figure bettered only in 1601 and 1602. As the new industries flourished, there was a revival in the traditional commerce in spice. Production in the Arsenal was immensely stimulated by the war of the Holy League against the Turk. The shipyards turned out 100 galleys in two months in the spring of 1570 and supplied over half the Christian fleet at Lepanto.[36]

The peak had been reached by 1575. In that year began a terrible pestilence which reduced the city's population by something like a third. Lepanto had not proved a decisive victory and the costs of war continued to rise. Shipping was increasingly prey to pirates and business prospects grew gloomy with the collapse of important banking houses in the 1580s. In the following decade, Venice, like Europe, was once again in the depths of recession.[37]

How did the boom and slump cycle of the sixteenth century affect the structures of the city's economy? If, as seems probable, the sixteenth century saw a diminution of the patriciate's activities in overseas commerce, then the change in the balance of Venetian economic life was not simply an increased weighting for manufactures. The instinct for profit and diversification grew stronger among small businesses in the metropolitan economy of the city itself.[38]

A luxury trade: the apothecaries

The 'beautiful white wax' which Casola noticed became increasingly important in the devotional life of a Catholic city in the age of the Counter-Reformation. In the 1550s, the goldsmiths' *scuola* spent a quarter of its outgoings on candles. The suppliers were the *speziali*, apothecaries, who had never been organised in an independent guild but whose trade was supervised by the government. (Perhaps this had made them wary of the chandlers' efforts to form their own *arte*.)

They were conspicuous at San Bartolomeo (where shops like the Golden Head are still in existence) and they were purveyors of three commodities of particular importance to Venetian commerce — spices, wax and sugar.

Their activities are best understood through a survey carried out in 1569 by the magistracy responsible for supplying the fleet with crews, the *Milizia da Mar*. Each apothecary was described and assessed by two others with particular attention to stock and capital resources and impressionistic comments about the state of each business.[39] The trade was divided into those who sold medicines and those who sold wax, spice and confectionery, though the distinction is never very clear.

In the 1569 list, there were 85 apothecaries who dealt in medicines, each with a separate business. Seven of them were wholesalers, one of whom dealt mainly in rhubarb. There were five women members, but none of these was amongst the 40 described as 'poor'. Of the others, Battista Silvestrini at the Crocodile in San Salvador and two others supplied medications to barber-surgeons in the galleys.

It is striking that respectable incomes could be generated from relatively slender capital resources. Giacomo Fin at the Venus was able, according to one estimate, to earn 200 ducats a year on the basis of 200 in capital. For the wealthy, risks were still high. Santo Locatelli at the Egg had lost his substance in a shipwreck which may have cost him 1500 ducats and he also stood surety for 300 ducats on Andrea di Franco, who had gone bankrupt.

The shops were located in 41 different parishes. There was a concentration of 28 businesses in the sestier of San Marco, 15 in Castello, 10 in Cannaregio, 9 in Santa Croce and 7 in Dorsoduro. So there was apparently some demand in all parts of the city.

By contrast, the spicers were much more heavily concentrated at Rialto. There were 122 practitioners of this branch of the trade: 31 of them in San Marco, a further 42 just across the Rialto in San Polo, and a further 17 were described as doing business 'in Rialto'. Of the spicers, 34 were wholesalers, a dozen of them engaged in international trade — in Alexandria, Antwerp, Lyons and Lausanne, or nearer home in Milan and Puglia. The same branch found room for 39 *poveri*. One of them, Salvador at the Cross near the fish market, was so badly-off that he had been in no position to meet local demand during an epidemic. 'When the plague was around he had nothing but empty boxes and a mortar.' Another, Zanantonio di Rossi at the Justice, had barely 2 ducats' worth of stock and often had to buy that retail or sell on behalf of another shopkeeper.

The same group of *poveri* also included three wholesalers, one of whom, Bartolomeo Giron, was not averse to portering to supplement his income. Tomaso at the Arm was also 'poor', but dealt in retail spices and wax which he bought wholesale and sold retail. Some of his spice was marketed at a fair in Lausanne. Thus, the area of economic life in which *poveri* and wholesalers could coexist was substantial and stretched as far as industrial activity.

'In all parishes, every apothecary sells spice, sugar and similar retail items,' was the comment of one assessor. The spices included pepper, ginger, cinnamon and drugs. Other favoured commodities were molasses and cloves. The latter may well have been important in easing the toothache caused by too much sugar. At least seven apothecaries were engaged in refining sugar, others turned it into marzipan. Many dealt in wax, some whitening it as a handicraft occupation, others employing chandlers to do so.

Status groups among the *speziali* were therefore very loosely defined. Wholesale, retail and manufacture were blended together by an impulse to do business on any scale: by the barrrel or by the jar, by the sack or by the bag full. It can of course be objected that the apothecaries, for all that they were described as an *arte*, were not really a guild, just a trade supervised by the government. To see whether guilds and commercial instincts were genuinely capable of operating in harness, the investigation needs to be taken much further. This we can do by examining the most dynamic and diverse of Venetian guilds — the mercers.

The mercers' guild and the Venetian economy

It is plain from their thirteenth-century statute that the mercers played a prominent part in the economy of medieval Venice. They supplied luxury goods to the Church, they profited from pilgrims and they were sometimes involved as suppliers of capital in industries like tanning and bleaching (above pp. 13, 20).

As the 'long sixteenth century' opened, the guild entered a phase of expansion which was to last into the eighteenth century, a long-term process which can be seen from the guild records to have begun in 1446. Already, the mercers were referring to themselves as 'the noblest trade in Venice and the richest'.[40] Their sense of superiority probably derived from the range of goods which they claimed exclusive rights to market and the number of other trades which they proceeded to gobble up.

The mercers sold haberdashery and 'dry goods' of all sorts. In 1446, they voiced their anxiety about non-members who were infringing their activities. In a larger-scale redefinition of the guild's competence and the scope of members' activities in the city's economy, the officers of 1446 sought to incorporate many more tradesmen and goods within the *arte dei marzeri*.

They reasserted their rights over their traditional commodities and went on to claim no less than twelve new categories of tradesmen and wares. They listed 'fustian sellers, spicers, goldsmiths, silk workers and others, fruiterers and second-hand dealers . . . makers of silk cord and linen thread, of fringes and silk belts' who would have to enrol. Shopkeepers who kept candlesticks or brassware, gloves, bowstrings and spinning-wheel cords 'and many other things' were enjoined to pay a subscription. So should journeymen who imported pewter from Flanders and those who made purses, hats (wool and straw), playing cards, foreign goods, tinned metal, mirrors, caps, woollen gloves, knives, scissors, paternosters, spectacles, combs (horn and wood) or shirts. The guild claimed to control dealings in goods from Lombardy and Tuscany, wedding chests, knives from Bologna, the Romagna, Modena — or anywhere else (!) — and indeed *all* goods made outside Venice: felt, jewels, caps, veils, kerchiefs, bonnets, pewter . . . and so on and so on.[41]

Small wonder that Casola was so impressed by shops which sold 'the special products for which other cities are famous'. By 1530, according to a list made by the patrician Marin Sanudo, the Merceria (where most of the mercers' shops were located) followed San Marco and the ducal palace on the official sight-seeing tour for visiting VIPs.[42] When Henry III came to Venice in 1574, he particularly asked to visit the shop of the dalla Vecchia. When a Venetian wished to extol the window displays of Jacobean London, he said they rivalled those of Bartolomeo Bontempelli at the Chalice (below, pp. 110, 145).

Of course, scattered references to businessmen who happened to be mercers do not prove the importance of the guild. But one sign that the guild itself grew with the fortunes of its members was the fate of the mercers' confraternity. In the late fifteenth century, the mercers became associated with the scuola di San Teodoro. In 1554 this was elevated to the status of a *Scuola Grande*, reflecting the importance and wealth of the guild of mercers rather than of just a few of its members (above, p. 47 and n. 16).

There was more to membership of the guild than association with a prestigious confraternity. The *arte* played a mundane but vital part in helping the Venetian economy to adjust to changing economic conditions. In the sixteenth century, particularly after 1560, some mercers were able to profit from the general economic boom, even after the plague of 1575–77. For, in the course of the seventeenth century, the retail sector which the mercers dominated absorbed a high proportion of the workforce no longer required for manufactures. By 1690 there were 1747 members of the guild in Venice: there were thus more mercers than there were boatmen, twice as many mercers as wool workers. The figures are Professor Rapp's. He has argued that a 'unitary guild system', in which members practised a single profession throughout their working lives, was eroded in the economic adjustments of the seventeenth century. The mercers' records suggest that a unitary system had never really crystallised and that guild structures were amorphous, but dynamic.[43]

The mercers' guild grew stronger through the expansion and

diversification of business. What looks like an insistence on old-fashioned monopolies in 1446 was in fact the basis for extraordinary development in the later sixteenth century.

The mercers and the guild system in the 1560s

New shops established in Venice had to be registered with the magistrates. A catalogue of who set up where to sell what survives from the 1560s.[44] The register is not confined to mercers and demonstrates their importance in a much broader economic context.

The register, whose contents are presented in Table 3.1, contains 584 entries relating to 517 shops, 50 trademarks and 27 medical licences. The total represents the establishment between 1561 and 1568 of three new businesses every fortnight or maybe one new shop every three working days.

Table 3.1: *Shops established, 1561–68*

trade	registrations	% of total
mercers	170	29.12
textiles	37	6.34
druggists	95	16.27
goldsmiths, painters, glass	40	6.85
booksellers	29	4.97
furriers	16	2.74
footware	24	4.11
household goods	53	9.07
fruiterers	19	3.25
other foodstuffs	53	9.07
barbers	10	1.71
surgeons	27	4.62
dual occupation	11	1.88
Total	584	100.00

source: see n. 44.

The figures suggest the predominance of retail premises (517 shops) over craft workshops (50 trademarks) but the overlap between them is too great to permit confident generalisation. It is more realistic to emphasise that guildsmen engaged in commercial activity, even at the retail level, could establish a business and watch it grow or turn their hand to something else ten times as quickly as those who had to invest time in training and money in tools.

A third of the shops can clearly be designated as dealing in mercery — a striking proportion and almost twice as large as any other category. Even so, the figure is almost certainly an underestimate. The mercers' own membership lists found room for canvas-makers and fruiterers and many of the other shopholders dealing in textiles, glass or household goods may have joined the *arte dei marzeri* at some stage. The intermingling of different activities can be demonstrated from a few individual cases.

In 1561, Antonio Valfredo set up at the City of Milan (now a hotel and restaurant) as a 'seller of belts, haberdashery, purses and hats'. An oil vendor like Antonio Morin at the Bison sold oil and soap as well as sausage and cheese. Piero at the Bergamo dealt in glassware and fruit. Francesco Patriani was a mercer who sold books, Giacomo Morando, bell founder at the Saint Anthony, took on the Falcon as a mercer in 1567.

These examples could be multiplied many times over. They should be seen in relation to the claims which the mercers had asserted within the retail sector in 1446. What could be interpreted as an effort to restrict and contain was really a move to diversify and expand. An occupational title in the mercers' guild may well indicate what someone sold most of rather than defining everything he was at liberty to market. The diversity of goods in which mercers dealt can be examined in greater detail and in closer relation to the institution of the guild itself, whose officers compiled a series of membership lists in the later sixteenth century.

These lists were drawn up for different purposes and only two of the six include members below the rank of master. Nevertheless, we can identify half a dozen broad categories which seem to match the claims made in 1446. These are as follows:

(i) mercery and textiles
(ii) haberdashery and clothing
(iii) luxuries and precision artefacts
(iv) metalware
(v) household goods and trinkets
(vi) dual occupation

The first category covers mercers, fullers, dealers in serge, knitters. The haberdashers were hatters, cappers, stringers, sellers of braid, thread, collars, gloves, belts, blankets, mattresses. The luxury trades were dominated by perfumers but included sellers of mirrors, scales, lutes, spectacles and stationery. Some members dealt in, or produced, metal fastenings and a few sold ornaments and toys for Venetian homes. Any of these trades could combine with another, and now and again a member might use two occupational titles, which places him (or her) in the final category.

The records reveal a remarkable variety of economic activity within the same guild. Equally striking is the small scale of each business which seems to have guaranteed a large measure of economic independence to individual members. Subsequent lists take us into the shadowy area where guilds and commercial enterprise overlapped.

Capital and business activities in 1567–68

The 1567 investigation of the apothecaries was coupled with a compilation of the capital resources and economic interests of the mercers and in their case, the information provided is rather more precise.[45]

Four hundred and forty-six members were named and details about each were supplied by witnesses questioned separately on different days. The details include estimates of capital, turnover, merchandise and interests outside Venice. The list probably refers to interests in mercery rather than to the global resources of each member: Iseppo Gandolfi was 'more often tending his property in Castelfranco than his shop'.

Even so, the total capital tied up in mercery was enormous — almost half a million ducats. The richest of the guildsmen must have rivalled patricians, for in the late sixteenth century a Venetian aristocrat was considered wealthy if he had an income of 1000 ducats a year.[46] This was well within the compass of many mercers, especially when one remembers that a high income could be generated from fairly slight capital resources.

The distribution of wealth within the guild was highly uneven, ranging from 60,000 ducats to nothing. Twenty mercers disposed of over 5000 ducats, 13 of more than 10,000. By contrast 171 had less than 100 ducats and 75 less than 20. The contrasts shown in Figure 3.2 and Table 3.2 were sharp: less than 5 per cent of members disposed of nearly half the total capital, 38 per cent controlled less than 2 per cent of the whole. But attention should also be given to the middling group which, in the best traditions of the *arti medie*, accounts for 16 per cent of total membership and 15.5 per cent of total capital. This was a level of security and probably of prosperity open to those in the lower groups.

Figure 3.2: *The distribution of wealth in the mercers' guild, 1567–68*

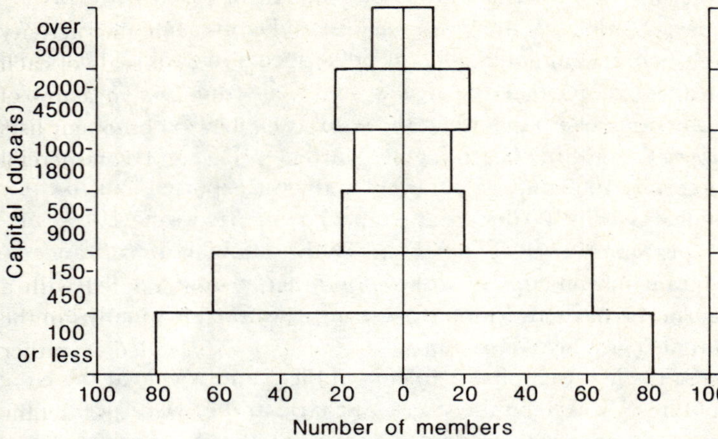

Table 3.2: *The distribution of wealth in the mercers' guild, 1567–68*

estimated capital	members	total capital	% of members	% of capital
over 5000 ducats	20	235,000	4.67	49.80
2–4000 ducats	45	121,500	10.51	25.75
1000–1800 ducats	36	51,000	8.41	10.80
500–900 ducats	40	22,100	9.35	4.68
150–450 ducats	125	34,500	29.21	7.31
100 ducats or less	162	7,840	37.85	1.66
total	428	471,940	100.00	100.00

source for both: MM, b. 446, *dichiarazioni testimoniali sullo stato economico di alcuni esercenti per l'applicazione della tansa (libro di inquisicion secundo), 1567–68.*

On successive pages are found Daniel Raspante 'who sometimes needs to go in search of bread' and Giacomo di Battista with 12,000 ducats in serges, silks, mohair and interests on the foreign exchange, probably in Antwerp whence his son had just returned after a stay of five or six years. Zilio da Ponte, the wealthiest member, was rated at 60,000 ducats, Antonio di Giacomo earned 16 or 18 soldi a day as a shop assistant — no more than a labourer in the building trade.[47]

Those are very stark contrasts, but 70 per cent of members disposed of over 100 ducats and in the information provided about them, retail, wholesale and manufacture tumble over each other in a bewildering variety of goods turned over at surprising speed. Some had interests in silk manufacture, but Paolo at the Egg had accumulated 5000 or 6000 ducats in prosaic tacks and buttons. Simone at the Scales sold veils and thread and was 'something of a big noise in the retail trade [*Fa assai strepito di cose menude*]'. Agostino Cigrini, guild warden in 1574, was reckoned to have only 1000 ducats, but even on that he exported hats to Crete in deals worth 100 ducats at a time; he imported wine, cheese and grapes, and had interests in cloth manufacture. Francesco Marangon sometimes worked for other people yet kept three journeymen; Zuan Morandi, a stringer, worked manually himself but also employed assistants.

Of the less well-off, Gierolemo di Piero and Nicolo at the King sold from baskets in the street. Zacharia at the Castle was 'in jail every other week for debt'. Andrea at the Annunciation had many days when he did not see a customer. But if a business failed, one could try something else. Francesco Bognolo became a runner for the magistrates, Antonio at the Vine went into domestic service.

The turnover of membership, 1550–75

The openendedness of the mercers' membership is still more obvious from a list compiled in 1575 of members of the guild aged between 18 and 45 along with their year of joining.[48] There are 874 names on the list and the outstanding feature, as shown in Table 3.3, is the figure of 205 members who had joined as recently as 1574. There is no evidence of the sudden addition of another sub-guild to the larger mercers' agglomerate: 38 per cent of members joined the guild less than two years before the list was compiled. Some mercers may have been abroad temporarily, but it seems likely that many assistants and masters remained only a short time attached to a particular business. The assistants may have formed a pool of casual labour moving from one shop to another, sometimes perhaps setting up independently, sometimes changing trades altogether. The *arte* seems to have taken in new members and allowed them to pass through, taking up opportunities and putting them aside as circumstances and resources dictated. The key point is that in a guild where salesmanship was more important than craftsmanship and a guildsman needed to be a businessman, the rigidity for which traditional corporations are often notorious is altogether lacking.

Table 3.3: *Dates of entry to the mercers' guild among the members of 1575*

year of entry	number of entrants	% age of members	year of entry	number of entrants	% age of members
1550	1	0.11	1564	31	3.55
1551	2	0.23	1565	25	2.86
1552	3	0.34	1566	13	1.49
1553	3	0.34	1567	24	2.75
1554	12	1.37	1568	49	5.61
1555	17	1.94	1569	24	2.75
1556	9	1.03	1570	36	4.12
1557	9	1.03	1571	75	8.58
1558	17	1.94	1572	43	4.92
1559	28	3.20	1573	37	4.23
1560	28	3.20	1574	205	23.46
1561	13	1.49	1575	127	14.53
1562	24	2.75	1576	1	0.69
1563	13	1.49	1577	5	
total	179	20.46		695	79.54
combined totals:	874	100.00%			

source: see n. 48.

The changing economic climate, 1575–1600

After the boom of the third quarter of the century came the gloom of the fourth. How was the world of guildsmen and artisans affected by the last, sombre decades of the sixteenth century?

Standing back for a moment from the mercers allows us to turn to three pieces of evidence which suggest how the changed conditions had begun to affect the lives of artisans: they concern prices and wages, taxation and debt.

The information on which Figure 3.3 is based is drawn from M. Aymard's work on grain prices and Professor Pullan's analysis of wage rates in the building trades.[49] Wheat prices are a helpful guide to conditions in Venice, since Venetians were unusually snobbish about white bread. The government permitted the introduction of other types of flour at their peril. Dark bread was regarded as disgusting while the use of millet could provoke rioting. In 1570, when Doge Pietro Loredan died, his corpse was taunted with the crowd's shouts of 'millet Doge'.[50] Sensitive to the social and political dimensions of protests like this, the government compromised with the people's choosiness by varying

Figure 3.3: *Real wages in Venice, 1567–1599*

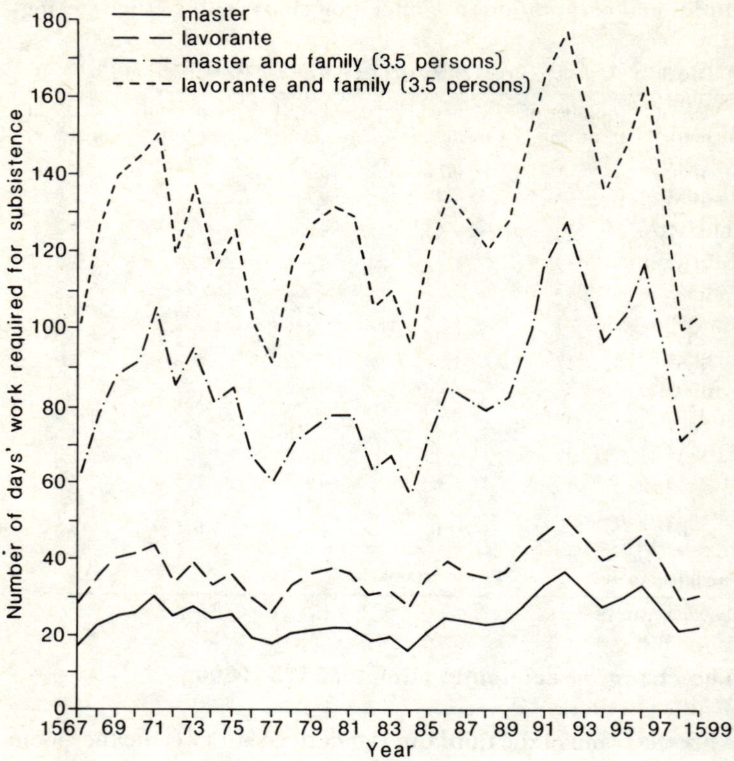

[1]source: see n. 49.

the standard size of a loaf rather than its cost, a policy implemented with the ill-tempered compliance of the bakers' guild.[51]

The effects of changes in the wheat price are, however, difficult to determine. The price was especially high in 1571 and 1592, but the impact on individuals and families must have varied greatly. A master without dependants in 1571 would only have needed to work for 30 days (about one working day in nine) to feed himself; for 36 in 1592 (one in seven). But much would depend on how many others had to live off the one income. A master with a family of four and two apprentices to feed would have had to work at least 180 days in 1571 and 216 in 1592. And of course the assistant with a family of, say, seven would be in a desperate position in either case, needing the equivalent of over 300 days' work in 1571 and 350 in 1592, figures which certainly exceeded what the economy could offer. We need much more information on the other elements of a household budget — drink, clothing and so on — and a much clearer idea of family and household size before the material standard of living of artisans can be properly assessed, but there can be little doubt that 1571 and 1592 were years of crisis for a large proportion of the guild population as well as for the poor.

Even when further information is brought to light, it will need to be understood in relation to the everyday functioning of the economy, especially in terms of the credit mechanisms available to people short of ready cash in years of high bread prices. Certainly, the years after 1594 saw a sharp rise in the value of claims made against debtors which were registered at the *Giustizia Vecchia*. These are shown in Figure 3.4. The number of claims fell back rapidly after 1600 and faster still after 1610, but the value of claims peaked in 1599 and soared again in 1602.

What did Venetians expect to get on credit? Table 3.4 shows that over half the total number and one-third of the total value of claims made between 1594 and 1610 were for wine, goods and services. It is an unremarkable conclusion from the evidence that a heavy drinker with a large family would have experienced special difficulties in the 1590s.

Even these figures, however, indicate that there were one or two safeguards. High wheat prices (1571, 1592) and high numbers of claims (1599, 1602) are not coincidental, which may suggest that credit facilities could ease hardship in a difficult year. Moreover, the cases of claims for unpaid wages indicate that employees as well as employers could resort to law for payment of what was due to them.

Figure 3.4: *Claims against debtors, 1594–1610*

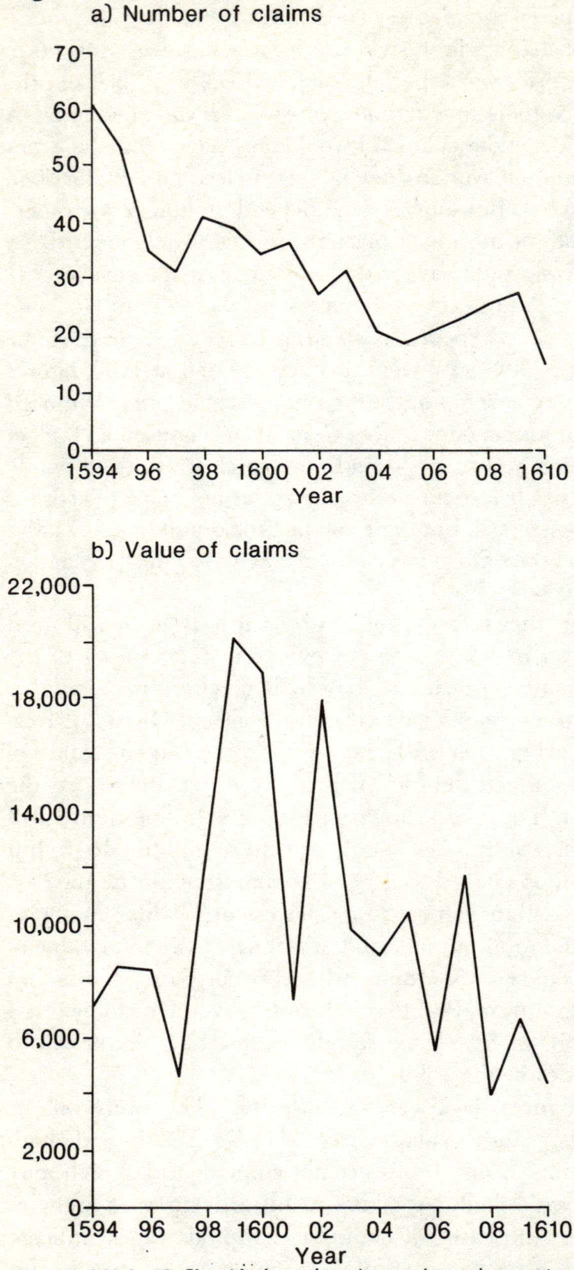

source: GV, b. 52, filza 43, *domande, scritture e risposte in causa per crediti e differenze varie fra gli artigiani*, 1524–1658.

Table 3.4: *Claims against debtors, 1594–1610*

type of claim	claims recorded	value of claims (lire)	% of claims	% of value
wine bills	177	22,037.65	33.08	13.33
goods and services	117	24,140.45	21.87	14.61
drugs and medicines	58	7,448.75	10.85	4.51
against employees	92	20,587.20	17.20	12.46
against employers	22	37,320.40	4.10	22.58
loans outstanding	35	7,199.80	6.54	4.35
personal services (food, errands, cash)	34	46,553.85	6.36	28.16
totals	535	165,288.10	100.00	100.00

source: GV, b. 52, filza 43, *domande, scritture e risposte in causa per crediti e differenze varie fra gli artigiani*, 1524–1658.

The squeeze of the 1590s also put pressure on the guilds themselves. Their overheads were soon on the rise. As we shall see in Chapter 6, the government's demands for men and money for the reserve fleet were becoming increasingly heavy as the century wore on. To make matters worse, taxation on raw materials and finished goods was also on the increase. This can be demonstrated by reference to a rare series of figures in the records of the ironmongers which shows how the price of charcoal varied in the period 1520–1624. The price which they paid to suppliers stayed fairly level from 1530 until 1572, when it rocketed to 44 soldi, 16 of which (over a third) were represented by tax. As can be seen from Figure 3.5, the next sharp rise was in the early 1590s.

There is some evidence, therefore, that the 1570s saw the beginnings of a threefold pressure on guilds and their members. The cost of foodstuffs soared, especially in 1571 and 1592. In the 1590s, credit facilities normally available to the populace may have become less accessible, and there was increasing pressure on the cash resources of the guilds themselves. Guildsmen needed more money for food, goods and services and guild contributions. What was their response to the new demands?

The anatomy of enterprise

The question just posed needs to be addressed at two different levels: the political, which is deferred until Chapter 6, and the economic, to which we can now turn, concentrating once again on

Figure 3.5: *The cost of charcoal, 1520–1630*

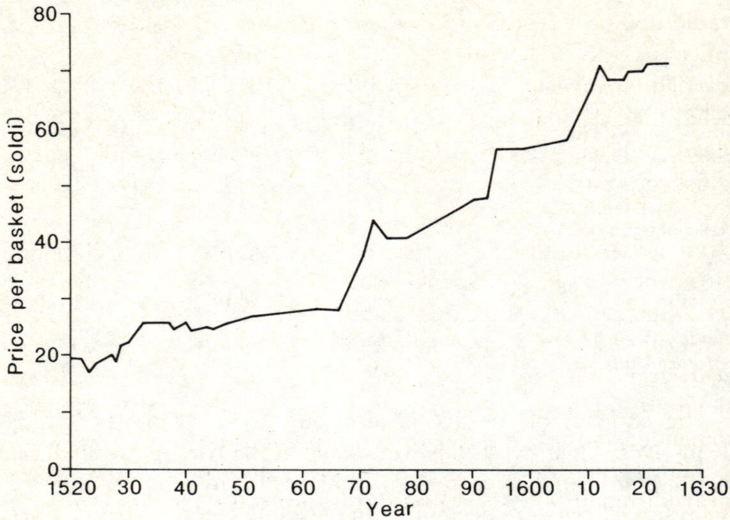

source: Arti, b. 127, *fabbri, atti diversi, 1506–1559*, and b. 128, *fabbri, atti diversi, 1600–29*

the mercers' records for information on the guild's institutional structures and the fortunes of individual members.

The scale of business enterprise

A survey drawn up by the mercers' officers in 1593 and analysed in Table 3.5, showed nearly 80 per cent of masters and one apprentice in four had fees to pay which they owed to the guild.[52]

Table 3.5: *Outstanding fees among members of the mercers' guild, 1593*

occupational group	number of debtors	% of debtors	% of debt	members 1586	% in debt
mercers	76	21.90	24.41	210	36.19
textiles	12	3.46	2.78	45	25.67
haberdashery	83	23.92	25.78	216	38.43
luxuries	24	6.91	6.73	86	27.91
metalware	19	5.48	4.34	48	39.58
household goods	9	2.59	2.08	23	39.13
food	19	5.48	1.93	48	39.58
dual occupation	2	0.58	1.14	3	66.67
itinerants	3	0.86	1.54	18	16.67
unspecified/misc.	100	28.82	29.27	267	37.45
total	347	100.00	100.00	964	Av. 35.67

source: see n. 48.

As can be seen from Table 3.5, the burden of the total debt was evenly distributed among the mercers' different trades. What the table does not reveal are the marginal notes made by the compilers next to each name. In 51 cases (14 per cent), the debt was carried forward, perhaps to give shopkeepers extra time to call in what their customers owed them. Some debtors to the guild were dead; only six were bankrupt. They should be carefully distinguished from 79 who had shut up shop ('*non fa più botega*'). In one sense, this suggests that small businesses were finding it hard to keep going in the 1590s. In another it shows that the high turnover of guild membership still enabled members to move on as opportunities in a particular field dissolved. Wholesale bankruptcy was avoided and individual misfortune did not have wider repercussions in the guild as a whole: this was due to the flexibility of status groups within the guild and the small staff dependent on the fortunes of any single business.

Figures in the extreme right-hand column of Table 3.5 are drawn from another list, the most comprehensive of the sixteenth century, which was made in 1586. There are 964 names in it, entered in five separate booklets which place members in the following categories:

wholesalers	245
retailers	121
'juniors'	282
'poor'	285
women	31
Total	964

The list is more comprehensive than that of 1575 (which only included mercers aged 18 to 45) but it is still striking that membership should be so numerous after the plague of 1575–77. In some ways, the amorphous quality of the guild's status groups enabled it to absorb casual labour and recover some of its losses, thus contributing to the formidable recuperative capacity of the Venetian economy.[53]

The first two categories seem to correspond to 'masters', the 'juniors' to apprentices, and the 'poor' to assistants or journeymen, but on closer inspection these categories dissolve. The 'poor' included many independent shopholders, as we shall see, and the 'juniors' were not defined by age. In 1471, the guild had ruled that the *zoveni* were 'all those who earn 50 ducats a year or less in our shops, either in salary or living expenses or as their share of the capital'.[54]

Wholesalers and retailers were defined — and then only loosely — by volume of business. In 1581, wholesalers were designated as:

> those who deal in silk (nap and twisted) and anyone who produces this silk, those dealing in canvas or cloth of any type from the West, or kersies and serges . . . all types of tapestry, cloaks and mohair from the Levant.

Some wholesale mercers were part of Venice's 'middle class', the *cittadini* (they had to be, to trade in the Levant), but they did not form an élite at the apex of the guild. For 'if anyone should have exceptionally large dealings in veils, thread, metal or other retail mercery, if they are soundly established, they also shall be inscribed among the wholesalers'. This is justified by the idea that 'not quality but quantity puts a man in good circumstances'.[55] That makes surprising reading at a time when guilds in Venice and elsewhere were allegedly crippling Italy's commercial prospects by insisting on high quality, high cost products which could not compete on the open market with cheap goods available in bulk from producers in the Netherlands and England.[56]

There was no question of wholesalers' subjecting other groups to their own interests. This is a significant point which can be demonstrated in two ways. First, as shown in Table 3.6, it is clear that few masters had more than two assistants.

Table 3.6: *Occupation and status in the mercers' guild, 1586*

occupational group	1	2	3	4	5	total
mercers/textiles	152	66	162	129	10	519
haberdashery	52	29	39	91	5	216
luxuries	21	10	21	31	3	86
metalware	17	7	8	15	1	48
household goods	3	2	7	10	1	23
food	—	3	28	7	10	48
dual occupation	—	1	—	1	1	3
itinerants	—	3	15	—	—	18
miscellaneous	—	—	2	1	—	3
total	245	121	282	285	31	964

1. Wholesalers, 2. Retailers, 3. 'Zoveni', 4. 'Poveri', 5. Women.

source: see n. 48.

Of those engaged in mercery, 218 masters (152 + 66), as it were, 'shared' 291 'juniors' and 'poor' (162 + 129). Amongst haberdashers there were 81 masters and 130 *poveri* and *zoveni*. In the metal trades there were 24 masters and only 23 potential dependants.

However, if the status groups were so loosely defined, could not these figures conceal the dependence of masters on each other? If the 1586 list is rearranged according to shops, the experiment produces the three groups of members shown in Table 3.7. About

Table 3.7: *Patterns of dependence in the mercers' guild, 1586*

	capomaestri					
	wholesale	retail	'zoveni'	'poveri'	women	total
i. SHARING PREMISES						
mercers/textiles	75	8	82	18	—	183
haberdashery	29	5	27	10	1	. 72
luxuries	9	3	14	6	—	32
metalware	8	1	6	4	—	19
household goods	1	—	1	—	—	2
food	—	—	—	—	—	—
dual occupation	—	—	—	—	—	—
itinerants	—	—	—	—	—	—
Total	122	17	130	38	1	308
ii. APPARENTLY INDEPENDENT						
mercers/textiles	64	14	7	48	—	133
haberdashery	16	6	1	31	—	54
luxuries	11	4	2	16	—	33
metalware	8	3	1	5	—	17
household goods	2	2	—	7	—	11
food	—	—	1	1	—	2
dual occupation	—	—	—	—	—	—
itinerants	—	—	—	—	—	—
Total	101	29	12	108	—	250
iii. WITHOUT SHOPS						
mercers/textiles	13	44	73	63	10	203
haberdashery	7	18	11	50	4	90
luxuries	1	3	5	9	3	21
metalware	1	3	1	6	1	12
household	—	—	6	3	1	10
food	—	3	27	6	10	46
dual occupation	—	1	—	1	1	3
itinerants	—	3	15	—	—	18
miscellaneous	—	—	2	1	—	3
Total	22	75	140	139	30	406
Overall totals	245	121	282	285	31	964

source: see n. 48.

32 per cent of total membership were engaged in some form of joint enterprise (and the firms were sometimes family partnerships rather than employers and dependent employees). We can be sure that 250 shops were quite independent (group ii) and it is important to emphasise that 108 of these were run by people who were described as 'poor'. In other words, 38 per cent of those inscribed in the guild's membership list as *poveri* ran their own businesses, which is perhaps the best evidence of the high degree of independent enterprise in the guild. The total membership of 964 represents something like 400 separate shops in 1586. By 1594, that figure had, if anything, increased.

In that year the mercers compiled another list which catalogued the location of shops in different areas of the city. The list, whose contents are analysed in Table 3.8, was confined to independent heads of shops. There were 446 shops in 1594. If there were 400 in 1586 and if 79 had gone out of business by 1593 (above, p. 103) they had certainly been very speedily replaced.

Table 3.8: *The distribution of mercers' shops, 1594*

occupational group	sestier S.Marco	Cast.	Cann.	S.Polo	S.Croce	D'D	Total
mercers/textiles	91	22	2	26	19	3	163
haberdashery	55	13	6	24	1	1	100
luxuries	31	—	1	10	—	—	42
metalware	24	3	1	5	—	—	33
household goods	9	—	1	—	—	—	10
dual occupation	—	2	—	—	—	—	2
miscellaneous	—	—	—	—	—	1	1
unspecified	66	—	24	1	—	4	95
total	276	40	35	66	20	9	446
% age of total	61.88	8.97	7.85	14.80	4.48	2.02	100.00

source: see n. 48.

From the 1594 list, we see that business was predictably concentrated in the Merceria which linked Rialto and San Marco. Here there were 276 shops, and a large number of the 66 shops in San Polo just the other side of Rialto should be regarded as part of the same complex. (The level of concentration this represents can be emphasised by saying that a modern pedestrian passes roughly 300 shop fronts in a walk from San Polo via Rialto and along the Merceria to the clock tower at San Marco.)

The variety of goods in the heartland of Venice's market life was extraordinary: cloth and clothes, fancy goods, hats and braid, haberdashery, fasteners, perfume. Here was where the mercers concentrated their enterprise and the distribution of shops in other parts of the city was comparatively sparse.

When John Evelyn visited Venice in the late seventeenth century, he was struck by the variety of goods and by the speed of turnover:

> Hence I pass'd thro' the Merceria, which is one of the most delicious streetes in the world for the sweetnesse of it, and is all the way on both sides tapistred as it were with cloth of gold, rich damasks and other silks, which the shops expose and hang before their houses from the first floore, and with that variety that for neere half the year spent chiefly in this Citty I hardly remember to have seene the same piece twice exposed . . .[57]

From the collection of inventories in the Venetian Archive, it is possible to obtain a fuller, though more mundane, picture of what was kept in a mercer's shop and how it was marketed.

Stock and turnover

Otis the mercer, who died in 1580, is not found on the mercers' lists compiled before that date and unfortunately his inventory does not record the name of his shop. Most probably, since this was a well-established business, he was an immigrant to Venice in the 1570s, perhaps from Germany or Flanders, as his name suggests. This would explain whey he was not in Venice for the 1567–68 list and was probably too old for the 1575 compilation which only covered the 18–45 age-group.

He had committed considerable resources to his haberdasher's business.[58] The stock in the shop at his death consisted of 107 separate items worth a total of L.11,539.7 soldi (1861 ducats). He stocked a wide variety of haberdashery and some cloth: braid, twine from Corfu, silk and gold thread, fringes, silk, velvet, serges, twill and taffeta. But the most striking items are his 21 different sorts of buttons, counted in dozens and running to the extraordinary figure of 62,562, worth L.1269.17 soldi (about 205 ducats). He evidently supplied a number of tailors, because five of them left small items in pledge to him. That there was a market for so much trumpery is a reminder of the sheer substance of the luxury trades in the Venetian economy.

Given the range of resources amongst mercers and the problems of relating occupation and status in any simple way, it would be rash to compare one inventory with another. However, a separate and still more valuable inventory survives for Stefano Zarnesi, mercer at the Fan, who died in 1608. We can be sure he was a guild member for he was about to become an officer of the guild when he died.[59] His father-in-law, named as executor, was Lorenzo Pomeli, perfumer at the San Jopo in San Moise, a *povero* in 1586, still in business in 1594 and contributing to the guild's candle money fund in 1612.

Stefano's considerable estate was made up as follows:

stock	L.54,127.04 soldi	(8730 ducats)
shop furnishings	L. 1127.12 soldi	(181 ducats)
cash in shop	L.13,947.00 soldi	(2249 ducats)
debts owed to him	L.58,620.00 soldi	(9454 ducats)

The shop contained a huge variety of goods: 228 different sorts of wares were listed, including cloth, canvas, kerchiefs, veils, thread (of standard, good and superior qualities), fustians, fringes, cord, lace, braid, tassels and pewter. The most valuable items were two bales of linen worth L.2367.18 soldi. It is an intriguing thought that such a figure represents only about 5 per cent of the value of stock in the shop, which underlines the variety of goods and the relatively small quantities in which they were held.

The figure of 2000 ducats for cash in the shop strongly suggests that this was a substantial and prosperous business. But it is dwarfed by the scale of debts owed to Stefano at his death: L.58,620 (nearly 9500 ducats) were still owed for goods. The figure represents 473 separate transactions at an average of L.120, rather a lot for incidental haberdashery and another reminder of the central and substantial place occupied by fancy goods in the economy. All the same, as can be seen from Figure 3.7, the average of each transaction is rather misleading. Of the debts, 340 (about 72 per cent) were worth less than L.100, 208 (44 per cent) were worth less than L.20 and more than a third were worth less than L.10 each.[60]

How many such deals were struck in a day, a week or a year is unclear, but this was undoubtedly a busy shop. The list of those owing money to Stefano includes nuns, nobles, other mercers, dyers, apothecaries and many visitors, from Este, Noale, Bassano, Verona, Treviso and Bergamo. Stefano gave credit of more than L.3000 to Antonio Poliaza from Padua, Paolo Vigo had come all the way from Salò but went away with only L.4's worth of goods. Lorenzo Loredan owed L.7.5 soldi, the Jew Marcho dalla Baldora over L.500.

The 9500 ducats owed by debtors represent almost exactly 60 per cent of Stefano's assets. The extent of these credit facilities indicates a high level of business confidence, and must have increased enormously the velocity of turnover. The risks involved

Figure 3.6: *The Scale of transactions in a mercer's shop, 1608*

L.2,000	***
L.1,500	*
L.1,000	****
L. 750	*****
L. 500	**************
L. 450	*
L. 400	********
L. 350	******
L. 300	*****
L. 250	*********
L. 200	****************
L. 150	************************
L. 100	*************************************
L. 90	*******
L. 80	*********
L. 70	**********
L. 60	
	*******************
L. 40	***********
L. 30	****************
L. 20	**************************************
L. 10.	**
	*******************
L. 0	**
	**
	*****************************

Each asterisk represents one transaction

source: ASV, *Giudici di Petizion, Inventarii, busta 343/8 no. 90*

and whether others were prepared to take them cannot be ascertained until a series of similar inventories is brought to light and systematically analysed. From this single compilation, it is evident that Stefano, a shopkeeper, was one link in a chain of credit which extended back to his own suppliers. At his death, he himself had debts of over 4700 ducats to 37 creditors. Ten of them were due sums in excess of L.1000, and the largest was owed to a relative, Tomaso Zarnesi, who could claim L.6831. The total figure represents almost exactly half of what Stefano himself was owed. One wonders whether he had made it a rule-of-thumb to keep his debts to wholesalers at half the level of what he gave out on credit, thus risking that 50 per cent of the debts would need to be 'bad' to threaten his solvency. Once again, this is speculation until further research is done. What is plain is that Stefano ran a business at the Fan which extended credit to all types of customer which speeded the turnover of goods, and in turn he balanced that against what he owed his own suppliers.

The connection of both Otis and Stefano to the mercers' guild is shadowy, and raises the question of whether they and others like them were in fact taking economic life in a direction which led away from guilds. This seems unlikely not just because Stefano was, after all, a guild officer, but because one even more enterprising businessman remained firmly attached to the traditional institutions of *arte* and *scuola*.

A success story: Bartolomeo Bontempelli

The lists which date from the 1560s showed the prosperity of members of the mercers' guild, some of them international businessmen dealing wholesale and sometimes even on the foreign exchange (above, pp. 94–6). The profits to be made by guild members were high, though they would not necessarily have derived from dealings in mercery alone.

Bartolomeo Bontempelli was born in Val di Sabbia, near Brescia, in 1538.[61] He set up shop in Venice in the 1560s and by 1568 was said to have capital resources amounting to some 6000 ducats at two shops, the Chalice and the Moon. Other sources show that he had hundreds more ducats invested in the public debt. He acquired full Venetian citizenship in 1579 and by this time his mining interests in Agordo could produce a deal with the Archduke of Austria worth 70,000 florins. His charitable donations were enormous by any standards. To the Hospital of the Mendicanti he gave 36,000 ducats and the endowment was strengthened by the recurrent income which the hospital received through the interest on a sum of 100,000 ducats which Bontempelli provided in his will.[62] In his lifetime he was the dedicatee of a devotional treatise, and his portrait survives in the corner of a large altarpiece by Sante Peranda (a follower of Tintoretto who became fashionable in Venice in the early seventeenth century) which he commissioned for the church of San Salvador at Rialto.[63]

This extraordinary guildsman was internationally famous. When in 1618 — two years after Bontempelli's death — the chaplain to the Venetian Embassy in London remarked on the window displays of London shops, he said that they were decorated 'precisely in the same way as the unique Bartolomeus dal Calese used to do at Ascension tide in Venice'.[64] Bontempelli was known to the English ambassador Dudley Carleton as 'he that doth so much beautify the carnaval with his divers suits of cloth of gold'. That was written while Carleton was considering an offer from Bontempelli of a 'complete furniture of my whole house, specifying hangings, plate, beds and linen, and all this *senza interesse*, only because I was minister to a prince so well beloved of the state to which he is subject'.[65]

The observations made of Bontempelli are significant. It is striking that both commentators make a connection between Bontempelli's business activities and Venetian festivals, Ascension tide and carnival, a connection which may not be fortuitous and which is investigated in detail in Chapter 4. The offer to furnish the residence of the representative of a Protestant state should perhaps be seen in the light of a pledge Bartolomeo made to the Venetian government in 1606: 10,000 ducats every time Venice went to war with the papacy. The implications of this and the general relationship between the Venetian business world and the Counter-Reformation Church will be reviewed in Chapter 5.

Mine-owner, silk merchant, purveyor of household furnishings, famous businessman — and guildsman: Bontempelli was a member of the guild's committee in 1569, 1571 and 1579. In 1582 he was the guild's warden. He did not hold office again, probably because of the burdens he shouldered as a member of the Scuola Grande di San Rocco.[66] Bartolomeo Bontempelli, who can look like the herald of a 'new' age of commercial enterprise on the grand scale, remained firmly attached to the 'medieval' world of guild and confraternity.

Summary

The mercers' records show them to have been far and away the most important of the guilds of Venice. They incorporated a vast number of trades within a huge agglomerate. Cappers, stringers, purse-makers, lace-makers and others regarded themselves as separate *arti* within the larger framework. Small wonder that in 1617, the canvas-makers complained that the mercers should be content to have subjected so many other guilds and trades.[67] Does this make the mercers the exception rather than the rule?

A comparison: the ironmongers

The *arte dei fabbri* was another *arte media*, standing midway between a handicraft and a trade organisation, between 'blacksmiths' guild' and 'ironmongers' company'. Scattered documentation from 1531 and 1603 suggests that the guild shared certain characteristics with the mercers.

A membership list of 1531 shows the guild's openness to immigrant labour.[68] Not all need have been *recent* immigrants, of course, but place of origin was clearly no ground for exclusion from the guild. In 1531, the members were listed as follows:

from Ballabio	56	Albanian	1
from Val di Sassina	20	Greek	1
from Mandollo	12	Friulians	2
from Lecce	28	Brescians	2
from Bergamo	18	Cremonese	1
Venetians	33	Cremaschi	2

The vast majority of the guild's members were identified with a place of origin on the Terraferma, barely one-sixth were described as Venetians. Once again, there was a looseness of occupational titles. Members were basically divided amongst smiths and cauldron-makers, but 17 different occupations appear on the list, including balance-makers, blade-makers, grinders, locksmiths, a bell-founder and two 'merchants'. Their shops were concentrated along the Calle dei Fabbri which runs almost parallel to the Merceria between Rialto and San Marco. Although 48 different parishes were represented, the main foci were at San Salvador (18), San Lucca (39) and San Zeminian (26), the parishes through which the Calle dei Fabbri passes.

In 1603, a ballot was held to choose those members who were to be available for the reserve fleet.[69] The requirement was 51 names, to be chosen from a membership of 185. At least 71 premises were represented and the scale of each enterprise was clearly very small: 16 masters worked alone, 17 with one assistant, 17 with two and 14 with three. Two employed four each and Berto at the Cross was quite exceptional in naming six assistants. Most members were again immigrants from the mainland, though the places of origin had changed since 1531: there were 49 members from Niminalengo, 29 from Cividal di Belluno, 21 from Cadore, 8 from Asolo and 18 Germans.

The blacksmiths/ironmongers thus formed a guild open to immigrant labour and offered work in small businesses. The experience of Venetian guilds suggests that their structures were traditionally loose, the institutional framework light and flexible. Much more evidence remains to be uncovered in the Venetian Archive and Museo Correr, but it does not seem premature to suggest that when guild structures look 'rigid' or 'obsolete' it is important to ask why. In the 1580s the mercers issued the following order in accordance with government instructions:

> This is to be observed by cotton and cloth merchants and others who sell mercery. . . . If they are selling anything else, they must within the month reorganise the shop and give notice of the presence of a genuine master . . . so that when galleymen are levied . . . noone can say they have already been balloted with the canvas makers or second-hand dealers but must be ready for every service and all appropriate taxes within our guild.[70]

The purpose of the order was clear: to simplify the administration of standby and call-up for the fleet. The fixing of status ('genuine master'), the drawing of lines of demarcation, these were a response to government orders and could only hinder the process of adjustment in which guildsmen were engaged, only slow the pulse of economic vitality.

The weight of the burden of service and the serious crisis it provoked in the relations of guilds and government are the subject of Chapter 6. In spite of government demands, guilds continued to adjust to changes in the economic climate in the seventeenth century. According to Professor Rapp's figures, the number of wool workers (beaters, carders and combers) fell from 1222 to 222 between 1595 and 1690, weavers from 856 to 224. The number of mercers increased from 567 to 1747 over the same period.[71] A guild like the mercers offered employment opportunities in the boom conditions before 1575, and in a period of transition like the 1590s, and it helped contain the implications of decline after 1600. Did the guilds of other cities face similar problems of adaptation and how successfully did they cope with them?

Comparisons and contrasts

Much of what appears above depends on a reinterpretation of guild agglomerates like the Venetian mercers. It was argued that the mercers' expansion to cover many trades, the impressive amount of capital tied up in those trades, and the spread of capital through hundreds of small businesses are evidence of the continued vitality of the guild system in an age of opportunity.

That vitality withered somewhat under the burden of the fisc, but not because its roots were old.

The comparisons have been chosen to fit very roughly the two phases of the Venetian experience: structural adjustment in the fifteenth century, metropolitan boom after about 1530. The aim of what follows is to isolate the elements of change and continuity in the economic life of early modern cities and to attempt an assessment of the part played by guilds in preserving tradition and fostering innovation. Most of the comparisons are struck against commercial centres: traditionally important cities and sixteenth-century boom towns. In most cases, it is suggested that guilds should not be viewed as forces which of necessity retarded economic development. And in a highly speculative coda, the thesis is extended from commerce to manufacture.

Structural changes in the economy of *Florence* were well under way before the 'long' sixteenth century opened. Perhaps the revolutionary events of the *Ciompi* uprising hastened changes which occurred only later in other cities. Woollen cloth retained a certain importance in the fifteenth century, but the textile sector of the Florentine economy was increasingly dominated by silk and silk-related trades. Industries like building retained a strikingly traditional economic organisation.[72] Professor Goldthwaite's pioneering book shows features of the Florentine building industry very similar to those of Venetian guilds. Enterprises in general remained small, though the heads of work gangs or the owners of kilns were sometimes small-scale capitalists. There was an easy mobility between artisanal activity and commercial life and this may help to account for the pervasiveness of business skills like keeping accounts and offering credit. According to the *catasto* of 1427, the stonemasons Giuliano and Andrea di Romolo had a shop with goods worth 200 florins and a list of debtors owing a total of 545 florins.[73]

Guild traditions of high-quality workmanship were preserved despite the weakness of lines of demarcation between particular trades. Their role in creating the splendours of renaissance architecture has long been overlooked. Investment in the 'luxury' sector

> calling for more skilled workers, for a greater variety of skill and for more highly developed skills brought about a transformation of the economy in the most basic factor of production — human capital itself. This was the notable achievement of the economy of Renaissance Florence — and, in the final analysis, this is what the Renaissance was about.[74]

We know very little about the economy of Florence in the sixteenth century — long or short — but in its general outlines it looks as though commercial decline was staved off in part by the proliferation of small-scale enterprises within a growing number of guilds.[75] As in Venice, the last three decades of the sixteenth century were uncertain and crisis-ridden, though the city did not enter irreversible decline until the plague of 1630.[76]

In 1561 there were nearly 2200 shops in Florence — six to every 100 inhabitants in the area of Santa Croce. If we exclude shops which *might* have been run on large resources of capital (wool, silk, flax, dyeing or metal trades) two thirds of the total were still run by artisans and retailers. There were 101 mercers, 96 shoemakers, 69 tailors and 42 goldsmiths. Visitors remarked on the lack of mechanical crafts in the shops.[77]

According to Montaigne, much the same could be said of *Rome*.[78] In the mid-sixteenth century, the city's population of about 100,000 people quadrupled in size at different times of the year. The economy was increasingly devoted to catering for a floating population of pilgrims, tourists and churchmen (unsurprising since the average size of a cardinal's household was about 150 persons). There were plenty of shops for the tourists to visit. By 1622, there were more than 5500 shops in the city, 1582 selling clothing, a figure which in turn includes 382 mercers.[79]

The number of outlets far outstripped the productive capacity of the economy, but there were signs of vitality in the building trades which, as in Florence, put together the fabric of the Renaissance city. Some of the projects were very large-scale: the building site at Saint Peter's could command a workforce of 2500. Few of those involved worked for periods of more than a few days, evidence perhaps of the flexibility of the traditional organisation of work and work-sharing which we have examined in Venice and briefly surveyed in Florence.[80] What must be stressed yet again is that the trades were organised in guilds: to meet the luxurious needs of Rome's inhabitants and visitors, there was 'a remarkable revival and extension of guild life in the sixteenth century'.[81]

The building boom in Renaissance Rome was in part a response to the destruction wrought by Charles V's unpaid mercenaries in 1527.[82] By the end of the century, warfare was exerting a less positive influence. The heavy taxes necessary to meet the papacy's mounting debts had begun to hamper enterprise, and confidence in the city's credit systems was on the wane.[83]

A city more readily associated with banking in the sixteenth century was *Genoa*, the home of the San Giorgio bank and of those who funded Charles V's wars. In many ways, Genoa seemed to have shed its medieval carapace by the fifteenth century. Commercial capitalism was represented by the banks; an entrepreneur such as Giovanni Triadano was said to be setting 300 people to work in his silk business. Wage-earners, who were rarely paid in coin, saw their living standards fall into decay. At another level, commercial development was rooted in traditional business practice like the *commenda* and traditional institutions like the guild. Capitalism was a 'popular' phenomenon. Despite Triadano's 300 dependent workers, most silk was produced by 2000 or so weavers who owned their own looms and sometimes small amounts of other capital besides.[84]

Genoa's trading prosperity was in many ways gained at the expense of the port of *Barcelona*. The Catalan city's population of 35,000 was large by fifteenth-century standards, and the economy displayed some features which foreshadowed by 100 years the more spectacular expansion enjoyed by other European towns in the sixteenth century. The city was a great Mediterranean entrepot. Its luxury manufactures — soap, glass, sugar, silk and leather — developed, it is said, thanks to the victory of free enterprise over guild restrictions. This was reflected in the declining status of master craftsmen, especially weavers, who often became dependent wage-labourers. Against this, one should set the fact that Barcelona's development as a port was aided by the organisation of guilds of dockers, and some guildsmen, particularly shearers and dyers, were instrumental in fostering the growth of a 'capitalist' economy.[85]

Political instability and Genoese competition rather than the guild system account for the fact that Barcelona never took part in the sixteenth-century boom.[86] In the Iberian peninsula, economic expansion after 1500 is most closely identified with the Atlantic Ocean and with the city of *Seville*. There too, large numbers of small investors were involved in the Atlantic trade, some of them artisans from the city's 60 guilds, most of which were engaged in luxury trades.[87]

In *Lyons*, whose sixteenth-century boom echoed all over Europe, economic innovation was mingled with archaism, but the consequences of expansion were rather different from those experienced elsewhere. By about 1550, Lyons had a population of some 70,000. As in other early modern cities, a figure like this was created and sustained by a high level of immigration — perhaps two-thirds of the population had not been born in Lyons.[88] The city's prosperity derived from silk, printing and banking. Capital invested by resident communities of foreign merchants was the crucial lubricant of the wheels of commerce. Native industries produced conflicts of capital and labour more familiar in an industrial age, particularly in the silk industry. A loom cost the equivalent of 40 days' pay and the means of production were as a consequence often in the hands of merchants rather than craftsmen.[89] In 1564 there were about 1200 looms in the city and 220 of them worked at the say-so of just two merchants. Two others, Voisin and Durier, were said to employ 800–1000 people. Concentrations of dependence such as this made the city's slump as spectacular as its boom. M. Gascon estimates that 60 per cent of all silk looms in Lyons were idle within three decades of the establishment of the industry.[90] In the printing industry, growth was unhampered by guild restrictions and employees worked in something more like a factory than a workshop in associations which looked more like trade unions than guilds.[91]

As in Barcelona, the guilds of Lyons played little part in the export trades and the survival of 53 corporations in 1579 is largely explained by their provision of goods for local markets. In 1545 there were 333 mercers in Lyons and we have 'an insufficiency of vocabulary to give a precise idea of the importance of the profession'.[92] However, it seems unlikely that the mercers of Lyons were in any sense an *arte media* standing between respectable artisans and the world of *grand commerce*. On the contrary, the traditional world of shopkeepers and artisans was under pressure at one end of the scale from rich merchants, at the other from the growing numbers of the poor.[93] A wage-labourer could expect to spend three quarters of his income on bread, a cordwainer might sleep on straw in lodgings where most of his other belongings would be claimed by creditors at his death.[94]

The general weakness of guild structures in Lyons and their incapacity to influence economic development to any great extent may have accelerated the deterioration of artisan living standards. However, lower wages did not widen profit margins to any appreciable degree and acted as a disincentive to artisans who saw no prospect of sharing in the wealth they helped to produce. The situation was worsened by the Wars of Religion and the demands of the fisc.[95] The history of Lyons therefore offers a sharp contrast to Venice in terms of the influence of guilds on economic life. It looks all the more distinctive when compared to the city it strove to outdo in a great 'contest of stamina'.[96]

By the 1560s, *Antwerp* had a population of some 90,000.[97] Its place at the centre of international trade and the attractions of its money market suggest a fully-fledged commercial metropolis which had advanced far beyond the potential of a traditionally important town like Bruges. One contributory cause is alleged to be that guild specialisation had never been far advanced. All the same, it must be remembered that the city's day-to-day life was built on the foundations of three huge agglomerates — boatmen representing the service sector, a cloth guild for manufactures and a guild of mercers for just about everything else. From these corporations came the craftsmen of the city's great luxury industries: tapestries, furniture, sugar and spices.[98]

Textile manufacture was based on 300 or so small enterprises, almost invariably having less than eight looms and usually a staff of four or five people.[99] The Guild of Saint Luke helped fuel the city's export-led expansion with 'a section of luxury crafts almost entirely working for an international market', producing everything from harpsichords to fancy buttons.[100] The retail sector expanded with the city's economy and credit facilities were extended to customers for as long as two years.[101] Perhaps it was their high standards which enabled the city's crafts to outlive the city's prosperity. Even in 1618 the city supported 164 diamond cutters.[102]

Refined skills in Antwerp — unlike Lyons — commanded high rewards. High wages, however, did not produce a squeeze on profits, which remained buoyant even in the lower reaches of enterprise. As in Seville, an increasing number of small merchants engaged in overseas trade and this stratum of the 'middling sort' included skilled, independent craftsmen. Earnings were usually dependent on individual ability rather than status — a characteristic familiar from the Venetian mercers — and the loss of independence by artisans and a rise in the number of workers attached to individual firms coincided not with Antwerp's apogee, but with its decline.[103]

M. van der Wee attributes the expansion of the Antwerp economy to the 'astonishing resilience and social vitality of the urban masses'. These same 'masses' however included manual workers who might live in 'comparatively expensive middle-class houses'.[104] Part of the 'social vitality' of the populace appears to have derived from their opportunities to compete for a place in the commercial world, and high wages presumably aided their quest, though this aspect of guild life in Antwerp remains obscure. At all events, guilds did little to hinder Antwerp's growth. The cause of decline was the Sack of 1576, with its 5 million florins' worth of damage and the consequent emigration of a large number of skilled workers.[105]

Antwerp thus yielded pride of place to *Amsterdam.* The military impregnability of this city, its place at the centre of a state which had broken out of the mould of 'feudalism' and dynasticism set up immediate parallels with Venice. In the seventeenth century, status in Amsterdam was determined by money, the money which the Bourse sucked in and made grow.[106] Capitalism flourished in banking and in industries like sugar-refining and printing. By 1619 one glass furnace could demand a workforce of 50 people.[107]

The continuities, however, are as striking as the innovations. 'Medieval' institutions — including guilds — remained very much alive. The guild system opened to admit immigrant workers, thus making room for the imported skills of refugees. Many of these skills were deployed in the production of luxury goods in small-scale enterprises where the ability of the individual was at a premium. The demand for skilled labour produced the incentive of high rewards and there was no preoccupation with the cost of labour. Accordingly, there was a proliferation of guilds in Amsterdam. As in Venice, they responded to market forces and shifted the emphasis 'from production for a local market to control of labour conditions for an international market'.[108]

The demand for skilled labour to produce expensive luxuries ensured a measure of social mobility and the formation of a 'bourgeoisie' which stretched from the Syndics of the Cloth Guild commemorated by Rembrandt to the craftsmen whose walls were adorned with paintings. Peter Mundy observed in 1640 that the Dutch were

> all in general striving to adorn their houses especially the outer or street room with costly pieces; butchers and bakers not much inferior in their shops, which are fairly set forth, yea many times blacksmiths, cobblers etc., will have some pictures or other by their forge and in their stall.[109]

Bartolomeo Bontempelli as depicted by Sante Peranda would not look out of place amongst Rembrandt's *Staalmeisters.* Mundy's comments on forges and stalls echo something of what Vasari said of Renaissance Florence, where the inventories of artisans almost invariably included a Madonna and where Andrea del Sarto or Pontormo might find customers amongst mercers, joiners and tailors.[110] Guildsmen helped to shape urban culture. They often had the means to enjoy it.

Similar sorts of people were no doubt to be found in Shakespeare's audiences. In the seventeenth century, *London* surpassed and outlasted both Antwerp and Amsterdam. Its population grew from something like 100,000 in 1580 to 400,000 in 1650, and once again the expansion depended on massive immigration, perhaps 5500 people a year.[111] Professor Fisher's view of London's function as an 'engine of economic growth' identifies investment and division of labour as the main sources of fuel.[112] How this operated at the everyday level is still surprisingly obscure. Beyond the general categories of 'cloth' and 'services', little is known about the city's occupational structure.[113] The role of the guilds is also difficult to define. One reason for the emergence of the city as a port superior to Southampton was the formation of a guild of pilots who could guarantee safe guidance for shipping in the Thames.[114] But the city's companies do not seem to fit Professor Fisher's criterion of the division of labour. On the contrary, the companies were rather like those of Antwerp or indeed the Venetian mercers: agglomerates which avoided sharp demarcation. The main reason for this was the 'custom of London' which gave a member of a livery company the opportunity to practise a trade associated with any other company. In the case of Antwerp, it has been argued that this hindered the division of labour, but in London it certainly facilitated economic change and may have fostered the kind of small investor familiar in Antwerp or Seville.[115] Moreover, the guilds still supervised the professional training of a huge section of the English workforce: in 1600 some 15 per cent of London's population were apprentices.[116]

The evidence suggests that in great metropolitan centres like Antwerp, Amsterdam and London (but not Lyons), guilds did respond to market forces and helped to regulate both the development of the urban economy and its contraction. We have yet to examine what happened in towns specialising in manufacture: did they point the way forward to a time when demand for luxury goods would no longer play such a vital part in economic life?

In *Nuremberg*, the *Verlagssystem* seems to have triumphed. Eschewing the high labour costs of the city's crafts, merchants put work out to the countryside. Traditionally, many of Nuremberg's 25,000 inhabitants were organised in some 150 trades specialising in high-quality items: hinges, locks, tiles, 'little objects of daily use' on which craftsmen lavished 'time-consuming care'.[117] It was a style of organisation which lacked a genuine guild structure, but which rewarded high skills with high wages (and it was one which helped to shape the art of Dürer) but by the end of the century the richest man in the city was an industrial entrepreneur called Bartolomäus Viatis. He was born in 1538 (the same year as Bontempelli) the son of a Bergamasc who emigrated to Venice, where he set up as a shopkeeper. His immense fortune — he was worth 1.4 million guilders at his death — derived largely from marrying the boss's daughter when he went on business to Nuremberg, and partly from the manufacture of textiles 'put out' to Northern Bohemia, Upper Saxony, and Silesia.[118] Despite the freedom of action enjoyed by a figure like Viatis, and despite the lack of a strong guild system, there was no real sign of economic advance in the city itself. Nuremberg enjoyed no part of the 'boom' after about 1550, but this was due to the cost of war rather than high labour costs fostered by craft organisations.[119]

In any case, the 'putting out' system was by no means universal in the production of cloth. *Lille* and *Leyden* provide a model which is the reverse of that of Nuremberg.[120] There, traditional patterns of production were only slightly altered by entrepreneurs in the sixteenth century. The outstanding feature of the two towns was the survival of 'small commodity' production based on guild organisations. Most cloth was made by independent masters who produced between 30 and 75 cloths a year in firms of perhaps four or five skilled artisans. There were two main reasons for the survival of this type of production. First of all, the system was protected by medieval legislation. This ensured for instance that no mere dealer controlled the supply of raw materials to guild members and that payments were generally made in cash, not in the form of advances of raw materials. There are echoes here of the statutes of thirteenth-century Venice and there is a further parallel in the political impotence of guilds in Lille and Leyden. The 'unhampered oligarchy' which characterised political structures in these towns ensured that mercantile interests could have changed the legal framework *had it been in their interests to do so*. But — and this is the second reason for the guilds' survival — it was not. Merchants recognised the value of guilds in terms of their capacity to adapt to market forces and to take the strain off public welfare facilities by sharing employment opportunities and running their own benefit schemes. This had the welcome effect of reducing the risk of social disturbance: both guilds and oligarchs could protect their own interests by defending the 'common good', and these structures survived 'well into the seventeenth century'.[121]

A similar species of social contract seems to have operated in a much smaller centre, *Nördlingen*, which in 1580 had a population of about 8500. Once again the crafts (which represented some 60 trades) were apolitical organisations but encouraged considerable occupational mobility.[122] Only in the late seventeenth century did the situation change as the Wörner family drew scores of master craftsmen into a web of indebtedness and dependence. The city council continued to defend *burgerliche Nährung* or 'economic self-sufficiency for every citizen' until the eighteenth century.[123] But by then, even allowing for the intensely localised character of economic development and immense variations in the chronology of change, we have stretched the elasticity of the 'long' sixteenth century too far. The task remaining is that of drawing together some conclusions about the period 1450–1650.

Conclusion

The subheading is something of a misnomer, for, as the comparative section of this chapter shows, a discussion of guilds in the 'long' sixteenth century tends to do little but draw attention to confusion, contradiction and problems of definition. On the basis of what can be said about a guild like the Venetian mercers, the Antwerp Guild of Saint Luke or the London Companies, a positive reassessment of guilds on the basis of fresh research is called for. In Venice, the guilds were open to immigrants from the Terraferma, and to artisans from various trades. This made them capable of growing with the expanding economy and of regulating the rate of decline by redistributing work between the different sectors of economic activity. Firms remained small, which in turn allowed the diversification of interests, particularly in the flourishing distributive sector, where opportunity was generated by traditional business instincts and by the confident extension of credit. The formation of a huge agglomerate like the mercers was not an erosion of guild traditions, but rather an extension of them: the response of guildsmen to changing economic circumstances.

It is an understatement to say that guilds have for some time had a bad press from historians. On the basis of not very much research, guilds are roundly arraigned for stifling innovation and for keeping wages high.[124] Around 1600 a miner in Agordo — working perhaps for Bontempelli? — could reckon to earn about 20 ducats a year. At the same time, woolworkers in Venice could expect about 140 ducats — and were asking for more. This is taken as a sure sign of uncompetitively high labour costs.[125] Where there is evidence that guildsmen sought to defend traditional structures, this is interpreted as obsolescence and rigidity, if by chance there are signs that guilds began to adapt, this is presented as breakdown. On this the most eminent economic historians are agreed.

According to Professor Coleman, a guild agglomerate was not really a guild at all:

> when further investigation reveals that the mercers [of Maidstone] included not only mercers and grocers, but also weavers, dyers, threadmakers, goldsmiths, physicians, surgeons and 'all petty chapmen', then we can be reasonably certain that economically meaningful guild life there was dead.[126]

And good riddance. Historians as different in approach as Professor Wilson and Mr Hill agree that the Commonwealth's attack on corporations removed a major barrier to England's economic advance.[127]

The survival of guilds in Italy, on the other hand, does much to explain the decline of the peninsula. Professor Cipolla asserts that 'Italian industry . . . mainly because it was controlled by traditionalistic guild regulation persisted in producing by ancient methods excellent goods which were out-dated'.[128] M. Braudel (who admitted some time ago that 'the copious guild archives have not been seriously investigated') has recently confirmed that in Europe as a whole, 'labour in the towns was imprisoned in the straightjacket of guilds'.[129]

There seems to be a basic misconception here: that guilds were units of production or distribution. If we look at them as units of producers and distributors which were expected by members to function in a way which went beyond the purely economic, and especially if we look at guild-based economic organisation in relation to shops, then the perspective changes quite dramatically. The guilds' alleged smothering of innovation should be set against the degree of commercial adaptability demonstrated by the Venetian mercers. And in any case, what does 'innovation' mean in a pre-industrial world? Short of recognising the future of coalmining or developing a huge iron industry, it is hard to see what guilds were expected to do beyond allowing members to adapt to market forces and patterns of demand whilst seeking to preserve traditional standards and economic independence. It is the absence of iron in Italy and coal in Holland which explains the failure of these countries to experience an industrial revolution, not the presence of guilds.[130]

With regard to the guilds' responsibility for reducing competitiveness through protecting high labour costs, M. van der Wee has demonstrated that high wages for a skilled labour force were the outstanding feature of the Antwerp economy, but guild agglomerates are denied a positive role. The corporations merely 'killed the possibilities of further division of labour'. Upward social mobility is related to a concept as vague as 'the social vitality of the urban masses'.[131] There is a similar paradox in Dr Barbour's book on Amsterdam. While guilds proliferated in the seventeenth century and adjusted to the demands of the international market, they were obstacles to economic development.[132] It is even more perplexing that in Barcelona or the Hansa towns, guilds are said to have survived only because they restricted themselves to local markets.[133]

The bewilderment created by assertions designed to dish the guilds from any angle might lead historians to study individual guilds in particular cities — as Dr Larmour advises — and not attempt comparisons at all.[134] Certainly, much more research on guild records in different cities is required before their role in the early modern economy can be properly understood.

For the time being, one might suggest that the rigidity for which guilds are often indicted is really the rigidity of our analytical categories, easily baffled by groupings of people in organisations which stood at the intersection of economic, charitable and political life. Guilds and guildsmen stand in need of reassessment in terms of their relationship to the organisation of production in genuine industries like construction or textiles, and in the fashioning of luxuries. But it must be borne in mind that the patterns of production were inextricably tied to commerce, that is to say, to distribution and marketing. It is misleading to see business purely in terms of great merchants, for trade and commercial enterprise were part of guild life as well, part of a world which stretched from the production unit, the workshop, to the world of *grand négoce*, from a poor mercer like Daniel Raspante via Bontempelli to the world of the Fuggers: after all, the great German banking family had once been weavers by trade.[135] What hindered the process of adaptation were wars and the taxes to pay for them. War was the enemy of enterprise, as was the religious dogma which helped to stir up conflict.

One of the most striking illustrations of the way in which guilds and commercial enterprise operated in harness is to be found in the opportunities for work and profit provided by great civic occasions, which the guilds often helped to organise. Some public holidays were solemn occasions dominated by the propaganda of Church and State, others were licensed chaos: some were opportunities to advertise and to make a sale.

Notes

1. F. Braudel, *The Mediterranean and the Mediterranean World in the Age of Philip II*, trans. S. Reynolds, 2 vols. (London, 1975), vol. 1, p. 895.

2. R. Mols, 'Population in Europe, 1500–1700', in C. M. Cipolla (ed.), *The Fontana Economic History of Europe, vol. 2: The 16th and 17th Centuries* (London, 1974), pp. 38–9.

3. E. Le Roy Ladurie, *The Peasants of Languedoc*, trans. J. Day (Urbana, Ill., 1974), p. 51.

4. Mols, 'Population', pp. 39–44; Braudel, *The Mediterranean*, vol. 1, pp. 319–54.

5. Braudel, *The Mediterranean*, vol. 1, pp. 328–34.

6. F. Braudel and F. Spooner, 'Prices in Europe from 1450 to 1750', in *CEH*, vol. 4, pp. 413, 429–43.

7. H. Kellenbenz, 'The Organisation of Production', in *CEH*, vol. 5, pp. 463–5, 486; J. R. Hale, *Renaissance Europe, 1480–1520* (London, 1971), pp. 149–51.

8. Kellenbenz, 'Organisation of Production', p. 470.

9. F. Braudel, *Civilisation and Capitalism, 15th–18th Centuries*, trans. S. Reynolds, 3 vols. (London, 1982), vol. 2, *The Wheels of Commerce*, esp. pp. 247, 229–32.

10. F. C. Lane, *Venise: A Maritime Republic* (Baltimore, Md., 1975), p. 156.

11. Braudel, *The Mediterranean*, vol. 1, pp. 427–33.

12. R. T. Rapp, *Industry and Economic Decline in 17th-century Venice* (Cambridge, Mass., 1976), esp. p. 102.

13. F. C. Lane, *Andrea Barbarigo, Merchant of Venice, 1418–1449*, (Baltimore, Md., 1944), p. 68. See also R. Delort, 'Un aspect du commerce venitien au 15e siècle: Andrea Barbarigo et le commerce des fourrures, 1430–40', *Le Moyen Age*, vol. 71, no. 2 (1965), pp. 29–70.

14. Quoted in Ph. Braunstein and R. Delort, *Venise: portrait historique d'une cité* (Paris, 1971), pp. 125–6.

15. G. Luzzatto, *Storia economica di Venezia dal 11 al 16 secolo*, (Venice, 1961), p. 166; M. F. Mazzaoui, *The Italian Cotton Industry in the Late Middle Ages, 1100–1600* (Cambridge, 1981), p. 98.

16. F. C. Lane, *Venetian Ships and Shipbuilders of the Renaissance* (Baltimore, Md., 1934), pp. 80–1.

17. Arte della Seta, b. 552, *capitolare nuovo dell'ufficio e arte de testori di panni di seta et oro, 1746*, fols. 20r, 23v, 32v, 49v, 319v.

18. Ibid., fols. 29v, 37v–38r.

19. Arte della Seta, b. 553, *capitoli, lezi, cronache*, fol. 18r.

20. Arte della Seta, b. 552, *capitolare nuovo*, fols. 21v–22r.

21. Ibid., fols. 43r, 57v.

22. D. Sella, 'The Rise and Fall of the Venetian Woollen Industry', in B. S. Pullan (ed.), *Crisis and Change in the Venetian Economy*, (London, 1968), pp. 88–105.

23. PC, b. 54, no. 182, *filza lanifizio*, doc. of 17 May 1448.

24. Ibid., capitolo 125 of 20 July 1538, reiterating an order of 1413.

25. PC, b. 57, *lanifizio: terminazioni ecc. circa panni et università drappieri, e processi*, fasc. B, no. 4, 14 April 1450.

26. PC, b. 54, no. 182, *filza lanifizio*, doc. of 28 March 1517; Lane, *Venice*, p. 314.

27. Lane, *Venice*, pp. 308–21 (pp. 314–16 on the chandlers); M. Lowry, *The World of Aldus Manutius: Business and Scholarship in Renaissance Venice* (Oxford, 1979).

28. Arti, b. 182, *linaroli, ordinazioni per l'arte, 1436*, capitolo 37 of 1458; b. 183, *luganegheri, capitoli dell'arte*, docs. of 8 April 1498 and 13 November 1512, fols. 2r and 4r of a set of documents marked 'che non possino esser comprati porci se non per conto arte'.

29. Arti b. 436, *peltreri e stagneri, mariegola, 1477–1803*, fol. 32v; b. 445, *pistori, mariegola, 1333–1691*, fol. 59r.

30. Arti, b. 436, *mariegola*, fol. 32r.

31. G. Perocco and A. Salvadori, *Civiltà di Venezia*, 3 vols. (Venice, n. d.), vol. 3, p. 610.

32. P. de Commynes, *Mémoires*, ed. J. Calmette, 3 vols. (Paris, 1925), vol. 3, p. 113; W. Wey, *Itineraries* (London, 1857), pp. 5–6. I am grateful to Peter Burke for this reference.

33. *Canon Pietro Casola's Pilgrimage to Jerusalem in the Year 1494*, ed. and trans. M. M. Newett (Manchester, 1907), pp. 129, 142.

34. R. T. Rapp, 'Real Estate and Rational Investment in Early Modern Venice', *Journal of European Economic History*, vol. 8, no. 2 (1979), pp. 269–91; A. Tenenti, *Piracy and the Decline of Venice, 1580–1615*, trans. B. and J. Pullan, (London, 1967); U. Tucci, 'The Psychology of the Venetian Merchant in the 16th century', in J. R. Hale (ed.), *Renaissance Venice*, (London, 1974), pp. 346–78.

35. W. Thomas, *The History of Italy (1549)*, ed. G. Parkes (Ithaca, N.Y., 1963), p. 66; PC, b.60, *traghetti incanti libertà, 1572–8;* Lane, *Venice*, p. 347.

36. B. S. Pullan, *Rich and Poor in Renaissance Venice: The Social Institutions of a Catholic State* (Oxford, 1971), p. 289 and n. 12; Sella, 'Woollen Industry', pp. 108, 110; F. C. Lane, *Venice and History: The Collected Papers of Frederic C. Lane* (Baltimore, Md., 1966), pp. 25–35; idem, *Venice*, p. 364.

37. A. Stella, 'La crisi economica veneziana della seconda metà del sec. 16', *AV*, vol. 58 (1956), pp. 17–69; Tenenti, *Piracy*. On the European context, P. Clark (ed.), *The European Crisis of the 1590s* (London, 1985).

38. Tucci, 'Psychology', p. 374.

39. MM, b. 446, *dichiarazioni testimoniali sullo stato economico di alcuni esercenti per l'applicazione della tansa (libro de inquisicion secundo), 1567–8.*

40. Arti, b. 312, *marzeri, mariegola, 1471–1787*, fol. 6r.

41. Ibid., fol. 10r.

42. M. Sanudo, *De origine, situ et magistratibus urbis Venetae: ovvero la città di Venetia (1493–1530)*, ed. A. Carraciolo Aricò, (Milan, 1980), p. 62.

43. Rapp, *Industry*, pp. 60, 62 for the figures; p. 20 and n.12 for the 'unitary' guild system.

44. GV, b. 49, reg. 79, *registro di costituti per la notificazione di insegne da porsi sopra i negozii, 1560–97.*

45. See above, n. 39.

46. Lane, *Venice*, p. 333.

47. B. S. Pullan, 'Wage Earners and the Venetian Economy, 1550–1630', in idem (ed.), *Crisis and Change*, p. 179: the wage for a master in the late 1560s was 18 soldi.

48. Arti, b. 397, *marzeri, nomi di fratelli, 1586–1692.*

49. M. Aymard, *Venise, Raguse et le commerce du blé pendant la seconde moitié du 16e siècle*, (Paris, 1966), p. 17, which suggests a subsistence level of 4 staia of wheat per person per year, and p. 110 for wheat prices, 1567–99; Pullan, 'Wage Earners', p. 158 for wages.

50. Pullan, *Rich and Poor*, p. 295.

51. Arti, b. 445, *mariegola*, fols. 69r–70r.

52. For the sources, see above, n. 48.

53. Pullan, 'Wage Earners', pp. 159–63.

54. Arti, b. 314, *marzeri, capitoli e parti, 1508–1608*, reg. of 1564–1591, fol. 124r.

55. Ibid., fol. 129v.

56. C. M. Cipolla, 'The Economic Decline of Italy', in Pullan (ed.), *Crisis and Change*, p. 135.

57. *The Diary of John Evelyn from 1641 to 1705–6*, ed. W. Bray (London, 1889), p. 160.

58. GP, *Inventarii*, b. 337, no. 75. I am greatly in the debt of Dottoressa Michela del Borgo for suggesting that I should consult this collection.

59. Zarnesi's election is recorded at Arti, b. 314, *capitoli e parti*, reg. of 1591–1608, fol. 171v, where he was noted as present at a meeting of 14 April 1608.

60. We can be sure that these are separate transactions and not outstanding instalments. The inventor, was based on another book and the leaf number of each entry is recorded next to the name of the debtor. Thus on p. 339 we find Giacomo Pezis owing L. 1 686. 8 soldi, while Mafio mandoler appeared on p. 342 owing only L. 5. 14 soldi. Neither had appeared previously.

61. See the entry by U. Tucci in *Dizionario biografico degli italiani*, (Rome, 1960 onwards), vol. 12, Bonfadini–Borrello, pp. 426–7.

62. Pullan, *Rich and Poor*, p. 368.

63. On Sante Peranda, see P. Burke, *Venice and Amsterdam: A Study of 17th-century Elites* (London, 1974), p. 91.

64. *CSPV*, vol. 15, p. 102.

65. *Dudley Carleton to John Chamberlain 1603–1624: Jacobean Letters*, ed. M. Lee, Jr (New Brunswick, N. J., 1972), p. 172.

66. His tenure of office is recorded under those years in the mercers' archive, Arti, b. 314, *capitoli e parti*, reg of 1564–1591, fols. 56r, 106v, 128r. On his responsibilities at San Rocco, see Pullan, *Rich and Poor*, pp. 81–2.

67. Arti, b. 313, *marzeri, capitolare, 1595–1797*, fol. 44v.

68. Arti, b. 109, *fabbri, capitoli sciolti, 1531–1734*, doc. of 10 January 1531.

69. Ibid., doc. of 16 August 1603.

70. Arti, b. 314, *capitoli e parti*, fol. 124r.

71. Rapp, *Industry*, p. 103.

72. R. A. Goldthwaite, *The Building of Renaissance Florence: An Economic and Social History* (Baltimore, 1981), pp. 44, 397, 402; G. Corte and J. -G. da Silva, 'Note sur la production de la soie à Florence au 15e siècle', *Annales*, vol. 20, no. 1 (1965), pp. 309–11.

73. Goldthwaite, *Building*, pp. 47, 96, 306, 309, 312, 314, and on the di Romoli, p. 277.

74. Ibid., p. 51.

75. Ibid., p. 256; J. N. Stephens, *The Fall of the Florentine Republic* (Oxford, 1983), pp. 136–8.

76. S. Berner, 'Florentine Society in the late 16th and early 17th centuries', *Studies in the Renaissance*, vol. 18 (1971), p. 212.

77. P. Battara, 'Botteghe e pigioni nella Firenze del' 500: un censimento industriale e commerciale all'epoca del granducato mediceo', *ASI* no. 95, vol. 2 (1937), pp. 8–11 for the list of shops, p. 7 on Santa Croce, p. 16 on numbers of crafts, p. 18 on lack of mechanical crafts.

78. Quoted in J. Delumeau, *Vie économique et sociale de Rome dans la seconde moitié du 16e siècle* (2 vols. Paris, 1957–9), vol. 1, pp. 365–6.

79. P. Partner, *Renaissance Rome, 1500–1559: A Portrait of a Society*, (Berkeley and Los Angeles, 1976), pp. 46, 135; Delumeau, *Rome*, vol. 1, p. 377.

80. Delumeau, *Rome*, vol. 1, p. 366.

81. Partner, *Renaissance Rome*, p. 103.

82. Ibid., pp. 33–4; Delumeau, *Rome*, vol. 1, pp. 368–70.

83. Delumeau, *Rome*, vol. 1, p. 145.

84. J. Heers, *Gênes au 15e siècle* (Paris, 1961), p. 236 on the number of weavers, p. 245 on the independence of weavers, p. 250 on Triadano. The abridged Italian edition (trans. P. Mastrorosa, Milan, 1984) is subtitled 'Mediterranean civilisation, large-scale capitalism and popular capitalism'.

85. C. Carrère, *Barcelone: centre économique à l'époque des difficultés, 1380–1462*, 2 vols. (Paris and The Hague, 1967), vol.1, pp. 83–103, 352, 373, 488–9.

86. J. H. Elliott, *Imperial Spain, 1469–1716* (London, 1970), pp. 38–40.

87. R. Pike, *Aristocrats and Traders: Sevillian Society in the 16th Century* (London, 1972), pp. 25, 99–102, 132, 141.

88. R. Gascon, 'Economie et pauvreté au 16e et 17e siècles: Lyon, ville exemplaire et prophétique', in M. Mollat (ed.), *Etudes sur l'histoire de la pauvreté*, 2 vols. (Paris, 1974) vol. 2, pp. 748, 755.

89. Idem, *Grand commerce et vie urbaine au 16e siècle: Lyon et ses marchands 1520–1580*, 2 vols. (Paris, 1971), vol. 1, pp. 310–14.

90. Ibid., vol. 2, pp. 622–4.

91. N. Z. Davis, 'A Trade Union in 16th-century France', *EcHR*, 2 ser., vol. 19, no. 1 (1966), pp. 48–69.

92. Gascon, *Lyon*, vol. 1, p. 374, vol. 2, pp. 611, 722.

93. Ibid., vol. 1, p. 351.

94. Ibid., vol. 2, pp. 737, 741.

95. Ibid., vol. 2, pp. 586, 759, 808, 874.

96. S. T. Bindoff, 'The Greatness of Antwerp', in *NCMH*, vol. 2, p. 66.

97. H. van der Wee, *The Antwerp Market and the European Economy*, 3 vols. (The Hague, 1963), vol. 2, p. 227.

98. Ibid., vol. 2, p. 132.

99. Ibid., vol. 2, pp. 379–80.

100. Ibid., vol. 2, pp. 225–6.

101. Ibid., vol. 2, p. 324.

102. J. A. van Houtte, 'Déclin et survivance d'Anvers', in *Studi in onore di Amintore Fanfani*, 5 vols (Milan, 1962), vol. 5, p. 725.

103. Van der Wee, *Antwerp*, vol. 1, pp. 46–7, vol. 2, pp. 85, 95, 132, 280, 321, 331, 334, 377–8.

104. Ibid., vol. 2, pp. 384, 386.

105. Van Houtte, 'Déclin et survivance', p. 707.

106. C. H. Wilson, *The Dutch Republic* (London, 1968), pp. 27, 120.

107. V. Barbour, *Capitalism in Amsterdam in the 17th Century* (Baltimore, Md., 1950), p. 68.

108. Ibid., pp. 16, 71.

109. Quoted in C. R. Boxer, *The Dutch Seaborne Empire, 1600–1800* (London, 1965), pp. 170–1.

110. Goldthwaite, *Building*, p. 404.

111. R. Finlay, *Population and Metropolis: The Demography of London, 1580–1650* (Cambridge, 1981), pp. 6–8; A. L. Beier, 'Social Problems in Elizabethan London', *Journal of Interdisciplinary History*, vol. 9, no. 2 (1978), p. 205; G. D. Ramsay, 'The Recruitment and Fortunes of some London Freemen in the mid-16th Century', *EcHR*, 2 ser., vol. 31, no. 4 (1978), pp. 526–40; R. G. Lang, 'Social Origins and Social Aspirations of Jacobean London Merchants', *EcHR*, 2 ser., vol. 27, no. 1 (1974), pp. 28–47; S. R. Smith, 'The Social and Geographical Origins of the London Apprentices, 1630–60', *Guildhall Miscellany*, vol. 4, no. 4 (1973), pp. 195–206.

112. F. J. Fisher, 'London as an "Engine of Economic Growth"', in P. Clark (ed.), *The Early Modern Town: A Reader* (London, 1976), p. 206.

113. Beier, 'Social Problems', pp. 210–11.

114. A. A. Ruddock, 'London Capitalists and the Decline of Southampton in the Early Tudor Period', *EcHR*, 2 ser., vol. 2, no. 1 (1949), p. 148.

115. G. D. Ramsay, 'Industrial Discontent in Early Elizabethan London: Clothworkers and Merchant Adventurers in Conflict', *London Journal*, vol. 1, no. 2 (1975), pp. 228, 237; Finlay, *Population and Metropolis*, pp. 10–11.

116. Finlay, *Population and Metropolis*, p. 66.

117. Strauss, *Nuremberg*, p. 27.

118. G. Aubin, 'Bartolomäus Viatis: ein nürnberger Grosskaufmann', *Vierteljahrschrift für Sozial- und Wirtschaftsgeschichte*, vol. 33, (1940), p. 147. See also W. Schultheiss, 'Der Vertrag der nürnberger Handelsgesellschaft: Bartholomäus Viatis und Martin Peller von 1609 bis 1615', *Scripta Mercaturae* (1968), pt. i, pp. 1–20.

119. Strauss, *Nuremberg*, pp. 182–6.

120. R. C. Duplessis and M. C. Howell, 'Reconsidering the Early Modern Urban Economy: The Cases of Leiden and Lille', *PP*, no. 94 (1982), pp. 49–84.

121. Ibid., p. 71; see also pp. 61–3, 72, 74, 80.

122. C. R. Friedrichs, *Urban Society in an Age of War: Nördlingen 1580–1720* (Princeton, N. J., 1979), p. 93.

123. Ibid., p. 259; and on the Wörners, pp. 239–87.

124. D. Sella, *Crisis and Continuity: The Economy of Spanish Lombardy in the 17th Century* (Cambridge, Mass., 1979), p. 99, 105.

125. Braudel, *The Mediterranean*, vol. 1, p. 430.

126. D. C. Coleman, *Industry in Tudor and Stuart England* (London, 1975), p. 22.

127. C. H. Wilson, *England's Apprenticeship, 1603–1763*, (London, 1965), p. 136; C. Hill, *Reformation to Industrial Revolution* (Pelican Economic History of Britain, vol. 2, 1530–1780, London, 1969), p. 169.

128. Cipolla, 'Decline of Italy', p. 135.

129. Braudel, *The Mediterranean*, vol. 1, p. 456; idem, *Wheels of Commerce*, p. 310.

130. D. Sella, 'The Iron Industry in Italy, 1500–1650', in H. Kellenbenz (ed.), *Schwerpunkte der Eisengewinnung und Eisenverarbeitung in Europa, 1500–1650* (Cologne-Vienna, 1974), pp. 91–105; J. de Vries, *The Economy of Europe in an Age of Crisis, 1600–1750* (Cambridge, 1976), p. 166.

131. Van der Wee, *Antwerp*, vol. 2, pp. 95, 135, 194; quotations from pp. 341, 384.

132. Barbour, *Amsterdam*, p. 71.

133. Carrère, *Barcelone*, vol. 1, p. 371; C. R. Friedrichs, 'Capitalism, Mobility and Class Formation in the Early Modern German City', in P. Abrams and E. L. Wrigley (eds.), *Towns and Societies: Essays in Economic History and Historical Sociology* (Cambridge, 1978), pp. 208–9.

134. R. Larmour, 'A Merchant Guild of 16th-century, France: The Grocers of Paris', *EcHr*, 2 ser., vol. 20, no. 3 (1967), p. 467.

135. P. Jeannin, *Les marchands au 16e siècle*, (Paris, 1957), pp. 37–79; on the Fuggers as weavers, R. Ehrenberg, *Capital and Finance in the Age of the Renaissance: A Study of the Fuggers and their Connections*, trans. H. M. Lucas (London, 1928), pp. 64–5.

4

The Festive Spirit: Guilds and Public Life, *c*.1250–*c*.1650

Introduction

Previous chapters have investigated only three-quarters of the guildsman's calendar. What of the 90 or so days when 'normal' work was suspended? What was expected of guilds on festive occasions? What part did they play in ceremonies and processions? And what meaning did 'public life' have to a guildsman?

The significance of festivals is usually assessed in political and cultural terms. Solemn occasions and festive entertainments were, in a sense, part of the propaganda which heralded the emergence of the modern state, and were an essential tool in the equipment of a successful ruler. For once, a Machiavellian interpretation can be traced back to Machiavelli himself. In summarising the qualities of Lorenzo the Magnificent, he wrote that one of Lorenzo's greatest accomplishments as a ruler was that 'he entertained the city with festivals at which were displayed tournaments and representations of ancient deeds and triumphs'.[1] Iconographical analysis of Medicean spectacle suggests that entertainments were suffused with a set of symbols which impressed themselves on the minds of onlookers.[2] As the Renaissance, and more especially as Medicean influence, gained ground in Europe, so did the ideological and propagandist trimmings which they provided for princes — public life in the Empire, in France and in England was characterised by a public exaggeration of the status of the prince.[3]

The emergence of 'princely magnificence' marked a double shift in the relationship between culture and politics. Within the ruling élites, the prince and his entourage established the court as the centre of patronage and power to the confusion of traditional oligarchies in the towns. A royal entry or a princely celebration in a city both overshadowed and outshone traditional expressions of communal solidarity. Thus, broadly speaking, there was a shift from the 'civic' to the 'courtly' style in urban ceremonial.[4] A whole genre of literature was devoted to the commemoration of these festivals. Jean de Galaup de Chasteuil wrote a description of the entry of Louis XIII into Aix in 1622 and in the dedication alluded to the way in which the populace was to be enlisted in the cult of the prince, for 'as kings are gods on earth, so their name must be continually adored in solemn festivals'.[5] The conscious development of a gap between a courtly élite and 'popular' culture was the second shift and was one aspect of a growing antagonism between the powerful and the lowly. Carnival was something of a truce in the struggle, for it turned the world upside down for a limited period of time. Such status reversal was permitted on the grounds that it reinforced the status quo, but sometimes attempts were made to make the reversal permanent, as happened in the bitter class violence at Romans in 1580.[6]

However, the lines of battle between the two cultures are easily overdrawn and were not always as clear as those between an educated churchman and a peasant.[7] Burckhardt's interpretation of festivals in Renaissance Italy stands as a caution against over-generalisation. He saw festivals as a wide variety of different occasions which can be attached to the same genre because they played a vital part in the life of society as a whole: public occasions meant something – but not necessarily the same thing, and not necessarily the different things intended – to different sorts of people.[8]

This chapter follows both Machiavelli and Burckhardt. It sets out to examine the importance of propaganda in the life of the Renaissance state, but it also seeks to emphasise the complexity of the 'civic' tradition and its legacy to the age of 'princely magnificence'. The discussion draws heavily on the ideas of modern historians who have drawn attention to the unfamiliar patterns of work and leisure in the pre-industrial age.[9] But it seeks to add an economic dimension. Festivals were often the seed-bed of political propaganda, but more than ideology was on display. From a guildsman's point of view, the celebration of the state's power was often intimately connected with the community's prosperity. Festivals generated work, and they were also occasions when it was possible to advertise and sell.

The Venetian experience

The solemn processions which played so important a part in Venetian public life embodied a symbolism deeply rooted in a perception of the Venetian past, a symbolism which the patriciate strove to impress on the populace. 'Public ritual' involved the creation and recreation of a 'civic myth' through the association of the Venetian polity with peace, justice and true religion, and the guarantee of all these was the solidarity of the aristocracy.[10]

Professor Edward Muir has suggested that the serene public image of Venetian civic ritual concealed a set of real political tensions. He argues that an ancient myth of opposition to tyranny was turned into an ideology of the patrician state and he uses ceremony as an index of conflicts within the aristocracy. An early emphasis on the figure of the Doge was countered by the image of an aristocratic polity in the fourteenth century. However, both these competing ideologies had sought to act as the focus for a political community whose stability rested on an extraordinarily strong sense of solidarity. According to this thesis, even though Venice did not come under the sway of a prince and his court, the sense of *communitas* which traditional ritual had fostered began to decline in the sixteenth century and there was a concomitant strengthening of elements of empty pageantry.[11]

Demonstrations of solidarity were especially important in the aftermath of the war against the League of Cambrai, when Venice's independence seemed on the point of collapse and even erasure.[12] Having stood alone against the League, the Venetian government was relieved to celebrate an alliance with the Empire in 1511. Sanudo recorded that San Marco was swathed in cloth of gold, the ducal palace decked in tapestries. The *Scuole Grandi* put on a dazzling display of reliquaries, and scenarios with political overtones, emphasising the special relationship which Venice enjoyed with heaven. Members of the Misericordia carried images of the Pope, the Kings of England and Spain; the brethren of San Marco bore the head of Saint Theodore and a thorn from the crown worn by Christ. The Carità displayed pieces of clothing worn by Christ and by the Virgin. More relics were shown by the Scuola di San Giovanni Evangelista. The figure of Justice which appeared in the display was imitated by members of San Rocco. A figure representing the city was reassured by the Dove of the Holy Spirit and by Saint Mark. The King of England was assured of an heir; the King of France burned in hell before the Pope.[13]

The city renowned for order and stability also celebrated a long period of licensed mayhem every year. Some festivals were occasions when the people could make their own entertainment, especially in the topsy-turvy world of carnival dextrously analysed by Peter Burke.[14]

The odd mixture of solemnity and anarchy which was characteristic of Venetian public life is vividly recorded by visitors. Petrarch did not write about carnival, but he was much impressed by the celebrations and games which greeted victory in Crete in 1364:

> The great square, the church itself, the towers, roofs, porches, windows were not so much filled as jammed with spectators. An inestimable, an incredible throng covered the face of the earth. Under our eyes the swarming, well-mannered offspring of the flourishing city augmented the joy of the festival. The general gaiety was reflected and redoubled by one's recognition of it on one's neighbour's face.[15]

Sir Henry Wotton saw the Republic draw heavily on its reserves of wealth and popular support during the Interdict crisis of 1606:

> Yesterday was the Feast of Corpus Christi, celebrated by express commandment of the State (which goeth farther than devotion) with the most sumptuous procession that ever had been seen here, wherein the very basins and ewers were valued in common judgement at 200,000 pound sterling, besides many costly and curious pageants, adorned with sentences of Scripture fit for the present as *Omnis potestas est a Deo, Date Caesari quae Caesaris et Deo quae Dei, Omnis anima subdita sit potestatibus sublimioribus, Regnum meum non est de hoc mundo*, and the like. The reasons were two as I conceive it. First, to contain the people in good order with superstition, the foolish band of obedience. Secondly, to let the Pope know (who wanteth not intelligencers) that notwithstanding his interdict, they had friars enough and other clergymen to furnish out the day.[16]

Clearly what struck him was the solidarity of Venetians, a solidarity which underpinned political stability and generated wealth.

However, a history of Venetian festivals based on descriptions of different occasions with different purposes through different sets of eyes in different periods is founded only on a miscellaneous set of impressions often provided by visitors who were not necessarily intimately acquainted with the everyday life of the city. Even when the observers were Venetian, they were often high-born spectators rather than low-born participants.[17] Might it in fact be argued that propaganda was intended for members of foreign élites (like Wotton) rather than for the local population? Do the sources enable us to ask what were the shape and substance of ceremony as far as guildsmen were concerned?

The brotherhoods in public life

Pushing the implications of questions like that a little further raises the controversial problem of whether a visitor like Henry Wotton was more easily taken in than the Venetian people themselves. The spectacle of the Venetian state in all its wealth and majesty was undoubtedly awesome. However, people like guildsmen and artisans were in many ways better placed to appreciate that such occasions were grand overstatements than were ambassadors who watched from on high.

The earliest description we have of the guilds in a public display suggests that artisans were capable of using public ceremonies to make their own statements in public life. In 1268, the guilds gave a rapturous reception to the newly-elected Doge, Lorenzo Tiepolo, well aware of his *'debonairetés'* towards the people. Each of the guilds went to salute him, parading 'with their trumpets and banners before them' and bearing flagons of wine. Even food-sellers — who could not have used their own wares — wore 'rich garlands of pearls, and silk threaded with gold'. The comb-makers may have wished to represent the *popolo*'s aspirations to liberty when they stood before the Doge and released a cage full of birds.[18]

If the people did *not* take to a new Doge, then they made their feelings plain, even in the sixteenth century. Andrea Gritti was loathed by patricians and populace alike and on his election as Doge the people paraded an effigy of 'their' candidate, Antonio Tron, in protest.[19]

There were other ways, too, in which ceremony could go wrong, hiccups of which participants were probably more aware than spectators. In 1512, the Ten had to take action to eliminate 'disorders of the kind which occurred in the procession on Good

Friday because of the jostling of the *Scuole Grandi* in Piazza San Marco'. In future, 'whoever is first to enter an alley way shall pass first'. The government was worried about the wardens of the *Scuole*, each anxious to see his own confraternity first to show off its finery, but not concerned to organise the orderly return of the brethren to the guildhall after the ceremonies.[20] Despite this order, Sanudo reported that in 1519, on St Mark's Day (when Venice should have been at its most harmonious) there was a scuffle between the Scuole Grandi di San Marco and San Rocco on their way into the Basilica.[21]

Since they were involved in processions and were on the receiving end of policy as well as propaganda, guildsmen might be expected to see public festivals in a different light from learned, aristocratic and sedentary observers. Partly for these reasons, the most convincing and concrete account of what public life may have meant to guildsmen is provided by a member of the guild of bookmen, Francesco Sansovino.[22]

As a guildsman (and in 1578 an officer of the guild), Sansovino is a particularly useful source of information on the role of the brotherhoods in ceremonies.[23] As a bookseller he would have been more aware than many of the limits of authority, for many of his colleagues spent much of their time trying to dodge the Inquisition. One of his fellow officers in 1578, Francesco Zilletti, was suspected of keeping heretical books; another, Damiano Zenaro, was given a stern warning not to do so. By 1587, Giacomo Bognolo had no less than 26 prohibited titles in his shop — including four by Luther. And Gasparo Bindoni was known to have eluded the grasp of the Holy Office.[24]

It must be emphasised that Sansovino and his colleagues may well have been more mindful of the respect due to the civic authorities than to the Holy Office of the Roman Church, but clearly their trade thrived on enterprise and independence of mind rather than humble compliance. This is perhaps reflected in Sansovino's writings on ceremonial which show a bracing realism often lacking in other sources. He is at pains to point out the diversity of functions which festivals fulfilled in Venetian life. They took place, he wrote, 'at different times, for different purposes and different occasions'.[25] And he goes on to provide a basic typology — 'habits and customs', 'welcomes for foreign princes', 'ducal processions' — indicating the elements which commonly appeared in different sorts of festival.[26]

'Habits and customs' were occasions of traditional public

assembly. As if to demonstrate the way in which public and private life overlapped, some of the events he describes were family occasions — marriages, births, christenings and funerals. In the case of the latter, the *scuole* formed an important link between the family and Venetian society as a whole. Some of the *scuole piccole* attended (presumably the ones attached to the church where the funeral took place) and if the deceased had been a member, then his *Scuola Grande* would also turn out.[27]

There were other public events which were specifically 'Venetian' celebrations. On 'Fat Thursday', pigs were butchered by blacksmiths to celebrate an ancient victory over the Patriarch of Aquileia.[28] There was another celebration of victory in 1571 when the town went wild at the news of Lepanto: shops were draped in tapestries and brocades, and some of them displayed great masterpieces of Renaissance art.[29] There had been a string of celebrations throughout the fifteenth century. A year of festivities marked Francesco Foscari's election as Doge in 1423, the 'most solemn peace' with Ferrara was celebrated at carnival in 1485 and intermittently (in 1457, 1462, 1471 and 1556) there were coronations of the Dogaressa. That of 1556 brought to Sansovino's mind the parades of 1268. Each of the guilds was given a room in the palace in which to mount a display, and each hired a group of musicians.[30]

The second category covered 'visits of foreign princes'. There are sound reasons for giving them separate attention for they demonstrate how for centuries the world's greatest rulers had been coming to Venice in peace and acknowledging the city's independence. Sansovino lists popes like Benedict III, Leo IX, and most important of all Alexander III, who was given shelter as a fugitive. Sansovino names the Holy Roman Emperors Louis II, Otto II, Frederick II and Frederick III, and he is careful to include the Lords of Byzantium: most notably John VIII in 1423.[31] Relics of these visits — and the aura which surrounded them was scarcely less than that which ringed the bones of saints — were regularly displayed. The symbols of the Doge's power had been presented to him by popes and emperors. The head of the Venetian state was thus able to enjoy, quite literally, the best of both worlds. The Doge had seven titles granted to him from Byzantium, he was acknowledged to rule a *regnum* as early as 840 and was using the title *Dux Dei gratia* by the mid-twelfth century. In his processions were displayed a white candle, a throne and a ceremonial parasol from the Pope. Perhaps the most significant symbols of Venetian sovereignty went back to Pope Alexander III. He was given refuge by the Venetians during his struggle with Barbarossa and eventually it was the Venetians who acted as mediators between the Pope and the Emperor. Alexander rewarded the Doge with eight silken flags and a ring. The flags, according to Sansovino, 'signify absolute sovereignty without any superior power'. The ring was the one used on Ascension Day for the Doge's ceremonial wedding to the sea.[32]

Few rulers could parade so flamboyantly such tangible evidence of their independence of empire and papacy, and of all other earthly rulers. This may have been especially poignant for the King of war-torn France, Henry III, who was given a rapturous welcome by the Venetians on his way home from Poland in 1574.[33]

The irregular shows for visiting princes were underpinned by some 30 regular occasions which involved the Doge in visits to various parts of the city to commemorate the special role of particular groups of Venetians at particular moments in the city's history. These great *Andate* form Sansovino's third category. They took place 'either in accordance with rite of Holy Church, or by public order, sometimes for dangers escaped, sometimes in thanksgiving'.[34] Eight of them involved elaborate triumphs and all were Christian festivals with a special meaning for Venetians. Alle due Castelli took place on Ascension Day to commemorate victory over Otto, son of Barbarossa. San Vito's day was remembered for the crushing of the Tiepolo conspiracy; Sant'Isidoro was used by the Senate to remind Venetians and visitors of the fate of Marin Falier, the traitor-Doge. Santa Marina was a celebration of the retention of Venice's mainland territories despite the international conspiracy of the League of Cambrai; victory at Lepanto fell on the feast of Santa Giustina. Deliverance from the plague in 1577 was celebrated (then as now) with a procession across a bridge of boats to the Church of the Redeemer on the Giudecca.[35] The most important of the *andate*, predictably, took place on St Mark's Day, though it was rivalled by Corpus Christi which involved the participation of pilgrims *en route* for the Holy Land.[36] There were 22 other festivals celebrated without triumphs and, as if to emphasise the subordination of the Church, these tended to have a Christian significance not peculiar to Venice — Christmas, Epiphany, Holy Week for instance — and only five times a year was there a sermon in the Church of San Marco.[37]

Professor Muir's splendidly detailed list gives a firm indication of the substance of the Venetian festive calendar. He lists 65 saints' days and 10 moveable feasts and notes that 21 visits, alliances or 'one-off' occasions were celebrated between 1361 and 1598.[38]

Why was so much of the year devoted to such occasions? According to some, festivals gave the Venetian authorities numerous opportunities to impress on Venetian subjects and on visitors the matchless unity of the aristocracy, something which was encouraged even in 'everyday' political life. 'Our ancestres', wrote Contarini, 'did deeme it a thing of great moment for the maintenance of the citizens in amitie and love, if they did often meet and assemble together.'[39] Sansovino wrote that the nobility met every day in public at Rialto 'for no other reason but to see each other together, to grow acquainted through conversation in order to preserve for ever unity and concord amongst themselves'.[40] Such meetings in a sense made public the political proceedings of the city, and more formal occasions were used to hammer the point home. In 1455 a processional order was fixed: 'when they are invited to do so, the Procurators and members of the *Collegio* are obliged to walk with each other in processions and solemnities . . . for the honour of our city and state.'[41]

Four times a year, the Doge gave a banquet for nobles as 'a restricted sacrament of true amity'.[42] However, the principle of association which was clearly so important for patricians in fact extended to the rest of Venetian society.[43] Seventeen of the people of Poveglia were drawn into the life of the state on Ascension Day when they too were given a banquet by the Doge. In the parish of San Lorenzo, nobles and commoners demonstrated their brotherhood on the *Festa dei Diedi*. In the great procession at Corpus Christi, nobles walked with pilgrims, thus associating public power with piety and humility.[44]

The idea of associating, becoming a *socius*, a brother of other Christians and other Venetians, brings the discussion back to the private activities of the scuole discussed in Chapter 2. And indeed the *scuole* could amplify their expressions of fraternity into public occasions.[45] This is particularly well illustrated by funerals. It is consonant with Venetian suspiciousness of individual glory that private persons became public personalities only when they were dead. Antonio Tron had been the unsuccessful rival of Andrea Gritti in the ducal election of 1523. When he died in 1524, his cortège was formed by the six *scuole* of which he had been a member. A Doge could, of course, expect greater pomp. At the funeral of Leonardo Loredan in 1521, 119 *scuole* were present. But in the same year, 96 *scuole* turned out for the funeral of the French ambassador. Eminent churchmen might also receive a 'state' funeral. The confraternities were represented by 210 banners at Cardinal Zen's funeral in 1501, 111 *scuole* were present for the obsequies of Cardinal Corner in 1525. All the shops were closed for two hours and there was a solemn procession of all the *scuole* to celebrate the canonisation of Lorenzo Giustinian in 1519. The death of the Pope's representative was publicly mourned by 64 *scuole* in 1514 and 82 attended the funeral of the *condottiere* Alviano the following year.[46]

The transfer of private fraternity to the public stage was even more conspicuous in the case of the *scuole delle arti*, various of which were given a special role to play on different occasions. It is vital to emphasise that only twice a year were all the guilds bound to be represented — on St Mark's Day as Venetians, for Corpus Christi as Christians.[47] These 'comprehensive' festivals must be distinguished from occasions which gave a particular role to one or more of the *arti*.

On the other hand, public life did not create a hierarchy amongst the guilds. Processing or just walking around the Basilica and the ducal palace, guildsmen could see a figure of Christ giving his blessing not to saints but to boat-makers, bakers, butchers, vintners, builders, barbers, coopers, carpenters, blacksmiths and fishermen — all humble, all exalted in the material fabric of the city. The columns which support the ducal palace are topped by depictions of officials: a notary and someone from the weights and measures department — and there were more builders. Industry was sanctified in the Church and honoured in the state in an obvious and permanent fashion.[48]

However, at certain times of the year, special gestures were made toward the guilds themselves. If her coronation was celebrated, the Dogaressa, patroness of the guilds, rewarded their decoration of the palace and their regatta with a banquet — just as the Doge did for the nobles.[49] And some trades had a special part to play on particular days. The head of the fishermen dressed as Doge at the latter's coronation.[50] One of the oldest of Venetian festivals celebrated the case-makers' rescue of 12 Venetian brides carried off by pirates. The smiths slew a white bull and pigs on *zuoba grasso*.[51] On the eve of the feast of St Mark the painters, furriers, silk weavers, smiths and *Scuole Grandi* were obliged to present candles at the Basilica and were given the privilege of seeing the phial of miraculous blood which was kept in the church.[52]

The *scuola*'s ideal of Christian brotherhood was taken up in public festivals, and the confraternities spanned the gaps between private and public life, between religious and state occasions. The confraternities gave a pious character to celebrations of the state's majesty, the *scuole delle arti* gave a Venetian air to religious feasts. This harmony was sung out by a large chorus of people engaged in a process which might be described as 'status association': people who were usually of different standing, on certain occasions became brothers of the same status. Brotherhood became a public phenomenon, guildsmen became members of the public life of the state. For guildsmen, feast days were times when the world was turned inside out rather than upside down.

That alone does not express the full significance of festivals as far as guildsmen were concerned. On certain occasions, the sense of brotherhood may have been uppermost, on others the rules of normality were reinforced or suspended, but festivals also had a material importance which should not be overlooked.

Trade fairs and advertising: the economics of display

Historians have often wrestled with the elements of political propaganda which Renaissance festivals contained, but they have paid scant attention to economic propaganda. In the case of Venice, festivals are an illustration of the close links which existed between the commercial economy and the sovereign state. Onlookers were expected to marvel at the city's wealth as well as its power, and they were expected to come and buy as well as to come and gawk. Referring back to an earlier example, it is interesting to reflect that Bontempelli's wares were connected in Dudley Carleton's mind with carnival and in Orazio Busino's with Ascension tide (see, p. 110). And in surviving accounts of Venetian festivals, the description of goods and the description of ceremonies are usually not far apart.

The guilds' procession for Lorenzo Tiepolo in 1268 stressed the wealth of the *arti*, their skill and craftsmanship. The furriers' outfits were trimmed with ermine and fox and the skins of wild animals, the weavers were draped with the fustians they had made. The doublet-makers put on a sort of fashion parade, for they were dressed in white jackets embroidered with fleurs-de-lis and decorated with pearls. The mercers displayed silk cloth 'of all the beauty one could devise', the glassmakers carried flagons and other of their wares, the goldsmiths were awash with jewels. The fishmongers even managed to sell some sturgeon to the Doge.[53]

In the fifteenth century, the pilgrim William Wey marvelled at relics and processions, but he was also impressed that Venetians were eager to supply those *en route* to the Holy Land with equipment for the voyage.[54] Pietro Casola was startled by the way in which the Corpus Christi festivities demonstrated the power of the Doge over the Church. He had been delighted by the quantity and quality of wax in the shops and he commented on the fine candles carried in procession. Some of the clergy seemed like mannequins in a shop window:

> For I saw certain pluvials that between the border and the cape had so many large and beautiful pearls that they appeared to me worth all the vestments in our city [i.e. Milan]. I cannot decribe the abundance of the brocades of every kind, because there were so many that my eyes became confused and I lost count.

The procession took place on the Thursday, and Casola spent the weekend sightseeing. By Monday he was prepared to pay 60 ducats for his voyage to the East, having previously agreed 45, and on Tuesday he bought a mattress and a chest for the journey.[55]

In the early sixteenth century, even a joke set in a Venetian festival involved a description of the goods on display as well as the procession. Castiglione set the scene for a jest at the expense of an ignorant and innocent Brescian visiting Venice at Ascension tide:

> I heard a Brescian speak a joly grosse matter, which, being this yeare in Venice at the feast of Ascension rehearsed in a place where I was to certaine mates of his the goodly matters he had seene there, what sundrie merchandise, what plate, what sortes of spices and what cloth and silke there was, then how the Signoria issued out with a great pompe in the Bucentoro to wedde the Sea, in which were so many gentlemen well apparayled, so many sortes of instruments and melodies, that a man would have thought it a Paradise.

This was a man of 'fonde imagination' who, on seeing a trombone 'thought the blower thrust into his throat that part of ye Shagbut that is hid in putting it backe againe'.[56]

The trumpets and drums which accompanied the procession in 1268 had by the sixteenth century become much more sophisticated ensembles which clearly added much to the dreamy splendours of Venetian festivities. Much of the music served to heighten the sacred character of the Venetian state, some of it intensified the devotions of members of the *Scuole Grandi*. But some of it — like the nightingales on sale in the Merceria which so charmed John Evelyn — may have had the effect of piped music at a trade fair.[57]

Once one begins to look for it, the economic dimension emerges even in sources which do not readily identify it. The mercers were apparently famous for the display they mounted for Frederick III in 1452. Apart from something which sounds suspiciously like a set of go-go dancers, 'there were two armed galleys with other boats, all covered in silken cloth'.[58] The great celebrations which followed victory at Lepanto have been anlaysed for their artistic content but here too there is evidence of a great trade jamboree. The festivities were initiated by the German merchants who decked the Fondaco in tapestries illuminated with torches and lamps. The drapers covered the Rialto bridge in arras, bunting, canopies and lanterns. Some of the cloth formed a backdrop for paintings by masters such as Giovanni Bellini, Giorgione, Raphael, Pordenone, Titian and Bassano.[59] The Tuscan silk merchants put on a show clearly intended to outdo the Germans:

> If the Germans made rich and grand trophies
> Then the Tuscans with greater pomp today
> Made a more superb display [of their wares]
> With music they did so and splendid songs.

The display was obviously immensely noisy, which presumably served to attract attention to the precious fabrics on display.[60] There was a revolving pyramid which showed images of Neptune, Jupiter, Saturn and Mars, which from Stringa's description appears to have acted as a mobile display with illuminated compartments.[61] Another observer recorded a species of Father Christmas dressed in silk and velvet, counting money into a ewer as a reminder that this was a time to give treats to youngsters and to send marzipan and sweets to one's friends. There was also a float which represented Ascension Day — the day when the Doge 'wed' the sea and the occasion of Venice's biggest market — with children blowing glass trumpets and merchants showing their wares.[62]

For the visit of Henry III in 1574, the whole city seemed to be a theatre.[63] Arrangements for the visit had been carefully coordinated and the King was welcomed by some 200 boats provided by the guilds.[64] The mercers recorded how they made their preparations.[65]

On 5 July the guild received an order to prepare a brigantine. The mercers decided to hire a skipper, 20 oarsmen, a bombardier and twelve halberdiers, all of whom were given colourful costumes. The boat itself was covered in a pink canvas decorated with fleurs-de-lis and tongues of flame made of cloth of gold. Another canvas was painted with fleurs-de-lis in gold on deep blue (the King's colours) and there was also a tapestry with a white comet woven into it. Another canopy — pink with red and white tassels — was made for the poop. The ship's lantern was replaced with the guild's emblem. With the goldsmiths, the mercers took pride of place in the flotilla and followed the Bucintoro to a triumphal display on the Lido before accompanying the King back to his apartments at Ca' Foscari.

The display cost the mercers a total of L.1115.15 soldi — about 180 ducats. Very roughly, this figure can be broken down into the elements of a theatrical budget:

costumes and set:	L.659.14 soldi	(106 ducats:	59.14%)
hire of brig:	L.215.06 soldi	(35 ducats:	19.30%)
properties:	L.153.19 soldi	(25 ducats:	13.68%)
music:	L.61.03 soldi	(10 ducats:	5.48%)
porterage and misc.:	L.25.13 soldi	(4 ducats:	2.30%)
total	L.1115.15 soldi	(180 ducats:	100.00%)

The display owed much to hefty expenditure on costly cloth, gilt props, music and lavish decoration. The 106 ducats spent on materials exceeded the capital resources of one mercer in three in 1568.[66] The brig and crew cost L.215.06 soldi. The 27 crew members received 12 soldi each and a free meal of bread, cheese and wine. The trumpeter on the other hand earned L.58.02 soldi in pay and expenses.

So, the occasion was good business for suppliers of cloth and for 'star' peformers like the trumpeter. It gave half a day's work and a meal to the 'extras' and stagehands — halberdiers and oarsmen. Was all this merely expensive and carefully staged flattery?

According to another source, Tomaso Porcacchi, the King, having been duly impressed by Palladio's triumphal arch on the Lido, was literally dazzled by the guilds' displays. The mast of the brig furnished by the *specchieri* was decorated with mirrors which flashed in the sun, hurting the eyes of the spectators. They were outshone, however, by the goldsmiths who decorated their boat with a 'lantern made completely from cups and chalices of gold and silver, and from every angle the boat shone, thanks to the great quantities of silver on display all over it'.[67]

Amidst thunderous artillery salutes, the King visited a glassworks and witnessed a skilful demonstration by artisans. As he strolled beneath the arches of the ducal palace (which were decorated with his colours), he walked on red carpet — a scarlet cloth laid down for him to walk on. More skills were shown off by Nicolo dalla Pigna, a grocer, who presented the King with a fanciful image of the Golden Age made in sugar. After-dinner entertainments included dramatic and musical presentations. And there was a visit to the shops: 'All this time the shops have been handsomely decked with displays of vast quantities of goods such that many foreigners, men and women, who had thronged to Venice, marvelled at their beauty.' The King, perhaps in response to the displays on the brigs, went in person to see gems and a royal sceptre at the shop of the dalla Vecchia. After a visit to the humming workshops at the Arsenal, he crossed the city to the Frari, where noblewomen modelled white silk, jewels and pearls said to be worth 180,000 ducats.[68]

Occasions such as this saw Venice full of visitors and although the preparation of the festivities may have been tiresome for the guilds, some members may have welcomed the chance to advertise their goods before wealthy potential customers. In 1597 the mercers spent much more money, almost 500 ducats, on a display to mark the coronation of the Dogaressa, Zilia Dandolo. In 1595, the guild's finances had been in a poor state and subscription rates were doubled, but members voted 55 to 11 to allocate 500 ducats to their 1597 display. Given the small number (66) who voted on the issue, it may well be that the interests of the wealthy members predominated. Professor Muir has traced evidence to suggest that the expenditure was controversial and perhaps rose as high as 3000 ducats. Perhaps this explains why the guild committee was anxious to placate members, for they offset the cost of a banquet on the day with a contribution of 40 ducats from their own pockets 'so that no one can say the officers caused the guild any ill'.[69]

The format of the 1597 display differed from that of 1574 and this is reflected in a different breakdown in costs. There was a boat to decorate once again, but the guild was also involved in preparing a display in the ducal palace. The costs recorded were as follows:

costumes:	L.1290.02 soldi	(208 ducats: 43.03%)
brig and decoration:	L.491.08 soldi	(79 ducats: 16.39%)
properties:	L.32.00 soldi	(5 ducats: 1.07%)
porterage:	L.112.09 soldi	(18 ducats: 3.75%)
musicians:	L.266.16 soldi	(43 ducats: 8.90%)
display in the palace:	L.373.04 soldi	(60 ducats: 12.45%)
banquet:	L.431.17 soldi	(70 ducats: 14.41%)
total	L.2997.16 soldi	(483 ducats: 100%)

The guilds' boats pulled into line at the palace of Alvise Grimani, the Doge's brother. The Dogaressa arrived in the Bucintoro in which she was accompanied by gentlewomen dripping with jewels 'which sparkled wherever they went'. The mercers' boat was adorned with crimson, damask of red and yellow, pennants of white taffeta decorated with the Doge's coat of arms in gold. A red and white livery was worn by the crew of twelve and by the two trumpeters hired for the occasion. The guild dined together at the monastery of Sant'Antonio and then formed up with the other *arti* in the Piazza while the Dogaressa attended a service in San Marco.

The mercers acclaimed themselves as the most splendid of the corporations. Their officers, in black damask and velvet, paraded round the Piazza before entering the ducal palace to set up their display in the Ufficio Forestieri. A showcase was filled with gold, silver and silk, cloth of gold was hung from floor to ceiling; there were twelve stalls of velvets 'all worked with gold' and a silken carpet. The columns of the balcony which looked on to the Piazza were swathed in silk and music played constantly. The celebrations lasted three full days during which time the Doge himself visited the display and complimented the guild on its show.

The scene in the rest of the ducal palace is recorded by Giovanni Stringa in his *additione* to Sansovino. Each guild, he wrote, had hired flautists and viol players and there were major displays by tailors, cobblers, furriers, armourers, painters, weavers, glassmakers. The carpenters, smiths, sculptors and builders combined in one huge advertisement for the construction industry.[70]

Much of this was done to honour the Dogaressa as patroness of the guilds. But the response of foreign dignitaries or Venetian noblemen and women who visited the display may have generated the possibility of future sales. As Pompeo Molmenti casually suggested, the display took on the character of an industrial fair.[71]

The impressiveness of the occasion owed much to the elements of traditional ceremonial which it brought together. First, there was the religious element: the early festivities had gone ahead in the manner of Corpus Christi.[72] Second, the trade fair in the ducal palace involved an invitation to the guilds in the tradition of 'status association'. Finally, the great procession which followed on St Anne's Day was dominated by those most glorious embodiments of the principle of brotherhood, the *Scuole Grandi*. The slogan borne aloft by the brethren of San Rocco seemed to sum up what a Venetian celebration was about. It still reads like a formula to explain Venice's success:

> Avenging Justice, Corn a-plenty,
> Copious riches, cheerful labour,
> Public joy.[73]

Did such advertisements of stability reflect a social reality on festive occasions? Revelry, money changing hands, thousands of visitors *in giro*: the fuel for disorder surely only needed a spark. How did the Venetian authorities cope with the potential problems? The general tenor of carnival was violent and in some years there seemed to be a murder every night.[74] All the same, Stringa emphasised that 'there was not the slightest trouble or disturbance' during the celebrations after Lepanto.[75] And celebrations of harmony and prosperity would have seemed somewhat feeble had they not been accompanied by careful provisions for the comfort of visitors. Some festivals can make the government appear to be the pupils of Machiavelli. From another angle, they look like a tourist board.

Careful regulations governed taverns and there were strong prohibitions on drunkenness. Strict laws were issued from the fourteenth century onwards against illegal drinking haunts or *furatole*. Those who hosted such premises ran the risks of fines, confiscation of stock and destruction of property. Those who wassailed in taverns or went on a rowdy tour of the bars could be condemned to the galleys. Even the drunkard, however, enjoyed the protection of the law. Those who left a pledge for their wine had a month's grace and a public warning before the taverner could auction what he held *in pieggio*.[76]

Visitors were expected to lodge in hostels set aside for their particular *nazione* and anyone offering accommodation had to register their premises at the *Giustizia Nova*. This concern that public life should not be separable from public order had an economic dimension for guildsmen and artisans. In 1530–31, those offering lodgings to visitors included barbers, charcoal porters, tailors, painters, porters, mirror-makers, comb-makers, a weaver, a carpenter, a government official, a shoe-maker, a glover, a courier, a blanket seller and an engraver. Guildsmen could sell their services as well as their wares.[77]

This chapter has sought to emphasise the economic importance of 'holidays' in metropolitan Venice. Rather than reducing the working year, public festivities may have extended it, for they offered opportunities for the advertisement of luxury goods, stimulated the growth of the service sector and generated casual employment. In public displays like Corpus Christi in 1606, visitors like Sir Henry Wotton were impressed by Venice's stability and its riches. The guilds helped to project these characteristics as social realities, emphasising that stability rested on the broad base of public life and the deep-rootedness of prosperity. Some visitors — including perhaps Wotton — unwittingly contributed to such wealth and stability too, buying the goods and services which the guilds helped to market. Venetians were advertising and selling when 'normal' economic life had ostensibly ceased: selling a few lengths of cloth, or a souvenir, offering a room in the crowded city. Visitors 'of fond imagination' were probably taken in in more ways than one. When Auguste d'Aubigné wrote in praise of Henry IV, he said that such was the respect for France and the French amongst Venetians, 'when a French gentleman passed through their town they would run to greet him'.[78] Flattery or business acumen? Venetian festivals were often celebrations of the solemn majesty of the state, designed with visitors as well as residents in mind. They also played a vital part in the economy of a city devoted to business. What would have happened to a gullible Brescian or a French courtier — or Sir Politick Would-Be — when confronted by Ben Jonson's crafty salesman?

> For your Venetian, if he see a man
> Preposterous in the least, he has him stript
> He has, he strips him.
>
> (*Volpone*, IV, i, 11.39–41)

Comparisons and contrasts

Venetian public life embodied a medieval civic tradition which displayed the virtues of a sovereign republic and a commercial economy. The guilds played an important part in developing this tradition: the *scuole* advertised the idea that brotherhood was a principle which all Venetians acknowledged as vital, the *arti* advertised the prosperity of the Republic. On occasion they may have enhanced it by selling their wares to visitors and the commercial aspect of public life seems to have strengthened in the course of the sixteenth century.

The resilience of this civic tradition may help to explain why Venice can seem to have been by-passed by some of the great currents of Renaissance and Reformation — currents which washed over other cities. Venice had no court and maintained the appearance of republicanism despite occasional celebrations of princely magnificence. Nor was the pattern of the festive calendar significantly altered by the upheavals associated with religious division. Elsewhere public life was much affected by nascent absolutism and by religious conflict, and these spectacular changes have distracted attention from the economic significance of display. In Florence, ritual was an attempt to create 'a representational sovereignty not necessarily coextensive with material strength that could deal on equal terms with feudal and papal Europe'.[79] The attempt failed and city governments, republican or princely, proved incapable of demonstrating that Florentines were noble without sacrificing the solidarity of citizens. This helps to explain the protracted political oscillations of the republic before it eventually completed a transition to princely absolutism in the course of the sixteenth century.[80]

The occasions of public ceremony — solemn and joyous — were similar to those of Venice: special days in the Christian calendar, welcomes to foreign visitors, 'rituals of danger' which celebrated or sought deliverance from external threat.[81] But they never achieved the expression of harmony and solidarity regularly on show in Venice. One of the main reasons for this was the reluctance of the Florentine Republic to give artisans a 'festive identity'. They were banned from civic representations as artisans — a sharp contrast with the process of 'status association' which operated in Venice. The contrast becomes even more emphatic when one recalls that in Florence historic defeats of the lesser guildsmen such as the expulsion of Walter of Brienne and the crushing of the *Ciompi* were celebrated to remind artisans of their place. This was a deliberate slap in the face and an arrogant statement of the fact that 'the *popolo di Dio* were not part of the *popolo di Firenze*'.[82]

The exclusion of artisans from the life of the Republic made its position more insecure by exposing the *popolo* to the blandishments of potential tyrants. Walter of Brienne sought to outflank the major guilds by winning the support of unenfranchised artisans who were to become pillars of the Medicean regime. Indeed, their incorporation into Florentine public life by the Medici in the late fifteenth century coincides with a period of political stability and may help to explain it.[83]

But all too often, public gatherings in Florence, far from easing political tensions, tended to exacerbate them. Again in stark contrast to Venice, the brotherhood of Florentines was never easily demonstrated. In the Florentine commonwealth 'competition between interests was rarely absent from public show'.[84] Palm Sunday 1496 was chosen by Savonarola for the celebration of Christian brotherhood. There were tears of joy and 'a craze of fraternity' but at the cry of '*Viva Cristo*!', feared as the signal for an uprising, the mood changed abruptly: people had forgotten their station. Those who had encouraged the procession now doubted the wisdom of having let it go on.[85] So nervous do occasions of public assembly seem to have been in Renaissance Florence that not even welcomes to foreign princes were extended with conviction. One faction might be placated, another offended. Even the Medici fought shy of splendour for foreign dignitaries and tended to avoid the problem by having all the receptions for themselves.[86]

These characteristics may well have restricted the profitability of public ceremony in Florence. Luxury items of 'extravagant cost' were displayed every year on the Feast of St John, a celebration whose 'length, cost and participation left visitors awed at the wealth of a body politic that could afford such expenditures'.[87] Nor were the goods for display only. According to Piero Cennini in 1475, 'almost all the artisans and those with warehouses who do business in such places put whatever precious things they have outside . . . for the greater honour of the city and perhaps for greater profit'.[88] But if important or merely wealthy visitors were not inevitably drawn to the city, then displays like that impressed and tempted few but the Florentines themselves. On public occasions in Venice, guildsmen such as Bontempelli helped to demonstrate the city's prosperity and sometimes may have shared in it, but in Florence such a mechanism was never clearly identifiable in principle, still less in function.

In the fifteenth century, the Republic was reluctant to involve the lesser guildsmen in public display, and the Medici were cautious in welcoming foreigners. When the Medici established a duchy after 1530, the court life of the principate may have become a welcome source of work for skilled tradesmen. For the lying in state of Cosimo I after his death in 1574 an upholsterer and nine assistants had to work day and night. For the funeral itself the church of San Lorenzo was draped in black cloth, and huge quantities of cardboard were required for temporary monuments. The preparations gave work to at least 30 painters, sculptors and other craftsmen. Large amounts of wax were imported from Venice, 20,000 pieces of gold leaf were supplied from Bologna.[89]

Rather before Cosimo's death, Medicean influence had begun to make itself felt on the court festivals of Valois France. This was in large measure due to Catherine de' Medici, herself an excellent producer, but she did not put paid immediately to celebrations of civic prosperity.[90] When Henry II visited Lyons in 1549, the wealth of the city and the martial might of the princely state were celebrated simultaneously.[91]

Henry had been on a tour of inspection of royal fortresses. When he arrived in Lyons, he found the city decked out with royal devices. There was a cavalcade which involved the clergy, the magistrates, 'the principal artisans', and the various foreign communities. The heads of the guilds walked together. Then came the artisans themselves, in very large numbers: 446 dyers, 225 silversmiths, 459 silk-makers, 285 saddlers, 306 builders, 315 carpenters, 255 shoemakers. Those who trafficked on the Rhone numbered 423. There were 225 founders, 175 hatters, 126 pewterers and 414 printers, all sumptuously dressed. The

Genoese consul had been first to welcome the King and there were parades by the Lucchese, the Florentines, the Milanese and the Germans, all anxious, one presumes, to advertise their presence in the city. This was followed by a series of jousts and displays of weapon handling. Later, there were entertainments on water, watched by the King from a small red brig covered in red velvet fringed with silver. The Florentines put on a play which involved two colourful pantomime cockerels, and their display earned the actors 500 *scudi* from the King, and a further 300 from his Queen.[92]

This royal largesse is the only solid evidence of money being earned on this occasion, but the fact that guildsmen turned out so splendidly and in such numbers made their march past an economic profile of the city. Rouen entertained the King in much the same way the following year.[93]

Such displays became impossible when France was plunged into civil war, which brought religious riot to the streets of Lyons.

> Lyons has changed indeed . . .
> The profit of Mercury, the dance of Venus,
> And presumption, too, each man has left aside

So ran one popular poem of 1562 in celebration of the city's having purged its idolaters and usurers.[94]

The 'profit of Mercury' deserted Bruges rather before then, though a visit by Charles of Habsburg in 1515 provided an opportunity, it might be said, to arrest the pace of decline.[95] When the future emperor entered the city, he was greeted by 4500 torches and a striking series of *tableaux vivants*. The houses of merchants were decked out to make the city look like a market and to court favour with its Prince.[96] At one point, Charles passed a street in which

> a merchant of the city had joined two high and mighty houses with great beams . . . these were triumphantly draped from top to bottom and all the way across with fine cloth of gold and silver, brocades and various types of different coloured velvets from which hung large numbers of the Prince's coat of arms. And beside each tier burned 200 torches fixed on pewter stands. The neighbours did the same, each according to his means, so along the whole length of the street to the Pont Saint Jean, all the houses on both sides were swathed and clad in

> cloth of yellow, red and white, and other rich tapestries and an abundance of torches. But one of the tapestries, showing fine ladies and damsels, seemed to be everywhere: on all the doors, windows and galleries, so that it did not allow passers-by to look at the rest.[97]

The chance to advertise the city's products, and perhaps to sell some of them to the 500 members of Charles's entourage, were presumably welcome to a city which had yielded pride of place to Antwerp, and in the case of Antwerp, too, festivals can act as an index to the city's fortunes.[98]

While Albrecht Dürer was in Antwerp in 1521, he visited the workshops where preparations were being made for the triumphal entry, again for Charles, who was now Emperor. The shops must have been huge in terms of space and staff: there were to be no fewer than 400 arches, each 40 feet wide. The display was rumoured to be worth 4000 florins to the painters and joiners of the city.[99]

In the procession for the Feast of the Assumption, Antwerp's other guilds made a splendid show. The artist's eye was obviously of an exceptional sharpness, but it is still striking that Dürer remembered each trade by its emblem. Each was in costly attire: goldsmiths, painters, sculptors, silk weavers, stonemasons, joiners, carpenters, fishermen, sailors, butchers, leather sellers, cloth-makers, bakers, tailors, cordwainers, all kinds of craftsmen and dealers, merchants of every sort. There were costly candles and a series of waggons which carried scenes from the Old Testament. The procession took more than two hours to pass the house where the artist was staying.[100]

Another opportunity for a dazzling display arose in 1550, when Charles V's heir, the future Philip II, was welcomed to a city decorated with crimson and gold. The parade was led by communities of foreign merchants, Lucchese, Milanese, English, Spanish, Portuguese, Genoese and Florentines. Each prepared a spectacular arch — that of the Genoese was 100 feet high, 70 feet wide and 90 feet deep. The English decorated theirs with figures of Ocean, Britain, and Tritons, the Germans staged mock combats. In all, the arches of the foreign merchants provided work for 907 artisans. The display presented by the city itself gave several months' work to 895 carpenters, 234 painters, 16 wood carvers and nearly 500 other artisans, not to mention 137 actors.[101]

The importance of a cosmopolitan population to a great

metropolis was clearly lost on Philip and the prosperity of Antwerp was wrecked by his wars. In 1582, scarcely recovered from the disastrous sack of 1576, the municipal authorities were caught unprepared for a visit from the Earl of Leicester and the Duke of Anjou. The *joyeuse entrée* was a tawdry affair and the city missed the opportunity to generate employment and money, for it had to use equipment from a previous display. As Holinshed remarked, the city could not

> in so short a time make anie meane apparell new, nor anie rare costliness of imageries, pillers, triumphall arces, or other pageants: but were constreined to make a shift with such things as they had in a readinesse aforehand of their owne store.

The occasion, which had clearly suffered from lack of advance planning, was marred further by a sudden attack on the city by the army of the Duke of Parma.[102]

However, even in the seventeenth century, when there was little prosperity to celebrate, a great public occasion could still provide a great deal of work in Antwerp. In 1635, Rubens designed a magnificent display to welcome the Cardinal Infante Ferdinand as Governor of the Netherlands. The major arch was topped with the motto *orbi sufficit unus*.[103] The earth needed only one sun, the world needed only one ruler, a Habsburg. As if to acknowledge the triumph of the prince over the town, the courtly world over the civic, another of Rubens' arches was a lament for the decay of Antwerp. It showed Mercury, the god of trade, deserting the city, and a slumbering river god symbolising the closure of the Scheldt to maritime traffic. Rubens had depicted 'the decline of commerce resulting from continuance of the war in the Netherlands'.[104]

The same arch produced a fee of 1500 guilders for a team of five painters. The carpenter Cornelis van Mol received 1275 guilders (after an original agreement of 680).[105] Most probably he employed a large team of workers, and presumably the fee covered materials as well as labour. But to give some idea of the sum involved, the figure could be set against the 1.2 guilders which a carpenter or bricklayer could have expected to earn in a day in 1635.[106] There were at least nine component arches and stages in the display, and the cost of six is known to us. Together they amounted to over 22,000 guilders.[107] Without knowing the cost of materials, these are difficult figures to interpret, but they give a clear impression of the extent to which resources and labour were committed to a public display, and they suggest that what was, in essence, a holiday involved a sudden quickening in the volume and rhythm of work: the carpenter Michiel Boussoy was contracted to complete the Stage of Welcome, which was 80 feet high and 78 feet wide, in 34 days, the Portico of the Emperors (100 feet wide and topped by an obelisk of 70 feet) in a fortnight.[108]

This celebration of dynastic power at a time of urban economic decline might be interpreted as wasteful, or at best unproductive. In London, courtly and civic entertainments were more systematically distinguished from each other. Royal ceremonial became increasingly elaborate at the courts of the Tudors and Stuarts.[109] There was something of a civic decline, too: in Coventry, communal celebrations had begun to lose meaning by 1500.[110] But in London, the civic tradition asserted an increasingly powerful influence on public life. In continuing to celebrate a city rather than a state, a community rather than a ruler, in developing the economic potential of ceremonial against a European background of princely magnificence and religious upheaval, the great metropolis of London offers some striking similarities to Venice.

As Thomas Platter remarked in 1599, the capital seemed to embrace the whole country: 'London is not said to be in England, but rather England in London.'[111] Venetian observers made much the same point, and set up intriguing comparisons with Venice itself. London could seem like 'a sort of republic of wholesale merchants', the aldermen 'governed the city absolutely, almost as though it were an independent Republic'. There was even some suggestion that the maritime virtues of the English outshone those of the Venetians themselves.[112]

The organisation of civic life in London depended on the twelve great companies and 60 smaller guilds, though it was the former who dominated the most striking public event, the Lord Mayor's Show.[113] Instituted in 1535 by the Mercers' Company, the celebration superseded the traditional Midsummer Feast.[114] In the latter part of the century, expenditure on the event, which fell on the company which provided the Mayor, increased markedly. In 1568, the Merchant Tailors honoured Sir Thomas Roe with a pageant costing £317, in 1602 they paid £747 for celebrations for Sir Robert Lee, which included a pageant designed by Anthony Munday.[115]

The Show became increasingly opulent in the early seventeenth century. Table 4.1 gives some examples from the records of the

Haberdashers and Grocers. The costs are huge. The Haberdashers' display in 1604 cost the equivalent of over 10,000 days' work. The artillery salute which the Grocers provided in 1613 sent up in smoke the equivalent of 1,000 days' work in the London building trades. Once again, such entertainments should be seen as a boost to economic life rather than a drain on it. As in Venice, the pageants take on a different character if we take into account the work which they generated and their publicity value, rather than the time and resources which they apparently consumed. This is perhaps reflected in the fact that the Haberdashers consistently spent the major part of their budget on costumes (nearly 70 per cent in these examples), the Grocers on gunpowder, while expenditure on meals and musicians remained a similar proportion throughout for both. The first item of expenditure in 1604 was £134 14s 0d for costumes. John Grimkin made the pageant and provided a model lion, mermaids and a chariot for £46. Thomas Kendall supplied the children's outfits for £22. For the 34 trumpeters, there was 13s 4d each, and the Company made a demand for 38 dozen torches provided at 16 shillings a dozen. The Grocers' 1613 accounts show £30 spent on the galley, £25 on trumpeters, a hefty £149 to Anthony Munday 'for the devyse of the Pageant' and £40 to Thomas Middleton for writing it. On this occasion, Grimkin charged £310. In 1620 17 broadcloths were purchased for £136 19s 0d, 100 gowns were made for a shilling each, 45 coats at 1s 3d and 103 pairs of sleeves at 1s 9d the pair: work for haberdashers and a chance to show it off.[116]

In the early seventeenth century, the pageants seem to have been designed to project London as a great trading metropolis. At this time, Venetian observers were remarking on London's warehouses, shops and shop windows and 'good artificers' like apothecaries, booksellers and plume sellers.[117] In 1617, Thomas Middleton's pageant, appropriately titled 'The Triumphs of Honour and Industry', saw the Thames swarming with boats 'like the gondolas about the Bucintoro'.[118] The grocers distributed 'sundry confections, sugar, nutmegs, dates and ginger' which they threw to the onlookers like free samples.[119] (This may have been very sensible publicity. The English were already addicted to sweets between meals and were 'always munching through the streets like so many goats'.[120])

The Lord Mayor's Show was the central public occasion in London life but there was a more general proliferation of leisure

Table 4.1: *The cost of pageants for the Lord Mayor, 1604–22*

	costumes, props, set, pageant				barge and military salute				odd-jobs, tips, and porterage				dinners and expenses				musicians				total			
Year	£	s	d	%	£	s	d	%	£	s	d	%	£	s	d	%	£	s	d	%	£	s	d	%
1604[a]	346	17	5	64.65	81	2	6	15.12	24	14	2	4.61	52	11	4	9.80	31	5	0	5.82	536	10	5	100.00
1613[b]	304	12	10	27.83	597	4	4	54.56	63	16	5	5.83	68	18	6	6.30	59	19	10	5.48	1094	11	11	100.00
1614[b]	282	2	0	31.95	375	11	4	42.54	109	18	3	12.44	65	5	3	7.39	50	2	0	5.68	882	18	10	100.00
1620[a]	535	15	7	71.40	70	5	0	9.36	46	10	7	6.20	60	2	8	8.01	37	15	0	5.03	750	8	10	100.00
1622[b]	233	14	8	33.17	293	4	9	41.61	74	11	4	10.58	53	1	10	7.53	50	2	0	7.11	704	14	7	100.00

a. Haberdashers — sources: *MSC* III (1604), pp. 61–8; GHL Haberdashers' Co., 15869, Yeomanry Wardens' Triumph Accounts.
b. Grocers — source: GHL Grocers' Co. 11590, Triumphs Accounts, 1613–41.

activity in the city and it was pronouncedly commercial. Platter, like the Venetian ambassador, was amazed at the number of inns for 'eating, drinking, fiddling and the rest' and of course there were bear gardens as well as beer gardens.[121] But perhaps the most commercial of all entertainments was the theatre. It was Thomas Heywood, an author of plays and pageants, who wrote in his *Apology for Actors* (1612) 'what variety and entertainment can there be in any City of Christendome, more than in London?'.[122] According to the Chaplain of the Venetian embassy, Orazio Busino, apart from 'triumphs and revels' there were 'theatrical representations without end throughout the year'.[123] Two or three productions might compete for an audience.[124] In this sense, and in that it was not dependent on commission, London's theatre was intensely commercial.[125]

Although it has been rightly said that one could never mistake a pageant for *King Lear*, the Lord Mayor's Show focused attention on the luxury, pleasure and entertainment available in the metropolitan economy of which the commercial theatre was part.[126] Celebrations of metropolitan life could even be a direct challenge to the supremacy of Venice. In Munday's 1616 pageant, Oceanus told the Mayor:

> That minion of the world
> Venice to Neptune — A poor Lantscip is
> To these full braveries of Thamesis.[127]

At the Lord Mayor's Show in 1629, John Webster proclaimed London's supremacy in even more magnificent terms. He made this quotation his choice when he sought to summarise 'the conceit of the device':

> *Thetis.* What brave sea-music bids us welcome! Hark!
> Sure this is Venice and the day Saint Mark
> In which the Duke and Senates their course hold
> To wed our empire with a ring of gold.
>
> *Oceanus.* No, Thetis, you're mistaken; we are led
> With infinite delight from the land's head
> In ken of goodly shipping and yon bridge:
> Venice had ne'er the like: survey the ridge
> Of stately buildings which the river hem,
> And grace the silver stream as the stream them.
> That beauteous seat is London . . .[128]

London and Venice were both great commercial centres, both were dependent on maritime trade. In both, the corporations played a vital part in public life using civic entertainments to advertise the wealth of the city and to show the solidity of the institutions which created general prosperity. One city gave birth to modern drama, the other to opera, and the connection between these great cultural achievements and the early commercialisation of leisure deserves investigation. That, however, is tangential to the task in hand which is to summarise the part played by guilds in nurturing entertainment as an economic enterprise.

Conclusion

It is hazardous to generalise about Venetian festivals because they took many different forms. They could be solemn or carnivalesque, regular or extraordinary, and they might enjoin the participation of the entire city or just of certain groups within it. Perhaps their most contradictory aspect is that the suspension of the ordinary routine of work which they involved could lead to a quickening of the pace of economic life. But whether they were devotional exercises or commercial ones, festivals played a vital part in the life of the guilds. In ceremonies and festivities, guildsmen who were excluded from the everyday functions of the state took part in the life of a polity blessed by heaven. They reinforced the validity of their participation in some events by generating prosperity as well as celebrating it. The confraternities gave public expression to the principle of brotherhood around which their private devotions were organised, and their public appearances usually marked occasions which had a greater significance in the history of Venice than in the calendar of the Church. The *scuole* were convenient vehicles of a principle of 'status association' which helped ordinary Venetians to feel part of the Christian state. On some occasions, such as the Ascension Day fair, or during the celebrations which greeted the arrival of a distinguished visitor, there were opportunities to renew the state's commercial base through advertisement and sales.

The organisation of public life was much less successful in Florence, partly because of a failure to develop mechanisms of 'status association' or an underlying confidence in statehood. A similar crisis of political identity may have prevented Antwerp from capitalising on the economic possibilities of public display, though even in the seventeenth century, a princely visit could still provide a considerable stimulus to the labour market. More similarities to the Venetian experience are to be found in the case of London, a great metropolitan centre whose major civic occasion was a celebration of wealth and prosperity organised and funded by the guilds and companies. Like Venice, London developed a considerable service sector and an entertainments industry which, until the theatres were closed in 1642, may have surpassed the pleasures of Venice itself.

The evidence that a Catholic city like Venice and a Protestant capital like London prospered due to their precocity in making leisure part of commercial enterprise should perhaps prompt a reassessment of the place of festivals in social life before the Industrial Revolution. According to some historians, such as Professor Trexler, Professor Coleman or Mr Hill, saints' days and festivals were an interruption to the routine of work and therefore a drag in the tide of economic advance.[129]

However, such views seem to derive from the idea that the key transformation in European economic life was from seasonal agricultural labour to regular urban industrial work.[130] This identifies a significant complex of changes, but it neglects the importance before the Industrial Revolution of commercial activity — services, distributive trades, entertainment — which, as was argued in Chapter 3, was the driving force of enterprise in early modern times. As M. Braudel suggested with reference to the volume of business at the German warehouse in Venice, 'the seasonal determinism that so clearly affects rural life has continually been thwarted by the will of man, particularly in the towns'.[131] Perhaps some of the holidays and festivals of the traditional calendar actually helped to iron out seasonal variation by generating extra activity through attracting visitors and increasing the turnover of the urban economy. More concretely, the comparative section of this chapter has sought to demonstrate that even in a Protestant capital, holidays and entertainments were often part of commercialised leisure.

In the way argued at the end of the previous chapter, a historical understanding of guilds can only be gained by coming to terms with a remote and unfamiliar world. However, holidays in Venice and London were not the rites of primitive societies, and it is misleading to analyse them as though they were.[132] Festive occasions were often opportunities for commercially-minded people to foster the confidence of businessmen and consumers — visitors and residents — in the foundations of the city's prosperity.

The sixteenth century was part of the pre-industrial age, but this does not mean that resourcefulness and enterprise were alien to its institutions, merely that these qualities flowed through channels unfamiliar to the twentieth-century mind. Guild structures and traditional holidays did not of necessity hamper enterprise, but as the experience of Antwerp suggests, and as the next two chapters will seek to demonstrate, intolerance and absolutism did.

Notes

1. *Florentine History*, trans. W. K. Marriott (London, 1909), p. 359.

2. B. R. Hanning, '"Glorious Apollo": Poetic and Political Themes in the First Opera', *Renaissance Quarterly*, vol. 32, no. 4 (1979), pp. 485–513.

3. J. H. Shennan, *The Origins of the Modern European State, 1450–1725* (London, 1974), pp. 9–68; F. Yates, *Astraea: The Imperial Theme in the 16th Century* (London, 1977); S. Anglo, *Spectacle, Pageantry and Early Tudor Policy* (Oxford, 1969).

4. D. Hay, *The Italian Renaissance in its Historical Background* (Cambridge, 1970), p. 172; H. G. Koenigsberger, 'Republics and Courts in Italian and European Culture in the 16th and 17th centuries', *PP*, no. 83 (1979), pp. 32–56. A. G. Dickens (ed.), *The Courts of Europe: Politics, Patronage and Culture, 1400–1800* (London, 1977); H. R. Trevor-Roper, *Princes and Artists: Patronage and Ideology at Four Habsburg Courts, 1517–1633* (New York, 1974); M. Levey, *Painting at Court* (London, 1971).

5. *Discours sur les arcs triomphaux* (Aix, 1624), dedication.

6. P. Burke, *Popular Culture in Early Modern Europe, 1500–1800* (London, 1978); E. Le Roy Ladurie, *Le carnaval de Romans* (Paris, 1979).

7. N. Z. Davis, *Society and Culture in Early Modern France* (London, 1975), pp. 209–25.

8. J. Burckhardt, *The Civilisation of the Renaissance in Italy*, trans. S. G. C. Middlemore (Oxford and London, 1945), pp. 245–9.

9. Most notably K. Thomas, 'Work and Leisure in Pre-Industrial Society', *PP* no. 29 (1964), pp. 50–66.

10. There are two old but illuminating works on Venetian festivals. G. Renier Michiel, *Le feste veneziane*, 3 vols. in 6 (Milan, 1929); G. Tassini, *Feste, spettacoli, divertimenti e piaceri degli antichi veneziani* (Venice, 1890). More analytical and more relevant are G. Fasoli, 'Venezia, nascita di un mito', in *Studi in onore di G. Volpe*, 2 vols. (Florence, 1958), vol. 1, pp. 455, 478; A. Pertusi, '"Quaedam regalia insignia"', *SV*, vol. 7 (1965), pp. 3–123; E. Muir, 'The Ritual of Rulership in 16th-century Venice: A Study in the Construction of Myth and Ideology' unpublished PhD thesis (Rutgers University, N. J., 1975); idem, *Civic Ritual in*

Renaissance Venice (Princeton, N. J., 1981). I am most grateful to Professor Muir for permission to quote from his work.

11. Muir, 'Ritual of Rulership', esp. pp. 37, 179–80, 199; Renier Michiel, *Feste*, vol. 1, part i, p. xii.

12. Muir, 'Ritual of Rulership', pp. 10–15; F. Gilbert, 'Venice in the Crisis of the League of Cambrai', in J. R. Hale (ed.), *Renaissance Venice* (London, 1974), pp. 274–93.

13. *DMS*, vol. 12, cols. 130–6.

14. Burke, *Popular Culture*, pp. 178–204; idem, 'Le carnaval de Venise: esquisse pour une histoire de longue durée', in P. Ariès and J.-C. Margolin (eds.), *Les jeux à la Renaissance* (Paris, 1982) pp. 55–63.

15. Quoted in *Letters from Petrarch*, selected and trans. M. Bishop (Bloomington, Ind., 1966), p. 238.

16. Quoted in B. S. Pullan, *Rich and Poor in Renaissance Venice: The Social Institutions of a Catholic State* (Oxford, 1971), p. 59.

17. Burke, *Popular Culture*, pp. 22–8.

18. M. da Canal, *Les Estoires de Venise*, ed. A. Limentani (Florence, 1972), pp. 270, 283–304, and on the comb-makers, p. 303.

19. R. G. Finlay, *Politics in Renaissance Venice* (London, 1980), p. 160.

20. Consiglio dei Dieci, *Parti Miste*, reg. 35 (1512–13), fol. 160v. I am grateful to Dr. Robert Finlay for this reference.

21. *DMS*, vol. 27, col. 193.

22. Sansovino's main work, which contains a continuation by Giovanni Stringa, is *Venetia: città nobilissima et singolare* (Venice, 1663, facs. edn., Farnborough, 1968). See also P. F. Grendler, 'Francesco Sansovino and Italian Popular History, 1560–1600', *Studies in the Renaissance*, no. 16 (1969), pp. 139–80.

23. Arti, b. 163, *libreri, registro atti, 1578–1658*, fol. 4v.

24. P. F. Grendler, *The Roman Inquisition and the Venetian Press, 1540–1605* (Princeton, N. J., 1977), pp. 17, 111, 164, 167 (Zilletti); 167, n. 15 (Zenaro); 183, 320–1 (Brugnolo); 20, 187, 195 (Bindoni).

25. *Venetia*, p. 406.

26. Ibid., pp. 406–38, 439–67, 492–526.

27. Ibid., pp. 402–5.

28. Ibid., p. 406. See also da Canal, *Estoires*, p. 26; *DMS*, vol. 27, col. 12.

29. Sansovino, *Venetia*, p. 415; E. H. Gombrich, 'Venetian Celebrations for the Holy League and the Battle of Lepanto', in *Essays in Renaissance and Baroque Art Presented to Anthony Blunt* (London, 1967), pp. 62–8.

30. Sansovino, *Venetia*, pp. 409–16.

31. Ibid., pp. 439–42.

32. Ibid., pp. 479–86, 498; Fasoli, 'Nascita di un mito', p. 473.

33. Sansovino, *Venetia*, pp. 442–5.

34. Ibid., p. 492.

35. Ibid., pp. 498, 502–3, 510, 513.

36. Ibid., pp. 505, 511.

37. Ibid., p. 519.

38. Muir, 'Ritual of Rulership', pp. 272–8.

39. G. Contareno, *The Commonwealth and Government of Venice* trans. L. Lewkenor (1599, facs. edn., Amsterdam, 1970), p. 21.

40. Sansovino, *Venetia*, p. 487.

41. D. Queller and F. Swietek (eds.), *Two Studies on Venetian Government* (Geneva, 1977), p. 57.

42. Sansovino, *Venetia*, p. 487.

43. Cf. Muir, 'Ritual of Rulership', pp. 72–3.

44. Tassini, *Feste, spettacoli*, pp. 62, 67, 81.

45. Renier Michiel, *Feste*, vol. 1, p. 18.

46. *DMS*, vol. 35, col. 330; vol. 31, col. 399; vol. 32, col. 45; vol. 4, col. 63; vol. 39, col. 242; vol. 34, col 264; vol. 17, cols. 547–9; vol. 21, cols. 274–5.

47. Muir, 'Ritual of Rulership', p. 72.

48. P. Molmenti, *Venice: Its Individual Growth from the Earliest Times to the Fall of the Republic*, trans. H.F. Brown, 3 vols. in 6 (London, 1906–8), vol. 1, part i, p. 189; F.C. Lane, *Venice: A Maritime Republic* (Baltimore, Md., 1975), fig. 13, pp. 158–9.

49. Sansovino, *Venetia*, p. 49.

50. Lane, *Venice*, p. 12. It should be noted, however, that the commoner was head of a community of fishermen not formally incorporated as a guild.

51. See Muir, *Civic Ritual*, pp. 135–64.

52. *DMS*, vol. 27, col. 107.

53. Da Canal, *Estoires*, pp. 284–304.

54. W. Wey, *Itineraries* (London, 1857), pp. 5–6, 84.

55. *Canon Pietro Casola's Pilgrimage to Jerusalem in the Year 1494*, ed. and trans. M. M. Newett (Manchester, 1907), pp. 135, 151, 153–4.

56. B. Castiglione, *The Courtier*, trans. T. Hoby (1561, London, 1928), pp. 145–6.

57. E. Rosand, 'Music in the Myth of Venice', *Renaissance Quarterly*, vol. 30, no. 4, (1977), pp. 511–37; T. Porcacchi, *Le attioni d'Arrigo Terzo* (Venice, 1574), fol. 28v.

58. Porcacchi, *Le attioni*, fol. 25r.

59. Gombrich, 'Celebrations', p. 63.

60. Ibid., p. 66.

61. Stringa writes this in his *Additione* to Sansovino, *Venetia*, p. 416.

62. Gombrich, 'Celebrations', p. 63.

63. Porcacchi, *Le attioni*, fol. 18v.

64. Ibid., fol. 15v.

65. Arti, b. 312, *marzeri, mariegola, 1471–1787*, fols. 79v–82r.

66. Above, p. 95.

67. Porcacchi, *Le attioni*, fol. 24v.

68. Ibid., fols. 28r–34r.

69. Arti, b 312, *mariegola*, fols. 70r–72v.

70. Sansovino, *Venetia*, pp. 412–16.

71. Molmenti, *Venice*, vol. 2, part i, p. 81.

72. Stringa in Sansovino, *Venetia*, p. 421.

73. Ibid., p. 432.

74. According to the observer quoted in Burke, *Popular Culture*, p. 187.

75. Sansovino, *Venetia*, p. 410.

76. On the early legislation, see the collection cited above p. 38, n. 46; also Arti, b. 405 *ter, mercanti di vin (bastioneri), raccolta di leggi,*

1348–1801, fols. 2v, 13v; GN, b. 2, reg. 4, *raccolta dei decreti, terminationi etc. riguardanti i pegni, cioe gli effetti dati dai privati ai negotianti di vino in garanzia dei loro debiti, 1348–1795*, fols, 3r, 5r, 35r–36r.

77. On the importance of registration, GN, b. 5, reg. 11, *campana*, fols. 19v, 44r. At fol. 144r there is a warning to the taverners at San Marco that they are to be prepared for the influx of visitors at the Sensa, 'so that foreigners can be comfortably lodged'. The list of those offering accommodation is contained in GN, b. 5, reg. 12, *stella*.

78. Quoted in Yates, *Astraea*, p. 212.

79. R. C. Trexler, *Public Life in Renaissance Florence* (New York, 1980), pp. 305–6.

80. Ibid., pp. xxi, 224; A. M. Nagler, *Theatre Festivals of the Medici* (New Haven, Ct., 1964); J. N. Stephens, *The Fall of the Florentine Republic* (Oxford, 1983) covers the political history of Florence in the early sixteenth century.

81. Trexler, *Public Life*, p. 214.

82. Ibid., pp. 222–3, 341.

83. Ibid., pp. 221, 404, 412, 416.

84. Ibid., p. 288.

85. Ibid., p. 339.

86. Ibid., pp. 298, 303.

87. Ibid., p. 240.

88. Quoted ibid., p. 247.

89. E. Borsook, 'Art and Politics at the Medici Court I: The Funeral of Cosimo I de' Medici', *Mitteilungen des Kunsthistorischen Institut in Florenz*, vol. 12, nos. 1–2 (1965), pp. 31–54.

90. Yates, *Astraea*, pp. 133–5, 150.

91. *La magnifica et triumphale entrata del Christianiss. Re di Francia Henrico secondo* (Lyons, 1549).

92. Ibid., fols. A3r–v, Bv, B2r, Cr, C2r–v, I2r, Nv.

93. For a most informative summary, see P. Benedict, *Rouen during the Wars of Religion* (Cambridge, 1981), pp. 1–11.

94. Quoted in Davis, *Society and Culture*, p. 160.

95. R. du Puys, *La tryumphante et solemnelle entrée* (1515; Bruges, 1850).

96. Ibid., pp. 12–21.

97. Ibid., p. 20.

98. Ibid., p. 7.

99. A. Dürer, *Tagebuch der Reise in die Niederlände* (Leipzig, n.d.), p. 18.

100. Ibid., pp. 20–2.

101. C. Graphaeus, *Spectaculorum in susceptione Philippi* (Antwerp, 1550), fols. P3r–v.

102. D. Bergeron, *English Civic Pageantry, 1558–1642* (London, 1971), p. 47.

103. For illustrations of this extraordinary occasion, see G. Gevaarts and P. P. Rubens, *Pompa Introitus Ferdinandi Austriaci Hispaniarum Infantis*, (Antwerp, 1641, facs. repr. Munich, 1971); for the motto , J. R. Martin, *The Decorations for the Pompa Introitus Ferdinandi*, (Corpus Rubenianum Ludwig Burchard 16, London, 1972), p. 102.

104. Martin, *Decorations*, p. 179.

105. Ibid., p. 181.

106. J. de Vries, *The Economy of Europe in an Age of Crisis, 1600–1750* (Cambridge, 1976), p. 186.

107. Those listed in Martin, *Decorations*, are (i) the Stage of Welcome, 1870

guilders (p. 40), (ii) the Triumphal Arch of Philip, 4200 guilders (pp. 66–7), (iii) the Portico of the Emperors, 6600 guilders, (p. 108), (iv) the Stage of Isabella, 'more than a thousand guilders', (p. 134), (v) the Arch of Ferdinand, nearly 6500 guilders, (p. 142), (vi) the Arch of Saint Michael's Abbey, nearly 2000 guilders (p. 204).

108. Ibid., pp. 40, 107.

109. Anglo, *Spectacle*; Yates, *Astraea*; R. Strong, *The Cult of Elizabeth* (London, 1977); S. Orgel, *The Illusion of Power: Political Theater in the English Renaissance* (Berkeley and Los Angeles, 1975).

110. On Coventry, C. Phythian–Adams, 'Ceremony and the Citizen: Coventry, 1450–1550', in P. Clark (ed.) *The Early Modern Town: A Reader* (London, 1976), pp. 106–28.

111. *Thomas Platter's Travels in England*, ed. C. Williams (London, 1937), p. 153.

112. *CSPV*, vol. 15, p. 58; vol. 10, p. 503; vol. 15, pp. 395–6 and p.246. See also D. Bergeron, 'Venetian State Papers and English Civic Pageantry', *Renaissance Quarterly*, vol. 23, no. 1 (1970), pp. 37–47.

113. *CSPV*, vol. 15, p. 59.

114. *Mallone Society, Collections III: A Calendar of Dramatic Records in the Books of the Livery Companies of London, 1485–1640*, ed. D. J. Gordon and J. Robertson (Oxford, 1954), *(MSC)*, p. xxv.

115. Ibid., pp. 47, 60, and on Munday's involvement, p. 58.

116. Sources are cited at Table 4.1.

117. *CSPV*, vol. 15, p. 257.

118. Ibid., p. 59.

119. Ibid., p. 60; Bergeron, 'Venetian State Papers', p. 45.

120. *CSPV*, vol. 15, p. 319.

121. *Platter's Travels*, p. 170, see also p. 189.

122. Quoted in S. Schoenbaum, *Shakespeare: A Documentary Life* (Oxford, 1975), pp. 102–3.

123. *CSPV*, vol. 15, p. 110.

124. *Platter's Travels*, pp. 166–7.

125. M. Heinemann, *Puritanism and Theatre: Thomas Middleton and Opposition Drama under the Early Stuarts* (Cambridge, 1980), p. 10. See also L. C. Knights, *Drama and Society in the Age of Jonson* (London, 1937); B. Gibbons, *Jacobean City Comedy* (London, 1968), A. Gurr; *The Shakespearean Stage* (2nd. edn., Cambridge, 1980).

126. Bergeron, *Civic Pageantry*, p. 4.

127. Quoted ibid., p. 175.

128. Quoted in G. Unwin, *The Gilds and Companies of London* (4th edn., London, 1963), p. 285.

129. Trexler, *Public Life*, p. 213; D. C. Coleman, 'Labour in the English Economy of the 17th century', *EcHR*, 2 ser. vol. 8, no. 3 (1956), pp. 290–2; C. Hill, *Society and Puritanism in Pre-Revolutionary England* (London, 1969), pp. 141– 211.

130. A point specifically made by Hill, *Society and Puritanism*, p. 142.

131. F. Braudel, *The Mediterranean and the Mediterranean World in the Age of Phillip II*, trans. S. Reynolds, 2 vols. (London, 1974), vol. 1, p. 266.

132. Cf. Benedict, *Rouen*, p. 1; Muir, *Civic Ritual*, pp. 57–8 and n. 111–16, p. 133 and n. 76.

5

Guildsmen and the Counter-Reformation, *c.*1550–*c.*1600

Introduction

The previous two chapters have examined the ways in which medieval guild structures adapted to the new economic climate which began to prevail after the middle of the fifteenth century. In Venice at least, it seems that the guilds played an important part in a process of general readjustment, and their survival into the eighteenth century should be attributed to their vitality rather than their ossification. However, the precise nature of the changes which guilds underwent is obscured by the shroud woven for them by the forces of absolutism, both confessional and political.[1] The impact of these forces is the subject of the final chapters.

As we have seen, confraternities were organised to perform works which were an expression of the Christian's love for his brother. Philanthropy was part of a devotional practice which promoted the cult of the saints and of the Virgin Mary in particular. In an age which saw the lines of battle drawn between Lutheranism and the Church of Rome and then between revolutionary Calvinism and Spanish Catholicism, confraternities became targets for the broadsides of reformers and shields behind which true believers could advance the Roman faith. Luther had written that the brotherhoods should be 'snuffed out and brought to an end'. He despised their gluttony and drunkenness and their neglect of the poor.[2] Such darts were turned aside by Catholic Reformers like Carlo Borromeo, who mobilised brotherhoods to defend some of the doctrines under attack, notably the Church's teaching on the Body of Christ whose transubstantiation at the hands of the priest was the most potent justification for a separate clerical order mediating between Christians and their God.[3]

The new religious pressures had profound implications for the social order and for economic life. It used to be thought that Protestantism encouraged capitalist activity, though any simple connection between the two phenomena is virtually impossible to establish.[4] After all, capitalism and traditional Catholicism had been quite compatible in medieval Italy and they seemed to be operating in harness in sixteenth-century Germany: Tetzel's infamous indulgences were collected for the Church of Rome by a representative of the greatest capitalists of the age, the Fuggers of Augsburg.[5]

According to Professor Trevor-Roper's majestic thesis, the Counter-Reformation — a distinctly *un*traditional form of Catholicism — drove commercial talent to places where entrepreneurs could operate without fear of persecution. Thus, the Lucchese founded a silk industry in Switzerland, industrious Flemings fled northward to escape Alba's 'Tribunal of Blood'.[6] Intolerance and dogma put great pressure on a body of ideas which Trevor-Roper defines as 'Erasmian':

> by Erasmian I mean not specifically the doctrines of Erasmus, but those general views to which the early reformers, Erasmus in particular, gave a clear form. These Erasmians were Christian and Catholic, but they rejected or ignored a great deal of the new external apparatus of official Catholicism: an apparatus which, since it absorbed energy, consumed time and immobilised property, without having any necessary connection with religion, was equally disliked by educated, by pious and by active men. So, instead of 'mechanical religion', and of monasticism which had come to represent it, the Erasmians extolled 'primitive' Christianity, private devotion, the study of the Bible; and they believed intensely in the sanctification of lay life.[7]

These were ideas which best suited the merchant, but it was these which were stifled by the Counter-Reformation. What has yet to be examined in detail is how reformed Catholicism hampered economic enterprise in countries where it had previously flourished. And in some ways Venice, of which Trevor-Roper makes an exception, provides an intriguing case history, even though the process of internal transformation cannot be attributed purely and simply to external pressure.[8]

As institutions in which the beams of religion and economics crossed, guilds are useful prisms through which to observe the social implications of the Counter-Reformation. In the *arti* and *scuole* of Venice, the cultural and economic dimensions were never far apart. The traditional vigour of lay religion and of small-scale entrepreneurialism were closely interdependent. As a result, the Church could not touch one and not the other. The Inquisition could not stem heresy without disrupting the travels of businessmen and tradesmen, who found the patterns of everyday life unpredictably dislocated. With this in mind, it is worth asking the question: did the restriction on free exchange and speculation which the Holy Office sought to impose on intellectual life affect economic activity as well?

The Venetian experience

The Interdict crisis of 1606 can be interpreted with various historical emphases. It was a struggle of Church and State, of Counter-Reformation papacy and Renaissance republic, of Tridentine universalism and a secular polity insisting on its sovereign independence. The struggle had enormous implications for the confessional contours of Italy and Europe, implications which historians have assessed through an examination of the religious attitudes of the ruling caste and of the 'Disemboweller of the Council of Trent', Paolo Sarpi, the most outspoken and radical champion of secular statehood.[9]

The Corpus Christi procession of 1606 took place despite the papal ban, and the people of Venice dutifully paraded their loyalty to the state. The event was an impressive symbol of the unity of Venetians in their resistance to a papacy apparently intent on destroying the sovereignty of the Republic.[10] It was a resistance embedded in a political tradition which had from the outset offered a cool reception to the vanguard of the Counter-Reformation. The Venetian government had insisted on being represented on the tribunal of the Holy Office as soon as it was revived in 1547. It was suspicious, too, of the Jesuits, and expelled them from Venetian territories once the Interdict was declared.[11]

Venice's defence of its traditions in the Interdict was in many ways highly effective, but the triumph was rhetorical rather than material. Although Sarpi and others encouraged a formal break with Rome, the Republic eventually drew back from Schism. War would almost certainly have resulted, and the influence which the Church maintained in the mainland possessions of the Republic made their ultimate loyalty uncertain. Even had their support been assured, Venice would have been hard-pressed to mobilise forces for a war which was bound to involve taking on the might of Spain.[12]

However magnificent the processions, and however waspish the rhetoric, there was also a sense in which the Interdict was not so much an excuse to assert Venice's independence of Tridentine Catholicism as it was a means of stopping the rot which had already set in. For it might be argued that the Counter-Reformation, especially the Inquisition, had been engaged in half a century of guerilla warfare for the hearts and minds of the Venetian people. Rome may have lost the war of words over the sovereignty of the Republic, but it had begun to subvert the traditions of commercial enterprise which underpinned it.

Trevor-Roper uses Venice as an exception to his general thesis. In the Republic, he maintains, the aristocracy remained predominantly a commercial élite.[13] It can be argued that his thesis is even more comprehensively applicable than he seems to think. This is partly because the Venetian state (as the final chapter will suggest) had begun to take on some of the characteristics of Catholic absolutism.[14] What concerns us here, however, is not the transformation of the Venetian state — in many ways an internal process — but the subversion by the Inquisition of commercial initiative in the world of the guilds. An examination of how this came about may add another dimension to the complicated problem of Venice's 'decline'.

Traditionally, the Church had played only a small part in the spiritual life of guildsmen, whose devotional organisations enjoyed a striking degree of independence from the parish and from the clergy in general. In the later part of the sixteenth century, however, the Church began to play a much more prominent role in the lives of Venetian guildsmen, and began changing the patterns of their institutional and personal life. The representatives of reforming Catholicism sought to redraw the patterns of behaviour, and restructure the routines of everyday life, transforming them into acts of obedience to Rome. This threatened not just the independence of the patrician Republic but also the cultural and economic traditions of ordinary people.

The Counter-Reformation and the guilds of Venice

Ostensibly the Counter-Reformation failed to penetrate the social institutions of Venice. The *Scuole Grandi* and hospitals were not subject to any clerical interference, even after the Visitation of 1581. The carapace of state sovereignty served to protect the 'medieval' character of the *Scuole Grandi*, and they continued to represent 'the comprehensible people's religion in Venice'.[15]

But while the formal and public role of the *scuole* remained much the same throughout the sixteenth century, they extended their work in the field of poor relief, and their new initiatives owed much to influences which came to be identified with the Counter-Reformation. The Company of Divine Love, which established its headquarters in Venice after the Sack of Rome in 1527, was organised and run by Gian Pietro Carafa, who also founded the Theatine Order and went on to become Pope Paul IV.[16] Ignatius Loyola went to Venice in 1536, and some of his early followers served their novitiate in Venetian hospitals.[17] The zeal of Roman reform in philanthropy was matched by the lavish cult of relics, and the splendour of holiness was further enhanced by great decorative cycles like the one painted for the scuola Grande di San Rocco by Tintoretto.[18]

The influence of the new Catholicism was stronger still amongst the *scuole piccole*. The supra-parochial brotherhoods of the late Middle Ages were increasingly rivalled by the scuole del Santissimo Sacramento. A confraternity for the cult of the eucharist had existed in Venice in 1395, but there were several more foundations shortly after 1500 and a more rapid expansion after 1540. This was a result of Paul III's great drive to establish such confraternities in every parish.[19] Many such *scuole* were recorded in Venice in the Visitation of 1581, and Francesco Sansovino wrote at about the same time that a *scuola* for the cult of the eucharist existed in every one of the city's churches.[20] Such organisations were a vital means of extending the influence of the Counter-Reformation: they tied devotional life more closely to the parish, and, in 1591, they became subject to Visitation.[21] In that they were reviewed by churchmen, they were unlike any other type of confraternity in Venice, and thus became a link which tied the Venetian laity more securely to the universal Church. Irregular attendance could be denounced as a sign of spiritual weakness, membership could be used as a defence against charges of heresy. In at least one instance, a scuola del Santissimo

Sacramento, the one at San Samuele, was used by the Holy Office to ensure that the activities of another confraternity remained orthodox.[22]

Turning to the trade guilds and their *scuole*, we find a more complicated picture, with the elements of tradition and innovation hard to distinguish. At least, this is what emerges from the analysis of an account book kept by the goldsmiths' guild for the years 1540–53.[23] What can be deduced from the figures is limited by the short timespan and by the absence of a similar series from other guild records, but the data allow some important generalisations.

Income and expenditure are analysed at Table 5.1 and Figure 5.1. As can be seen, members' contributions provided the guild with most of its income. Some two-thirds of funds were drawn from candle money and entrance fees. Of the rest, about a quarter derived from investments at the Bond Office. Before 1546, about 13 per cent of annual income came from rent on a property, but in that year the house was sold and the money invested in more bonds.

Table 5.1: *Income and expenditure in the goldsmiths' scuola, 1540–53*

Income (lire and solid)			*Expenditure* (lire and soldi)		
A. Fees from members			A. Administration		
1. Candle money	1116.16	(22.35%)	1. Market	359.16	(8.28%)
2. Guild dues	1375.6	(27.52%)	2. Errands etc.	582.16½	(13.41%)
3. Misc. fees	840.7½	(16.82%)	3. Govt/legal	564.18½	(13.00%)
Total	3332.9½	(66.69%)	Total	1507.11	(34.69%)
B. Other sources			B. Alms	864.2	(19.88%)
4 .Rent	207.7	(4.15%)	C. *Ceremonial*		
5. Investment	1300.13	(26.03%)	5. Priests	380.14	(8.76%)
6. Legal action	61.0	(11.22%)	6. Oil/wax	949.8½	(21.85%)
7. Galley tax	95.11½	(1.91%)	7. Porters	87.4	(2.01%)
			8. Musicians	154.12	(3.56%)
			9. Ornament	402.4	(9.25%)
Total	4997.1	(100.0%)		4345.15½	(100.00%)

source: see note 23.

The pattern of expenditure is less straightforward. More than a third of the guild's outgoings was spent on administration. As an illustration of the close links between devotional and economic activity and of the economic importance of religious festivals, it is worth noting that the religious sodality, the *scuola*, organised the

Figure 5.1: *Income and expenditure in the goldsmiths' scuola, 1540–53*

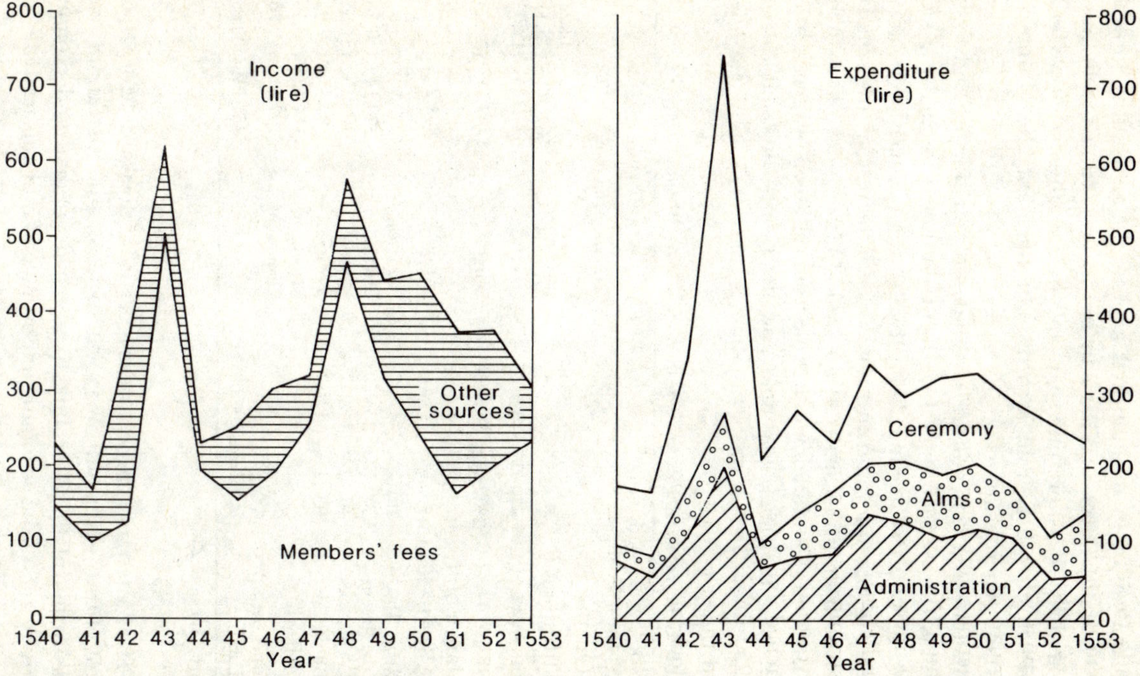

Source: see n. 23.

setting-up of the guild's stalls on Ascension Day. It was the *scuola* which hired canvas, carpenters and porters, and there were other running costs, too: stationery for the guild secretary, payments to guild officials and government officers.

Although the guild spent nearly one-fifth of its money on alms, the sums involved were paltry. Regular payments were made to between 15 and 18 *poveri*, but the average for each of them in any one year was about L.3½: a little more than three days' pay in the building trade.[24] These figures should be set against what the *scuola* disbursed on its devotions. The largest regular item of expenditure was the candlewax burnt at meetings and in procession. In 1545, wax accounted for more than a third of expenditure. In 1547, L.30.12 soldi were spent on '49 medium and 98 small candles for a meeting', in 1550, candles for two funerals cost L.48 — almost as much as the total distributed amongst the guild's poor that year. To underline the devotional character of the *scuola*, the peak of expenditure reached in 1543 is accounted for by payments totalling over L.250 for a silver cross. The money was raised from members, and the cross along with a new box to keep other ornaments in, a lock and key, and decorations represented 48 per cent of all outgoings in that year. Perhaps it advertised members' skills, like the emblems carried in public ceremonial.

On the whole the goldsmiths' confraternity was a traditional institution. It had no parochial base, and while expenditure on alms was slight in real terms, poor relief more or less matched what was spent on ceremonial, thus preserving the traditional balance of devotion and philanthropy. Significant in this respect too is the fact that the Church itself had little to do with the *scuola*. Payments to priests amount to less than 9 per cent of outgoings, and were no more than gifts of candles to the *piovan* or a fee to the sacristan of San Silvestro for cleaning up.

All this seems to bear out Professor Pullan's idea that, as social institutions, Venice's smaller *scuole* did not mobilise members' resources for much more than an altar or chapel here and there.[25] All the same, while the institutional traditions of the Venetian *scuole* survived, the lives of individual members were increasingly circumscribed by a novel insistence on outward and inner conformity, a conformity which a vigilant Holy Office often tested.

Guildsmen and the Inquisition

The records of the Inquisition offer a number of insights into the complex of attitudes and impulses which historians try to tie to different social groups with the label 'mentalities'. This is a particularly difficult task in the case of Venetian artisans. Each trial is in many ways a discrete, even unique, entity defined by its own personalities and proceedings.[26] Given the problems of identifying occupational title and status or wealth, it is not possible to make convincing connections between various trades and heretical tendencies. Since the Inquisition's jurisdiction took in much more than formal heresy, and since it did not always record how proceedings went forward or were concluded, it is hard to establish a valid set of statistics. This chapter does not pretend to solve these formidable problems, but it does try to use the breadth and diversity of the records in a positive way to examine the psychological and material preoccupations of artisans and businessmen — an exercise successfully carried out for publishers, sorcerers and Jews.[27]

The often repeated theme of previous chapters was that Venetian guilds were open-ended organisations which assembled with various degrees of formality to regulate the economic and religious life of members. Though guilds were closely watched by the government, the institutional Church had little influence on their establishment or development. The theme of what follows is that the Counter-Reformation as represented by the Inquisition sought to impose a new parochialism, not just on religious life, but also on the spirit of enterprise on which the adaptability of guild structures depended. The enterprise of guildsmen survived the assault, but the struggle proved a debilitating one.

This is not to say that all the artisans who came before the Inquisition as suspects were entrepreneurs or somehow more commercially minded than their accusers, many of whom were also their workmates or partners. Nor can one neglect the spiritual dimension. One stratum of the records, indeed several strata, reveal the real spiritual crisis of people who, in the aftermath of the Lutheran protest, were becoming concerned about some of the great issues of the Reformation. There is plenty of evidence, for instance, of a strong iconoclastic impulse amongst artisans. Not all were as violently opposed to the cult of the saints as a broker called Giuliano, who in 1558 said he would tear down the images of the Virgin and trample them under foot, or as Giacomo the silkworker who had actually dealt a blow to a statue of the Madonna. But there were clearly worries amongst artisans that the cult of the saints was idolatrous and that belief in the existence of purgatory and the validity of indulgences was unjustified by Scripture.[28]

A comprehensive and typical list of errors — Erasmian in that it asserts the spiritual independence of the laity — appears in the trial of Antonio dall'Oio, a Friulian weaver. The 20 charges he faced amounted to a rejection of the sacramental paraphernalia of religion and he justified his position by asserting that 'I don't find any of this in the Gospel'. He was against baptism and the mass, and he thought that 'the real sacrifice would be the fulfilment of the law'. He refused to worship the saints, or keep their feast days, and he would not adore images. He felt there was no need for auricular confession or confirmation, and he thought extreme unction should be administered 'without ceremony'. He was against monasteries and he approved of clerical marriage if chastity were impossible. He rejected purgatory, indulgences and the authority of the Church. He believed in Justification by Faith alone, not works, and he thought that free will could be exercised only through Christ. He believed in predestination, but not fasts and vigils. Real abstinence, he thought, was abstinence from sin.[29]

To point to a 'spiritual' stratum of the records is not to isolate a particular type of trial. Each has to be read at various levels. The two which concern us most are those which relate to trade guilds and devotional confraternities, the economic and the religious, and the process of seepage from one to the other. The contention of what follows is that the views defined by Trevor-Roper as Erasmian were often held by traders and tradesmen. This is the clear impression left by a selection of trials involving artisans from the period *c.*1547–*c.*1600. The selection is a random one which has encompassed 277 trials from 59 files — about a quarter of the trials for the period. The sample is drawn from files 7–48 for the years 1547–80, from every third file of the voluminous records of the 1580s, and from all six of the *buste* which form the sparse documentation surviving for the period 1590–1616. According to Dr John Martin, the number of artisans accused between 1547 and 1583 was 318.[30] The sample used here is therefore not all-embracing, but it includes a wide variety of occupational and status groups amongst suspects, witnesses, and witnesses who became suspects. Many of those interrogated demonstrate the kind of intellectual independence and resourcefulness which are consistent with the qualities which guildsmen were showing in their economic life. Though it deserves a book in its own right, a case can be made for using these records as representative of artisan 'mentalities'. Certainly, artisans charged or questioned can, in extreme cases, appear to be marginalised crackpots defending a miscellany of traditions which some historians call 'popular culture'.[31] But many of the trials are rather less momentous. What is striking about the evidence is the frequent triviality of the reasons for a summons — not trivial to an Inquisitor who thought a Christian soul was at stake, or to a worried suspect, but trivial in terms of the kinds of everyday actions and omissions for which people were suddenly accountable. Put another way, making a business visit to Lyons or Geneva, eating meat on Friday, failing to defer to the eucharist when it was borne past, or muttering that a recent sermon was 'a load of bollocks' ('*coglionarie*') were the kinds of 'offences' which could lead to a summons like this:

> X, you are summoned tomorrow morning at ten, to the Office of the Holy Inquisition in Venice on pain of 100 ducats, 18 months in the galleys and further penalties.[32]

A fine or a court case threatened an artisan's livelihood. From this point of view alone, the work of the Holy Office was a splinter under the guildsman's nails. One can only speculate as to the psychological impact of the new constraints on a community heavily dependent on the economic initiative of ordinary people.

That the speculation is worthwhile is strongly suggested by the case of Alessandro Caravia, a goldsmith who appears regularly on the list of contributors to the guild's candlewax fund. He was an outspoken critic of the pompous devotions of the *Scuole Grandi* and in a satirical poem called *Il sogno dil Caravia*, published in 1541, he attacked the great confraternities for their failure to offer more to those in want:

> For they do not offer shelter to the poor
> So numerous as they are in Venice,
> Hungry and naked, united in their need

He reminds the *Scuole Grandi* of their original principles and of the works of corporal mercy:

If they were to think on death,
Pondering on that as good brethren,
They would help the poor
Through their love for each other, . . .

They were founded to good purpose these Scuole
And they originally governed their affairs properly, . . .

Each loved his fellow as good brothers,
While now what one is against is promoted by another
They didn't need to spend their money
On architects and gilded objects,
They clothed the naked and looked after prisoners

He also extolled the cult of the eucharist which, he alleged, the *Scuole Grandi* neglected:

The sacrament is a greater treasure
Than all the others owned by the *Scuole Grandi*,
Though they be made of fine gold
And covered all over in jewels.[33]

Despite his praise for the eucharist in *Il sogno*, a later poem suggested to the authorities that Caravia was familiar with Protestant doctrines. This led to his interrogation by the Inquisition, in the course of which the orthodoxy of the earlier poem was called into question. Caravia was released and indeed lived to publish again. But although he had always paid his guild dues for candlewax, his will specified that no tapers were to burn at his funeral. Professor Pullan has cautiously described Caravia's beliefs as Erasmian, for, in his writings and will 'he consistently showed impatience with pomp and ceremony, with distractions from the essentials of the Christian faith, and with superstitious practices of all kinds'.[34] There is an intriguing resonance here with Trevor-Roper's point about the importance of Erasmian values to a world of free trade and free enterprise. The world of guildsmen contained many such echoes – which the Inquisition sought to silence.

In 1548, another goldsmith, Iseppo, was alleged to have said that 'it would be better to give alms than to keep oil lamps and candles burning before the images of saints'. According to his apprentice, Bernardin the capper said much the same. Francesco

Cagiola, a silkworker, said that as far as he was concerned, almsgiving was as important as a jubilee. Others remarked on the wastefulness of the practice: 'better to use the oil to fry fish' said Francesco the grocer (who must have sold the stuff). Gierolemo the silkworker thought it would be better used on salad; an opinion shared by Abramo the lute-maker. And there are many other examples.[35]

Amongst the artisans and traders who appeared before the Inquisition, the complaints against the wastefulness of devotional practices were symptomatic of a general dislike of the apparatus which made it difficult to live a Christian life in society and hampered spiritual communication between the Christian and his God. In questioning the traditional balance between devotion and philanthropy, Caravia and those of like mind were not heretics, they were merely responding to the real problem of material want in society, a problem which was becoming increasingly urgent. As in economic life, so in religion, guildsmen were moving with the times. So was the Church, but it was going in a different direction.

This may help to account for the strength of anti-clerical sentiment among guildsmen. It is consistent with Venetian habits and with the tenets of reformers that guildsmen were suspicious of the clergy. Priests had played only a small part in the life of the guilds in medieval Venice, and their attempt to intrude more forcefully revealed and perhaps intensified anti-clerical feeling. In 1572, Battista, a worker in enamels, was said to have criticised the wealth of cardinals on the grounds that they gave no alms. 'Canker on the priests . . . better to deal with a dog', was a remark alleged to have been made by Zeri d' Avanzo, a casual worker, adding that he would 'put 'em all in the galleys, starting with the pope'. The Bishop of Rome had been referred to as a tyrant, according to the denunciation against a hatter called Prospero, and Johann Herschetz, a German tailor, was said to have called him Antichrist. There were frequent remarks against the ecclesiastical hierarchy in general. Priests were pharisees according to an unnamed timber dealer who spoke to Stefano the boatman. The commercially-minded observed a similar instinct for gain in the clergy, which probably set them wondering why the clerical order was separate and superior. Francesco the grocer and Gierolemo the silkworker were both alleged to have said that churches were mere shops for priests. Abramo the lute-maker was supposed to have spoken against purgatory as just a way for priests to make money. There was more than bad-tempered grumbling in all this: criticism of the priesthood had a selective strain. Francesco Cagiola was denounced for calling priests 'fat pigs', but he himself had always made an exception of the Capuchins because they performed the sacrament of penance properly. Silvestro Bellachian, a butcher, agreed that he said the church of San Francesco della Vigna might as well be a brothel, but protested that the friars *did* keep whores there — before he was reduced to tears.[36]

But it was the work of the clergy rather than their character which seemed to arouse most suspicion, and this inevitably took guildsmen on to the uncertain ground of doctrinal irregularity. This is amply demonstrated by doubts and denials of the value of auricular confession. Lunardo de' Gabardi, a swordsmith, was reported for saying that confession was a novelty invented by priests and friars to make money. Francesco Cagiola had said of the sacrament that 'a bad master can't organise a good school', which also invalidated confession for a shoemaker, a silkworker, a broker, and a seller of eau-de-vie. Iseppo Zanco, who worked in the rope factory at the Arsenal, had apparently said quite openly that he had never confessed in his life and had no intention of doing so, 'so as not to tell his business to rogues of priests'.[37]

Mass, too, was criticised, on the grounds that it was not ordered by Christ or the scriptures. Absence from the service could result in a denunciation. And there was the niggling possibility of being informed against by a business acquaintance. Francesco, a stringer, testified against Battista, a casual worker, saying that in all the times they had been to fairs together, he had never seen Battista go to mass.[38]

Given the importance of the eucharist as a manifestation of the power of the clergy, comments on the sacrament and on the doctrine of transubstantiation seem to have been denounced especially frequently. Zuangiacomo, a turner, openly admitted under questioning that the eucharist was only 'a sign and a token'. This opinion was supposed to be shared by Zeri d'Avanzo, a casual worker. According to the testimony of Bartolomeo di Natali, Marc'Antonio Soprani, a grocer, had said that the eucharist was 'just a piece of bread'. Giacomo, a silkworker, recalled an argument about the sacrament when testifying against Paolo Gaiano, and a Flemish tanner called Piero was denounced for allegedly heretical views on the subject. Zulian the broker disputed the real presence since he had suffered food poisoning after taking communion.[39]

Challenging the teaching of the Church, even in an off-hand or jocular way, was perhaps asking for trouble. Much more unnerving are the instances of failure to revere the sacrament when it was carried in procession. Gierolemo, a jeweller, was alleged to be in the habit of hiding when it passed, as was a German pewterer called Johann. That at least appeared to have been a conscious action. But a point raised against a damask-seller from Bologna called Antonio, against a silkworker called Battista and against the weaver Anzolo Venturello was that they had not doffed their caps. In the case against Marc'Antonio Soprani, it was admitted that he had knelt as the sacrament passed, 'but in an ungracious way' ('*in brutto modo*').[40]

In these kinds of cases, the outcome of the trial is relatively unimportant. For the suspect, the verdict was always uncertain, and the strain imposed by the Inquisition on the nerves of ordinary Venetians going about their daily business was probably considerable: it even applied at mealtimes. The sabbath or the six weeks of Lent were further occasions when, wittingly or unwittingly, rules could be broken. Some suspects, like the mercer Giovanni Zonca, of whom more in due course, clearly opposed abstinence from meat on doctrinal grounds. Francesco Poetino, a tailor, justified ignoring the orders of the Church because 'Saint Paul says you must eat what you have'. There were practical reasons, too, he maintained. His wife was pregnant 'and could not eat oil or fried fish'. The family shared veal and chops with her 'because I haven't the means to do a lot of shopping around'. Medical grounds were used as an excuse by Battista de Anzolo, a silk manufacturer, who said he had a liver complaint, and Caravia maintained that he had kept two or three weeks of Lent but went on to meat because of his weak stomach. Giacomo Bresan, a bookseller, said it was impossible to be choosy when travelling on business — you ate what was put in front of you.[41]

Lenten and sabbatarian practices were closely linked to the observance of feast days, though the significance of non-observance is difficult to define in any simple way. Medieval guild statutes specified the saints' days which members were expected to observe, but, as we saw in Chapter 4, Venetians often turned religious festivals, especially the Feast of the Ascension, into trade fairs and market days, and they did so with official encouragement. Once again, it is hard to strike a balance between tradition and innovation, between commitment to abstract doctrinal positions and routine practice of a not very systematic or thoughtful kind. A timber dealer could remark to a boatman that one day was the same as the next. For some, it was imperative to work. Sugar refining and cloth manufacture were sufficiently complicated as production processes to have to go ahead on occasion regardless of the Church calendar. One silkmaker who 'made money . . . like muck', kept three looms going quite blatantly on feast days. These examples should be balanced against that of Giacomo the shoemaker who had told his sister-in-law, 'What do you expect? My children are ruining me and I have to work.' A gold-beater like Costantin Tessera could not have cared much about ecclesiastical constraints because he was given away by the noise he made. But even when work was easily concealed, it was frequently denounced.[42] How much commercial activity (as opposed to manufacture) was not detected is impossible to say, but it was presumably easier to bring an account book up to date or check a stock-list on a feast day than it was to make a pair of shoes or stretch a length of cloth.

The Inquisition was concerned not just for the keeping of saints' days, but also for the stamping-out of heretical opinion about the cult of the saints. Here again, the tribunal's interference between mind and hand had considerable impact on Venice's traders and tradesmen. It is increasingly plain that the struggle between Protestantism and the Counter-Reformation exposed for the first time that many parts of Europe, especially the more remote regions, were scarcely Christian. There, superstitious and even pagan practices could still be found in abundance well into the seventeeth century.[43] We know rather less about the impact of ecclesiastical reformers on lay cultures which had reached a high level of sophistication independent of the Church. What the records of the Inquisition exposed in Venice was not ignorance or foolishness, but a capacity for intellectual speculation on spiritual and secular matters and a diversity of opinion based on reading and discussion, both in pre-arranged meetings and in the casual exchanges of the working day. In these situations, artisans might express scepticism about the cult of the saints, or speak against purgatory, indulgences, jubilees and free will. The final section of this chapter examines the culture of guildsmen. Its argument has three essential elements: it seeks to suggest that artisan culture in sixteenth-century Venice should be understood in terms of a broad secular education and an acceptance of association and discussion; it investigates the implications of these characteristics for free enterprise in the world of the guilds; and most important, it suggests that the Inquisition's attack on intellectual freedom threatened free enterprise itself by imposing a new parochialism in every sphere, and it is around that idea that the discussion is organised.

The new parochialism

Confraternities in the later sixteenth century were increasingly organised around the nucleus of the parish. But the parochialism which the Counter-Reformation began to force on the guilds and their members took a number of forms. It was intellectual and economic as well as devotional, and it applied to individuals as well as to institutions. An attack on reading heretical books became an attack on reading itself, and was part of a still broader process: the attempt to subordinate a vigorous lay culture to the commands of the Roman Church. What needs to be emphasised at the outset is that the attack unleashed by the Inquisition was aimed at the independent spiritual life of laymen rather than at 'popular' traditions or at a culture which was strikingly 'worldly'.

Predictably enough, the spearhead of the advance set out to destroy the laity's access to the vernacular scriptures. It would appear from the records that a significant number of Venetian artisans had some contact with the Word in a directly comprehensible form. Possession of the Gospels '*in volgare*' was an offence which produced a number of denunciations — of Abramo the lute-maker, of Paolo de Albori the tailor, of Giovanni Sarotto, a merchant. Serafin de Magri a carpenter admitted possession, as did Lorenzo Vex a clockmaker. Andrea the silkmaker faced a similar accusation, partly on the basis that he had been heard to quote Habbakuk on idolatry, against the cult of the saints. Tomaso and Piero, both silkworkers, had been heard talking about a New Testament in the vernacular, and the dangers of forming a group to listen to readings from the scriptures seem to have made the Holy Office especially interested in a swordsmith called Zuangiacomo. Zulian the broker said that his Bible was his only book, but other guildsmen possessed a wider range of materials, and reading itself was a suspicious activity. 'He reads all the time', was the reason for the denunciation of Francesco di Rado, a silkworker, by his local priest, and the Holy Office was informed that the swordsmith Lunardo de' Gabardi 'stays up all night reading'. Such men are dangerous.[44]

The records of the Inquisition — always within the limitations of the sample — suggest that the level of literacy amongst artisans was high.[45] Once again, Zuangiacomo the swordsmith, who read a Bible to a shoemaker called Bartolomeo, said he was not literate, though he managed 'to put a few things together'.[46] But many suspects, perhaps the majority whose cases were pursued, were literate, and confessions of ignorance were part of a game of cat-and-mouse with the interrogators.

Where had they acquired this learning? We cannot know whether artisans had any contact with the large number of schoolmasters who taught in Venice in the late sixteenth century — there were at least 258 in 1587.[47] Inquisition records reveal a Francesco Scudieri from Cremona, the son of a cloth merchant, who described his own profession as 'man of letters who teaches music and Italian language to Germans and other northerners', and a broker who went on to teach at a school in Padua, so the world of the guilds did have some points of contact with the world of learning.[48] However, it might be worth trying to understand educational levels amongst tradesmen and traders in terms other than access to formal instruction in school, in particular in relation to the commercial skills which ordinary Venetians clearly possessed. Numeracy might have been more important than literacy in everyday trading, and to add or subtract in ducats and soldi required considerable intellectual agility. The potential speed of mental process in the culture of everyday life was perhaps most fully realised among compilers of inventories. After all, the contents of Stefano Zarnesi's shop (above, pp. 107–9), nearly 250 different entries carefully quantified and costed, took only five days to compile. At that rate, the calculations for things like 85½ *braccia* of cloth at L.19 the *braccia* can scarcely have been conducted laboriously. It is even possible that a businessman rather than the compiler himself (in this case, the father-in-law Lorenzo Pomeli rather than the notary Paolo Dario) may have been on hand to provide prices and measures.

Guildsmen may have become familiar with books as commodities rather than sources of knowledge. Venice was, after all, one of the most important centres of the printing industry in Europe, producing some 8 million books in the later sixteenth century, and publishers were swift to defend themselves against the imposition of the Index on economic grounds.[49] Books were valuable, too, to general merchants. Agostino Bonanome told the tribunal that he bought 'all sorts of merchandise' to Venetian clients, and his wares included books for Pietro Lungo and Gaspare Bindoni. A collector like the mercer Giovanni Zonca defended his possession of heretical books on the grounds that he had been too busy to read them — which was why they were covered in dust.[50]

Perhaps the handling of these valuable items led eventually to an interest in and even familiarity with their contents. That is speculative, but some significant examples indicate that guildsmen and artisans were quite comfortable with a sophisticated culture of the printed word. It is no real surprise to learn that a German clockmaker, Lorenzo Vex, owned a Lutheran Bible among his other books, but more striking that an ironmonger, Zanotto q. Bernardo, had been seen reading a book by Luther in the presence of his assistants. We could expect to find a publisher in possession of the *Decameron*. But the case of Paolo Gaiano, a weaver, is startling. His interrogators moved from purgatory, images, papal authority and the eucharist to an alleged remark about the wealth of the Church. In reply, Paolo recited a sonnet of Petrarch's which he had heard used in criticism of the Church during a conversation in someone's shop.[51]

The advanced cultural interests of some guildsmen are suggested in other cases. A tailor turned cook (to which of those professions would we attach his heresy?), Zuan Pietro, a Frenchman, had a book collection described by an acquaintance as 'war stories and plays', and a silk trader, Pier'Antonio de' Ungari also read war stories — though he includes Ariosto in this category. The circle of Domenego the shoemaker included a harpsichord-maker, Florian Benetto, who had copied out psalms for the group. He admitted he understood only a little Latin, adding, 'I haven't studied theology, but I do like to read the Bible.' Domenego himself maintained that he was illiterate, but in giving his opinion on infant baptism he supported what he said by saying, '*Deus vult omnes homines salvos fieri*'.[52]

How do we make sense of this world? How do we define the character of a cultural milieu in which a weaver recites Petrarch, a shoemaker quotes in Latin? For the examples go on: of a swordsmith's apprentice who reads *Orlando Furioso*, of a master in the same trade who plays the harpsichord, a belt-maker who plays the lute.[53] Two ditches which need to be filled in in order to define the subject are those represented by the words 'marginal' and 'popular'; the ditch represented by the word 'lay' needs to be raked out.

A figure like Caravia, a conventional guildsman in many respects, was also the correspondent of Aretino.[54] One of the painters who appeared before the tribunal, as is well known, was Veronese. He defended his version of the Last Supper (which had to be renamed 'The Banquet in the House of Levi' because of a black dwarf and table forks, which were regarded as unorthodox) on the grounds that he had merely exercised a freedom 'allowed to poets and madmen'.[55] This was more than a plea for the licence which must be allowed to genius. It was representative of the independent attitudes of a considerable section of the Venetian laity. A man who made a living writing price tags for books was defended as 'a glorious madman and drunk', 'a bizarre fantastic sort', 'a frantic wag'.[56] And under interrogation, artisans and traders demonstrated a surprising readiness to answer back, not always in a very disarming manner. There were some forthright defences of the authority of the Scriptures over that of the visible Church. Asked about ecclesiastical authority, the shoemaker Giacomo Cabiato said: 'if councils and papal constitutions are drawn from the Gospels, I believe in them. Otherwise no.'[57] A year later, in 1551, Zuangiacomo the swordsmith was mockingly asked about his circle of associates:

> There are very few of you whom God has inspired with the truth if there are no more than four of you.
>
> I don't know what to say. What do you want me to say? There aren't any more of us and if there were, I'd tell you. . . .
>
> What are the things you believe in?
>
> What Scripture says. Haven't I told you? . . .
>
> But everyone believes in the Scriptures.
>
> If everyone believed in the Scriptures, I wouldn't be here.[58]

Pressed to define his beliefs, the clockmaker Lorenzo Vex asserted that he believed in the Old and New Testaments, adding boldly, 'Do you want me to believe in anything else?'.[59] Giacomo Salviati, a factor in the silk trade, was known to be sceptical about purgatory because of the lack of scriptural evidence for its existence, Serafino de Magri, a literate carpenter, maintained under questioning that grace could be achieved with what he called 'internal commitment'.[60] Caravia, however, refused to be drawn in doctrinal matters and in so doing demonstrated a different defence mechanism. Because a passage in one of his poems seemed to smack of Protestantism, he was asked for his views on predestination, to which he replied, 'I know as much about predestination as that wall.'[61] The correspondent of Aretino was here using the same sort of defence as a peasant from Mestre brought in to testify against his master. Mio the ploughman had no idea about his master's religious practices — 'I don't concern myself with anything except walking behind an ox.' When asked whether he had ever called his master a Lutheran, he said he could never have done so, not knowing what 'Lutheran' meant.[62] It could, however, be a general term of abuse and had serious consequences for Marino de Nodi, a goldsmith. His wife admitted that she often called him: '"Lutheran", "pig", that sort of thing, but I've always seen him as living the life of a good Christian.'[63]

Not that confessions of ignorance invariably convinced the interrogators. Paolo the cutler said he had heard that Geneva was a bad place, but added, 'I've had no dealings with the place and I've never been there: what do you expect me to know?' But the Inquisitors recorded that 'he said many things which showed that he is not a simple or ignorant man'.[64] They knew what they were trying to repress.

The connection with Geneva in Paolo's case is one example of the link which Inquisitors perceived between freedom of movement and heresy. They were suspicious of devotional practices not based on the parish — and of course a penitent had to confess and communicate in his parish church.[65] They were especially suspicious in the case of informal groups, of casual encounters in shops, and, most important of all, of business visits to other countries. To understand the bondage which the new parochialism sought to establish, it is worth examining each of these areas in turn.

The insistence on parochial discipline for those who had abjured their error is mirrored not only in the parochialism imposed on devotional confraternities, but also in the suspicions raised in Inquisitors' minds by people who did not live as parochial Christians. Caravia said he went to mass at several churches and in this too he seems fairly typical. Domenego Gotardo, a grocer, said much the same, so did Battista the enamel-worker and Gierolemo the silkworker, who, like one of the shop assistants at the German warehouse, had no regular confessor either.[66]

Equally significant as a measure of the new parochialism were the constraints imposed by the Counter-Reformation on the traditional ease of association amongst the laity. Domenego the shoemaker was denounced by a mercer on the grounds that 'many people assemble at his home at San Felise to look at his works and listen to him preach Holy Scripture'. Another denunciation of the same group says that the artisans 'get together and read the vernacular Bible, interpreting the Scriptures in shameful ways'. The informant adds, 'I think it's a pretty big school' ('*credo che sia una schola grande*'), unconsciously applying the name of Venice's greatest lay charitable institutions to a bunch of heretics. It was probably natural to refer to a gathering of artisans as a *scuola*, but the links between nests of heretics and ordinary lay institutions were sometimes more concrete. The Tuscans who assembled their confraternity in an oratory at the Frari were denounced for practising flagellation.[67]

Other groups met in shops. This was said of the premises of Francesco the grocer, and similar allegations were made against a circle which met at San Moise. The confession of two of them linked their error to working in the same place. In this case, the connections between the artisans involved were economic rather than purely religious. As argued in Chapter 3, Venetian *botteghe* were the energetic units of enterprise which, through loose organisation and high turnover of stock and personnel, helped sustain the prosperity of the city. From the shops where confidence and trust had been established through free association, the Inquisition coaxed the worms of doubt. Martin the goldsmith may have overheard Iseppo, who practised the same grade, in conversation with a flour dealer. Pasquale the turner, another witness against Iseppo, reported that 'he usually comes to my shop to give me work, that is to turn forks and handles in lead, and one time he got on to talking about free will'.[68]

The examples can be multiplied. Paolo Battista, a Brescian lodging at the home of Zuane the silk dealer, testified that his landlord said 'lots of things against the faith at Rialto in his shop'. And according to another silk dealer, Zuane had got involved in an argument about religion at the shop of Bernardo della Porta. Francesco the grocer was accused of luring passers-by to his shop. (Is a salesman expected to drive them away?) Evidence against Agostino Oriani, another silk dealer, was gleaned from his workmate, Vardian Locadelli. A grocer came under suspicion for reading a prohibited book, *Mercurio et Charaonte*, in his shop. Marc' Antonio, another grocer, admitted that he had spoken about the war in Flanders 'as one does in the shops', emphasising that he was not alone in doing so. But in some shops an understandable nervousness was generated. Antonio the silkworker was often shouted at by his master to keep his opinions on works to himself, Francesco Chiari and Zuane de Giacomo were encouraged to get on with their own jobs and not listen to Paolo Gaiano 'going on for hours about religion'.[69]

Both Francesco and Zuane talk of '*prattica*'; practice, in the shop. This is a difficult word to tie down because it can refer both to religious observance and working habits, and as we shall see, it carried different weights of meaning for Inquisitors and traders. It is another example of the close links between attitudes of mind and economic activity, a point most strongly demonstrated in commerce, because less manual and more intellectual activity were involved. Fabio Locatelli, a mercer, defended one of his associates on the grounds that, yes, he had spoken of religion, 'but in the course of doing business, and in relation to matters of conscience in business affairs'.[70]

The Inquisition was at its most searching when it had evidence that a waverer had contact with foreigners or went abroad. The economic implications of this were vast but intricate. One does not seek to suggest that all heretics were merely honest businessmen, but some of them clearly regarded themselves as such, and we can never know how many potential deals were eventually called off because they involved a Huguenot broker in Lyons or a journey to Geneva — or even a foreign customer in Venice. Put another way, toleration of different opinions amongst customers and partners was consistent with Venetian commercial traditions and with business practice in the sixteenth century. The tradition and the practice were less important than the heretical *prattica* which could flow through the channels of commerce, and if the price of stemming heresy was the building of dams against business, then so be it.

Freedom of movement, between different trades, different shops and different countries, was crucial to Venetian economic life. The Holy Office threatened it at a variety of levels: for Venetian shopkeepers, for travelling artisans, for international merchants. Zanmaria Bagozzi may well have been astonished to be asked whether he knew anyone from Treviso: 'Different sorts of people come to my shop. I don't know whether they're from Treviso or not.' One could have expected a similar response from Stefano Zarnesi, whose customers came from all over the place, as we saw in Chapter 3 (above, p. 108). Zanmaria, a tapestry dealer, insisted that he had moved his premises nearer to the Ghetto to sell more tapestries to Jews, not to take up their religion. Andrea the silk dealer's frequent visits with a German merchant to San Zulian were to buy silk, not to contact heretics. In an economy where one followed one's opportunities, why was it suspicious that a grocer had moved half a dozen times to different parts of the city? Zanbattista, a woollen cloth shearer, had always done business with Lorenzo da Crema, 'and as far as goods are concerned, I've always found him honest', though he admits 'in the question of religion, he's been off the straight and narrow for ten or twelve years'. Tomaso the silkworker defended having given a meal to someone from Geneva: 'I didn't know he was a heretic, and there are lots of merchants who go here and there to make a living.' Zulian the broker was questioned about a German contact. He admitted discussing religion 'to get some brokerage with him, because he was on business, and as a broker I took action to make some money on the deal'. Lorenzo Vex, himself a German, admitted that his Bible had been printed in Zurich (and had been given to him by a factor of the Fuggers) but he maintained that other Germans who visited him came to have their clocks mended or buy new ones, not to plot heresy. If there were heretical books in bales of merchandise brought to Venice by Alessandro Bonanome, well, 'we're carriers of all sorts of merchandise', in Venice 'to pick up some stuff . . . silk, camlets, grapes, soap, lead, books. And I don't know what's in each bale because I don't know how they're packed' — and he admits that he has been too busy to take communion.[71]

Moving from one town to another in search of work seems also to have been fairly common — certainly as a cause of investigation. Zuangiacomo's wife Anzelicha said that as a swordsmith, he often had to go to Treviso or Vicenza for blades and handles. Domenego, whose silk business in Venice had folded, went to Bologna, Geneva and Lyons and was about to try his luck at the imperial court in Vienna. By contrast, Iseppo, who made lanterns, said there could never be any question of his going to Geneva because there was no work for him there. Battista the enamel-worker insisted he had only gone to Geneva to make a bit of money. Piero had gone to Lyons because he was a silk weaver and heard that the trade was flourishing there. Another trader on the move, a dyer called Francesco Fontana, justified his journey to Switzerland in terms of work opportunities. He had left Lyons when the plague struck, but the closure of the passes to Italy led him to Germany. He then found the Simplon shut and so he went to work in Geneva. He admitted that some people there spoke ill of the Church, but he defended his stay there on the grounds that there was no work in Catholic regions.[72]

Like tradesmen and small traders who came before the Inquisition, businessmen engaged in international commerce defended visits abroad on economic grounds. Pietro d'Ochino, a French bookman, had been asked to visit Lyons, he said, when Catholics and heretics lived there freely. He had gone about his business in Lyons, though he knew that his nephew and friends were influenced by heretical ideas. He had not denounced them because he did not consider it decent, and gave an emphatic justification of doing business with heretics: 'When it's a matter of making money, you can and must stick to making money. In Venice I've done business with Jews, worked with them — and cast Hebrew characters for them.'[73]

Three other cases demonstrate the pressure which the Inquisition's activities put on the business community. In 1563, a silk merchant, Nicolo Pellizzari, with interests in Vicenza, presented himself to the Inquisition in Venice. He was aware that he had been denounced and wanted to clear his name. But he was in a hurry. On 8 June, he said, 'since it's now time to settle accounts in Lyons and Besançon, and on the silk market, I beg your lordships to bear this in mind and leave me at liberty so that I can attend to the business'. He offers a surety, but emphasises that 'complete ruin and bankruptcy' for him and other merchants may otherwise result. He is told that he must return to Vicenza and stay within a radius of ten miles of the town. He returns to the court two days later offering to stay confined to his house in Vicenza and have contact with no one but his factors.

But something seems to have aroused the tribunal's interest. Nicolo may have got away on this occasion — the records are obscure — but in November he is once again before the tribunal. He admits having passed through Switzerland and receiving letters from Swiss correspondents, but 'I don't read them all. I pass them on to my factors . . . I only concern myself with the letters which appertain to my business affairs.' He is pressed, too, on a visit made to Lyons. He admits talking to a heretic, 'but he had been recommended by the Arnolfini firm . . . so I couldn't but butter him up . . . he didn't talk to me about religion, but he left me the responsibility of sending a bale of silk to Lucca.' He has also received letters from relatives in the firm in Geneva, Antwerp, Nuremberg and Lyons, and these, according to the Inquisition, were heretical. He offered to show his replies, and by December was pleading still more forcefully that his contact with Lyons was only commercial. He confesses to dealing with suspects in Lyons, but 'outside of business, I came to no arrangements with them'. His interrogators, however, point to letters from Camillo Bonanome which contain comments on current affairs, but then, 'I can't know the intimate details of character: he wrote on business and included some items of news as well . . . and certainly it looked as though in passing on the news, he was a bit inclined to favour the Huguenots.' But he insisted he needed the news 'in the interests of my business, since I'm constantly afraid the upheavals over there will leave me a poor old boy'. In his final deposition, he argues that he should not be the victim of letters written to him:

> As I said on previous occasions, when it's a question of business, I, like many other merchants, haven't been able to stop them [my correspondents] from writing to me their impressions and what they were feeling. . . . and the business I've had with those kinds of people I've had in respect of merchandise and without knowing I was doing wrong.

He offers to give the names of 50 people who will testify that he confesses and communicates every year.[74] This is surely a member of the family identified by Dr Kamen, the Pellizzari (Latinised in the trial to Pelliparius) 'who first came from Vicenza in 1553, flourished in both Basel and Geneva, and prepared the way for other immigrants'. Perhaps it was the disruption to business caused by this trial which led to their being overshadowed by the company of Arnolfini, mentioned by Nicolo in connection with his visit to Lyons.[75]

Similar tensions, and an example of the type of letter held against Nicolo, are to be found in a trial of 1569. According to one witness, Paolo Avanzi was part of a circle which met in a mercer's shop at Rialto — though when the time came for the markets to open, the group dispersed and heresy gave way to business. Paolo, who, like Nicolo, came to clear his name, was apparently involved in very lucrative spice trafficking, and had been looking to strengthen a contact with one Claude le Maître in Geneva. Included in the file is a letter from le Maître to a Florentine merchant, Michelangelo Baglioni. Current affairs are mentioned, but largely because of the disruption they cause to business. Le Maître tells Baglioni not to worry about the ginger and pepper which had evidently proved unobtainable:

> Here [in Geneva] you can get them at a better price from Lyons, and from Marseilles they're excellent value — if only there weren't all this nonsense all over France which makes the roads so unsafe. And it looks as though it will last longer than was thought.

Le Maître's sympathies seem to be Protestant, for he laments the persecution of those 'of the religion' of Lyons, and speaks of an army raised in Germany and marching to support Condé. But he adds, probably with a deal of self-interest, 'May God grant the best and assure that all the disorder gives birth to some good order.' And immediately he goes on to talk of an unexpected shipment of ginger from Alexandria, instructing Baglioni to purchase a list of commodities on his behalf.

Against this background, Paolo is called before the Inquisition in 1569. He is asked about his connection with Geneva and Lyons, and he explains that when Baglioni left Venice to return to Florence, he had put his business in Paolo's hands,

> and since his business interests were based in Lyons and Geneva . . . I thought I'd go off to Lyons and Geneva and acquaint myself with his contacts to put them at ease so they would continue to send their merchandise to the said firm.

When summoned again, he talks like Nicolo, and like others were have looked at: 'I've always attended to my trade and proceeded as a merchant would.' But he is pressed by his interrogators over his correspondence, which prompts a desperate defence:

> If in the course of business it seems that I have had contact with people who have been found to have wicked opinions, I did not know them as such, nor did I deal with them as such, but strictly for business, as Jews, Turks and people of every nation have dealt. Nor can merchants do other than deal with everybody and if anyone wants to take this on or forbid it, he'll find the majority of businessmen in the same position.

Paolo is given 'till Monday next' to formulate his abjuration.[76]

Someone who was certainly 'in the same position' was Giovanni Zonca, a mercer. He kept the Saint Sebastian behind the church of San Salvador, but he spent time abroad, including four years in Antwerp, where he indulged his interest in book-collecting. Again, letters were used against him. The correspondence, the course of the trial, and the sentence enable us to watch the intellectual horizons of a businessman shrink from the high life in Antwerp to house arrest in Venice.

It must be allowed that Zonca was scarcely a great businessman. His letters from Antwerp suggest he was having a rare time. In a letter to Giovanni Raxello he writes of the fun to be had watching youngsters ice skating during the bitterly cold weather. He wishes his correspondent luck in his alchemical endeavours, and encourages him to have as much fun as he can at carnival. Only after looking forward to a game of tennis does he talk about the price of tin, and then only to say that it is too dear in Antwerp and is best obtained direct from England.

He loves the atmosphere in Antwerp, partly because 'here one can speak freely', but largely because the oysters are better than in Venice — and so are the girls:

> It's great being here: everyone is a gentleman of the same condition, and we foreigners are as good as the leading lords. You can carry a weapon whenever you like — no one would say anything if you carried a cannon. . . . You take your girl by the arm and talk about whatever you like. . . . This is a land of madmen in terms of the liberty there is in everything.

He quickly falls in love (so presumably he used his new-found freedom to talk about more than doctrinal abstractions) and is soon quoting Ariosto in his letters home.

Giovanni was an avid book-collector: writing to a contact in Frankfurt for titles like *Pious Pasquito Ecstatic* and *The Tragedy of King Free Will*, to Toulouse for Peter Martyr's *Flight of Superstition*. In that same letter, the light of Renaissance inquiry gives way to the darkness of things to come. The Spaniards had been striving to set up the Inquisition in Antwerp, and the gates of the city were under guard. This is a point taken up by Zonca's French correspondent, Jean de Sere, who offers reassurance:

> I think the events in France in recent years will serve as a mirror for those who are always trying to turn things on their

head and go their own way without thinking ahead: and in this I think the council of the King of Spain will be good and that this Inquisition business will not go ahead.

It did: but it was not the Spanish Inquisition which pursued Giovanni, but the Holy Office in Venice. In 1571, Zonca returned to Venice, sending his luggage and books separately. He disappears until 1582, when he is denounced by one Lauro Zordan for the way he is living in his house in the country. Zordan urges that Zonca's shop be searched for heretical books. At his first appearance on 28 June, Zonca maintains that the informer was personally motivated since he was involved with Zonca in a court case over property in a village in the Trevisano. The local priest has not actually heard Zonca say anything about jubilees or purgatory, but 'in my soul I think it's certain that he's denied purgatory'. Giovanni's books are used against him. The inventory which the Inquisition has found includes an Old Testament, a New Testament in Latin and the Gospels, Livy, Ovid, Caesar, Apuleius, Plautus, Petrarch, Boccaccio, two histories of Venice (Bembo and Scalzi), Aretino, a history of the Kingdom of Naples, a history of the Indies — and Erasmus.

Zonca's defence was that he had not had time to read them — hence the dust — but he engaged in a long justification of eating meat in Lent. He asserted that he had always lived as a Christian, but like the other two businessmen we have looked at, he had to plead to be put under house arrest, 'otherwise neogtiating for merchandise will come to nothing . . . with a clear danger of bankruptcy' which, he argues, was what his enemies wanted. He offers any amount of money as security, but he is held until 11 August when he is shown the letters quoted above, and is informed that the tribunal has more concern for the suspect's soul than the suspect himself — though his interrogators refer to him as a witness.

Perhaps seeing the danger, Zonca pleads that when he was in Antwerp 'being young I gave myself over to having a good time and dallying with women'. Eventually, the Inquisition brings to light a familiar list of topics on which Giovanni is prepared to admit his doubts: papal authority, images, ceremonies, auricular confession, the intercession of saints, the nature of the sacrament, abstinence from meat, the role of monks, saints' days, pilgrimages, relics, excommunication. On 13 August, he admits that he had held these ideas 'until last Saturday', errors, which he confesses, were based on books like *The Harlot Priest*, *The Worldly Bishop* and 'a book on the Christian institutes: I can't remember the author, but he was a heretic'. And included at the top of the list are the *Colloquies* of Erasmus.

His confession saved him, but his penance was a heavy one for an international businessman, not in terms of physical torment, but in terms of a life that was redefined and reorganised by the clergy.

> Every Friday for a year, he must recite the seven pentitential psalms before an image of Christ. He must give a ten-pound candle to the church at Mogiano and one to his parish in Venice for the altar of the Most Holy Sacrament.
> Every day he must recite seven paternosters and seven ave Marias before a crucifix.
> He is to recite ten masses for the dead.
> 100 ducats to pious foundations [for attempting to speed up his case with bribes].
> He is to appear twice a month before the Inquisition.
> He is to be imprisoned for life.

In response to a letter he wrote from prison 3½ months later pleading that he could be released to look after his wife, he was allowed to live at home. This was 'provided that he never allows himself to be seen at the window, nor goes to the ground floor, especially not to the shop'.[77]

The business of the Interdict

It is important not to make too much of Zonca's case. The bribery he attempted suggests he was not entirely honest, and there is little evidence that he was an especially enterprising businessman. Moreover, his house arrest must have been lifted at some stage. In 1588 he was certainly free, for he was secretary to the committee of the mercers' guild.[78] The point to be made is that his experience in the commercial world brought him into contact with ideas unacceptable to reformed Catholicism, and from that point of view he can be set in the broader context of the other tradesmen and traders who came under the reproachful eye of the Inquisition — and indeed of those who did not. In the year of Zonca's trial, 1582, the head of the mercers' guild was our old friend Bartolomeo Bontempelli, whose shop was near Zonca's in San Salvador. His later offer to furnish the residence of the representative of a Protestant state should perhaps be seen in the light of the 10,000 ducats he offered the government every time Venice went to war with the papacy (above, p. 111). Is it too much to trace the themes of Zonca's career via Bontempelli's into the Interdict crisis itself? Paolo Paruta, the ambassador who was to explain to the Pope why Venice had chosen to be the first state to recognise Henry IV as King of France was certainly aware of Venice's dependence on commerce. As he wrote in his history of Venice (*c.*1580):

> The ancient founders of the city and establishers of her laws took great care that her citizens should engage in voyages and traffic on the sea, and with their industry and virtue endeavour to increase their private resources and public wealth, making the Venetian name both known and famous among the most distant foreign nations. The site of the city invited this way of life and activity and almost by itself inclined its inhabitants to such thoughts. Since the city had no lands of its own through whose fertility and the diligence of men it could grow rich, and indeed lacked the things necessary to sustain life, its needs first of all stimulated industry, from which was born the abundance of all things.[79]

Ultimately, however, neither wealth (such as Bontempelli's) nor propaganda (such as Sarpi's) nor even an awareness within the governing class of Venice's dependence on commerce (as displayed by Paruta) was to free the Republic from Tridentine Catholicism and from the power of Spain which loomed behind it.

By about 1600, the balance of economic power in Europe had begun to shift away from Venice in favour of the Dutch, whose tolerance for heterodox immigrants — a principle which drew strength from the ideas of Erasmus — was the key to economic and cultural advance. It is perhaps fitting that the ideas of Paolo Sarpi, the Disemboweller of the Council of Trent, were formed in a circle of acquaintances which met regularly in a Venetian shop, and it seems entirely appropriate that their speculations and exchanges at the *Nave d'Oro* took place in commercial premises owned by a Dutchman.[80]

Comparisons and contrasts

The institutions on which this study is based, the *arti* and *scuole* of Venice, demonstrate the overlap which existed in the world of the guilds between economic activity and religious life. In the sixteenth century, the economic life of the *arti* was subjected to new pressures of change, but the people who worked in the city's *botteghe* showed surprising versatility in adapting to the new conditions. Religious and economic life remained inseparable, however: on festive occasions, the devotions of confraternities and the commercial enterprise of shopkeepers continued to operate in spectacular harness.

The main body of this chapter has been concerned with the transformation of the cultural climate of the guildsman's world in the later sixteenth century. The influence of Roman theocracy filtered into the *scuole* through the Visitation and through new confraternities, more insidiously and more significantly, the *botteghe* were penetrated by the Holy Office.

The Venetian experience is hard to parallel in the case of other cities. While a good deal is known about confraternities in Catholic cities, an interpretation of all the activities of the Roman Inquisition has yet to appear.[81] The themes of the chapter are of course impossible to pursue in German cities, where the Inquisition did not operate, and where religious affiliation was often determined by the matrix of local circumstances, especially the occupational profile of the city and the political and economic interests of its rulers.[82]

The rationale of this section is as follows. The discussion begins with an examination of confraternities in some north Italian cities. The economic implications of the Inquisition's activities are then assessed in relation to the declared objectives of the Holy Office itself. The focus then turns to some French towns whose confessional identity was often uncertain: Troyes, Rouen, Lyons. The middle of the spectrum is then abandoned for its opposite ends, and Rome and Geneva are used to give an impression of the influence of theocracy in urban life, and these cities are in turn contrasted briefly with the economic success stories of the seventeenth century, Amsterdam and London.

In a number of Italian cities, confraternities spearheaded the advance of Catholic reform. They proved a popular phenomenon and were often characterised by the cooperation of zealous churchmen and devout laymen.[83] Here, the internal reform of the universal Church and the attack on Protestantism became one and the same, and confraternities provide some explanation for Catholic success. In Verona, new companies to promote the cult of the eucharist were formed by the bishop, Matteo Giberti, in the 1530s. Giberti was an admirer of Erasmus (and one of his correspondents) and the humanist's general influence seems to have affected the character of reform in the diocese of Bologna, even after the Council of Trent. Giberti was in turn admired by the uncompromising champion of rigid orthodoxy, Carlo Borromeo, who aimed to establish sacramental brotherhoods in every parish of the diocese of Milan. By the end of the sixteenth century, it was said that such confraternities existed in 556 of 763 Milanese parishes, and they were organised into a single diocesan brotherhood.[84]

Borromeo's ideas and actions should not be projected onto the whole Catholic reform, but in his hands, instruments of internal reform became weapons against Protestantism. The purpose of one eucharistic brotherhood in Rome was made abundantly clear in its statutes, for it was to 'repress once more the arrogant madness of modern heretics, who in this most sinful age speak against the Holy Sacrament'.[85] The use of confraternities to ensure the obedience of the laity to the Church of Rome is clearer still in the case of Genoa. There were some 200 confraternities in the city in the sixteenth century.[86] As in Verona, their formation had been strongly influenced by the new Orders. After the Council of Trent, eucharistic brotherhoods operated under much stronger parochial and diocesan structures. Despite the traditional vigour of lay devotional associations, what came to be imposed on the Genoese were the values of Borromeo and the Jesuits (who exercised direct control over eight brotherhoods in the 1580s). The new spirituality was very different from that of the old popular religion — and it was highly suspicious of mercantile activity.[87]

It is further testimony to the strength of the new devotion that it transformed the brotherhoods of Renaissance Florence, and perhaps the culture of the city-state. Even in the fourteenth century, Florentine schools had been notable for the variety of their curricula, and the diversity of opinion bred in them was sometimes linked to heresy in the minds of the ecclesiastical authorities.[88] The vitality of lay culture may even have found expression in the tough legislation drawn up to restrict the Inquisition during the period of popular government in the mid-fourteenth century.[89] It was argued in Chapter 2 that the religious life of the Florentine laity retained its diversity in the fifteenth century: it was to undergo radical changes in the sixteenth with the advent of the principate and the onset of the Counter-Reformation. Even the devotional activities of the craft guilds became tied to parochial discipline, and the cult of the eucharist was increasingly prominent. After 1530, at least 24 new sacramental confraternities were founded — but no *laudesi* or flagellant companies, the traditional types of Florentine devotional association.[90] One example encapsulates the process through which an older institution was transformed.The Compagnia della Carità was founded in 1379 and fell into disuse in the sixteenth century. It was re-established for the cult of the eucharist in 1538. In 1544 it was united with the Company of the Purification and that of San Nicolo dei Tolentini. Four years earlier, all had been linked to the arch-confraternity of the Santissimo Sacramento in Santa Maria Sopra Minerva in Rome, 'the model sacramental confraternity of the Catholic Reformation'.[91]

We know much less about the work of the Holy Office in Italy than we do about the new confraternities. It is perhaps worth pointing out what was expected of the Inquisition by Borromeo himself in order to establish how the operation of the Holy Office was envisaged, and how efficiently it functioned in Venice. Borromeo was not only a dynamic promoter of confraternities and arch-confraternities for the cult of the eucharist, he worked tirelessly to coordinate the surveillance of lay society by the Visitation and the prosecution of disobedience by the Inquisition. Sometime around the middle of the sixteenth century, Borromeo produced memoranda for those appointed to carry out Visitations. The document reveals what the Visitors' priorities should be and what aspects of the Inquisition's work were of especial importance.[92]

Heretics top the list. They are followed by those who harbour them and those who share their heresies with others. Lower down the list come preachers, whose orthodoxy is to be checked, and those laymen who show signs of contempt for the authority of the Church. Two of the categories singled out by Borromeo — sorcerers and Jews — were especially prominent in the proceedings of the Inquisition in Venice.[93] It would also appear that the third, fourth and fifth memoranda inspired the work of the Holy Office amongst Venetians. The Visitation is to check

Whether there are dealings [*commertio*] amongst heretics or suspects, and how word is passed to those families which are active [*praticano*] in heretical countries either in business [*mercantia*] or by other pretext.

Whether they send their children to Germany or to other provinces in suspect regions to learn the language or trade [*trafico*] or to live in the courts of princes.

Of prohibited and scandalous books, and what care is taken over the bringing of books into the country, and whether due warning is given to merchants and to whoever has dealings [*a chi pratica*]; whether they bring books which are heretical or suspected by the Inquisition to the bookshops.

It is the Inquisition which is to ensure that the community is free from the plague of heresy.[94]

The Venetian trials seem to indicate that the Inquisition was following these precepts. Exchanges of heretical ideas may clearly take place through commercial transactions: commercial contact is therefore to be monitored. Freedom of movement might involve an excursion to a land tainted with heresy: it must therefore be curbed. People who deal in books might be dealing in heresy: they must be closely watched. The tension between the theocratic vision and the business of everyday life is revealed in the language: the *commertio*, *mercantia* and *trafico* of the laity must be subordinated to a decidedly religious *pratica*: something which the Inquisition sought systematically to enforce in Milan, where the Inquisitor was instructed to forbid merchants to engage in *commercium literarum* which involved more than trade.[95]

It must be stressed that this was not an assault by 'religious' on 'secular' culture.[96] As we have seen, the devotions of confraternities were always allied to the economic activities of members of guilds: What was under attack was the idea that laymen could inhabit a world which had its own channels of communication and exchange — both intellectual and economic — which might assert the layman's independence of clerical influence. In a city like Venice, the gulf between the lay and theocratic visions of social life was as broad as that between Protestant and Catholic, and though the contours of the gorge were less jagged, the abyss was just as profound.

Perhaps the best-known example of the Inquisition's systematic dismantling of a commercial culture is provided by the city of Lucca. The great silk industry was stripped of entrepreneurial talent as the Holy Office sought to make the laity obedient to Rome. There too heresy was regarded as a plague. It was thought that Lutheran books were sent to Lucca 'by way of merchants'. Businessmen who had been to Germany or Flanders were regarded with particular suspicion. The resultant emigration to reformed cities included no one who was under sentence from a secular court. Their flight was an acknowledgement that enterprise was no longer free. 'Popular rationalism' departed from Lucca, and it went in step with popular capitalism.[97] Simultaneously, the Inquisition was turning the merchants of Vicenza, Cremona and Locarno into refugees.[98]

In the case of French towns, the picture is more complicated because of the instability of the denominational framework. The research which Professor Natalie Davis has carried out and inspired has suggested that in the towns, religious sympathy and occupation were closely linked. Artisans in general and skilled workers like printers, painters, jewellers and silk workers were especially susceptible to reforming ideas, partly because literacy rates were higher than average in these trades.[99] Parallels with Venice remain difficult to draw with any conviction because of the problems involved in defining social status on the basis of occupation. Sometimes in French towns any pattern in the relationship between occupation and heresy is qualified out of existence by local circumstances. In Rouen, Calvinism 'drew its adherents from virtually all strata of society and from a bewildering variety of occupations', though clothworkers were conspicuous by their absence from the Protestant ranks.[100] In Meaux by contrast, artisans in the textile trades had been to the fore in the religious unrest of the early 1520s.[101] Could it be that the real determinant of how far reformed ideas were promoted or restrained was the operational strength of judicial institutions, a strength which varied greatly from one town to another, and from one year to the next? And one might speculate that as in Venice, the struggle between Protestantism and Catholicism was intensified by the assault of theocracy on the culture of the urban laity.

In France, the instability of central government made the progress of the Counter-Reformation less inexorable but more explosive than in Italy. In the towns of Champagne, as in Florence, there were signs of decline in the older confraternities by about 1530. As in Florence, the old Corpus Christi brotherhoods underwent severe shrinkage. In Troyes, membership of the confraternity at the church of Saint Pantalon fell from 57 to 14 between 1515 and 1585, at Sainte Marie Madeleine from 72 to 5 between 1542 and 1562, at Saint Jean from 39 to 18 between 1544 and 1564.[102] These sodalities were superseded by a number of new eucharistic brotherhoods founded to counter Protestantism.[103] In Troyes the confraternity founded to defend the mass at Saint Jean had 142 members in 1575. The figure leapt to 254 in 1580 before slipping back to 123 in 1585.[104] Equally violent fluctuations were evident in Rouen during and after the period of Catholic fervour brought on by the ascendancy of the League in the early 1590s. In Venice, the patterns of daily life were insidiously redrawn, in Rouen 'life was jolted out of its normal rhythms' as the Catholic authorities and the Jesuits advanced the cult of the eucharist and of relics, and the screw tightened on parochial discipline.[105]

Religious and secular authorities seemed anxious to reduce an energetic urban laity to obedience. In Rouen, there was a 'tendency to abolish the division between cleric and layman, the secular realm and the sacred, so that priests became magistrates and magistrates sanctified their power by priestly rite'.[106] In Champagne, the High Court acted like the Holy Office and followed a Borromean policy of prosecution: possessors of wicked books, secret assemblies, signs of irreverence for the mass, the Virgin and saints. As in Venice, the court recognised heresy more easily than the accused.[107] The courts in Lyons sometimes recorded exchanges with artisans which are similar to those found in Venice:

> Do you think it's up to you to read the Bible, since you're just an artisan and without knowledge?
>
> God taught me by his Holy Spirit. It belongs to all Christians to know it in order to learn the way to salvation.[108]

On the whole, the culture of the urban laity in France was 'enriched' by such conflict, its concerns became broader, its articulacy more assertive. The ideas generated by religious controversy were circulated in increasing numbers of books, the culture of tradesmen and traders in towns detached itself from that of the rural laity.[109] In a town like Reims, the level of literacy made many artisans the cultural equals of the clergymen they knew. Ideas were spread with the free movement of an artisan like Michel Poncelet from Meaux to Geneva to Troyes, where he helped establish groups which met to read the Bible. There is no particular pattern to the exchanges between laymen — a physician, a tanner, a scabbard-maker had little in common — but there was a recognition of lay autonomy which went beyond simple anti-clericalism.[110] The printers of Lyons, like those in Venice, produced numerous 'heretical' editions under the noses of the Catholic authorities and in defiance of Jesuit propaganda which boomed out the message that 'God does not want to declare his secrets to a bunch of common people'.[111] In terms of literate artisans not prepared to be cowed by religious authority, and in terms of its flourishing book trade, Lyons provides some striking similarities with Venice. The crucial difference in France, however, may well be that the Inquisition was vastly less effective than it was in Italy or Spain.[112]

All the same, there is little to suggest that French Protestantism released economic energies elsewhere pent up by the Inquisition. Indeed, the expectations of artisans in Lyons were disappointed by the Calvinist Consistory, which censured flirting and prosecuted drunkenness and which accused the printers of seeking 'carnal liberty under the false title of Gospel'.[113] Some righteous Protestants took pleasure not just in seeing Venus dance out of Lyons, but also in seeing her take Mercury with her. 'Idolatry and dealings of usury and lewdness' were associated with the time when Lyons had 'clerics and merchants a-plenty'.[114]

The merchants may of course have left because of the instability caused by the wars of religion, the conflict which Baglioni's correspondent lamented (above, p. 192). After all, when Antwerp was sacked by Spanish Catholic soldiers, Spanish Catholic merchants left for Rouen, and when turmoil came to Rouen they moved on again.[115]

The weight of authoritarian theocracy on lay culture can be measured by some important similarities between the Rome of the Counter-Reformation and Calvin's Geneva. In Rome in the sixteenth century, money was available for palace building or for war against Protestantism — but not for manufacture — for buildings which glorified God and for handouts which emphasised the dependence of the laity — but not for investment in skills which might give them autonomy. The capital of the Catholic world had room for innumerable whores and beggars, but work as the productive everyday activity of the laity was routed. The poor were passive before the charisma of the saints.[116]

Geneva's economy had flourished in the fifteenth century.[117]

There were no guilds at all to hinder enterprise before 1557, and only nine by 1600.[118] But despite an influx of skilled immigrants like the Buontalenti of Lucca, and despite the crisis experienced by its main competitor, Lyons, after 1580, the city showed no sign of economic recovery. This was due in large part to the insecurity of roads used by Spanish armies and to the suspicion of authorities in Catholic states like Venice or Milan of goods exchanged with heretics. However, a partial explanation may lie in the rigidity of the social control exercised by the religious authorities in Geneva itself. The Consistory operated against offences which in some ways were the mirror images of those prosecuted in Venice. Public humiliation (such as kissing the ground) would result for a barber who tonsured a priest, for a goldsmith who made a chalice, for anyone who said a prayer in Latin or made a vow to a saint, or owned a copy of Amadis de Gaul — and the Consistory reserved the power of excommunication. Calvin's legacy was the 'acute awareness of being a holy city'. The new Jerusalem set itself against the old Rome, and, as Tawney said, the city which stood against monasticism set about turning the world into a monastery.[119]

At least one observer, Artus Desirée, bracketed Geneva and Rome together. Neither was the home for Erasmianism or an independent laity.[120] Erasmian influence, in its general sense, was strongest where the Inquisition was kept out and where Calvinism was carefully restrained:

> Hence Amsterdam, Turk, Christian, Pagan, Jew
> Staple of sects and mint of schism grew:
> That bank of conscience where not one so strange
> Opinion but finds credit and exchange.
>
> (Marvell, *The Character of Holland*, 11.71–4)

In the early seventeenth century, a third of the population of Amsterdam were immigrants, and ideas were part of the myriad of circulating goods.[121]

A robust lay culture was developing in London, too. With its violent pastimes and its vagrants it was perhaps a less civilised place than Amsterdam (or indeed Venice), but around 1600, three-quarters of shopkeepers and craftsmen in the city may have been literate, and even in Stepney and Whitechapel half the craftsmen could read or write. By mid-century, a turner in Eastcheap, Nehemiah Wallington, owned a few books and kept a diary, and he enjoyed a religious liberty matched only in Amsterdam.[122]

Conclusion

Introducing the rise of Amsterdam and London inevitably raises the difficult question of why Venice declined. The deterioration of Venice's fortunes relative to other states is usually seen to have begun with the plague of 1575–77, which reduced the population by something like a third. The recovery thereafter was remarkable, but what made economic decline absolute and irreversible was the wave of pestilence which struck in 1630 and from which there was to be no sustained recuperation. Even so, as Professor Rapp has shown, the Venetian economy was still able to make major adjustments in the seventeenth century, and the guild system played a vital part in regulating the pace of decline, just as it had helped Venetians to take advantage of the sixteenth-century boom.[123]

The evidence examined in this book suggests that the decline of Venice cannot be couched in simple economic terms. There were demographic crises in 1575 and 1630, and these obviously had profound economic implications. But those engaged in economic activity in the metropolis still showed an astonishing vitality. The aristocracy did not desert commerce for the noble life in mainland villas, they invested in land because the returns were better than in sea-borne trade.[124] And if this was an age of decline in terms of the nobility's level of commitment to maritime commerce, it was also the age of mercers like Bontempelli.

This chapter has suggested that at least one more dimension should be added to the problem — the attack on commercial culture by the Holy Office. This is hard to quantify in any simple way, but the 1570s and 1580s, decades of plague, piracy and bank failure, were also the decades when the Inquisition's activities were at their most intense: 795 trials were begun in those years.[125]

The balance of opinion amongst modern historians has shifted away from the idea that the Inquisition was a bloodthirsty institution which epitomised the bigotry of the Counter-Reformation. Inquisitors were generally much less brutal than secular judges and often demonstrated a genuine pastoral care for the salvation of the accused.[126] However, pastoral care implied pastoral authority and obedience to it. Inquisitors themselves, especially after Pius V's decree of 1566, were the agents of papal universalism and sought to bring the laity to obedience in matters of faith.[127] They often worked from a comprehensive fourteenth-century manual reworked by the canonist Francesco Peña in 1578. The rack and the stake may not have been used all that often, but Peña left his readers in no doubt of their role. 'The ultimate end of the trial and condemnation to death,' he wrote, 'is not to save the soul of the accused, but to maintain public order and to terrorise the people.'[128] The evidence suggests that the activities of the Holy Office brought about an important change in the balance of business and religion in Italian culture. And since Italian business and Italian culture were traditionally the most advanced in Europe, the implications for Europe as a whole were vast. In the Middle Ages, commercial activity was generally able to outpace the restraints of the Church, and ecclesiastical authorities seem to have accepted that this was the case.[129] It was from a commercial, though far from irreligious, environment that the Renaissance emerged as a great assertion of the cultural capacities of the laity. But in the mid-sixteenth century, the Church caught up: the bawdiness of Aretino gave way to sermons and saints' lives, commercial culture gave way to theocracy.[130] While the activities of the Inquisition may have obstructed lay economic activity in Catholic cities, Protestant towns were by no means bound to expand. On both sides of the denominational barrier, theocracy inhibited speculation by seeking to restrain the autonomy of the laity. What could be achieved when such constraints were broken or absent is demonstrated by Amsterdam and London respectively. While it is by no means the whole story, and while a complex of other considerations must be taken into account, it might still be pointed out that in London and Amsterdam, the great economic success stories of the seventeenth century, there were plenty of guilds, but no Inquisition.

Notes

1. For a discussion of these two forms of absolutism, see G. Parker, *Europe in Crisis, 1598–1648* (London, 1979), pp. 49–65.

2. 'To the Christian Nobility of the German Nation on the Reformation of the Christian Estate (1520)', in *Works*, ed. J. Pelikan and H. T. Lehmann, 53 vols. (Philadelphia, Pa., 1955 onwards), vol. 44, p. 192; 'The Blessed Sacrament of the Holy and True Body of Christ, and the Brotherhoods (1519)', in the same edition, vol. 35, p. 68.

3. J. Delumeau, *Catholicism between Luther and Voltaire*, trans. J. Moiser (London, 1977). pp. 13–15; for a local example, see P. Benedict, *Rouen during the Wars of Religion* (Cambridge, 1981), pp. 62–3.

4. For a convenient summary of the views of Weber, Tawney and others, see P. Besnard, *Protestantisme et capitalisme: la controverse post-Wéberienne* (Paris, 1970). For a penetrating discussion of the problem in its historical context, see H. Kamen, *The Iron Century: Social Change in Europe, 1550–1660* (London, 1971), pp. 84–128.

5. R. Ehrenberg, *Capital and Finance in the Age of the Renaissance: A Study of the Fuggers and their Connections*, trans. H. M. Lucas (London, 1928), p. 73.

6. H. R. Trevor-Roper, *Religion, the Reformation and Social Change* (London, 1972), p. 23.

7. Ibid., p. 24.

8. Ibid., p. 27.

9. W. J. Bouwsma, *Venice and the Defense of Republican Liberty: Renaissance Values in the Age of the Counter-Reformation* (Berkeley and Los Angeles, 1968); G. Benzoni, *Venezia nell'età della Controriforma* (Milan, 1973), pp. 50–78; D. Wootton, *Paolo Sarpi: Between Renaissance and Enlightenment* (Cambridge, 1983).

10. B. Pullan, *Rich and Poor in Renaissance Venice: The Social Institutions of a Catholic State* (Oxford, 1971), pp. 59–61.

11. B. Pullan, *The Jews of Europe and the Inquisition of Venice, 1550–1670* (Oxford, 1983), p. 3; F. C. Lane, *Venice: A Maritime Republic* (Baltimore, Md., 1975), p. 397.

12. Wootton, *Sarpi*, pp. 48–9.

13. Trevor-Roper, *Religion*, p. 27.

14. Wootton, *Sarpi*, pp. 5–6 and below, Chapter 6.

15. Pullan, *Rich and Poor*, p. 62.

16. Ibid., pp. 235, 237, 258; L. von Ranke, *The History of the Popes*, trans. E. Foster, 3 vols. (London, 1866), vol. 1, pp. 213–41.

17. Pullan, *Rich and Poor*, pp. 264, 266.

18. B. Pullan, 'Le Scuole Grandi e la loro opera nel quadro della Controriforma', *SV*, vol. 14 (1972), pp. 83–109; G. Perocco and A. Salvadori, *Civiltà di Venezia*, 3 vols. (Venice, n.d.), vol. 3, p. 824 for an illustration of the reliquaries of the Scuola Grande di San Rocco in front of Tintoretto's *Crucifixion*.

19. P. Hills, 'Piety and Patronage in '500 Venice: Tintoretto and the Scuole del Sacramento', *Art History*, vol. 6, no. 1 (1983), pp. 31, 33; Pullan, *Rich and Poor*, p. 121, n. 86.

20. Above, p. 60; F. Sansovino and G. Stringa, *Venetia: città nobilissima et singolare* (Venice, 1663, facs. repr., Farnborough, 1968), p. 290.

21. Pullan, *Rich and Poor*, p. 344.

22. SU, b. 59, proc. Colina, Pietro Paolo, test. 30 June 1588. The defendant refers the tribunal to the Scuola of the Sacrament on the Giudecca for proof of his ardent devotion; b. 61, proc. Versemon Giovanni e compagni includes certificates for Martin, warden of the German shoemakers, from the sacristan of the eucharistic brotherhood at San Samuele.

23. Arti, b. 425, *orefici, cassa amministrazione, 1540–53.*

24. Calculated from B. Pullan, 'Wage Earners and the Venetian Economy', in idem (ed.), *Crisis and Change in the Venetian Economy* (London, 1968), p. 173.

25. Pullan, 'Scuole Grandi', p. 97.

26. Pullan, *Jews of Europe*, p. xiv.

27. P. F. Grendler, *The Roman Inquisition and the Venetian Press, 1540–1605* (Princeton, N. J., 1977); Pullan, *Jews of Europe*. R. Martin, 'Witchcraft and the Inquisition in Venice, 1550–1650', Unpublished PhD thesis (University of Manchester, 1986).

28. The examples quoted are from SU, b. 13, proc. Bartolomeo Toscan, Giuliano Salvioni, test. 23 October 1558, Zordan de Bernardo; b. 66, proc. Giacomo samiter (who is accused by his wife). For other instances: b. 7, proc. Gierolemo lavoratore di perle *et al.*, test. 11 October 1548; b. 7, proc. Bartolomeo Sartor, test. 21 April 1549; b. 7. proc. Alvise di Michiel confessore, test. ? May 1548 (against Zeri d' Avanzo, a silk trader); b. 11, proc. Francesco Merlara medicus, test. 1 August 1553, against Battista samiter; b. 15, Domenego Gotardo spicier, fols. 6r. and 7v; b. 15, proc. Antonio dalle Gelosie, Muzio calegher, test. 16 March 1560; b. 17, proc. de Giovanni, Giuseppe (a lantern-maker), test. 16 May 1562; b. 20, proc. Gio.batt. e Marcantonio speziali alle due colombe, test. 8 May 1565; b. 30, proc. Soprani Marc'Antonio, fol. 2v; b. 31, proc. Lorenzo Vex (a clockmaker), fol. 5r; b. 32, proc. Piero Antonio de Ungari (a silk-maker), fol. 3r; b. 40, proc. Albori Paolo (tailor), test. 5 May 1576; b. 45, Grison Giovanni (a pork butcher), test. 16 May 1579; b. 46, proc. Grisolan Gio.batt (a dyer), test. 21 June 1580.

29. SU, b. 14, proc. dal'Oio Antonio, test. 26 October 1557.

30. These figures are given in the index (no. 303) of the records of the Holy Office in the Venetian Archive. J. J. Martin, 'In God's Image: Artisans and Heretics in Counter-Reformation Venice', Unpublished PhD thesis (Harvard University, 1982), pp. 126–8. I am grateful for permission to cite this information.

31. The most obvious example of such a figure is the Friulian miller discussed in C. Ginzburg, *The Cheese and the Worms: The Cosmos of a 16th-century Miller*, trans. J. and A. Tedeschi (London, 1980).

32. SU, b. 46, proc. Grisolan Gio.batt. (a dyer), test. 25 June 1580. Zuanbattista's remarks are reported by Matteo, a cloth shearer; b. 48, proc. Zonca Giovanni, inserted at fol. 31v–32r, dated 28 June 1586.

33. A. Caravia, *Il sogno dil Caravia* (Venice, 1541), verses 166, 212, 214, and, on the sacrament, verses 188–9.

34. Pullan, *Rich and Poor*, p. 117 and n. 77.

35. SU, b. 7, proc. Gierolemo lavoratore di perle *et al.*, test. of Martin (a goldsmith), 11 October 1548; b. 7, proc. Bernardin Garzatore di barette, test. of Jacomo Pordenari (apprentice), 14 February 1549; b. 24, proc. Cagiola Francesco ormesiner, fol. 5v; b. 16, proc. Francesco speziale in his test. of 13 July 1561; b. 17, proc. Gierolemo di Luca samiter, test. of Mattio (silk-worker), 2 February 1561; b. 39, proc. Lauter Abramo, test. of a woman called Elena, 5 May 1575.

36. SU, b. 33, proc. Prospero capeller, fols. 1r, 17r; b. 7, proc. Alvise di Michiel, test. of Tomaso furlan and Margherita, May 1549; b. 46, proc. Herschetz Giovanni (a tailor), den. 27 February 1580; b. 12, proc. Stefano de Ongari (a boatman), test. 28 May 1555; b. 16, Francesco

speziale, test of Gierolemo sagrestano, 28 March 1560; b. 17, proc. Gierolemo de Luca samiter, test. of Matteo (a silk-worker), 2 February 1561; b. 39, Lauter Abramo, test. Aurelio q. Domenego (a painter), 8 May 1575; b. 24, proc. Cagiola Francesco ormesiner, fols. 1v, 2r, 3v; b. 28, proc. Silvestro Bellachian (a butcher), fol. 2r.

37. SU, b. 40, proc. de Gabardi Lunardo spadaro, undated den.; b. 24, proc. Cagiola Francesco ormesiner, fol. 1v; b. 8, fasc. 3, proc. Giacomo Cabiato calzolaio, test. 15 December 1550; b. 13, proc. Bartolomeo Toscano, Giuliano Salvioni, test. of Serafin (an almond seller), 13 October 1558; b. 32, proc. Bartolomeo Grisoni, den. at fol. 1r; b. 19, no. 11, proc. Zanco Giuseppe, test. of Nicolo (a carpenter) of 8 July 1561.

38. See for example, SU, b. 7, proc. Francescinam, test. of Paolo di Battista (the lodger), 18 September 1548; b. 46, proc. bolzer Gio.batt., test of Hippolita Mantuana, 23 June 1580; b. 31, proc. Lorenzo Vex, fol. 4v.

39. SU, b. 7, proc. Gierolemo lavoratore di perle *et al.*, test. of 27 October 1548; b. 7, proc. Alvise de Michiel confessore, test. of Tomaso furlan, May 1549; b. 30, proc. Soprani Marcantonio fol. 2r; b. 20, proc. Gaiano Paolo, fol. 30r; b. 45, proc. Pietro Fiamengo, undated den.; b. 13, proc. Bartolomeo Toscan, Gierolemo Salvioni, test. of Gierolemo Cornetti (a mercer), 23 October 1558.

40. SU, b. 7, proc. Gierolemo lavoratore di perle *et al.*, test. of Anzolo (a fur-seller), 14 October 1548; b. 67, proc. Giovanni Peltrer Teutonicus, undated den.; b. 7, proc. Antonio Bolognese Damaschiner, test. of Vicenzo Comino, also a damask worker, 10 January 1548; b. 11, proc. Francesco Merlara medicus, fol. 20v; b. 19, proc. de Franciol, Lazzarol *et al.*, test. of Zuanne (a weaver), 19 April 1565; b. 61, proc. Soprani, Marc'Antonio, test. of Zuane de Lazaro, 20 February 1588.

41. SU, b. 48, proc. Zonca Giovanni, fol. 119v; b. 8, fasc. 17, proc. Francescum Poetinum, test. of Francesco's son Cesare, 26 April 1550, and of Francesco himself 28 April 1550; b. 11, proc. Tomaso baveller, test. of Battista de Anzolo, 4 June 1555; b. 13, proc. Alessandro Caravia, test. of 14 February 1558; b. 59, proc. Giacomo Bresan, test. of Zuanbattista di Zanantonio, 18 February 1587.

42. SU, b. 12, proc. Stefano di Ongari barcaruol, test. of 28 May 1555; b. 44, proc. Felino Giuseppe, fols. 3r, 4r; b. 24, proc. Tentori/Chiovaroli — the appeal is made by the dyers and stretchers themselves; b. 11, proc. Francesco Merlara, medicus, fol. 24v; b. 38, proc. Giacomo calzolaio, test. of the tailor Bernardo's wife, 28 August 1574; b. 41, proc. Tessera Costantino, test. of Zuangiacomo milanese (a gold beater), 30 April 1577; b. 29, proc. Andrea Zavater Grison, test. of Antonio (a tailor), 4 January 1571; b. 29, proc. Giovanni Sfulgher (a merchant), fol. 4r; b. 31, proc. Lorenzo Vex (a clockmaker), fols. 10r, 11v; b. 46, proc. Bolzer Gio.batt., den. of 23 June 1580.

43. Parker, *Europe in Crisis*, pp. 298–9; Delumeau, *Catholicism*, pp. 166–8.

44. SU, b. 39, proc. Lauter Abramo, test. of Cornelia, 5 May 1575; b. 40, proc. de Albori Paolo sartor, test. of Francesco (a tailor), 5 January 1576; b. 55, proc. Valasso Francesco, Sarotto Giovanni, den. of 12 September 1585; b. 69, proc. de Magri Serafin, test. of 12 December

1592; b. 31, proc. Lorenzo Vex, fol. 4r; b. 15, proc. Andrea ormesiner, test. of Bastian q. Giacomo, 2 May 1559; b. 11, proc. Francesco Merlara medicus, fol. 29r; b. 11, proc. Zuangiacomo spader, fols. 2v–3r; b. 20, proc. Rado Francesco Toscan den. of 3 June 1565; b. 40, proc. di Gabardi Lunardo Spadaro, test. of Piero Zaccher, 5 May 1576.

45. The model established by N. Z. Davis in *Society and Culture in Early Modern France* (London, 1975), p. 210 simply does not work in the case of Venice.

46. SU, b. 11, proc. Zuangiacomo spader, fol. 2v.

47. V. Baldo, *Alunni, maestri e scuole in Venezia alla fine del 16 secolo* (Como, 1977), p. 43.

48. SU, b.15, proc. Scudieri Francesco, test. of 8 April 1560; b. 11, proc. Zuangiacomo spader, fol. 13r.

49. P. F. Grendler, 'The Roman Inquisition and the Venetian Press, 1540–1605', *Journal of Modern History*, vol. 47, no. 1 (1975), pp. 53, 62.

50. SU, b. 30, proc. Alessandro Bonanome, fol 2r; b. 48, proc. Zonca Giovanni, fol. 63r.

51. SU, b.31, proc. Lorenzo Vex, fols. 3r–4v; b. 33, proc. Zanotto q. Bernardo, fol. 4v; b. 39, proc. D'Ochino Pietro, test. of 11 August 1575; b. 20, proc. Gaiano Paolo, fols. 2r–v.

52. SU, b. 17, proc. Zuan Piero Francese, test. of Rigo Neron (a mercer), 19 February 1561; b. 32, proc. Piero Antonio de Ungari, fol. 8v; b. 35, proc. Domenego de Lorenzo calegaro *et al.*, fols. 4r, 5r, 6v, 12v.

53. SU, b. 8, fasc. 17, proc. Francescum Poetinum, test. of Anzela, 24 April 1550 and Cesare, 26 April; b. 7, proc. Rocco centurer, test. of Francesco Griffo (a physician), 29 January 1549.

54. Pullan, *Rich and Poor*, p. 117 and n. 76.

55. SU, b. 33, proc. Cagliari Paolo detto Veronese, test. of 18 August 1575. see also J. Bossy, *Christianity in the West, 1400–1700* (Oxford, 1985), p. 121; Benzoni, *Venezia*, p. 46.

56. SU, b. 23, proc. Bartolomeo Fontana, fols. 4v, 34r, 37v.

57. SU, b. 8, fasc. 3, proc. Giacomo Cabiato, test. of 15 December 1550.

58. SU, b. 11, proc. Zuangiacomo spader, fol. 4r.

59. SU, b. 31, proc. Lorenzo Vex, fol. 4r.

60. SU, b. 26, proc. Giacomo Saliceti, fol. 2v; b. 69, proc. de Magri Serafin, test. of 12 December 1592.

61. SU, b. 13, proc. Alessandro Caravia, test. of 31 January 1558.

62. SU, b. 29, proc. Giovanni Sfulgher, fols. 13r–v.

63. SU, b. 61, de Nodi Marino orese, test. of 27 October 1588.

64. SU, b. 20, proc. Paolo cortelliner, test. of 1 February 1568.

65. See for example, the sentence on the case of Francesco Poetino, SU, b. 8, fasc. 17, following his abjuration of 13 May 1550.

66. SU, b. 13, proc. Alessandro Caravia, test. of 14 February 1558; b. 15, proc. Domenego Gotardo spicier, test. of 2 September 1560; b. 33, proc. Prospero capeller, fol. 19r; b. 17, proc. Gierolemo di Luca samiter, test. of 20 March 1561; b. 39. proc. Dugati Gaspare, test. of Bortolomeo, a shop assistant, 9 August 1575. For other examples, b. 7, proc. Gierolemo lavoratore di perle *et al.*, test. of Francesco (a cutler), 2 September 1548; b.11, proc. Tomaso baveller, test. of Vincenzo Quariato, 15 September 1553; b. 12, proc. Iseppo orese, test. of Lodovico (goldsmith), 31 October 1555.

67. SU, b. 32, *1572–79, denunzie a solo nome*, den. of 10 February 1573; b. 35,

proc. Domengo di Lorenzo calegher *et al.*, den. of 1 September 1573; b. 66, proc. San Giovanni (confraternita), den. of 8 May 1590.

68. SU, b. 16, proc. Francesco Speziale, undated den.; b. 7, proc. Gierolemo lavoratore di perle *et al.*, abjuration of Giacomo and Simon (both turners), 9 November 1548, test. of Iseppo (a goldsmith), 30 October 1548, test. of Pasquale q. Giacomo, 9 November 1548.

69. SU, b. 7, proc. Francescinam, test. of 18 September 1548, and test. of Zanmaria de Antonio, 25 September 1548; b. 36, proc. Oriani Agostino Mantoan, fol. 3r; b. 44, proc. Felino Giuseppe, fol. 10v; b. 61, Soprani Marc'Antonio, fols. 7r–v; b. 7, proc. Antonio Bolognese damschiner, test. of Marino (a silk worker), 7 January 1548; b. 20, proc. Gaiano Paolo, fol. 30v.

70. SU, b. 7, proc. Tasso Giuseppe, test. of 21 March 1591.

71. SU, b. 8, fasc. 5, proc. Zuan Maria Bagozzo (a mercer), test. of 29 July 1550; b. 11, proc. Zuangiacomo spader, fol. 10v; b. 15, proc. Andrea ormesiner, test. of 30 August 1559; b. 61, proc. Soprani Marc'Antonio (grocer), test. of 12 May 1588; b. 13, proc. Lorenzo da Crema, test. of Zanbattista di Schio (a cloth-shearer), undated; b. 24, proc. Tomaso baveller, test. of 12 October 1569; b. 13, proc. Zulian sanser, test. of 17 November 1558; b. 31, proc. Lorenzo Vex, fols. 5v–6r; b. 30, proc. Alessandro Bonanome, fols. 1v, 2v.

72. SU, b. 11, proc. Zuangiacomo spader, fol. 6r; b. 16, proc. Domenico Toscan, test. of Alvise (a silkworker), 26 October 1560; b. 17, proc. De Giovanni, Giuseppe, test. of 6 June 1562; b. 33, proc. Prospero capeller, fol. 42v; b. 37, proc. Montanaro Gottardo which includes the file for Beretto Piero, of which see fol. 8r; b. 45, proc. Fontana Francesco tentor, test. of 4 April 1579.

73. SU, b. 39, proc. D'Ochino Pietro (French bookman), fols. 3r, 17v, 20r, and test. of 26 November 1575.

74. SU, b. 19, no. 8, proc. Nicolai di Battista de Peliphariis, fols. 1r–2v, 4r–5v, 6r, 7r, 8r, 12r, 14r–15v.

75. On the Pelizzari and the Arnolfini, see Kamen, *Iron Century*, p. 90.

76. SU, b. 29, no. 24, proc. Paolo Avanzi, test. of Bartolomeo Bartozzi, 21 July 1568, letter of 13 November 1567, and fols. 11v, 22v, 31r, 32v.

77. SU, b. 48, proc. Zonca Giovanni. Letters quoted are those of 9 January 1563, 20 February 1563, an undated extract which precedes a letter of 3 April 1563. The letter to Frankfurt is of 4 September 1565, that to Toulouse of 9 April 1566, the one to Jean de Sere in Paris is of 8 May 1565. The inventory of luggage follows a letter of 26 May 1571. These documents, some of which are bound, precede a foliated record of the trial. References used here are to fols. 17v, 28r, 50r–51r, 63r–v, 97r–v, 113r, 115r, 118r–120r, 123r–125r, 137r. His letter and the reduction of his sentence to house arrest are undated, but follow the record of the trial.

78. Arti, b. 312, *marzeri, capitoli e parti, 1508–1608*, reg. 1564–1591, fol. 178v.

79. Quoted in Bouwsma, *Republican Liberty*, p. 239. See also Lane, *Venice*, p. 393.

80. Wootton, *Sarpi*, p. 9.

81. This gap will shortly be filled by Mr Nicholas Davidson's book on the Inquisition.

82. For example, see H. Baron, 'Religion and Politics in the German Imperial Cities during the Reformation', *English Historical Review*, vol. 52 (1937), pp. 405–27, 614–33; R. W. Scribner, 'Civic Unity and the Reformation in Erfurt', *PP*, no. 66 (1975), pp. 29–60; idem, 'Why was there no Reformation in Cologne?', *Bulletin of the Institute of Historical Research*, vol. 49, no. 120 (1976), pp. 217–41; G. Strauss, 'Success and Failure in the German Reformation', *PP*, no. 67 (1975), pp. 30–63.

83. G.-G. Meersseman, 'La riforma delle confraternite laicali in Italia prima del Consilio di Trento', in *Problemi di vita religiosa in Italia nel '500* (Padua, 1960), p. 29.

84. Pullan, *Rich and Poor*, p. 121, n. 86; P. Prodi, 'The Application of the Tridentine Decrees: The Organisation of the Diocese of Bologna during the Episcopate of Cardinal Gabriele Paleotti', in E. Cochrane (ed.), *The Late Italian Renaissance, 1525–1630* (London, 1970), pp. 226–43; P. Tacchi-Ventura, *Storia della Compagnia di Jesù in Italia*, 2 vols. in 4 (Rome, 1950–51), vol. 1. i, p. 224.

85. Quoted in Tacchi-Ventura, *Compagnia di Jesù*, vol. 1, i, p. 224.

86. E. Grendi, 'Morfologia e dinamica della vita associativa urbana. Le confraternite a Genova fra i secoli 16 e 18', *Atti della Società Ligure di Storia Patria*, new ser., no. 5 (1965), p. 249.

87. Ibid., pp. 256, 260, 261, 276.

88. C. T. Davis, 'Education in Dante's Florence', *Speculum*, vol. 40, (1965) pp. 420–2.

89. M. B. Becker, 'Heresy in Medieval and Renaissance Florence. A Comment', *PP*, no. 62 (1974), pp. 153–61; but cf. J. N. Stephens, 'Heresy in Medieval and Renaissance Florence', *PP*, no. 54 (1972), p. 40.

90. R. F. E. Weissmann, *Ritual Brotherhood in Renaissance Florence, 1200–1600* (New York, 1982), p. 163.

91. Ibid., pp. 200–1, 205, 208.

92. The document is reproduced in H. C. Lea, *The Inquisition in the Spanish Dependencies* (London, 1908), pp. 532–3. I am grateful to Dr Martin McLaughlin for checking the accuracy of the translation.

93. Pullan, *Jews of Europe*, and now Martin, 'Witchcraft and the Inquisition'.

94. Lea, *Inquisition*, pp. 532–3.

95. Quoted ibid., p. 530.

96. Stephens, 'Heresy', p. 60.

97. M. Berengo, *Nobili e mercanti nella Lucca del '500* (Turin, 1965), pp. 377, 385, 389, 391, 402, 441.

98. Kamen, *Iron Century*, p. 90.

99. Davis, *Society and Culture*, p. 210.

100. Benedict, *Rouen*, p. 78.

101. H. Heller, 'Famine, Revolt and Heresy at Meaux, 1521–5', *Archiv für Reformationsgeschichte*, no. 68 (1977), p. 135.

102. A. N. Galpern, *The Religions of the People in 16th-century Champagne* (Cambridge, Mass., 1977), pp. 205, 207, 208.

103. Ibid., p. 106.

104. Ibid., p. 190.

105. Benedict, *Rouen*, pp. 190–6.

106. Ibid., p. 187.

107. Galpern, *Champagne*, p. 116.

108. Quoted in Davis, *Society and Culture*, pp. 220–1. I am grateful to Professor Philip Benedict for his advice on the presentation of this example.

109. Davis, *Society and Culture*, p. 225.

110. Galpern, *Champagne*, pp. 125–9.

111. Quoted in Davis, *Society and Culture*, p. 221.

112. Benedict, *Rouen*, p. 93.

113. Quoted in Davis, *Society and Culture*, p. 11.

114. Quoted ibid., p. 160.

115. Benedict, *Rouen*, pp. 155, 212.

116. J. Delumeau, *Vie économique et sociale de Rome dans la seconde moitié du 16e siècle*, 2 vols. (Paris, 1957–59), vol. 2, pp. 940, 942.

117. J.–F. Bergier, *Genève et l'économie européenne de la renaissance*, (Paris, 1963), pp. 1–357.

118. E. W. Monter, *Calvin's Geneva* (New York, 1967), p. 21

119. Ibid., pp. 137–8, 195, 235; R. H. Tawney, *Religion and the Rise of Capitalism* (London, 1938), p.123.

120. Quoted in A. Dufour, 'Le mythe de Genève au temps de Calvin', *Schweizerische Zeitschrift für Geschichte*, new ser., vol. 9 (1959), pp. 511–12.

121. C. H. Wilson, *The Dutch Republic* (London, 1968), pp. 26–7; C. R. Boxer, *The Dutch Seaborne Empire, 1600–1800* (London, 1965), pp. 155–86.

122. P. Burke, 'Popular Culture in 17th-century London', *London Journal*, vol. 3, no. 2 (1977), p. 157 on literacy rates, pp. 145–50 on Nehemiah Wallington. Strasbourg, where 40 per cent of the citizens, including artisans and workmen, were apparently literate, and where a furrier might read Virgil, provides another example of a vigorous and literate culture among artisans. See M. U. Chrisman, *Lay Culture, Learned Culture: Books and Social Change in Strasbourg, 1480–1599* (New Haven, Ct., 1982), pp. 69, 75; T. A. Brady, *Ruling Class, Regime and Reformation in Strasbourg, 1520–55* (Leyden, 1978), pp. 95–122 describes the world of the guilds in Strasbourg.

123. B. S. Pullan, 'Introduction', in idem (ed.), *Crisis and Change in the Venetian Economy* (London, 1968), pp. 8–14; R. T. Rapp, *Industry and Economic Decline in 17th-century Venice* (Cambridge, Mass., 1976), passim.

124. R. T. Rapp, 'Real Estate and Rational Investment in Early Modern Venice', *Journal of European Economic History*, vol 8, no. 2 (1979), pp. 269–91.

125. This is the figure recorded in the Index (no. 303) of the records of the Holy Office in the Venetian Archive.

126. E. W. Monter, *Ritual, Myth and Magic in Early Modern Europe* (Brighton, 1983), pp. 61–2.

127. The decree is reproduced in Lea, *Inquisition*, pp. 531–2.

128. N. Eymeric and F. Peña, *Le manuel des Inquisiteurs*, ed. and trans. L. Sala-Molins (Paris and The Hague, 1973), p. 130.

129. In general see J. T. Noonan, *The Scholastic Analysis of Usury*, (Cambridge, Mass., 1957). In particular see R. S. Lopez, 'Italian Leadership in the Medieval Business World', *Journal of Economic History*, vol. 8, no. 1 (1948), p. 65; R. de Roover, *San Bernardino of Siena and Sant'Antonino of Florence: The Two Great Economic Thinkers of the Middle Ages*

(Boston, 1967), pp. 13, 36, 41; I. Origo, *The World of San Bernardino* (London, 1963), pp. 77–99.

130. In the letters of Francesco Datini, 'only two things have any importance — religion and trade. On the first page of Datini's great ledgers stood the words, "In the name of God and of Profit"', according to I. Origo, *The Merchant of Prato* (London, 1963), p. 9. On the links between this commercial but religious world and the culture of the Renaissance, see R. Romano, 'Il mercante italiano tra medioevo e rinascimento', in his collected essays, *Tra due crisi: l'Italia del rinascimento* (Turin, 1971), pp. 85–100; on Florence, see C. Bec, *Les marchands écrivains: affaires et humanisme à Florence, 1375–1434* (Paris and The Hague, 1967); on Venice, see U. Tucci, 'Il patrizio veneziano mercante e umanista', in his collected essays, *Mercanti, navi, monete nel '500 veneziano* (Bologna, 1981), pp. 15–42. On the changes in cultural life in the mid-sixteenth century, see P. F. Grendler, *Critics of the Italian World, 1530–60* (Madison, Wis., 1969), pp. 9, 19.

6

Guilds, War and the State, *c.*1550–*c.*1650

Introduction

This book began with an examination of guilds as the component units of the medieval polity. It was suggested that in Venice the relationship between the guilds and public authorities remained stable even amid the disasters of the fourteenth century. Subsequently, it was argued that guildsmen often showed great enterprise in the sixteenth century when the European economy as a whole began to expand, but that their initiative was sometimes inhibited by the forces of theocracy. At the same time, guilds were having to adjust to the development of the secular state, with its vast implications for traditional institutions. We have already mentioned the innovations made in the field of poor relief. Far more important than the provision of welfare, however, was the state's appropriation of human and material resources in order to wage war.

In domestic politics, the efforts of the central power to establish a monopoly of legitimate violence had been under way for centuries, but as suggested in Chapter 1, sovereign authority was never easily asserted in a feudal world where public power was frequently in private hands.[1] However, from the late fifteenth century onwards, the capacity of the feudal localities to compete with the central power was eroded — gradually, even imperceptibly — by a slow revolution in the duration, scale and cost of war. The cost of new fortifications and the provision of weapons (including firearms) for larger armies humbled the overmighty subject in a way few warrior monarchs could, and rulers were able to get round to fighting each other rather than fighting those they ruled. The culmination of the long process was the absolutist state of the seventeenth century, often an overtly military institution.[2].

Before then, however, the relationship between violence and statehood was highly unstable, and the emergence of the absolutist state was hindered by the continued vigour of a wide variety of political formations. Manageable territorial entities governed by centralised sovereign institutions — the nation-states of the future — had by no means triumphed over universal empires or autonomous localities. Despite the 'military revolution', the standing army was not generally used as a means of coercion in domestic politics before the seventeenth century, and there remained plenty of opportunity for conflict and debate within traditional representative institutions.[3]

As mouthpieces of political expression, or as regulators of economic life, guilds traditionally fulfilled certain 'public' functions. How were they to be incorporated into the fabric of the modern state? In the years around 1600, their destiny was still unclear. No 'national' economy had emerged to which their resources might be subordinated, the absolutist state was not yet steady enough to neuter the guilds and fatten them up for the fisc. Indeed, it was still possible that they might even set limits on the power of the state. In most instances the government rolled back the guilds. In Venice the guilds rolled back the government.

The Venetian experience

Although the structures of the Venetian state were highly developed in the Middle Ages, the Republic seems to stand apart from the general developments of the sixteenth century outlined above. Despite the trend toward absolute monarchy, Venice remained staunchly republican, despite confessional conflict, Venice remained both Catholic and anti-clerical, despite the tendency for state power to be identified with the army, Venice remained pronouncedly civil in its institutional life. The uniqueness of Venice was enhanced by its internal stability. The avoidance of revolution in a world in turmoil generated an extraordinary mystique which became a myth. Its details have been rehearsed so often that only a brief summary is called for here. Venice was supposed by many to be a society which acknowledged the authority of a constitution which balanced monarchy (the Doge), aristocracy (the Senate) and democracy (the Great Council) in perfect measures.[4]

More recently, scholars have pieced together a far less idyllic reality from the documentary records of the Venetian state and the modern perspective on the Renaissance polity is rather different. Venice was primarily an oligarchy. Patricians elected the Doge and they did so from a forum, the Great Council, which guaranteed democracy only for themselves. In so far as society at large benefited from such rule, then constitutional principle was far less important than the careful extension of a wide range of social institutions. The stability of the Venetian state rested on reality, not myth — on the sovereign rule of law, on a pragmatic approach to problems of disorder and poverty, and, from the fifteenth century onwards, on centralised authority over the territories which Venice ruled on the mainland.[5]

What did this complex of sovereign patrician institutions look like from underneath? From the guilds' viewpoint, the Venetian state is probably best defined as a collective absolutism.[6] This was especially obvious in matters of taxation, since no representative institutions in the city itself had any say in the organisation of state finance. In the course of the sixteenth century, this tendency, which was also characteristic of the burgeoning absolutisms of the seventeenth, was dangerously exaggerated by the effects of the 'military revolution'. As the Holy Office inhibited enterprise in the guild system, economic possibilities were restricted further by the need to devote increasing resources to defence commitments. Dominion over the mainland state had required the formation of a substantial standing army in the fifteenth century, and Venice's military commitments grew steadily thereafter.[7] However, the demands which the state made upon the guilds in the sixteenth century were designed to meet the problem of how to sustain a credible capability for war at sea.

The guilds of Venice linked state and society, forming a bond between the sovereign patrician Republic and the commercial capacity of the metropolitan economy. The relationship established between guilds and government in the Middle Ages was a durable one, but it shuddered in the early seventeenth century. The clash of interests, a clash between state and society, did not result in armed rebellion or social disorder, but the conflict was, by Venetian standards, a fierce one, and its outcome strange. For, despite their subordinate position in the Venetian polity, the guilds were able to gain a victory over the patrician state.

The problem of defence: scale and cost

In the sixteenth century, Venice experienced a naval revoltuion whose essential features matched those of the military revolution which gripped Europe as a whole. On sea as on land, warfare required larger forces deployed for longer periods, and it became much more expensive in terms of manpower and money. For Venice, war was a continuous battle of attrition. There was no clear distinction between 'intense military conflict and long periods of peaceful commerce'.[8] War with the Turk was a constant threat, and the fleets of the Republic were plagued by pirates of all nations. Venice's navy had to grow larger to cope with the privateers who menaced its commerce. One corsair, Ochiali, commanded a pirate fleet of 80 galleys.[9] Between 1470 and 1537, the Venetian reserve fleet consisted of 30 light galleys, very occasionally of 50. In 1537, the fleet was expanded to a normal peacetime strength of 50, though in years of crisis like 1537–40 and 1570–73, the number rose to 100 or more.[10] The second of those crises had seemed to culminate in a Christian triumph in 1571, but Lepanto was a false climax. The bill for victory was, in Venice's case, about 900,000 ducats, but the triumph of Don John's fleet had not been planned as a decisive battle, and it did little apart from providing a brief fillip to Christian morale.[11] For Venice, perhaps 60 per cent of the costs of victory were recurrent. The unremarkable year of 1587 saw expenditure of nearly 500,000 ducats on the fleet, in 1594 the cost of armed readiness was 628,000, in 1602 it was 720,000. The fleet sustained by these sums had meanwhile contracted under the pressure of increased costs: the construction and fitting out of a light galley doubled in price between 1563 and 1600. The problems which the government faced were gravely intensified by the plague of 1575–77.[12] Venice lost a third of its population, the productive capacity of the Arsenal was reduced, and worst of all, it became increasingly difficult to find enough men to serve in the crews. The prospect of life aboard ship was scarcely an attractive one. As Pantero Pantera observed,

> were it not for the wants and foolishness of many vagabonds and emancipated villains full of the lowest vices which lead them in the end to sell themselves, it may well be believed that no man could ever be found who would willingly submit to so unhappy a life full of such miseries and horrid accidents.[13]

The guilds and the manpower problem

The 19 horsepower which each galley produced required the muscle of 156 oarsmen. Until the end of the fifteenth century, the fleet relied entirely on volunteers. But even in the morale-sapping campaign of Zonchio (1499–1503) there were problems of under-manning and signs that pay and conditions in Venetian war fleets were deteriorating.[14] The expansion of the fleet necessitated by the war of 1537 was accompanied by important innovations in fleet organisation. The Senate acknowledged that 'forever and perpetually there will be a need to supplement the reserve fleet' and in 1539 the government created a new magistracy, the *Milizia da Mar*, to administer the supply of naval personnel. In the course of the 1540s, an energetic programme of reform was put forward and partially implemented by Cristoforo da Canale: the fleet's volunteer manpower was increasingly supplemented with convicts and conscripts.[15] Since 1449, those who opted to serve at sea instead of going to prison had been treated like other oarsmen. In 1545, Venice fitted out its first galley to be crewed entirely by convicts, and by 1547 had equipped five in this way. It was thought that the harsh discipline would make such galleys efficient fighting machines, but, like conscripts from the mainland, the *sforzati* were no match for the Turks.[16] There was even evidence that conditions in the Sultan's fleet were superior, especially for free oarsmen. In 1562, Marcantonio Donini, secretary to the governor of the Venetian colony in Constantinople, wrote that men were leaving Venetian territories and taking service in the Ottoman fleets, 'to earn in four months on the galleys of the Sultan what they earn in a year on Your Lordship's galleys'.[17] Despite heavy conscription from the Greek islands, often with the use of the press gang, a heavy burden of service fell on the people of Venice itself. In 1539, the trade guilds, and the *Scuole Grandi* (but not the *scuole piccole*) were told to supply 4000 oarsmen for 25 galleys, and the arrangement was subsequently regularised by the *Milizia da Mar*.[18]

The *arti*, *Scuole Grandi* and *traghetti* were assigned quotas of oarsmen. *Galeotti* were chosen by lot. Members of the *Scuole Grandi* were exempt from personal service, and they hired substitutes, but in most of the guilds, those on whom the lot fell served in person. All the boat stations carried the obligation of galley service.[19] By virtue of their work and the physical fitness it demanded, the *traghetti* were well equipped to offer the Venetian fleet a trained reserve. William Thomas observed in 1543 that Venetians,

> because they have such a number of boatmen that continually live by gain upon the water within the city, they need not to seek further for mariners to furnish their galleys withal. For it was credibly told me that there are no less than twelve thousand boats daily serving in those channels, and almost no boat rowed but of a sufficient mariner.[20]

As the century wore on, the government had to seek very much further. Between 1617 and 1621, over 1000 demands were made on the guilds for galleymen — a measure of how far defence problems had intruded into the world of the guilds, and, by that stage, of the guilds' reluctance to cooperate in solving them.[21]

Service to the state was nothing new to artisans. The galleys which destroyed the Genoese at Chioggia in 1381 were manned by guildsmen apparently eager to serve the commune and hurriedly trained as oarsmen.[22] In the sixteenth century, however, the demands were greater and were sustained for decades. Professor Lane estimated that a quarter of the guild workforce faced call-up, a figure which represents a third of those eligible for service. Even before Lepanto, Arsenal workers often crewed the ships they had helped to build, and the manpower shortage became much greater after the plague of 1575–77. Thereafter, the burden on the guilds increased dramatically. In 1582 they were expected to contribute towards the costs of the 4000 oarsmen they themselves were to supply by paying a total of 110,000 ducats to the Mint in the form of reserve deposits. This represented 25 ducats for each galleyman, about half the cost of supporting him on campaign. In 1587, the collection had reached 80,642 ducats, and in the same year, the *Scuole Grandi* were incorporated into the mechanism.[23]

There was a reaction, sporadic at first, but gathering intensity after about 1600. The records of the *Milizia da Mar* include a series of documents which give some idea of the social, the economic, the human cost of Venice's maritime defences, and which illuminate a decisive episode in the history of the Republic. It is difficult to determine when a levy required men to turn out to fight and when it demanded that men be kept available. This in itself is a measure of the revolution. The impression which the documents leave is that stand-by was a condition of unbearable tension for all, while active service was a justifiable necessity for the few. The prospect of enduring the hardships of an oarsman's life left its mark on economic activity and on business confidence. More important still, it induced a shift in the guildsman's perspective on the Venetian state. Government policies exaggerated the tendency toward recession in the aftermath of the plague, and relations between the guilds and the state underwent a genuine crisis in the years 1610–12.

Signs of strain: the 1590s

At the very moment when the government needed to exploit the city's resources of manpower, economic recession and heavy taxes were driving away the immigrants on whom the recovery of the population depended.[24] The problem emerged as soon as the plague departed in 1577. In that year the magistrates reviewing the statutes of the guilds registered their disquiet in the face of

> a most damaging and corrupt practice in all the *scuole* of the trade guilds, in that the majority who join, having got what they wanted from the guilds for years at a time, leave the city and go elsewhere when asked to pay taxes for war or other emergencies.[25]

There is further evidence that the mechanism by which immigrants filled the gaps left by plague was counterbalanced by the taxes which drove out replacements. In 1578, the boatmen complained about foreigners 'who can leave the city whenever there's a tax to pay'. Like the potters, they blamed the flight of immigrants on the galley tax.[26]

The problem was not a purely financial one: there was also the question of who actually had to serve. This produced an unprecedented insistence on status and privilege amongst guildsmen, and a spate of snob-squabbling which the *scuole* had always tended to moderate. The guilds of Venice were never guilds of masters and guilds of men, or guilds of merchant capitalists and guilds of dependent craftsmen. They were organisations which found room for people whose relationship to the means of production and whose capital resources were varied and variable. In the discouraging 1590s, signs of tension between merchants and producers became more frequent as pressure on the *scuole* increased.

One of the strengths of the *arti medie* had been the avoidance of the explosive tensions generated by indebtedness in the textile industries. In the 1590s, the cloth shearers recorded the development of an ominous dependence of wage labour on merchant capital. At the start of the decade, the guild was committed to creditors for 6000 ducats. By 1593 many of the masters were working as labourers for merchants, and the guild sought to 'increase our poor business generally despite the merchants'. The following year, it was thought that the guild needed a further 7–10,000 ducats. By 1604, 4000 ducats were required to prevent members from 'dying in want'. The example makes a number of important points about the Venetian guild network. The guild was small — only 163 masters — and even in hard times it was not submerged in one vast *arte della lana*. Regulation of debt was strict and was designed to preserve the independence of as many members as possible. Most of the money borrowed went to shopkeepers to protect jobs.[27] It is not surprising that when the *Scuole Grandi* wished to stress the scale of their charitable activities, they pointed out that they supported as many poor people as the wool and silk industries.[28]

The *Scuole Grandi* themselves were heavily taxed. Professor Pullan has estimated that benefit schemes in the Scuola Grande di San Rocco might have grown by as much as 30 per cent between 1590 and 1620 but for the claims made by the fisc.[29] In 1607, the Scuola Grande di San Marco offered a vote of thanks to its secretary, who had organised the recruitment of *galeotti*. Three years later, the warden presented the magistrates with evidence of a deficit of 700 ducats on current accounts. 'Salaries, financial commitments, alms and even medicines for poor members' had all been reduced, but the Scuola still faced closure.[30]

Even the limited potential of the *scuole delle arti* in the field of poor relief was cramped still further by the levies. In 1592 the tailors trebled their fees to meet the demand for tax, alms and repairs to their hospital. Two years later, the guild had to borrow 500 ducats 'to meet the urgent requirement of 23 *galeotti*'.[31]

It became increasingly difficult to sustain a *scuola* which existed for the good of all. In 1591, the merchant tanners described their *scuola* as 'of the greatest benefit, both public and private',

> public because of the number of men given to the fleet . . . and other support in emergencies, private because . . . no one can tyrannise or dominate business and the markets, but in buying

and selling, goods are shared out equally, to the common benefit of rich and poor.

The guild was threatened, however, by six wealthy men who sought to control the whole trade, 'a great harm and evil, not only as far as poor shopkeepers and traders are concerned, but for the whole city'.[32] Even eggs seemed to be menaced by a monopoly enjoyed by three or four dealers, and this led the poulterers to found a *scuola* in 1597, a traditional way of safeguarding fair trade.[33]

In isolation, such examples do not amount to much, but they are given a broader context by the demands of the government, for fiscal policy emphasised social divisions amongst guildsmen. For the first time, merchants began to insist on their separateness and superiority, and sought to claw their way to legal privileges above craftsmen and boatmen. The stimulus for this development was provided by the government. Complaining about their allocation of *galeotti* in 1594, the drapers reminded the government that the guild counted nobles among its members. They warned that if the demands were not reduced, they would simply cease trading, with consequent 'ruin and desolation' of the people.[34] The drapers were then excused personal service. Members of the *Scuole Grandi* had always been exempted if they could afford to send a substitute. In 1594, the same privilege was awarded to the drapers and to merchants of wool and silk. In 1596, it was extended first to the goldsmiths and then to the mercers.[35] It was the government, then, which separated richer guilds from poorer ones, and, for the purposes of manning the fleet, effectively created a distinction between 'greater' and 'lesser' guilds. As was made clear in Chapter 3, status and occupation were not so easily equated. There were plenty of mercers of modest means, and plenty of merchants in guilds still liable for personal service. The latter began to seek the privilege of exemption and they did so by setting themselves apart from less wealthy tradesmen and traders.

The moment of crisis: 1610–12

Rising taxes and falling membership provoked the guilds to resist the government's demands. They did so by submitting to the *Milizia da Mar* a series of petitions pleading the injustice of the levy assessments in respect of their numbers and financial resources. The incidence of these petitions is sparse before 1590. However, reassessments of the guilds' obligations in 1595, 1603 and 1610 produced a crisis in 1611, a crisis of state and society. The guilds stressed their loyalty and patriotism: but the size and frequency of the government's demands proved unbearable.[36]

There are three main types of petition. First, and the ones on which this chapter concentrates, are those in which the guilds ask for revisions in the government's estimates of the numbers of men which they were expected to supply. Usually, the appeal for a reduction is preceded by pleas of poverty and assertions of loyalty. This applies whether the submission is made by merchants, craftsmen or boatmen, or by informants exposing groups of artisans functioning as guilds but not contributing to the levies. The second category describes the transfer of ferry station licences (*libertà di traghetto*) from one holder to another. The government was particularly concerned to supervise these transactions since each station carried an obligation of personal service. Finally there is a series of denunciations of illegal bargains struck over the licences, frequently because a station has fallen vacant.

A measure of hyperbole must be allowed for in these documents: hardship could easily be exaggerated to establish a bargaining position with a view to reaching a compromise. But there were limits on the deceits which were practicable. False information itself might lead to denunciation, and in any case, private assemblies of the guilds were often attended by a public notary (above, p. 25). These protests were not lodged for rhetorical effect — and the firmest proof of this is the government's eventual response.

The character of the economic organisation which the guilds helped to foster meant that they did not lend themselves to clear delineation as taxable units. What applied to the mercers seems to have obtained generally. Lines of demarcation between guilds were not always all that clear, and membership was not all that fixed: it was government policy, not guild-based economics, which forced the pace of their definition. According to the assessment of 1610, sellers of eau-de-vie were expected to furnish 30 oarsmen. They pointed out that the guild had only ten members, and insisted that it seemed larger only because shoemakers, hot food sellers and other tradesmen bought from them to retail on their own behalf. Sellers of glass beads, of whom

40 oarsmen were expected, had already been assessed, they said, as members of the mercers' agglomerate (which as we know included some 80 occupations). The coopers, bakers and smiths all protested that their quotas could not be calculated on the basis of a figure for membership which included apprentices. In the case of labourers employed by the cloth stretchers, 'they only help serve and have nothing to do with us', and barges on the route to Este were often rowed by those who came 'arbitrarily, now and again, to help out in our boats'.[37]

The seriousness with which the guilds viewed the impositions, and the care with which they prepared their own case, can be discerned in the smiths' records of 1612. The guild drew up a set of notes showing what was to be emphasised in their appeal:

Item: find out from the magistrates the number of smiths on which the 1605 levy was based.
" find out the same figure for 1610.
" show that 90 masters have died since then.
" show that the membership lists include lads under 18.
" now there are only 293 members, including 20 or so who are already committed to serve as bombardiers.
" illustrate this from the book recording payments of candle money.
Note: the number of able-bodied *galeotti* among the 293 would be scarcely 80.

The petition itself shows that the estimates of 1605 had been cut from 147 to 100 at a time when the guild had 131 able-bodied masters. In 1612, 120 were demanded from only 98 who were fit for service. (It is intriguing to note that the guild allowed room to bargain by saying that it could not support more than 72 *galeotti*, a reduction of eight on the figure mentioned in their draft memoranda.) The demand is cut from 120 to 110, though the list of those liable for service is to be submitted within the week.

The smiths' petition dwells on the guild's economic problems, 'principally due to the fact that there is no longer an export market for our iron- and copperware'. The price of charcoal had soared in the last third of the century (above, p. 102). It was 70 soldi a basket in 1612, and the high level of tax had reduced Venetian competitiveness. Copperworkers have been leaving for other cities, and trade for those who remain has declined by four-fifths.[38]

Perhaps this was the background to a protest registered in none-too subtle fashion by some unruly members:

> Our meeting having assembled in the ironmongers' guildhall as usual, the warden and officals sat down at the tribunal with the holy cross and two lighted candles, there were some who had the audacity to go above and, with scant fear of God and our glorious patron Saint Alo, they pissed over the tribunal and soaked it.[39]

As far as we know, this was the only protest of that type, but the blacksmiths were by no means alone in lamenting the state of business in 1611–12: the levy of 1610 caused protests which make this abundantly plain. The butchers would have liked to supply their allocation of 36 oarsmen 'if only membership hadn't fallen off so much'. The gold-beaters spoke of a decline of business and membership, and complained of foreign competition. The beltmakers had been bedevilled with commercial setbacks. The coopers complained of 'few goods, small earnings and very little business'. The grain sellers' membership seemed 'reduced to nothing', there was a 'notable decline' in the number of cabinetmakers. The turners were doing scarcely any business, the bargemen at Este were close to beggary, the brokers complained of 'infinite damage to trade', the wood merchants of 'a thousand misadventures'. Similar complaints of diminishing membership and increased taxation came in 1611 from tanners who said that members had left Venice 'running after work like birds after food'. The basketmakers, bakers, and potters said much the same: times were bad, government demands were making them worse.[40]

In their relatively new role as taxable entities, the guilds were subject to relentless demands. As early as 1595, the Senate acknowledged that the guilds were committed to heavy repayments of interest. The problem of indebtedness proved long-term. In 1611, the painters needed perhaps two extraordinary contributions from members to bring the galley fund up to the required amount. In 1608, the smiths tried to raise 2000 ducats to pay off one debt at the Mint before the next 500 fell due. In 1617, the cost of 22 oarsmen was 1200 ducats, which would have paid for two-thirds of the charcoal which the guild bought the previous year at prices already herniating with tax. A debt of 1000 ducats taken out in 1592 had still to be repaid in 1625. Another loan, this time of 400 ducats, was taken out to placate the first creditor, but further extraordinary fees would still have to be levied on members. By 1617, the bakers had debts of 1100 ducats despite an annual tax of one ducat on each shop. In the same year the fruiterers borrowed 2000 ducats to pay for *galeotti*. A previous loan of 500 ducats had to be used to pay off outstanding interest, and 300 ducats a year would have to be raised from members.[41]

The government's insistence on demarcation, and the weakening of the *scuole delle arti* as associations in which all members were, in principle, equal, set merchants and craftsmen apart and at odds. The fluid boundary between tradesmen and traders, hardening in the 1590s, crystallised further in the early 1600s. In 1606, the wine merchants asked for a reduction in their quota and an end to personal service. They could not afford such an imposition — financially or socially — as well as paying for 'the education of our children in the liberal arts in order that they should do honour to the state'. The leather merchants, 'held in some esteem' and of 'good name and credit' are 'somewhat disturbed to hear that for the 13 *galeotti* imposed on us, Your Illustrious Lordships intend to put us on the same footing as boatmen, odd jobbers and other manual trades of no standing'. The city's six gold merchants would, of course, not wish to be relieved of the 'yoke of service to our Prince', but they wish to petition separately, and not to be associated with underling beaters and twisters: 'we have nothing to do with their *scuola*'. The wood merchants do not wish to face a ballot or enjoy 'terms which are inferior, or the practices of ferrymen and other mechanicals'. Cotton merchants discount 'unhappy wretches like apprentices and journeymen' from their membership. The grain sellers insist that 'apprentices and unskilled workers' swell their numbers misleadingly 'for they're here, there and everywhere'. The tanners, on the other hand, based their petition on the exploitations of 'those most hard and cruel adversaries of ours, the merchants'.[42]

Some guilds were so loosely defined that they were not registered with the government. Denunciations of unauthorised professional groups were couched in terms of how many oarsmen they might be worth. In 1609, four allegedly illegal guilds were reported — chandlers, beadmakers, sugar refiners and soapmakers — and the informant asked for no less than eight boat station licences in return for exposing them. Sometimes, the accusations of individuals were angrily rebuffed. The ferrymen at the station at San Felise resented the secret denunciation lodged against them 'with mortal damage and prejudice against us poor sailors already committed to years of public service'. On the same day, the boatmen at Santa Sofia rounded on an informer, himself an illegal licence-holder despised by other members, 'we have earned our licences by paying out money and by sweating blood, some of us by risking our lives as oarsmen in public service'.[43]

What such service might entail can be glimpsed in the narrower focus of individual distress. There were numerous pleas of hardship, the most poignant that of Millia, widow of Benedetto di Iseppo. In 1606, Benedetto had had to sell 'all that we unfortunates had' in order to send an oarsman to the galleys in his stead: he was too sick to go in person. In order to find someone willing to go, a bonus of 10 lire a month had to be offered. In 1610, Benedetto's ferry licence had been sold at public auction even though it should have passed to his son. Without husband, father or ferry licence to earn money, how is the galleyman to be paid off? Gasparo de Tonin's widow lamented that her husband 'unable, unlike others, to meet his obligation with money, promptly met it with his body'. On his discharge, he returned home a sick man, and although he escaped death for a while 'our ruin was two-fold because he was always ill and having to be cared for'.[44]

In 1610–12, the cases of individual and collective hardship produced a reaction against taxation which sits oddly with the myth of the serene and tranquil republic which was beginning to catch the European imagination. Increasingly, guild protest addressed itself to the state's demands. In 1610, the boat station at Mirano was denounced for concealing the true number of its members. The guild insisted that untaxed licences had always existed 'to earn bread for poor boatmen'. The ferrymen did not expect to be taxed after having served in the fleet:

> If members have given their own blood in public service, that was not done in order that at every turn they should feel a hand in their purse, snatching at what they'd earned with the sweat of their brows.

The guilds' loyalty to the Doge — and it is the Prince himself who is identified rather than the republic — is not to be questioned, but loyalty has its limits. In 1610, the straw-weavers grumbled that members have too many obligations: 'to the Water

Board, and the tax on boats, and high rents, and now this thing we're not supposed to notice' (a sour reference to the so-called *tansa insensibile*). In 1611, there was a string of such protests. The levy on the barbers was 'quite certainly a burden exceeding our capabilities'. The tax on the beadmakers 'afflicts and grieves us mortally'. The coopers protest that 'when you see that large numbers of poor men like us are continually in public service in ships, at the Arsenal and at the Office of Wine and Oil, a quota of 44 oarsmen is oppressive'. The water-carriers point out that labour services are already a nuisance, for they cannot work in the rain, but when business picks up, 'then the Board of Health threatens us with punishment unless we transport a hundred barges of water without payment'. The couriers feel that their quota of 30 is 'to tell the truth, unfitting'. The cheese-sellers, who are supposed to send 36 oarsmen, see this number 'exceeding by a long way our capabilities . . . we say respectfully that this is a mistake'. Both the cloth tenterers and the bakers describe the levy as 'unbearable', the turners are 'at the height of desperation'. Boatmen from the mainland also remonstrate vigorously. The bargemen on the Padua run said that an allocation of 79 oarsmen on 79 members was 'a thing which cannot be tolerated'. From Rovigo, the boatmen protested against the 'new obligation and yoke which is no more to be suffered'. The boats at Este, already carrying hemp, munitions and soldiers for the state, resist the intolerable level of additional taxation. From Moncelese came the complaint that supplying eight galleymen 'would assuredly put every man jack of us in a desperate state and make us abandon our homes'. And the new strain in the relations between the guilds and the government is epitomised in the rough eloquence of the boatmen at Portogruaro. Already, members have been forced to work as sailors on wine barges and the like in order to raise the required tax. 'We were forced to put 700 ducats in the Mint, payable over ten years: those ten years are now up, but it just goes on for ever.'[45] What did this protest amount to, and how much weight did it carry?

The government backs down

In 1610, the government demanded 6577 oarsmen from the guilds. In 1612, the figure was reduced to 4746, a cut of about 28 per cent. In 1611, the quotas initially scribbled on surviving guild petitions were cut by exactly the same proportion.

Table 6.1: *The reduction of the levy in 1611*

guild	assessments		guild	assessments	
	1	2		1	2
turners	16	14	potters	36	24
bakers	60	52	basketmakers	20	17
tanners	40	30	lumber merchants	30	15
cratemakers	40	33	couriers	8	2
boatmen	20	15	water carriers	20	19
wood haulers	40	30	coopers	44	10
cloth tenterers	12	8	gold thread makers	20	16
grain weighers	17	15	bead-makers	40	12
cheese-sellers	36	30	barbers	70	60
goldleaf beaters	15	10	butchers	36	25
grain and flour sellers	24	20	distillers	30	0
			gold merchants	2	2
cotton, linen, and canvas-sellers	30	24	leather merchants	13	13
			cloth shearers	90	86
coopers	36	30	beltmakers	12	8
			totals	857	620

source: see n. 30.

The new figures scribbled on the *suppliche* correspond to those compiled from other sources by Professor Rapp. It is clear that the petitions against the levy of 1610 resulted in a general downward revision of the government's estimates in 1612. The petitions of the *traghetti* seem to have been spectacularly successful: their obligation of 690 oarsmen was removed altogether.[46]

This was not the end of the conflict. As we have seen, the blacksmiths took great care to present a strong case against the imposition in 1612. The burden on the *Scuole Grandi* increased during an 'acute shortage of manpower' in 1617–18.[47] In the same year, the government increased the pressure on the guilds by forcibly closing the shops of recalcitrant *botteghieri*: 38 tailors had their shops sealed up for failing to pay the galley tax. In 1620 similar punishment was meted out to 16 basket-makers, 8 boat builders, 10 fruiterers, 24 smiths, 24 tanners, and 10 barbers.[48] Shops were units of enterprise, taxes shut shops. In 1626, the Senate tightened its control over guild finances, objecting to the wasteful habits of guild officers and making a concerted effort to turn the *scuole delle arti* into easily taxable units. The guilds' financial independence 'does great harm to members and to the public good when it is necessary that the state avail itself of those resources which the *scuole* are obliged to give when the reserve fleet has to be armed'.[49] All the same, the assessments never again rose to the figure put forward in 1610, and by the 1630s, the government was clearly backing down still further. After the plague of 1630, the size of the reserve fleet was reduced in 1633, and in 1639 the social barrier separating those who served in the fleet and those who were not expected to do so was, for the guilds, entirely removed. Their obligations became entirely financial. The Ottoman danger had receded, but the number of volunteers had also grown smaller. The magistrates acknowledged that the workforce could not afford to lose thousands of traders, and reserve crews were to be selected in the government's words, from 'foreigners, vagabonds and any guildsmen prepared to volunteer'.[50] This removed the artificial distinction between 'greater' and 'lesser' guilds created in 1596. The difference between those who served in person and those exempted proved temporary. In 1639 there was a return to the idea that the guilds were, at least in principle, equal. And as Professor Rapp has shown, the *arti* then continued to reorganise the workforce to cope with a period of economic contraction.[51]

The survival of the *arti medie* was a triumph for guild tradition, but it did not doom the Venetian economy to stagnation or decline. It marked a successful defence of a way of life which was commercially viable and politically effective. In economic terms, the guilds remained open-ended and elusive of rigid definition. Predictably, the guild which grew most in the seventeenth century was that of the mercers, who had been exempted from personal service in 1596. By 1660, there were as many mercers in the city as there were licence-holders on the ferry stations: 1243. As is plain from the evidence discussed elsewhere, the status of many mercers, none of whom was obliged to serve in person, was well below that of merchant traders in other guilds whose membership was expected to supply oarsmen rather than hire substitutes. It made no sense to exempt such a large guild when the status of members did not distinguish them greatly from other guilds, especially when the expansion of membership must be attributed to the guild's absorption of manpower from other sectors of the economy and not to an increase in the size of the workforce as a whole. In the course of the seventeenth century, the mercers' membership grew threefold, while the woollen industry's labour force fell by three-quarters.[52]

It was the government, then, which produced rigidity in the guild system, not the traditions of the guilds themselves. Those traditions were founded on the articulate defence of commercial enterprise. Personal freedom at work was incompatible with docile acceptance of the fisc's demands. The forcefulness with which the guilds presented their case drew strength from a robust culture and from the oldest of Venetian traditions: respect for the rule of law and for the decisions of the courts. The channels which made justice accessible to guildsmen in the thirteenth century were kept open in the seventeenth, partly by guild resistance to government demands. The guilds' recognition of the commercial base of the Venetian economy and their perception that justice was the keystone of the polity survived the assaults of Church and state. That survival may prove to have been one of the great sources of continuity and stability in the history of the Venetian Republic.

Some final comparative thoughts

The myth of Venice, the myth of the state renowned for its justice, the myth set out in the courtroom scene of the *Merchant of Venice* and in *Volpone*, greatly exaggerated the institutional stability of the Venetian polity and the manner in which power was exercised.[53] Paradoxically, the myth of Venice's uniqueness spread at a time when the republic was in the mainstream of European development.[54] The commentator Giovanni Botero argued that one of Venice's outstanding characteristics was its avoidance of the instabilities caused by political innovation. He made a strong connection between war and changes in the style of government, and implicitly made of Venice an exception. Victory was no longer to be won suddenly for nowadays 'war is dragged out as long as possible, and the object is not to smash, but to tire out, not to defeat, but to wear down',[55]

> to pay for it you use ordinary incomes, so it is necessary to find extraordinary sources which become ordinary, thus seeking to remedy one evil with a greater one, states fall from one disorder to another and eventually are ruined and lost.[56]

Botero recognised the threat to political and social order for 'innovation brings hatred, and the setting aside of ancient tradition cannot happen without resentment'.[57] His words seemed to reflect the experience of many parts of Europe where princes had stripped cities of their resources and where resentment of the fisc had burst into social violence. In France and in the Spanish monarchy, the solidarities of traditional society gave way to royal absolutism, in north Germany the princes reduced the independence of the Hanseatic towns.[58] From all this, Venice stood apart. Traiano Boccalini commented that Venice's capacity to cope with its international problems was yet another aspect of the city's uniqueness: 'it seemed very strange that the Senate of that commonwealth studied more and more the peace yet with great diligence and assiduity did perpetually prepare for war and that Armed Peace was only seen in the flourishing Venetian state.'[59]

The evidence examined in this chapter suggests that the creation of the *Milizia da Mar* and the extension of its activities in the later sixteenth and early seventeenth centuries were an important structural innovation which imposed a species of intendancy on the people of Venice. That change, prompted by the state's defence commitments, should be seen in relation to the increasingly princely style of Venetian government. From the fifteenth century onwards, there were signs that the sovereign medieval polity was taking on the features of monarchical absolutism. The ruling caste had long enjoyed an absolute power over society at large, a power most obviously expressed in their monopoly of executive office and in fiscal matters: loans were always forced and, within the city, there were no estates to be outflanked.[60] In the Middle Ages there had been a number of acknowledgements, however, of the transcendent breadth of the political community, the '*ben comun*'. Traditionally, a new Doge was presented to the populace with the words, 'This is your new Doge and it please you'. In 1423 'and it please you' was summarily dropped from the formula. The consent of the populace was no longer sought even symbolically. From 1462 onwards, all references to the 'Commune of the Venetians' disappeared from the Doge's oath. Thenceforward the state was referred to as *La Serenissima*.[61] At the same time, an increasingly princely authority was exercised over the mainland state, where subject cities were held in check by a standing army and by the cooperation of feudal aristocracies.[62] The Doge himself became a sovereign head of state and was sometimes a flamboyant *principe* rather than the sober head of a patrician republic. True, Francesco Foscari was deposed, but for his laziness in the business of government, not for his eagerness to become a tyrant.[63] In the course of the sixteenth century, the pivotal role of the Doge in government and in ceremonial became still more pronounced. 'A

Venetian prince may do as he pleases,' wrote Gierolemo Priuli in 1505.[64] When the Interdict was rebuffed a century later, it was the Doge's authority rather than that of the state alone which shielded 'republican liberty'. The Father Superior of the Jesuits was curtly informed that

> the Doge was absolute master and could ordain and dispose of the persons and goods of his subjects, and a prince of 1200 years' standing ought not to be so treated. The Republic was not so small as was thought: it depended immediately on God and upon no other: it was a sovereign state.[65]

The majesty of the Doge's office, enhanced by holders like Leonardo Loredan, Andrea Gritti, Marino Grimani, Leonardo Donà, and Nicolò Contarini, was also recognised from below.[66] It may be recalled that the guilds' *suppliche* acknowledged their loyalty and obligation to the prince. In 1609, a boxmaker called Bastian Grasso was involved in a demarcation dispute with the carpenters' guild after making some targets, which had been confiscated during the dispute. An official from the Arsenal had the confiscation lifted since the targets were needed for gunnery practice, and Bastian himself was released with a warning not to make any more targets. His justification for making them in the first place without being a member of the appropriate guild was that

> these targets were the Prince's business, as are other things needed at the Arsenal . . . I obeyed what the Prince commanded. And what's more, when some carving was done on the Bucintoro, the Prince got outsiders to do it, because he's master of whatever he chooses (*padron di quel li piase*).[67]

> *Quod principi placuit legis habet vigorem.*[68]

The fact remains however, that neither princely government nor the demands of the fisc excited armed resistance among the Venetian people. The uniqueness of Venice in the sixteenth and seventeenth centuries, as in the fourteenth, lay in its apparent immunity to rebellion in a world of conflict. Venice witnessed nothing more serious than one or two isolated riots by Arsenal workers and the legal disputes of guilds and government.[69] This is explicable in several ways. The first is that despite changes in the character and structure of the state, Venice was never ruled by a dynastic prince, and never developed a court or a swarm of venal office-holders, often the focus of resentment in other states.[70] Furthermore, in the city itself, the Venetian government did not have the alien character of a distant central or centralising power.[71] There is perhaps a parallel with London here. The city authorities were closely involved with the function of the state, and apart from 'Evil May Day', the apprentices' riot of 1517, and disputes in the cloth industry in the 1560s, and in 1675, the city was relatively peaceful. And like Venice, the English state attained political stability on the basis of the sovereign rule of law.[72] However, even a casual comparison of that sort makes the point that to compare 'Venice' with the experience of larger territorial states — 'England', 'France', 'Spain', 'the Empire' — would require careful examination of what happened in the Republic's subject cities on the mainland, a huge task which requires much more archival research. Until that work is done, one's conclusions can apply only to the city itself, isolated from the rural surroundings which could turn urban unrest into provincial rebellion.[73] And in the city there were obvious safeguards which were the products of conscious policy and of reason of state: careful regulation of the grain supply and the systematic encouragement of institutionalised philanthropy had an important prophylactic effect on urban social problems which elsewhere engendered violence.[74]

The evidence examined in this study suggests another reason for the stability of the city of Venice: the enduring versatility of its guild system. Those excluded from political power inhabited the world of shops where the small scale of enterprise could limit the impact of individual misfortune, where employment opportunities were more important than handouts, where the commercial ethic was pervasive. It was a world where associations of ordinary people moderated some of the desperate insecurity of pre-industrial life, and promoted economic and intellectual self-sufficiency within a framework of mutal dependence and brotherhood. On the whole, guildsmen were able to adapt to expansion and recession in economic life. Their traditions were most seriously threatened by a theocracy jealous of lay independence and by a government which extended the reason of state into cooperation with the Inquisition and into the gearing of society for war. Pointing out that commercial enterprise was faltering, and articulating their case through the traditional channels of appeal, the guilds succeeded in making the Venetian government change its mind. Commerce and justice were the foundations of the state. In the early seventeenth century the maintenance of these traditions was more important to the guilds than to a government concerned to prove that it had a place amongst Europe's princely states.[75]

The guilds' petitions may be set in the context of M. Braudel's 'comeback of the small state' in the early seventeenth century, and they give substance to Professor Tenenti's idea that the peculiarity of Venice lies in its survival in the early modern period as an essentially medieval polity.[76] One explanation for this 'comeback' or 'survival' in a world of upheaval is that the Venetian state acknowledged its limitations rather than insisting on an arrogation of further powers. In Venice, the guilds provided an underlying stability amid the vagaries of economic life, and checked the excesses of the city's sovereign institutions. In doing so they helped to create in the relations betwen state and society a symbiotic vitality belied by political decline and physical decay. In 1611, the Venetian government backed down. In 1639, it backed down still further, just as Europe as a whole entered its traumatic 'days of shaking'.[77]

In so far as the Venetian experience finds a parallel, one might point to the collective absolutism developed in the United Provinces, or by the English Parliament after 1640.[78] However, the closest analogy in terms of the survival of medieval corporativism is provided by the German *Ständestaat*, where 'the medieval commune and guild town persisted, accentuating its communitarian features'.[79] These features were obscured by the commotions of the Thirty Years' War, but in a town like Nördlingen, medieval solidarities and guild structures remained politically and economically active in the seventeenth century. The Thirty Years' War, cataclysmic as it was, did not destroy their viability: that was the task of later imperial wars. They, not traditional craft organisations, were the cause of economic decline.[80]

The distinctive features of absolutism were its sense of sovereignty and the exercise of reason of state, both of which widened the gap between state and society. Inadequate provision of relief in time of plague or famine, and excessive demands for men and money in time of war could be a source of turbulence. In Venice, the government's initiatives in the field of poor relief and its reduction of its demands on society for its war effort helped preserve a measure of stability in the relationship betwen society and the state.[81]

In his book *Della Ragion di Stato*, Giovanni Botero remarked that 'since the well-being of artificers depends on marketing their products and wares, they are of necessity friends of peace in which trade may flourish and commerce flow'.[82] He might have used Venice to illustrate his point. This book has sought to add a measure of everyday reality to the myth of Venice. It has also suggested that in understanding the decline of Venice, we may need to remove a few dimensions from the myth of progress. Guilds are useful observation posts from which to view grandiose processes such as 'capital accumulation' and 'state formation'. In medieval Venice, the guilds functioned in a precociously sovereign state and a highly commercialised economy. This unusual pattern of coexistence helps to explain why Venice can look modern in a medieval world, medieval in a modern one, and may have been part of Venice's insulation against violent change.

Historians occasionally point out that the intervention of the state in social life has not always been beneficial.[83] Yet state intervention against guilds is still generally assumed to have removed obstacles to progress, whilst their survival could only mean 'backwardness'. In seventeenth-century England, textiles, metalwork and mining developed without guild interference. In France, textile production benefited from the *Verlagssystem* which bypassed the guilds: when the corporations were strengthened or extended, they merely became integral parts of the ossifying privilege system of the Ancien Régime.[84]

In the light of the Venetian experience, we might now ask whether guild opposition to the innovations of the state was merely the instinctive defence of practices long outmoded. In Venice, the guilds accepted absolute authority in so far as it meant the sovereign rule of law administered by a clearly defined political establishment. But in 1611, they resisted absolute authority in so far as it meant the arbitrary imposition of obligations dictated by reason of state. In the final analysis, the guilds of Venice, and perhaps guilds in other cities, are best understood as an illustration of what Machiavelli said in the ninth chapter of *The Prince* about the aspirations of ordinary people in a constitutional principality:

> the people are more honest in their intentions than the nobles are, because the latter want to oppress the people, whereas they want only not to be oppressed.

Notes

1. J. R. Strayer, *On the Medieval Origins of the Modern State* (Princeton, N.J. 1970), esp. pp. 7–9.

2. G. Parker, *Europe in Crisis, 1598–1648* (London, 1979), pp. 66–75; J. R. Hale, *War and Society in Renaissance Europe, 1450–1620* (London, 1985); A. Corvisier, *Armies and Societies in Europe, 1494–1789,* trans. A. T. Siddall (Bloomington, Ind., 1979), pp. 63–130; P. Anderson, *Lineages of the Absolutist State* (London, 1974), pp. 29–42; P. Zagorin, *Rebels and Rulers, 1500–1660*, 2 vols. (Cambridge, 1982), vol. 1, pp. 87–121.

3. Hale, *War and Society*, p. 238, and in general, pp. 232–52.

4. G. Contareno, *The Commonwealth and Government of Venice*, trans. L. Lewkenor (1599, facs. edn. Amsterdam, 1970); F. Gaeta, 'Alcune considerazioni sul mito di Venezia', *Bibliothèque d'Humanisme et Renaissance*, vol. 23 (1961) pp. 58–76; W. J. Bouwsma, *Venice and the Defense of Republican Liberty: Renaissance Values in the Age of the Counter-Reformation* (Berkeley and Los Angeles, 1968), pp. 52–94; R. G. Finlay, *Politics in Renaissance Venice* (London, 1980), pp. 27–36; E. Muir, *Civic Ritual in Renaissance Venice* (Princeton, N.J., 1981), pp. 13–54; Z. S. Fink, *The Classical Republicans: An Essay in the Recovery of a Pattern of Thought in 17th-century England* (Evanston, Ill., 1945), pp. 28–51.

5. See especially, B. S. Pullan, *Rich and Poor in Renaissance Venice: The Social Institutions of a Catholic State* (Oxford, 1971); A. Ventura, *Nobiltà e popolo nella società veneta del '400 e '500* (Bari, 1964); M. Mallett and J. R. Hale, *The Military Organisation of a Renaissance State: Venice, c. 1400–1617* (Cambridge, 1984); G. Cozzi, *Repubblica di Venezia e stati italiani* (Turin, 1982), pp. 81–216.

6. B. S. Pullan, *A History of Early Renaissance Italy* (London, 1973), p. 301; D. Wootton, *Paolo Sarpi: Between Renaissance and Enlightenment* (Cambridge, 1983), pp. 5–6, 113–17.

7. Mallett and Hale, *Military Organisation*, pp. 105–52, 213–20, 409–84.

8. J. F. Guilmartin, *Gunpowder and Galleys: Changing Technology and Mediterranean War at Sea in the 16th Century* (Cambridge, 1974), p. 22.

9. F. Braudel, *The Mediterranean and the Mediterranean World in the Age of Philip II,* trans. S. Reynolds, 2 vols. (London, 1974), vol. 2, p. 879; A. Tenenti, *Piracy and the Decline of Venice, 1580–1615*, trans. B. S. and J. Pullan (London, 1967), pp. 150–1; R. Romano, 'Economic Aspects of the Construction of Warships', in B. S. Pullan (ed.), *Crisis and Change in the Venetian Economy* (London, 1968), p. 82.

10. F. C. Lane, 'Wages and Recruitment of Venetian Galeotti, 1470–1580', *SV*, new ser., vol. 6 (1982), p. 17. The army was also having to expand; see J. R. Hale, 'From Peacetime Establishment to Fighting Machine: The Venetian Army and the War of Cyprus and Lepanto', in *Il Mediterraneo nella seconda metà del '500 alla luce di Lepanto* (Florence, 1974), pp. 163–84.

11. G. Parker, 'Lepanto (1571): The Costs of Victory', in his *Spain and the Netherlands, 1559–1659: Ten Studies* (London, 1979), pp. 128–9.

12. Pullan, *Rich and Poor*, p. 324.

13. P. Pantera, *L'armata navale* (Rome, 1614), p. 136.

14. Guilmartin, *Gunpowder and Galleys*, p. 67; Lane, 'Galeotti', p. 21. See also J. R. Hale, 'Men and Weapons: The Fighting Potential of 16th-century Venetian Galleys', *War and Society*, vol. 1 (1975), pp. 1–23.

15. MM, b. 251, *decreti del senato in copia, 1519–1685*, doc. of 18 September 1537; C. da Canale, *Della milizia marittima*, ed. M. Nani Mocenigo (Rome, 1930); A. Tenenti, *Cristoforo da Canal: la marine vénitienne avant Lépante* (Paris, 1962); Lane, 'Galeotti', pp. 30–1.

16. F. C. Lane, *Venice: A Maritime Republic* (Baltimore, Md., 1975), p. 368; idem, 'Galeotti', pp. 30, 33; Da Canale, *Milizia marittima*, pp. 47, 157, 175.

17. Quoted in Ph. Braunstein and R. Delort, *Venise: portrait historique d'une cité* (Paris, 1971), p. 113.

18. Lane, 'Galeotti', pp. 32, 37–8.

19. Lane, *Venice*, p. 367.

20. W. Thomas, *The History of Italy (1549)*, ed. G. Parkes (Ithaca, N. Y., 1963), p. 67.

21. MM, b. 382, *registro continente ordini, riferte, ecc. relative ai debitori delle arti (libro lungo), 1617–21.*

22. D. di Chinazzo, *Cronica de la guera da veniciani e zenovesi*, ed. V. Lazzarini (Venice, 1958), p. 71.

23. Lane, 'Galeotti', pp. 38, 41; Pullan, *Rich and Poor*, pp. 152–3.

24. B. Pullan, 'Wage-Earners and the Venetian Economy, 1550–1630', in idem (ed.), *Crisis and Change*, p. 159.

25. Quoted in Arti, b. 501, *sartori, capitoli e parti, 1492–1683*, fol. 89v.

26. Arti, b. 7, *barcaruoli, mariegola, 1451–1767*, fol. 32v; b. 11, *boccaleri, mariegola, 1300–1804*, fol. 109r.

27. GV, ser. xv, *parti e capitoli*, b. 143, filza 130, *cimadori da panni, parti, 1596–1791*, docs. of 29 October 1590, 31 December 1593, 17 May 1594, 20 January 1604, 9 October 1594.

28. Pullan, *Rich and Poor*, p. 137.

29. Ibid., p. 156.

30. MM, b. 723, *suppliche delle arti e per libertà di traghetti della Dominante e fuori*, 31 March 1607, Scuola Grande di San Marco.

31. Arti, b. 501, *capitoli e parti*, fols. 91v, 94r.

32. GV, ser. xv, *parti e capitoli*, b. 188, filza 197, *mercanti da cordoani, parti, 1592–1715*, doc. of 3 April 1592. Cf. above, p. 6.

33. GV, ser. ii, *terminazioni*, b. 23, filza 17, *filza di terminazioni ed atti delle conferenza e del collegio delle arti, 1528–1780*, doc. dated '1597'.

34. MM, b. 722, *filza di suppliche, scritture etc. delle arti e scuole per le quote di galeotti*, doc. of 16 November 1594.

35. Arti, b. 313, *marzeri, capitolare, 1595–1797*, fols. 1r–v.

36. MM, b. 723, *suppliche;* R. T. Rapp, *Industry and Economic Decline in 17th-century Venice* (Cambridge, Mass., 1976), pp. 70–7.

37. MM, b. 723, *suppliche*, of 22 January 1610 (aqua di vita); 26 May 1611 (cristalleri et paternostreri); 23 February 1611 (barileri); 5 May 1612 (forneri). On the smiths, see Arti, b. 128, *fabbri, atti diversi, 1600–29*, doc. of '1612'. Also MM, b. 722, *filza di suppliche*, of 24 March 1612 (chiovaroli); 23 February 1611 (barche d'Este).

38. Arti, b. 128, *atti diversi*, fasc. 242.

39. Ibid., doc. marked 27 January 1612.

40. MM, b. 723, *suppliche*, of 19 February 1610 (beccheri); 26 May

1611 (tiraoro et battioro); 30 June 1611 (centurieri); 23 February 1611 (barileri); 17 March 1612 (biavaroli); 7 April 1612 (casselleri); 5 May 1612 (tornidori); 23 February 1611 (barche d'Este); 15 March 1611 (sanseri); 30 June 1611 (mercanti di legname); 9 June 1611 (conzacurami); 30 June 1611 (cesteri); 5 May 1612 (forneri); 30 July 1611 (boccaleri).

41. MM, b. 251, *decreti del senato*, proclamation of 25 November 1595; MM, b. 723, *suppliche*, of 14 February 1611 (pittori); Arti, b. 128, *atti diversi*, docs. of 1608, 5 May 1617, 26 May 1625; Arti, b. 152, *forneri*, *atti diversi, 1447–1797*, doc. of 4 October 1617; GV, ser. xv, *parti e capitoli*, b. 153, filza 194, *fruttaroli*, *parti*, *1490–1636*, doc. of 29 May 1617

42. MM, b. 723, *suppliche*, of 27 May 1606 (mercanti di vin); 27 March 1606 (mercanti da cordoani); 31 July 1609 (mercanti di oro); 30 June 1611 (mercanti di legno); 17 March 1612 (biavaroli); 26 April 1612 (conzacurami).

43. Ibid., of 12 January 1609. For other examples see the suppliche of 5 March 1610, 28 May 1611, 7 June 1611, 18 February 1605.

44. Ibid., 26 July 1610; 10 November 1610.

45. Ibid., of 9 February 1610; 22 January 1610 (arte della stuore); 7 May 1611 (barbieri); 26 May 1611 (cristalleri et paternostreri); 28 May 1611 (botteri); 31 May 1611 (aquaroli); 11 June 1611 (corrieri); 22 March 1612 (casaroli); 24 March 1612 (chiovaroli); 5 May 1612 (forneri); 5 May 1612 (tornidori); 1 August 1606 (barche del portello di Pavoda); 30 June 1611 (barche di Rovigo); 23 February 1611 (barche d'Este); 13 March 1612 (barcaruoli da Moncelese); 3 April 1612 (barche da Portogruaro).

46. Rapp, *Industry*, p. 74.

47. Pullan, *Rich and Poor*, p. 155.

48. MM, b. 382, *ordini, riferte ecc.*, 8 March and 4 April 1618, 3 August 1620.

49. PC, b. 47, op. 122, *terminationi ed ordini per il buon governo delle scuole, ecc., 1520–1637*, p. 19.

50. Pullan, *Rich and Poor*, p. 151; F. Besta, *Bilanci generali della Repubblica di Venezia*, (Milan, 1912), p. 542.

51. Rapp, *Industry*, pp. 138–67.

52. Ibid., p. 103.

53. Cozzi, *Repubblica di Venezia*, pp. 81–144, or idem, 'Authority and the Law in Renaissance Venice', in J. R. Hale (ed.), *Renaissance Venice* (London, 1974), pp. 293–345; R. H. Perkinson, '*Volpone* and the Reputation of Venetian Justice', *Modern Language Review*, vol. 35, no. 1 (1940), pp. 11–18.

54. Fink, *Classical Republicans*, pp. 28–51; R. Mousnier, 'The Exponents and Critics of Absolutism', in *NCMH*, vol. 4, pp. 104–31; Wootton, *Sarpi*, p. 6.

55. G. Botero, *Relatione della Repubblica venitiana con un discorso intorno allo stato della Chiesa* (Venice, 1605), fol. 20v.

56. Idem, *The Reason of State*, trans. D. and P. Waley, together with *The Greatness of Cities*, trans. R. Peterson (1606) (London, 1956), pp. 182–3.

57. Ibid., p. 51.

58. H. R. Trevor-Roper, *Religion, the Reformation and Social Change* (London, 1972), pp. 56–61; Zagorin, *Rebels and Rulers*, vol. 1, pp. 228–74;

F. L. Carsten, 'Medieval Democracy in the Brandenburg Towns and its Defeat in the 15th Century', in S. L. Thrupp (ed.), *Change in Medieval Society* (New York, 1964), pp. 297–308; Ph. Dollinger, *The German Hansa*, trans. D. S. Ault and S. H. Steinberg (London, 1970), pp. 328–9; H. Pirenne, *Early Democracies in the Low Countries: Urban Society and Political Conflict in the Middle Ages and the Renaissance*, trans. J. V. Sanders, intro. by J. H. Mundy (New York, 1963), pp. 214–38; D. M. Bueno de Mesquita, 'The Place of Despotism in Italian Politics', in J. R. Hale, R. Highfield and B. Smalley (eds.), *Europe in the Late Middle Ages* (London, 1970), pp. 301–31.

59. T. Boccalin, *I ragguagli di Parnasso: or, Advertisements from Parnassus*, trans. Henry, Earl of Monmouth (London 1657), p. 10; on Boccalini in general, see Wootton, *Sarpi*, pp. 74–6.

60. F. C. Lane, *Venice and History: The Collected Papers of Frederic C. Lane* (Baltimore, Md., 1966), p. 87.

61. Idem, *Venice*, pp. 252–3.

62. Ventura, *Nobiltà a popolo*; Cozzi, *Repubblica di Venezia*, pp. 261–92; Mallett and Hale, *Military Organisation*, p. 88; Trevor-Roper, *Religion*, p. 58; J. H. Shennan, *The Origins of the Modern European State, 1450–1725* (London, 1974), p. 32. For a regional example, see A. Tagliaferri, *Struttura e politica sociale in una communità veneta del '500* (*Udine*) (Milan, 1969), pp. 18–22; for an Italian comparison, see F. Gaeta, 'La naissance de l'état moderne en Italie: Milan ou Venise?', in *17e Colloque International de Tours: théorie et pratique politiques à la renaissance* (Paris, 1977), pp. 459–70; for the European context, see C. H. Wilson, *The Transformation of Europe 1558–1648* (London, 1976), pp. 66–89.

63. Finlay, *Politics in Renaissance Venice*, pp. 116–17.

64. Quoted ibid., p. 109: and see in general ibid., pp. 109–62; and D. S. Chambers, *The Imperial Age of Venice, 1380–1580* (London, 1970), pp. 86–93. On ceremony and the role of the Doge, see Muir, *Civic Ritual*, pp. 251–96.

65. P. Pirri (ed.), *L'interdetto di Venezia dal 1606 e i Gesuiti: silloge di documenti con introduzione* (Rome, 1959), p. 108.

66. In general, see A. da Mosto, *I Dogi di Venezia* (Milan, 1960). On Loredan's high-handedness, see Finlay, *Politics in Renaissance Venice*, pp. 77–9, 111–12; on Gritti's dismissal of the Great Council, ibid., p. 104, on his unprecedented step of conferring alone with a foreign ambassador, ibid., p. 113. On Gritti's prominent role in legal reform, see Cozzi, *Repubblica di Venezia*, pp. 293–312. On Grimani's courting of popular favour, see Muir, *Civic Ritual*, pp. 270, 286, 293, 296. On ducal politics around 1600, G. Cozzi, *Il Doge Nicolo Contarini: ricerche sul patriziato veneziano agli inizi del '600* (Venice and Rome, 1958).

67. Arti, b. 302, *marangoni*, *processi*, filza C, fol. 102r.

68. Mousnier, 'Exponents and Critics', p. 109.

69. B. S. Pullan, 'The Significance of Venice', *Bulletin of the John Rylands University Library of Manchester*, vol. 56 (1974), p. 446.

70. The limited market in offices is discussed in R. Mousnier, 'Le trafic des offices à Venise', *Revue Historique du Droit Français et Etranger*, ser. 4, vol. 30 (1952), pp. 552–66. On the absence of a court, Pullan, 'Significance of Venice', p. 451; Wootton, *Sarpi*, p. 6. On the court in Italy, see the penetrating essay by L. Martines, 'The Gentleman in

Renaissance Italy: Strains of Isolation in the Body Politic', in R. S. Kinsman (ed.), *The Darker Vision of the Renaissance: Beyond the Fields of Reason*, (Berkeley and Los Angeles, 1974), pp. 77–94; on the court as a focus of resentment in other European states, see Trevor–Roper, *Religion*, pp. 57, 61–70, 80–8; H. G. Koenigsberger, 'Republics and Courts in Italian and European Culture in the 16th and 17th Centuries', *PP*, no. 83 (1979), pp. 32–56.

71. Zagorin, *Rebels and Rulers*, vol. 1, pp. 87–121, 228–74. For a case history, see S. Haliczer, *The Comuneros of Castile: The Forging of a Revolution, 1475–1521* (Madison, Wis., 1981).

72. On 'Evil May Day', see G. Unwin, *The Gilds and Companies of London* (4th edn., London, 1963), pp. 247–9; on the 1560s, see G. D. Ramsay, 'Industrial Discontent in Early Elizabethan London: Clothworkers and Merchants Adventurer in Conflict', *London Journal*, vol. 1, no. 2 (1975), pp. 227–39. On seventeenth-century disturbances, see S. R. Smith, 'Almost Revolutionaries: The London Apprentices during the Civil Wars', *Huntington Library Quarterly*, vol. 42, no. 4 (1979), pp. 313–28; R. M. Dunn, 'The London Weavers' Riot of 1675', *Guildhall Studies*, vol. 1, no. 1 (1973), pp. 13–23. On the legal framework of the Tudor state, see G. R. Elton, 'The Rule of Law in 16th-century England', in his *Studies in Tudor and Stuart Politics and Government*, 3 vols. (Cambridge, 1974–83), vol 1, pp. 260–85.

73. Zagorin, *Rebels and Rulers*, vol. 1, pp. 233–4.

74. Pullan, 'Significance of Venice', p. 459; idem, 'Poverty, Charity and Reason of State: Some Venetian Examples', *SV*, vol. 2 (1960), pp. 17–60; idem, *Rich and Poor*, pp. 216–422, 641–2. See also R. S. Lopez, 'Venice and Genoa: Two Styles, One Success', *Diogenes*, no. 71 (1970), pp. 39–47.

75. Wootton, *Sarpi*, pp. 5–6, 74–6, 115–17.

76. Braudel, *The Mediterranean*, vol 2, pp. 701–4; Tenenti, *Cristoforo da Canal*, p. 99. For some astute suggestions as to how guilds acted as pressure groups and helped to preserve the representative principle, see S. J. Woolf, 'The Problem of Representation in the Post-Renaissance Venetian State', in *Liber Memorialis Antonio Era: Studies presented to the International Commission for the History of Representative and Parliamentary Insitutions, 26* (UNESCO, Cagliari and Brussels, 1961 and 1963), p. 75.

77. Trevor-Roper, *Religion*, p. 46.

78. E. H. Kossmann, 'The Singularity of Absolutism', in R. Hatton (ed.), *Louis XIV and Absolutism* (London, 1976), pp. 13–16; Mousnier, 'Exponents and Critics', p. 127.

79. A. Black, *Guilds and Civil Society in European Political Thought from the 12th Century to the Present* (London, 1984), p. 144.

80. C. R. Friedrichs, *Urban Society in an Age of War: Nördlingen, 1580–1720* (Princeton, N. J., 1979), p. 297.

81. Mousnier, 'Exponents and Critics', p. 104; Kossmann, 'Absolutism', p. 10.

82. Botero, *Reason of State*, p. 101.

83. E.g. C. H. Wilson, 'Taxation and the Decline of Empires: An Unfashionable Theme', in his *Economic History and the Historian: Collected Essays* (London, 1969), pp. 114–27. I am grateful to Professor Geoffrey Parker for this reference; J. H. Elliott, 'Revolution and Continuity in

Early Modern Europe', in G. Parker and L. M. Smith (eds.), *The General Crisis of the 17th Century* (London, 1978), p. 130; B. S. Pullan, 'The Roles of the State and the Town in the General Crisis of the 1590s', in P. Clark (ed.), *The European Crisis of the 1590s: Essays in Comparative History*, (London, 1985), p. 286.

84. E.g. C. H. Wilson, *England's Apprenticeship, 1603–1763* (London, 1965), p. 136; P. Deyon, 'Manufacturing Industries in 17th-century France', in Hatton (ed.), *Louis XIV and Absolutism*, pp. 226–42; P. Goubert, *The Ancien Régime: French Society, 1600–1750*, trans. S. Cox (London, 1973), pp. 211–22.

Appendix I:
The Sestieri of Venice: Churches, Scuole, Altars *c.*1250–*c.*1650

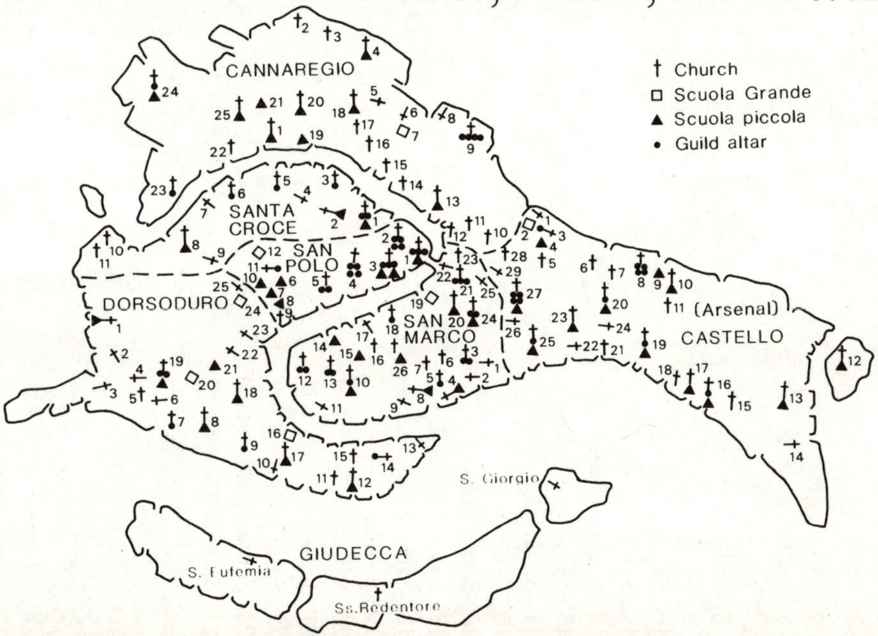

sources: Based on G. Perocco and A. Salvadori, *Civiltà di Venezia* 3 vols. (Venice, n.d.) vol 2, p.741: G. Lorinzetti Venice and its Lagoon trans. J. Guthrie (Trieste, 1961); archivil references

Key:

SESTIER DI CANNAREGIO

1. San Lunardo (scuola di San Lunardo)
2. San Bonaventura
3. Sant'Alvise
4. Santa Maria dell'Orto (scuola di San Cristofalo dei Mercanti)
5. San Marziale.
6. Santa Maria della Misericordia
7. Scuola Grande della Misericordia
8. Santa Caterina
9. Gesuiti (altars for tailors, bakers, furriers, coopers)
10. Santa Maria dei Mircacoli
11. San Canciano
12. San Zuan Grisostomo
13. Santi Apostoli (scuola di Santi Apostoli)
14. Santa Sofia
15. San Felice
16. Santa Fosca
17. Santa Maria Maddalena
18. Santa Maria dei Servi (barbers' *scuola*)
19. Scuola del Cristo
20. San Marcuola (bombardiers' *scuola*)
21. Jewish *scuola* and synagogues
22. San Geremia
23. Santa Lucia (altar for nobles)
24. San Giobbe (altar for boatmen, scuola di San Diego)
25. San Gierolemo (scuola di San Gierolemo)

SESTIER DI CASTELLO

1. San Lazaro dei Mendicanti
2. Scuola Grande di San Marco
3. San Zanipolo (altar for bookmen)
4. Scuola di Sant'Orsola
5. Ospedaletto
6. San Daniele
7. Santa Giustina
8. San Francesco della Vigna (altars for cabinetmakers, caulkers, crystal-makers, the Blessed Virgin)

9. Scuola di San Pasquale Baylon
10. Santa Maria della Celestia (scuola della Celestia)
11. Santa Trinità
12. San Pietro di Castello (scuola di San Pietro)
13. Sant'Anna (scuola di Sant'Anna)
14. San Giuseppe
15. San Francesco di Paola
16. San Domenego (altar for caulkers, *scuola* of the Blessed Virgin)
17. San Niccolo di Bari (hospital for sailors)
18. San Biagio
19. San Martino (altar for hemp-spinners, scuola di Santa Chiara)
20. San Zuan in Bragora (altar for sand porters, scuola di San Giorgio dei Greci)
21. Pietà
22. San Zaccaria
23. San Giorgio degli Schiavoni (scuola degli Schiavoni)
24. Sant'Antonio
25. Sant'Apollonia (altar for linen sellers, scuola di Sant' Apollonia)
26. San Zuan Novo
27. Santa Maria Formosa (*scuola* of bombardiers, altars for orange sellers, fruiterers, to the Purification and San Giosafatte)
28. Santa Marina
29. San Lio

SESTIER DI SAN MARCO

1. San Teodoro
2. San Marco
3. San Filippo Giacomo (altars for barbers, bakers)
4. Santa Maria dell'Ascensione (*scuola* of the Blessed Virgin)
5. San Geminiano (altar for turners)
6. San Basso
7. San Gallo
8. San Moise (*scuola* of the blind)
9. Santa Maria Zobenigo
10. San Maurizio (altar for bakers, scuola degli Albanesi)
11. San Vitale
12. San Samuele (altars for builders, carpenters)

13. San Stefano (altars for wool merchants, caulkers)
14. Shoemakers' *scuola*
15. *Scuola* of cripples
16. Sant'Anzolo
17. San Benedetto
18. San Luca (altar for painters)
19. Scuola Grande di San Teodoro (mercers)
20. San Salvador (scuola di San Giacomo)
21. San Bortolomeo (altars for fustian weavers, cutlers, oarmakers)
22. San Severo
23. San Zuan Lateran
24. San Zulian (altars for mercers, combmakers, scuola del sacramento)
25. Santa Maria della Fava
26. San Fantin (scuola di San Fantin adjoining)

SESTIER DI SANTA CROCE

1. San Cassian (altars for coopers, innkeepers, *scuola* of the Blessed Virgin)
2. Santa Maria Mater Domini (*scuola* of the Blessed Virgin)
3. San Stae (altar for goldbeaters)
4. San Giacomo dell'Orio
5. San Zuan Degolà (altar for knife-grinders)
6. San Simeon Profeta (altar for wool-carders)
7. San Simeon Piccolo
8. Santa Croce (corporazione della Croce)
9. San Nicolo da Tolentino
10. Santa Chiara
11. Sant'Andrea della Zirada

SESTIER DI SAN POLO

1. San Giacomo di Rialto (altars for goldsmiths, spicers, caulkers, *scuola* of the Blessed Virgin)
2. San Zuan Elemosinario (altars for brokers, poulterers, Sant'Anna, furriers)
3. San Silvestro (altars for wine merchants, cabinetmakers, boatmen, scuole di Santi Alessandro e Vicenzo and di San Giuseppe)
4. Sant'Aponal (altars for stonemasons, almond sellers, apothecaries, and of the sacrament)

5. San Polo (altars for knitters, linen sellers)
6. Scuola della Passione
7. Scuola dei Milanesi
8. Shoemakers' *scuola*
9. San Toma
10. Scuola dei Fiorentini
11. Santa Maria Gloriosa dei Frari (altar for potters)
12. Scuola Grande di San Zuan Evangelista

SESTIER DI DORSODURO

1. Santa Maria Maggiore (*scuola* of the Blessed Virgin)
2. Santa Teresa
3. San Nicolo
4. Santa Marta
5. Anzolo Raffaele
6. San Sebastian
7. San Basegio (altar for pork butchers)
8. Ognisanti (*scuola* of brokers)
9. San Trovaso (altar for hemp spinners)
10. Gesuati
11. Incurabili
12. Spirito Santo (scuola del Spirito Santo)
13. Santa Maria della Salute
14. San Gregorio (altar for boatmen)
15. San Vio
16. Scuola Grande della Carità
17. Sant'Agnese (scuola del Corpo di Cristo)
18. San Barnaba (scuola di Sant'Agnese)
19. Santa Maria dei Carmini (altars for fishmongers, Sant'Alberto, scuola di San Liberale)
20. Scuola Grande dei Carmini (1767)
21. Furriers' *scuola*
22. Santa Margherita
23. San Pantalon
24. Scuola Grande di San Rocco
25. San Rocco

Appendix II: Membership of the Scuole According to Parish of Provenance

	scuole						
parish	S. Anna	Celestia	S. Cris.	Ss. Apost.	total	Sansov.	Visit.
S. Agnese	3	6	4	3	16	1800	3000
S. Agostino	—	—	22	2	24	700	650
S. Andrea	1	—	—	—	1	—	—
S. Alvise	3	—	—	—	3	—	—
S. Angelo	13	27	10	5	55	2400	2397
S. Anna	22	—	—	—	22	—	—
S. Antonino	—	—	2	—	2	—	700
S. Antonio	25	52	—	8	85	1200	—
S. Aponal	7	15	16	12	50	1900	1100
Ss.Apostoli	12	24	19	408	463	3300	3500
S. Barnabà	5	6	8	4	23	2200	2000
S. Basso	6	3	6	—	15	400	200
S. Benedetto	2	1	6	2	11	700	300
S. Biasio	7	7	3	1	18	350	500
S. Boldo	—	3	15	—	18	400	—
S. Bortolomeo	16	39	39	6	100	1000	1200
S. Cancian	11	14	11	28	64	2400	4500
S. Cassian	3	16	48	23	90	2500	2538
S. Caterina	—	—	1	5	6	—	—
S. Croce	1	5	9	2	17	2700	4000
S. Daniele	3	—	—	—	3	—	—

S. Domenico	9	—	—	—	9	—	—
S. Donado (Murano)	—	—	—	1	1	—	—
S. Eufemia (Giud.)	—	—	1	—	1	4300	5200
S. Fantin	2	5	2	2	11	500	200
S. Felice	2	8	18	30	58	1200	1000
Ss.Filippo e Giacomo	—	2	3	—	5	—	—
S. Fosca	2	5	32	5	44	2900	1000
S. Francesco della Vigna	2	2	—	—	4	—	—
S. Geminiano	7	31	2	2	42	1300	1400
S. Geremia	4	5	23	16	48	6600	10000
S. Giacomo dell' Orio	4	4	12	10	30	3000	6000
S. Giacomo di Rialto	1	—	—	—	1	—	—
S. Giovanni in Bragora	40	55	2	2	99	2300	2500
S. Giovanni del Tempio	2	1	—	—	3	—	—
S. Giovanni Decollato	1	5	5	1	12	—	688
S. Giovanni Evangelista	1	—	—	1	2	—	—
S. Giovanni di Rialto	—	—	1	4	5	—	—
S. Giovanni Grisostomo	10	8	14	17	49	900	800
S. Giovanni Novo	6	34	7	3	50	1600	2000
Ss.Giovanni e Paolo	—	2	1	3	6	—	—
S. Giuliano	23	64	16	7	110	2100	2000
S. Giustina	1	23	3	4	31	1300	1300
S. Gregorio	—	9	1	2	12	700	1700
S. Lazaro	1	—	—	—	1	—	—
S. Leonardo	—	3	9	3	15	500	600
S. Lio	24	26	27	6	83	1200	1183
S. Lorenzo	1	4	2	1	8	—	—
S. Luca	22	14	7	5	48	2000	4000
S. Lucia	—	—	2	1	3	—	700
S. Marco	13	8	3	1	25	—	—
S. Marcuola	11	11	52	29	103	8400	7000

S. Margherita	4	4	10	5	23	2000	2000
Madonna dell'Orto	—	—	9	—	9	—	—
S. Maria Assunta	—	—	—	2	2	—	—
S. Maria del Carmelo	—	—	1	—	1	—	—
S. Maria della Celestia	—	2	—	—	2	—	—
S. Maria Formosa	26	65	21	18	130	3700	3766
S. Maria del Giglio	9	21	7	4	41	1300	1267
S. Maria Maddalena	2	2	7	1	12	650	300
S. Maria Maggiore	—	—	—	1	1	—	—
S. Maria Mater Domini	1	2	8	1	12	800	700
S. Maria della Misericordia	—	—	1	—	1	—	—
S. Maria Nuova	6	16	10	31	63	—	900
S. Marina	19	43	18	25	105	2200	2000
S. Martino	46	77	6	1	130	2200	2000
S. Marziale	5	17	82	22	126	2900	4000
S. Matteo di Rialto	—	—	6	—	6	650	800
S. Maurizio	2	4	8	1	15	600	300
S. Moise	23	33	8	5	69	3300	3600
S. Nicolo dei Mendicoli	3	5	1	1	10	3500	3500
S. Pantaleone	5	10	20	—	35	3000	3000
S. Paternian	7	10	7	1	25	800	600
S. Pietro di Cast.	226	36	—	1	263	8000	12000
S. Polo	6	17	49	7	79	2200	2000
S. Pruovolo	9	25	1	1	36	—	1200
S. Raffaele	4	4	13	1	22	3200	4000
S. Salvatore	33	40	39	9	121	800	3000
S. Samuele	8	14	10	4	36	2000	—
S. Sebastiano	—	1	—	—	1	—	—
S. Severo	5	23	5	5	38	1300	1200
S. Silvestro	5	8	17	2	32	1600	1568
S. Simeon Grande	3	9	24	5	41	2700	3000

S. Simeon Piccolo	—	1	—	—	1	—	—
S. Sofia	7	10	14	101	132	2000	3000
S. Spirito	—	1	—	—	1	—	—
S. Stae	1	6	23	5	35	1300	1000
S. Stefano	—	—	—	1	1	—	1000
S. Stin	4	6	—	—	10	—	—
S. Tomà	4	11	8	3	26	1100	800
S. Trinità	26	104	4	2	136	2200	2300
S. Trovaso	2	13	8	—	23	2400	2500
S. Vio	—	6	2	1	9	1100	1000
S. Vitale	5	7	5	1	18	1150	1143
S. Zaccharia	—	3	—	3	6	—	—
'In Chastello'	18	—	—	—	18		
unidentified	36	66	436	348	886*		
total	889	1269	1352	1284	4794		
total local churches:	94						
parishes in each *scuola*:	72	74	74	70			

Note:

*In the other tables, this figure is 887, which includes the parishioner from San Donado on the island of Murano, a parish not covered by the sestieri but included in the alphabetical list presented here.

Appendix III: Notes on Currency and on the Venetian Calendar

1. Currency

All sums are expressed in ducats, lire and soldi, the lira used only as a money of account. The equivalents in the later sixteenth century were as follows:

1 ducat	=	L.6.4 soldi
1 lira	=	20 soldi
1 ducat	=	124 soldi

It must be emphasised that this can only be regarded as a basic guide to the intricacies of Venetian monetary history, which are best pursued in the following works:

F. C. Lane, and R. C. Mueller, *Money and Banking in Medieval and Renaissance Venice*, 2 vols. (Baltimore, Md., 1985–86).
N. Papadopoli-Aldobrandini, *Le monete di Venezia*, 4 vols. (Venice, 1893–1919).

2. The Venetian calendar

In Venice, the administrative year began on 1 March. In the text, dates are adjusted to the modern calendar, in the notes, the Venetian style is adhered to when reference is made to a documentary source.

Abbreviations

1. Manuscripts

All references to Venetian documents relate to the holdings of the Archivio di Stato unless otherwise stated.

The indices used within the Archive are abbreviated as follows:

Arti	Referred to in full throughout
Arte della Seta	" " " " "
GN	Giustizia Nova
GP	Giudici di Petizion
GV	Giustizia Vecchia
MM	Milizia da Mar
PC	Provveditori di Comun
SP	Scuole Piccole
SU	Sant'Uffizio

Details of these holdings may be consulted in A. da Mosto, *L'Archivio di Stato di Venezia*, 2 vols. (Rome, 1937–40). References to archival materials are elaborated as indicated below:

b.	busta
fasc.	fascicolo
filza	referred to in full throughout
op.	opuscolo
den.	denunciation
proc.	processo
test.	testimony

GHL refers to collections in the Guildhall, London.

2. Printed materials

The abbreviations used in the notes and bibliography are as follows:

Annales	*Annales, Economies, Sociétés, Civilisations*
ASI	*Archivio Storico Italiano*
AV	*Archivio Veneto*
CAV	G. Monticolo (ed.), *I capitolari delle arti veneziane sottoposte alla Giustizia e poi alla Giustizia Vecchia dalle origini al 1330*, 3 vols. (Rome, 1896–1914)
CEH	*Cambridge Economic History of Europe*, 7 vols. in 8 (Cambridge, 1941–78)
CSPV	*Calendar of State Papers and Manuscripts Relating to English Affairs, Existing in the Archives and Collections of Venice, and in other Libraries of Northern Italy*, ed. R. Brown *et al.* (London, 1864 onwards)
DMS	M. Sanudo, *I diarii*, ed. R. Fulin *et al.*, 58 vols. (Venice, 1879–1903)
EcHR	*Economic History Review*
JWCI	*Journal of the Warburg and Courtauld Institutes*
MSC	*Mallone Society Collections*
NAV	*Nuovo Archivio Veneto*
NCMH	*New Cambridge Modern History*, 14 vols. (Cambridge, 1957–79)
PP	*Past and Present*
RIS	*Rerum Italicarum Scriptores*, modern edition, 34 vols. (Città di Castello and elsewhere, 1900 onwards)
SV	*Studi Veneziani*
TRHS	*Transactions of the Royal Historical Society*

Bibliography

1. Primary sources

(a) Manuscripts

I — Archivio di Stato di Venezia

(i) Guild records

The archive of the *arti* is composed of the statutes and miscellaneous records of the *arti medie* of shopkeepers and craft guilds. There is surprisingly little material on textiles. I have used some 70 different files, which account for nearly all the guild documents available in the Archive for the period in question. The disputes listed under '*processi*' have yet to be systematically exploited: the random sample which I consulted suggested that these documents relate largely to eighteenth-century disputes. The findings of this book will probably be supplemented, modified and challenged on the basis of guild materials included in the holdings of the Museo Civico Correr.

(ii) The Giustizia Vecchia

This magistracy, which was responsible for the supervision of the guilds, has a large archive of documents which are arranged in an unusually well-organised manner. I have used in particular those in series 15, '*parti e capitoli*' — some 30 files of regulations and disputes affecting and involving various of the city's trades. The register of shop signs discussed in Chapter 3 is contained in series 9, '*costituti*'.

(iii) The confraternities

The records of the *scuole piccole* contain a number of useful statute books and 30 files were used in building the argument of Chapter 2.

(iv) The Commissioners of the Commune

The records of the Provveditori di Comun are very patchy indeed before the seventeenth century. However, the magistracy was charged with the supervision of *scuole* and with the regulation of the woollen industry (b.53 and 54). This material is cited in Chapter 3, along with a list of auctions of ferry stations (b.60, reg. 207). Much remains to be learned about the brotherhoods of Venice from a study of the *matricule scuole* (b.272–83) which show how *scuole* formed and reformed at different times in the course of the seventeenth century.

(v) The Silk guild

The *arte della seta* has its own archive (and its own magistracy: the Ufficio della Seta had its premises near San Zuan Grisostomo at Rialto). The evidence used here is drawn from two large collections of documents: the informative and much amended statute book (b.552) and a miscellaneous collection of chronicles and laws (b.553).

(vi) The Judges of Petition

The inventories contained in the records of this magistracy give valuable information on the material circumstances of guildsmen and artisans. I have pursued some 60 references, including those of Otis and Stefano Zarnesi discussed in Chapter 3. This collection could form the basis for a study of material life among ordinary Venetians: and it shows beyond all doubt how difficult it is to use occupational titles as a guide to status or wealth.

(vii) The Giustizia Nova

This magistracy was established in the thirteenth century to administer the marketing of foodstuffs. Very little material survives for the period before about 1600. Of that which does, there are two registers of documents (both in b.5) which list licences granted to people offering accommodation to visitors, and the names of people staying at different inns in the early sixteenth century. These registers were used to illustrate the importance of services in the metropolitan economy, especially during festivals (above, Chapter 4).

(viii) The Holy Office

A random selection of over 270 trials from about 60 files forms the basis of what is said in Chapter 5, where the strengths and weaknesses of this type of evidence are discussed in detail. Such records clearly offer a rich seam for future research on the material life and mentalities of the people of Venice.

(ix) The Milizia da Mar

This magistracy was set up in 1539 to administer the supply of naval personnel. I have consulted about 35 different items, most especially the *suppliche* in b.723, extensively used in Chapter 6. Much more information about everyday life in the city may yet be gleaned from the statute books of the boat stations housed at b.866 and following.

II — Biblioteca Marciana, Venice, Ms. It. cl. vii, 1571, 7642 (a collection of medieval legislation known as the '*Capitolare Antico*'.)

III — Guildhall, London

In preparing this book, I consulted some of the records of the London companies. Those which proved most useful were the Triumphs Accounts of the Haberdashers and Grocers, analysed in detail in Chapter 4. The absence of a major study of London's guilds to supplement that of Unwin remains one of the outstanding gaps in the field of early modern history.

(b) Printed sources

Besta, F., *Bilanci generali della Repubblica di Venezia* (Milan, 1912).
Boccalin, T., *I ragguagli di Parnasso: or, Advertisements from Parnassus*, trans. Henry, Earl of Monmouth (London, 1657).
Botero, G., *The Reason of State*, trans. D. and P. Waley, together with *The Greatness of Cities*, trans. R. Peterson (1606) (London, 1956).
—— *Relatione della Repubblica venitiana con un discorso intorno allo stato della Chiesa* (Venice, 1605).
Calendar of State Papers and Manuscripts Relating to English Affairs, existing in the Archives and Collections of Venice and in other Libraries of Northern Italy, ed. R. Brown *et al.* (London, 1864 onwards).
Caravia, A., *Il sogno dil Caravia* (Venice, 1541).
Carleton, D., *Dudley Carleton to John Chamberlain, 1603–24: Jacobean Letters*, ed. with an intro. by M. Lee, Jr (New Brunswick, N.J., 1972).
Casola, P., *Canon Pietro Casola's Pilgrimage to Jerusalem in the year 1494*, ed. and trans. M. M. Newett (Manchester, 1907).

Castiglione, B., *The Courtier*, trans. T. Hoby (1561, London, 1944).

Cessi, R. (ed.), *Gli statuti veneziani di Jacopo Tiepolo del 1242 e le loro glosse* (Venice, 1938).

Compagni, D., *Cronica*, ed. G. Luzzatto (Turin, 1968).

Contareno, G., *The Commonwealth and Government of Venice*, trans. L. Lewkenor (1599, facs. repr. Amsterdam, 1970).

Da Canal, M., *Les Estoires de Venise*, ed. A. Limentani (Florence, 1972).

Da Canale, C., *Della Milizia Marittima*, ed. M. Nani Mocenigo (Rome, 1930).

Dandolo, A., *Chronica per extensum descripta* and *Chronica breve* in *RIS*, vol. 12, part i (Bologna, 1938–40).

De Commynes, P., *Mémoires*, ed. J. Calmette, 3 vols. (Paris, 1925).

Descrittione della pompa funerale fatta nelle essequie del Ser.mo Sig. Cosimo de Medici (Florence, 1574).

Di Chinazzo, D., *Cronica de la guera da veniciani a zenovesi*, ed. V. Lazzarini (Venice, 1958).

Du Puys, R., *La tryumphante et solemnelle entrée* (1515, Bruges, 1850).

Dürer, A., *Tagebuch der Reise in die Niederlände* (Leipzig, n.d.).

Evelyn, J., *The Diary of John Evelyn from 1641 to 1705–6*, ed. W. Bray (London, 1889).

Eymerich, N. and Peña, F., *Le manuel des Inquisiteurs*, ed. and trans. L. Sala-Molins (Paris and The Hague, 1973).

Fonti sulle corporazioni artigiane del medio evo (*Deputazione Toscana di Storia Patria* (Florence, 1940 onwards).

Galaup de Chasteuil, J. de, *Discours sur les arcs triomphaux* (Aix, 1624).

Gaudenzi, A. (ed.), *Gli statuti delle società di Bolgna*, 2 vols. (Rome, 1889–96).

Gevaarts, C. and Rubens, P. P., *Pompa Introitus Ferdinandi Austriaci Hispaniarum Infantis* (Antwerp, 1641, facs. repr. Munich, 1971).

Grapheus, C., *Spectaculorum in susceptione Philippi* (Antwerp, 1550).

La magnifica et trumphale entrata del Christianiss. Re di Francia Henrico secondo (Lyons, 1549).

Luther, M., 'The Blessed Sacrament of the Holy and True Body of Christ, and the Brotherhoods (1519)', in *Works*, ed. J. Pelikan and H. T. Lehmann, 53 vols. (Philadelphia, Pa., 1955 onwards), vol. 35, pp. 45–75.

—— 'To the Christian Nobility of the German Nation on the Reformation of the Christian Estate (1520)', in the same edition, vol. 44, pp. 123–217.

Machiavelli, N., *The Prince*, trans. G. Bull (London, 1961).

—— *Florentine History*, trans. W. K. Marriott (London, 1909).

Mallone Society Collections III: A Calendar of Dramatic Records in the Books of the Livery Companies of London, 1485–1640, eds. D. J. Gordon and J. Robertson (Oxford, 1954).

Marchionne di Coppo Stefani, *Cronaca fiorentina*, in *RIS*, vol. 30 (Città di Castello, 1903).

Monticolo, G. (ed.), *Cronache veneziane antichissime* (Rome, 1890).

—— (ed.), *I capitolari delle arti veneziane sottoposte alla Giustizia e poi alla Giustizia Vecchia dalle origini al 1330* (*CAV*) 3 vols. (Rome, 1896–1914).

Pantera, P., *L'armata navale* (Rome, 1614).

Petrarch, F., *Letters from Petrarch*, selected and trans. M. Bishop (Bloomington, Ind., 1966).

Pirri, P. (ed.), *L'interdetto di Venezia del 1606 e i Gesuiti: silloge di documenti con introduzione* (Rome, 1959).

Platter, T., *Thomas Platter's Travels in England*, ed. C. Williams (London, 1937).

Porcacchi, T., *Le attioni d'Arrigo Terzo* (Venice, 1574).

Queller, D. and Swietek, F. (eds.), *Two Studies on Venetian Government* (Geneva, 1977).

Salter, F. R. (ed.), *Early Tracts on Poor Relief* (London, 1926).

Sansovino, F. and Stringa, G., *Venetia: città nobilissima et singolare* (Venice, 1663, facs. repr. Farnborough, 1968).

Sanudo, M., *I diarii*, ed. R. Fulin *et al.*, 58 vols. (Venice, 1879–1903).

—— *De origine, situ et magistratibus urbis venetae, ovvero la città di Venetia (1493–1530)*, ed. A. Carraciolo Aricò (Milan, 1980).

Thomas, W. *The History of Italy (1549)*, ed. G. Parkes (Ithaca, N.Y., 1963).

Villani, G. *Cronica. Con le continuazioni di Matteo e Filippo*, ed. G. Aquilecchia (Turin, 1979).

(c) Secondary works

Alberigo, G., 'Contributo alla storia delle confraternite dei disciplinati e della spiritualità laicale nei sec. 15 e 16', in the volume *Movimento dei disciplinati*, pp. 156–252.

Anderson, P., *Lineages of the Absolutist State* (London, 1974).

Anglo, S., *Spectacle, Pageantry and Early Tudor Policy* (Oxford, 1969).

Aubin, G., 'Bartolomäus Viatis: ein nürnberger Grosskaufmann', *Vierteljahrschrift für Sozial- und Wirtschaftsgeschichte*, vol. 33 (1940), pp. 145–57.

Aymard, M., *Venise, Raguse et le commerce du blé pendant la seconde moitié du 16e siècle* (Paris, 1966).

Baldo, V., *Alunni, maestri e scuole in venezia alla fine del 16 secolo* (Como, 1977).

Barbour, V., *Capitalism in Amsterdam in the 17th Century* (Baltimore, Md., 1950).

Baron, H., 'Religion and Politics in the German Imperial Cities during the Reformation', *English Historical Review*, vol. 52 (1937) pp. 405–27, 614–33.

Battara, P., 'Botteghe e pigioni nella Firenze del '500: un censimento industriale e commerciale all'epoca del granducato mediceo', *ASI* no. 95, vol. 2 (1937), pp. 3–28.

Bec, C., *Les marchands écrivains: affaires et humanisme à Florence, 1375–1434* (Paris and The Hague, 1967).

Becker, M. B., 'La esecuzione della legislatura contro le pratiche monopolistiche delle arti fiorentine alla metà del sec. 14', *ASI*, no. 117, disp. 1 (1959), pp. 8–28.

—— 'Church and State in Florence on the Eve of the Renaissance, 1343–82', *Speculum*, vol. 37, no. 4 (1962), pp. 509–27.

—— 'Florentine Popular Government, 1343–48', *Proceedings of the American Philosophical Society*, vol. 106 (1962), pp. 360–82.

—— 'A Study in Political Failure: the Florentine Magnates, 1280–1433', *Medieval Studies*, vol. 27 (1965), pp. 246–308.

—— 'Economic Change and the Emerging Florentine territorial State', *Studies in the Renaissance*, vol. 13 (1966), pp. 7–39.
—— *Florence in Transition to 1330*, 2 vols. (Baltimore, Md., 1967–68).
—— 'An Essay on the Quest for Identity in the Early Italian Renaissance', in Rowe and Stockdale (eds.) '*Florilegium Historiale*', pp. 296–308.
—— 'Heresy in Medieval and Renaissance Florence. A Comment', *PP*. no. 62 (1974), pp. 153–61.
—— 'Aspects of Lay Piety in Early Renaissance Florence', in Trinkhaus and Oberman (eds.), *Pursuit of Holiness*, pp. 177–98.
—— and Brucker, G., 'The Arti Minori in Florentine Politics, 1342–1378', *Medieval Studies*, vol. 18 (1956), pp. 246–308.
Beier, A. L., 'Social Problems in Elizabethan London', *Journal of Interdisciplinary History*, vol. 9, no. 2 (1978), pp. 203–21.
Beloch, K. J., 'La popolazione di Venezia nei sec. 16 e 17', *NAV*, new ser. vol. 3, part i (1902), pp. 5–49.
Beltrami, D., *Storia della popolazione di Venezia dalla fine del sec.16 alla caduta della Repubblica* (Padua, 1954).
Benedict, P., *Rouen during the Wars of Religion* (Cambridge, 1981).
Benzoni, G., *Venezia nell'età della Controriforma* (Milan, 1973).
Berengo, M., *Nobili e mercanti nella Lucca del '500* (Turin, 1965).
Bergeron, D., 'Venetian State Papers and English Civic Pageantry, 1558–1642', *Renaissance Quarterly*, vol. 23, no. 1 (1970), pp. 37–47.
—— *English Civic Pageantry, 1558–1642* (London, 1971).
Bergier, J.-F., *Genève et l'économie européenne de la renaissance* (Paris, 1963).
Berner, S. 'Florentine Society in the late 16th and early 17th Centuries', *Studies in the Renaissance*, vol. 18 (1971), pp. 203–46.
Besnard, P., *Protéstantisme et capitalisme: la controverse post-Wéberienne* (Paris, 1970).
Bindoff, S. T., 'The Greatness of Antwerp', *NCMH*, vol. 2, pp. 50–69.
Bini, T., *I Lucchesi a Venezia. Alcuni studi sopra i sec. 13 e 14* (Lucca, 1856).
Black, A., *Guilds and Civil Society in European Political Thought from the 12th Century to the Present* (London, 1984).
Borsook, E., 'Art and Politics at the Medici Court I: The Funeral of Cosimo I de' Medici', *Mitteilungen des Kunsthistorischen Institut in Florenz*, vol. 12, nos. 1–2 (1965), pp. 31–54.
Bossy, J., 'The Counter-Reformation and the People of Catholic Europe', *PP*, no. 47 (1970), pp. 51–70.
—— 'Blood and Baptism: Kinship, Community and Christianity in Western Europe from the 14th to the 17th Centuries', *Studies in Church History*, vol. 9 (1973), pp. 130–43.
—— 'The Social History of Confession', *TRHS*, ser. 5, vol. 25 (1975), pp. 21–38.
—— *Christianity in the West, 1400–1700* (Oxford, 1985).
Bouwsma, W. J., *Venice and the Defense of Republican Liberty: Renaissance Values in the Age of the Counter-Reformation* (Berkeley and Los Angeles, 1968).
Bowsky, W. M., *A Medieval Italian Commune: Siena under the Nine, 1287–1355* (Berkeley and Los Angeles, 1981).
Boxer, C. R., *The Dutch Seaborne Empire, 1600–1800* (London, 1965).
Brady, T. A., *Ruling Class, Regime and the Reformation at Strasbourg, 1520–55* (Leyden, 1978).

Braudel, F., 'La vita economica di Venezia nel sec.16', in *La civiltà veneziana del rinascimento* (Florence, 1958), pp. 83–102.

—— *The Mediterranean and the Mediterranean World in the Age of Philip II*, trans. S. Reynolds, 2 vols. (London, 1974).

—— *Civilisation and Capitalism, 15th–18th Centuries*, trans. S. Reynolds, 3 vols. (London, 1982), vol. 2, *The Wheels of Commerce*, vol. 3, *The Perspective of the World*.

—— and Spooner, F. 'Prices in Europe from 1450 to 1750', in *CEH*, vol. 4, pp. 374–486.

Braunstein, Ph., 'Le commerce du fer à Venise au 15e siècle', *SV*, vol. 8 (1966), pp. 267–302.

—— and Delort, R., *Venise: portrait historique d'une cité* (Paris, 1971).

Bridbury, A. R., *Medieval English Clothmaking: An Economic Survey* (London, 1982).

Broglio d'Ajano, R., 'L'industria della seta a Venezia', in C. M. Cipolla (ed.), *Storia dell'economia italiana* (Turin, 1959), pp. 209–62.

Brucker, G. A., 'The Ciompi Revolution', in Rubinstein (ed.), *Florentine Studies*, pp. 314–56.

Brulez, W., *Marchands flamands à Venise, 1 (1568–1605)* (Brussels, 1965).

—— 'Le commerce international des Pays-Bas au 16e siècle: essai d'appréciation quantitative', *Revue Belge de Philologie et d'Histoire*, vol. 46, no. 4 (1968), pp. 1205–21.

—— 'Bruges and Antwerp in the 15th and 16th Centuries: An Antithesis?', *Acta Historica Neerlandica*, vol. 6 (1973), pp. 1–26.

Brunetti, M., 'Venezia durante la peste del 1348', *Ateneo Veneto*, vol. 32, part i, fasc. 3 (1909), pp. 289–311, part ii, fasc. 1, pp. 5–42.

Bueno de Mesquita, D. M., 'The Place of Despotism in Italian Politics', in J. R. Hale, R. Highfield and B. Smalley (eds.), *Europe in the Late Middle Ages* (London, 1970), pp. 301–31.

Burckhardt, J., *The Civilisation of the Renaissance in Italy*, trans. S. G. C. Middlemore (Oxford and London, 1945).

Burke, P., *Venice and Amsterdam: A Study of 17th-century Élites* (London, 1974).

—— 'Popular Culture in 17th-century London', *London Journal*, vol. 3, no. 2 (1977), pp. 143–62.

—— *Popular Culture in Early Modern Europe, 1500–1800* (London, 1978).

—— 'Le carnaval de Venise: esquisse pour une histoire de longue durée', in P. Ariès and J.-C. Margolin (eds.), *Les jeux à la Renaissance* (Paris, 1982), pp. 55–63.

Carrère, C., *Barcelone: centre économique à l'époque des difficultés, 1380–1462*, 2 vols. (Paris and The Hague, 1967).

Carsten, F. L., 'Medieval Democracy in the Brandenburg Towns and its Defeat in the 15th Century', in S. L. Thrupp (ed.), *Change in Medieval Society* (New York, 1964), pp. 297–308.

Cecchetti, B., 'I nobili e il popolo di Venezia', *AV*, vol. 3, part ii (1872), pp. 421–46.

—— 'Le industrie in venezia nel sec.13', *AV*, vol. 4, part ii (1872), pp. 211–57.

—— 'Il vitto dei veneziani nel sec.14', *AV*, vol. 29 (1885), part ii, pp. 235–304, vol. 30 (1885), part i, pp. 27–96, part ii, pp. 279– 333.

Chambers, D. S., *The Imperial Age of Venice, 1380–1580* (London, 1970).

Chill, E., 'Religion and Mendicity in 17th-century France', *International Review of Social History*, vol. 7 (1962), pp. 400–26.

Chojnacki, S., 'Crime, Punishment and the '300 Venetian State', in Martines (ed.), *Violence and Civil Disorder*, pp. 184–228.

Chrisman, M. U., *Lay Culture, Learned Culture: Books and Social Change in Strasbourg, 1480–1599* (New Haven, Ct., 1982).

Cipolla, C. M., 'The Economic Decline of Italy', in Pullan (ed.), *Crisis and Change*, pp. 127–44.

—— *Before the Industrial Revolution: European Economy and Society, c.1000–c.1700* (London, 1976).

Clark, P. and Slack, P., *English Towns in Transition, 1500–1700* (Oxford, 1976).

Clark, P. (ed.), *The Early Modern Town: A Reader* (London, 1976).

—— (ed.), *The European Crisis of the 1590s: Essays in Comparative History* (London, 1985).

Cochrane, E. (ed.), *The Late Italian Renaissance, 1525–1630* (London, 1970).

Cohn, N., *The Pursuit of the Millennium* (London, 1970).

Cohn, S. K., *The Labouring Classes in Renaissance Florence* (New York, 1980).

Coleman, D. C., 'Labour in the English Economy of the 17th Century', *EcHR*, 2 ser., vol. 8, no. 3 (1956), pp. 280–95.

—— *Industry in Tudor and Stuart England* (London, 1975).

Contento, A., 'Il censimento della popolazione sotto la Repubblica veneta', *NAV*, vol. 19, part i (1900), pp. 5–42, part ii, vol. 20 (1900) part i, pp. 5–96, part ii pp. 171–235.

Coornaert, E., 'Des confrèries carolingiens aux gildes marchandes', *Mélanges d'Histoire Sociale*, vol. 2 (1942), pp. 5–21.

—— 'Les gildes mediévales (5e–14e siècles): definition– évolution', *Revue Historique*, vol. 199 (1947), pp. 22–55, 208–43.

—— 'Draperies rurales, draperies urbaines: l'évolution de l'industrie flamande au moyen age et au 16e siècle', *Revue Belge de Philologie et d'Histoire*, vol. 28, no. 1 (1950), pp. 59–96.

Corte, G. and Da Silva, J.-G., 'Note sur la production de la soie à Florence au 15e siècle', *Annales*, vol. 20, no. 1 (1965), pp. 309– 11.

Corvisier, A., *Armies and Societies in Europe, 1494–1789*, trans. A. T. Siddall (Bloomington, Ind., 1979).

Cozzi, G., *Il Doge Nicolo Contarini: ricerche sul patriziato veneziano agli inizi del '600* (Venice and Rome, 1958).

—— 'Authority and the Law in Renaissance Venice', in Hale (ed.), *Renaissance Venice*, pp. 293–345.

—— *Repubblica di Venezia e stati italiani* (Turin, 1982).

Cracco, G., *Società e stato nel medioevo veneziano* (Florence, 1967).

Da Mosto, A., *L'Archivio di Stato di Venezia*, 2 vols. (Rome, 1937–40).

—— *I Dogi di Venezia* (Milan, 1960).

Davis, C. T., 'Education in Dante's Florence', *Speculum*, vol. 40 (1965), pp. 415–35.

Davis, J. C., *The Decline of the Venetian Nobility as a Ruling Class* (Baltimore, Md., 1962).

Davis, N. Z., 'A Trade Union in 16th-century France', *EcHR*, 2 ser., vol. 19, no. 1 (1966), pp. 48–69.

—— 'Some Themes in Popular Religion', in Trinkhaus and Oberman (eds.), *The Pursuit of Holiness*, pp. 313–40.

—— *Society and Culture in Early Modern France* (London, 1975).

Delany, J. F., 'Mercy', in *The Catholic Encyclopedia*, 15 vols. (London, 1907–12), vol. 10, Mass-Newman, pp. 198–99.

De la Roncière, C. M., 'Pauvres et pauvreté à Florence au 14e siècle', in Mollat (ed.) *Etudes*, vol. 2, pp. 661–746.

—— *Prix et salaires à Florence au 14e siècle, 1280–1380* (Rome, 1982).

Delaruelle, E., 'La pietà popolare alla fine del medio evo', in *10° Congresso Internazionale di Scienze Storiche*, vol. 3 (Rome, 1955), pp. 515–42.

—— 'La spiritualité aux 14e et 15e siècles', *Cahiers d'Histoire Mondiale*, vol. 5, no. 1 (1959), pp. 59–71.

—— 'Les grandes processions de pénitents de 1349 et 1399', in the volume *Movimento dei disciplinati*, pp. 109–45.

Delort, R., 'Un aspect du commerce venitien au 15e siècle: Andrea Barbarigo et le commerce des fourrures, 1430–40', *Le Moyen Age*, vol. 71, no. 2 (1965), pp. 29–70.

Delumeau, J., *Vie économique et sociale de Rome dans la seconde moitié du 16e siècle*, 2 vols. (Paris, 1957–59).

—— *Catholicism between Luther and Voltaire*, trans. J. Moiser (London, 1977).

De Roover, R., *San Bernardino of Siena and Sant'Antonino of Florence: The two Great Economic Thinkers of the Middle Ages* (Boston, 1967).

—— 'Labour conditions in Florence around 1400: Theory, Policy and Reality', in Rubinstein (ed.), *Florentine Studies*, pp. 277–313.

—— 'A Florentine Firm of Cloth Manufacturers: Management and Organisation of a 16th-century Business', in his collected essays, *Business, Banking and Economic Thought in Late Medieval and Early Modern Europe* (Chicago, Ill., 1974), pp. 85–119.

Derville, A., 'Les draperies flamandes et artésiennes vers 1250–1350: quelques considérations critiques et problématiques', *Revue du Nord*, vol. 54, no. 215 (1972), pp. 353–70.

De Vries, J., *The Economy of Europe in an Age of Crisis, 1600–1750* (Cambridge, 1976).

Dickens, A. G. (ed.), *The Courts of Europe: Politics, Patronage and Culture, 1400–1800* (London, 1977).

Dollinger, Ph., *The German Hansa*, trans. D. S. Ault and S. H. Steinberg (London, 1970).

Doren, A., *Die Florentiner Wollentuchindustrie* (Stuttgart, 1901).

—— *Le arti fiorentine*, trans. G. B. Klein, 2 vols. (Florence, 1940–48).

Duby, G., 'Medieval Society', in his collected essays *The Chivalrous Society*, trans. C. Postan (London, 1977) pp. 1–14.

Dufour, A., 'Le mythe de Genève au temps de Calvin', *Schweizerische Zeitschrift für Geschichte*, new ser., vol. 9 (1959), pp. 489–518.

Dunn, R. M., 'The London Weavers' Riot of 1675', *Guildhall Studies*, vol. 1, no. 1 (1973), pp. 13–23.

Duplessis, R. C. and Howell, M. C., 'Reconsidering the Early Modern Economy: The Cases of Leyden and Lille', *PP*, no. 94 (1982), pp. 49–84.

Ehrenberg, R., *Capital and Finance in the Age of the Renaissance: A Study of the Fuggers and their Connections*, trans. H. M. Lucas (London, 1928).

Elliott, J. H., *Imperial Spain, 1469–1716* (London, 1970).

—— 'Revolution and Continuity in Early Modern Europe', in G. Parker and L. M. Smith (eds.), *The General Crisis of the 17th Century* (London, 1978), pp. 110–33.

Elton, G. R., 'The Rule of Law in 16th-century England', in his *Studies in Tudor and Stuart Politics and Government*, 3 vols. (Cambridge, 1974–83), vol. 1, pp. 260–85.

—— 'An Early Tudor Poor Law', in the same collection, vol. 2, pp. 137–54.

Evenett, H. O., *The Spirit of the Counter-Reformation*, ed. with a postscript by J. Bossy (Notre Dame, Ind., 1970).

Fano, N., 'Ricerche sull'arte della lana a Venezia nei sec. 13 e 14', *AV*, vol. 18 (1936), pp. 73–213.

Fasoli, G., 'Le compagnie delle arti a Bologna fino al sec. 15', *L'Archiginnasio*, vol. 30 (1935), pp. 237–80, vol. 31 (1936), pp. 56–80.

—— '"Comune Veneciarum"', in *Venezia dalla prima crocciata alla conquista di Costantinopoli* (Florence, 1958), pp. 71–102.

—— 'Venezia: nascita di un mito', in *Studi storici in onore di Gioacchino Volpe*, 2 vols. (Florence, 1958), vol. 1, pp. 445–79.

—— 'La "Chronique des Veniciens" de Martin da Canale', *Studi Medievali*, ser. 3, vol. 2, fasc. i (1961), pp. 42–74.

—— 'Gouvernants et gouvernés dans les communes italiennes du 11e au 13e siècle', *Recueils de la Société Jean Bodin*, vol. 25 (1965), pp. 47–86.

Favaro, E., *L'arte dei pittori in Venezia e i suoi statuti* (Florence, 1975).

Fink, Z. S., *The Classical Republicans: An Essay in the Recovery of a Pattern of Thought in 17th-century England* (Evanston, Ill., 1945).

Finlay, R., *Population and Metropolis: The Demography of London, 1580–1650* (Cambridge, 1981).

Finlay, R. G., *Politics in Renaissance Venice* (London, 1980).

Fisher, F. J., 'The Development of London as a Centre of Conspicuous Consumption in the 16th and 17th Centuries', in I. R. Christie (ed.), *Essays in Modern History* (London, 1968), pp. 75–90.

—— 'The Growth of London', in E. W. Ives (ed.), *The English Revolution, 1600–1660* (London, 1968), pp. 76–86.

—— 'London as an "Engine of Economic Growth"', in Clark (ed.), *The Early Modern Town*, pp. 205–15.

Fiumi, E., 'Fioritura e decadenza dell'economia fiorentina', *ASI*, no. 115, vol. 4 (1957), pp. 385–439.

Forsellini, M., 'L'organizzazione economica dell'Arsenale di Venezia nella prima metà del '600', *AV*, ser. 5, vol. 7 (1930), pp. 54–117.

Fourquin, G., *The Anatomy of Popular Rebellion in the Late Middle Ages*, trans. A. Chesters (Amsterdam, 1979).

Friedrichs, C., 'Capitalism, Mobility and Class Formation in the Early Modern German City', in P. Abrams and E. L. Wrigley (eds.), *Towns and Societies: Essays in Economic History and Historical Sociology* (Cambridge, 1978), pp. 187–213.

—— *Urban Society in an Age of War: Nördlingen, 1580–1720* (Princeton, N.J., 1979).

Gaeta, F., 'Alcune considerazioni sul mito di Venezia', *Bibliothèque d'Humanisme et Renaissance*, vol. 23 (1961), pp. 58–76.

—— 'La naissance de l'état moderne en Italie: Milan ou Venise?', in *17e Colloque International de Tours: théorie et pratique politiques à la Renaissance* (Paris, 1977), pp. 459–70.

Gallo, R., 'La Scuola Grande di San Teodoro di Venezia', *Atti dell'Istituto Veneto di Scienze, Lettere ed Arti*, vol. 120 (*Classe di Scienze Morali e Lettere*) (1961–62), pp. 461–95.

Galpern, A. N., *The Religions of the People in 16th-century Champagne* (Cambridge, Mass., 1977).

Gascon, R., *Grand commerce et vie urbaine au 16e siècle: Lyon et ses marchands, 1520–1580*, 2 vols. (Paris, 1971).

—— 'Economie et pauvreté au 16e et 17e siècles: Lyon, ville exemplaire et prophétique', in Mollat (ed.), *Etudes*, vol. 2, pp. 747–60.

Gerbet, M.-C., 'Les confrèries réligieuses à Caceres de 1467 a 1523', *Mélanges de la Casa de Velasquez*, vol. 7 (1971), pp. 75–113.

Geremek, B., *Salariati e artigiani nella Parigi medievale*, trans. G. Pinto (Florence, 1975).

Gibbons, B., *Jacobean City Comedy* (London, 1968).

Gilbert, F., 'Venice in the Crisis of the League of Cambrai', in Hale (ed.), *Renaissance Venice*, pp. 274–93.

Ginzburg, C. *The Cheese and the Worms: The Cosmos of a 16th-century Miller*, trans. J. and A. Tedeschi (London, 1980).

Goldthwaite, R. A., *Private Wealth in Renaissance Florence: A Study of Four Families* (Princeton, N.J., 1968).

—— *The Building of Renaissance Florence: An Economic and Social History* (Baltimore, Md., 1981).

Gombrich, E. H., 'Venetian Celebrations for the Holy League and the Battle of Lepanto', in *Essays in Renaissance and Baroque Art Presented to Anthony Blunt* (London, 1967), pp. 62–8.

—— *In Search of Cultural History* (Oxford, 1969).

Goubert, P., *The Ancien Regime: French Society 1600–1750*, trans. S. Cox (London, 1969).

Gramigna, S. and Perissa, A., *Scuole di arti mestieri e devozione a Venezia* (Venice, 1981).

Grendi, E., 'Morfologia e dinamica della vita associativa urbana. Le confraternite a Genova fra i sec. 16 e 18', *Atti della Società Ligure di Storia Patria*, new ser. no. 5 (1965), pp. 241–311.

Grendler, P. F., *Critics of the Italian World, 1530–1560* (Madison, Wis., 1969).

—— 'Francesco Sansovino and Italian Popular History, 1560–1600', *Studies in the Renaissance*, no. 16 (1969), pp. 139–80.

—— 'The Roman Inquisition and the Venetian Press, 1540–1605', *Journal of Modern History*, vol. 47, no. 1 (1975), pp. 48–65.

—— *The Roman Inquisition and the Venetian Press, 1540–1605* (Princeton, N.J., 1977).

Guilmartin, J. F., *Gunpowder and Galleys: Changing Technology and Mediterranean Warfare at Sea in the 16th Century* (Cambridge, 1974).

Gukowski, M. A., 'Chi fu a capo della sommossa dei Ciompi?', in *Studi in onore di Armando Sapori*, 2 vols. (Milan, 1957), vol. 1, pp. 707–14.

Gurr, A., *The Shakespearean Stage, 1574–1642* (2nd edn., Cambridge, 1980).

Hale, J. R., *Renaissance Europe, 1480–1520* (London, 1971)

—— 'From Peacetime Establishment to Fighting Machine: The Venetian Army and the War of Cyprus and Lepanto', in *Il Mediterraneo nella seconda metà del '500 alla luce di Lepanto* (Florence, 1974), pp. 163–84.
—— 'Men and Weapons: The Fighting Potential of 16th-century Venetian Galleys', *War and Society*, vol. 1 (1975), pp. 1–23.
—— *Florence and the Medici: The Pattern of Control* (London, 1977).
—— *War and Society in Renaissance Europe, 1450–1620* (London, 1985).
—— (ed.), *Renaissance Venice* (London, 1974).
Haley, K. H. D., *The Dutch in the 17th Century* (London, 1972).
Haliczer, S., *The Comuneros of Castile. The Forging of a Revolution, 1475–1521* (Madison, Wis., 1981).
Hanning, B. R., '"Glorious Apollo": Poetic and Political Themes in the First Opera', *Renaissance Quarterly*, vol. 32, no. 4 (1979), pp. 485–513.
Hatfield, R., 'The Compagnia dei Magi', *JWCI*, vol. 33 (1970), pp. 107–62.
Hay, D., *The Italian Renaissance in its Historical Background* (Cambridge, 1970).
Heers, J., *Gênes au 15e siècle* (Paris, 1961).
—— 'Les métiers et les fêtes mediévales en France du nord et en Angleterre', *Revue du Nord*, vol. 55, no. 218 (1973), pp. 193–206.
Heinemann, M., *Puritanism and Theatre: Thomas Middleton and Opposition Drama under the Early Stuarts* (Cambridge, 1980).
Heller, H., 'Famine, Revolt and Heresy at Meaux, 1521–5', *Archiv für Reformationsgeschichte*, no. 68 (1977), pp. 135–50.
Henderson, J., 'The Flagellant Movement and Flagellant Confraternities in Central Italy, 1260–1400', *Studies in Church History*, vol. 15 (1978), pp. 147–60.
—— 'Piety and Charity in Late Medieval Florence: Religious Confraternities from the Middle of the 13th Century to the late 15th Century', unpublished PhD thesis (Westfield College, University of London, 1983).
Herlihy, D., 'The Population of Verona in the First Century of Venetian Rule', in Hale (ed.), *Renaissance Venice*, pp. 91–120.
Hexter, J. H., '"Il principe" and "lo stato"', *Studies in the Renaissance*, vol. 4 (1957), pp. 113–38.
Hibbert, A. B., 'The Towns', in *CEH*, vol. 3, pp. 158–228.
Hill, C., *Society and Puritanism in Pre-Revolutionary England* (London, 1969).
—— *Reformation to Industrial Revolution* (Pelican Economic History of Britain, vol. 2, 1530–1780, London, 1969).
Hills, P., 'Piety and Patronage in '500 Venice: Tintoretto and the Scuole del Sacramento', *Art History*, vol. 6, no. 1 (1983), pp. 30–43.
Hoshino, H., *L'arte della lana in Firenze del basso medioevo: il commercio della lana e il mercato dei panni fiorentini nei sec.13–15* (Florence, 1980).
Huizinga, J. *The Waning of the Middle Ages*, trans. F. Hopman (London, 1972).
Humfrey, P. and Mackenney, R. S., 'The Venetian Trade Guilds as Patrons of Art in the Renaissance', *The Burlington Magazine*, no. 998, vol. 128 (1986), pp. 317–30.
Jeannin, P., *Les marchands au 16e siècle* (Paris, 1957).

Jones, P. J., 'Economia e società nell'Italia medievale: la leggenda della borghesia', in *Storia d'Italia, Annali 1: dal feudalesimo al capitalismo* (Turin, 1978), pp. 185–372.

Jordan, W. K., *The Charities of London, 1480–1660* (London, 1960).

Kamen, H., *The Iron Century: Social Change in Europe, 1550–1660* (London, 1971).

Kedar, B. Z., *Merchants in Crisis: Genoese and Venetian Men of Affairs and the 14th-century Depression* (New Haven, Ct., 1976).

Kellenbenz, H., 'The Organisation of Production', in *CEH*, vol. 5, pp. 462–548.

Kent, F. W., *Household and Lineage in Renaissance Florence: The Family Life of the Capponi, Ginoti and Ruccellai* (Princeton, N.J., 1977).

Kiernan, V. G. *State and Society in Europe, 1550–1650* (Oxford, 1980).

Knights, L. C., *Drama and Society in the Age of Jonson* (London, 1937).

Koenigsberger, H. G., *Estates and Revolutions: Essays in Early Modern European History* (London, 1971).

—— 'Republics and Courts in Italian and European Culture in the 16th and 17th Centuries', *PP*, no. 83 (1979), pp. 32–56.

Landini, P., *Istoria dell'oratorio e della venerabile arci-confraternita di Santa Maria della Misericordia della città di Firenze* (Florence, 1843).

Lane, F. C., *Venetian Ships and Shipbuilders of the Renaissance* (Baltimore, Md., 1934).

—— *Andrea Barbarigo, Merchant of Venice, 1418–1449* (Baltimore, Md., 1944).

—— *Venice and History: The Collected Papers of Frederic C. Lane* (Baltimore, Md., 1966).

—— Review of Cracco, *Società e stato*, in *Speculum*, vol. 43 (1968), pp. 497–501.

—— 'The Enlargement of the Great Council of Venice', in Rowe and Stockdale (eds.), '*Florilegium Historiale*', pp. 236–74.

—— *Venice: A Maritime Republic* (Baltimore, Md., 1975).

—— 'Wages and Recruitment of Venetian Galeotti, 1470–1580', *SV*, new ser., vol. 6 (1982), pp. 15–43.

—— and Mueller, R. C., *Money and Banking in Medieval and Renaissance Venice*, 2 vols. (Baltimore, Md., 1985–86).

Lang, R. G., 'Social Origins and Social Aspirations of Jacobean London Merchants', *EcHR*, 2 ser., vol. 27, no. 1 (1974), pp. 28– 47.

Larmour, R., 'A Merchant Guild of 16th-century France: The Grocers of Paris', *EcHR*, 2 ser., vol. 20, no. 3 (1967), pp. 467–81.

Larner, J., *Italy in the Age of Dante and Petrarch, 1216–1380* (London, 1980).

Lea, H. C., *The Inquisition in the Spanish Dependencies* (London, 1908).

Le Bras, G., 'Les confrèries chrétiennes. Problèmes et propositions', *Revue Historique du Droit Français et Etranger*, ser. 4, vols. 19–20 (1940–41), pp. 310–63.

Leclère, F., 'Recherches sur la charité des bourgeois envers les pauvres au 14e siècle à Douai', *Revue du Nord*, vol. 48, no. 189 (1966), pp. 139–54.

Leff, G., *The Dissolution of the Medieval Outlook* (New York, 1976).

Lerner, R. E., *The Age of Adversity: The 14th Century* (New York, 1968).

Le Roy Ladurie, E., *The Peasants of Languedoc*, trans. J.Day (Urbana, Ill., 1974).

—— *Le carnaval de Romans* (Paris, 1979).

—— *Montaillou: Cathars and Catholics in a French Village, 1294–1324*, trans. B. Bray (London, 1980).

Lestocquoy, G., *Les villes de Flandre et d'Italie: aux origines de la bourgeoisie* (Paris, 1952).

Little, L. K., *Religious Poverty and the Profit Economy in Medieval Europe* (London, 1978).

Logan, O. M. T., *Culture and Society in Venice, 1470–1790* (London, 1972).

Lopez, R. S., *Studi sull'economia genovese nel medio evo* (Turin, 1936).

—— 'Italian Leadership in the Medieval Business World', *Journal of Economic History*, vol. 8, no. 1 (1948), pp. 63–8.

—— 'Venice and Genoa: Two Styles, One Success', *Diogenes*, no. 71(1970), pp. 39–47.

Lorenzetti, G., *Venice and its Lagoon*, trans. J. Guthrie (Trieste, 1961).

Lowry, M. J. C., *The World of Aldus Manutius: Business and Scholarship in Renaissance Venice* (Oxford, 1979).

Luzzatto, G., *Studi di storia economica veneziana* (Padua, 1954).

—— *Storia economica di Venezia dal 11 al 16 secolo* (Venice, 1961).

MacKay, A. I. K., 'Ciudad y campo en la Europa medieval', *Studia Historica*, vol. 2, no. 2 (1984), pp. 27–53.

Mackenney, R. S., 'Arti e stato a Venezia tra tardo medio evo e '600', *SV*, new ser., vol. 5 (1981), pp. 127–43.

Mallett, M. E. and Hale, J. R., *The Military Organisation of a Renaissance State: Venice, c.1400–1617* (Cambridge, 1984).

Manselli, R., 'L'anno 1260 fu anno gioachimitico?' in the volume *Movimento dei disciplinati*, pp. 99–108.

Martin, J., 'In God's Image: Artisans and Heretics in Counter- Reformation Venice', unpublished PhD thesis (Harvard University, 1982).

Martin, J. R., *The Decorations for the Pompa Introitus Ferdinandi* (Corpus Rubenianum Ludwig Burchard 16, London, 1972).

Martin, R., 'Witchcraft and the Inquisition in Venice, 1550–1650', unpublished PhD thesis (University of Manchester, 1986).

Martines, L., 'The Gentleman in Renaissance Italy: Strains of Isolation in the Body Politic', in R. S. Kinsman (ed.), *The Darker Vision of the Renaissance: Beyond the Fields of Reason* (Berkeley and Los Angeles, 1974), pp. 77–94.

—— *Power and Imagination: City-States in Renaissance Italy* (New York, 1980).

—— (ed.), *Violence and Civil Disorder in Italian Cities, 1200–1500* (Berkeley and Los Angeles, 1972).

Martz, L., *Poverty and Welfare in Habsburg Spain: The Example of Toledo* (Cambridge, 1983).

Mazzaoui, M. F., *The Italian Cotton Industry in the Late Middle Ages, 1100–1600* (Cambridge, 1981).

Meersseman, G.–G., 'La riforma delle confraternite laicali in Italia prima del Concilio di Trento', in *Problemi di vita religiosa in Italia nel '500* (Padua, 1960), pp. 17–29.

—— *Dossier de l'ordre de la pénitence* (Fribourg, 1961).

Meiss, M., *Painting in Florence and Siena after the Black Death* (Princeton, N.J., 1978).

Miskimin, H. A., *The Economy of Early Renaissance Europe, 1300–1460* (Cambridge, 1975).
—— *The Economy of Later Renaissance Europe, 1460–1600* (Cambridge, 1977).
Mollat, M., *Les pauvres au moyen age* (Paris, 1978).
—— (ed.), *Etudes sur l'histoire de la pauvreté*, 2 vols. (Paris, 1974).
—— and Wolff, Ph., *The Popular Revolutions of the Late Middle Ages*, trans. A. L. Lytton-Sells (London, 1973).
Molmenti, P., *Venice: Its Individual Growth from the Earliest Times to the Fall of the Republic*, trans. H. F. Brown, 3 vols. in 6 (London, 1906–08).
Mols, R., 'Population in Europe, 1500–1700', in C. M. Cipolla (ed.), *The Fontana Economic History of Europe vol. 2: The 16th and 17th Centuries* (London, 1974), pp. 15–82.
Monter, E. W., *Calvin's Geneva* (New York, 1967).
—— *Ritual, Myth and Magic in Early Modern Europe* (Brighton, 1983).
Monti, G. M., *Le corporazioni nell'evo antico e nell'alto medio evo* (Bari, 1934).
Monticolo, G., *L'ufficio della Giustizia Vecchia à Venezia* (Venice, 1892).
Mousnier, R., 'Le trafic des offices à Venise', *Revue Historique du Droit Français et Etranger*, ser. 4, vol. 30 (1952), pp. 552–66.
—— 'The Exponents and Critics of Absolutism', in *NCMH*, vol. 5, pp. 104–31.
Movimento dei disciplinati nel settimo centenario dal suo inizio (Perugia-1260), *Appendice* 9 to *Bolletino della Deputazione di Storia Patria per l'Umbria* (Spoleto, 1962).
Mueller, R. C., 'Charitable Institutions, the Jewish Community and Venetian Society: A Discussion of the Recent Volume by Brian Pullan', *SV*, vol. 14 (1972), pp. 38–78.
Muir, E., 'The Ritual of Rulership in 16th-century Venice: A Study in the Construction of Myth and Ideology', unpublished PhD thesis (Rutgers University, N.J., 1975).
—— *Civic Ritual in Renaissance Venice* (Princeton, N.J., 1981).
Mundy, J. H., *Liberty and Political Power in Toulouse, 1050–1230* (New York, 1954).
Nagler, A. M., *Theatre Festivals of the Medici* (New Haven, Ct., 1964).
Najemy, J. M., *Corporatism and Consensus in Florentine Electoral Politics, 1280–1400* (Chapel Hill, N. C., 1982).
Newett, M. M., 'The Sumptuary Laws of Venice', in T. F. Tout and J. Tait (eds.), *Historical Essays* (Manchester, 1907), pp. 246–77.
Nicholas, D. M., *Town and Countryside: Social, Economic and Political Tensions in 14th-century Flanders* (Bruges, 1971).
Noonan, J. T., *The Scholastic Analysis of Usury* (Cambridge, Mass., 1957).
O'Neill, J. D., 'Alms and Almsgiving', in *The Catholic Encyclopedia*, 15 vols. (London, 1907–12), vol. 1, Aachen- Assize, pp. 328–30.
Orgel, S., *The Illusion of Power: Political Theater in the English Renaissance* (Berkeley and Los Angeles, 1975).
Origo, I., *The Merchant of Prato* (London, 1963).
—— *The World of San Bernardino* (London, 1963).
Ottokar, N., *Il comune di Firenze alla fine del '200* (Florence, 1962).
Panofsky, E., *The Life and Art of Albrecht Dürer* (Princeton, N.J., 1971).

Papadopoli-Aldobrandini, N., *Le monete di Venezia*, 4 vols. (Venice, 1883–1919).
Parker, G., 'The "Military Revolution", 1560–1660: A Myth?', in his *Spain and the Netherlands, 1559–1659: Ten Studies* (London, 1979), pp. 86–105.
—— 'Lepanto (1571): The Costs of Victory', in the same volume, pp. 122–34.
—— *Europe in Crisis, 1598–1648* (London, 1979).
Partner, P., *Renaissance Rome, 1500–1559: A Portrait of a Society* (Berkeley and Los Angeles, 1976).
Perkinson, R. H., '*Volpone* and the Reputation of Venetian Justice', *Modern Language Review*, vol. 35, no. 1 (1940), pp. 11–18.
Perocco, G. and Salvadori, A., *Civiltà di Venezia*, 3 vols. (Venice, n.d.).
Pertusi, A., '"Quaedam Regalia Insignia"', *SV*, vol. 7 (1965), pp. 3–123.
Phythian-Adams, C., 'Ceremony and the Citizen: Coventry, 1450–1550', in Clark (ed.), *The Early Modern Town*, pp. 106–28.
Pike, R., *Aristocrats and Traders: Sevillian Society in the 16th Century* (London, 1972).
Pirenne, H., *Economic and Social History of Medieval Europe*, trans. I. E. Clegg (London, 1936).
—— *Early Democracies in the Low Countries: Urban Society and Political Conflict in the Middle Ages and the Renaissance*, trans. J. V. Sanders, intro. by J. H. Mundy (New York, 1963).
Pozza, M., *I Badoer: una famiglia veneziana dal 10 al 13 secolo* (Padua, 1982).
Preto, P., *Peste e società a Venezia, 1576* (Vicenza, 1978).
Prodi, P., 'The Application of the Tridentine Decrees: The Organisation of the Diocese of Bologna during the Episcopate of Cardinal Gabriele Paleotti', in Cochrane (ed.), *Late Italian Renaissance*, pp. 226–43.
—— 'The Structure and Organisation of the Church in Renaissance Venice: Suggestions for Research', in Hale (ed.) *Renaissance Venice*, pp. 409–30.
Pullan, B. S., 'Poverty, Charity and Reason of State: Some Venetian Examples', *SV*, vol. 2 (1960), pp. 17–60.
—— 'The Famine in Venice and the New Poor Law, 1527–9', *SV*, vols. 5–6 (1963–64), pp. 141–202.
—— 'Service to the Venetian State: Aspects of Myth and Reality in the Early 17th Century', *Studi Seicenteschi*, vol. 5 (1964), pp. 110–47.
—— 'Wage-Earners and the Venetian Economy, 1550–1630', in idem (ed.), *Crisis and Change*, pp. 146–74.
—— Review of Cracco, *Società e Stato*, in *Rivista Storica Italiana*, no. 81 (1969), pp. 182–7.
—— *Rich and Poor in Renaissance Venice: The Social Institutions of a Catholic State* (Oxford, 1971).
—— 'Le Scuole Grandi e la loro opera nel quadro della Controriforma', *SV*, vol. 14 (1972), pp. 83–109.
—— *A History of Early Renaissance Italy from the mid-13th to the mid-15th Century* (London, 1973).
—— 'The Significance of Venice', *Bulletin of the John Rylands University Library of Manchester*, vol. 56 (1974), pp. 443–62.

—— 'Catholics and the Poor in Early Modern Europe', *TRHS*, ser. 5, vol. 26 (1976), pp. 15–34.
—— Review of Rapp, *Industry*, *EcHR*, 2 ser., vol. 30, no. 1 (1977), pp. 207–8.
—— 'Poveri, mendicanti e vagabondi, sec. 14–17', in *Storia d'Italia, Annali 1: dal feudalesimo al capitalismo* (Turin, 1978), pp. 981–1047.
—— 'Natura e carattere delle Scuole', in T. Pignatti (ed.), *Le Scuole di Venezia* (Milan, 1981), pp. 9–26.
—— *The Jews of Europe and the Inquisition of Venice, 1550–1670* (Oxford, 1983).
—— 'The Roles of the State and the Town in the General Crisis of the 1590s', in Clark (ed.), *The European Crisis of the 1590s*, pp. 285–300.
—— (ed.), *Crisis and Change in the Venetian Economy* (London, 1968).
Queller, D., 'The Civic Irresponsibility of the Venetian Nobility', *Explorations in Economic History*, vol. 7 (1969–70), pp. 223–35.
Ramsay, G. D., 'Industrial Discontent in Early Elizabethan London: Clothworkers and Merchants Adventurer in Conflict', *London Journal*, vol. 1, no. 2 (1975), pp. 227–39.
—— 'The Recruitment and Fortunes of some London Freemen in the mid-16th Century', *EcHR*, 2 ser., vol. 31, no. 4 (1978), pp. 526–40.
Rapp, R. T., *Industry and Economic Decline in 17th-century Venice* (Cambridge, Mass., 1976).
—— 'Real Estate and Rational Investment in Early Modern Venice', *Journal of European Economic History*, vol. 8, no. 2 (1979), pp. 269–91.
Renier Michiel, G., *Le feste veneziane*, 6 vols. in 3 (Milan, 1829).
Renouard, Y., 'Mercati e mercanti veneziani alla fine del '200', in *La civiltà di Venezia del secolo di Marco Polo* (Florence, 1957), pp. 83–109.
Rodolico, N. 'The Struggle for the Right of Association in 14th-century Florence', *History*, vol. 7 (1922–23), pp. 178–90.
—— *Dal comune alla signoria* (Bologna, 1934).
—— *I Ciompi* (Florence, 1945).
—— *Il popolo minuto: note di storia fiorentina 1343–78* (Florence, 1968).
Romano, D., 'Charity and Community in Early Renaissance Venice', *Journal of Urban History*, vol. 11, no. 1 (1984), pp. 63–82.
Romano, R., 'Economic Aspects of the Construction of Warships in Venice in the 16th Century', in Pullan (ed.), *Crisis and Change*, pp. 59– 98.
—— 'Il mercante italiano tra medio evo e rinascimento', in his collected essays, *Tra due crisi: l'Italia del rinascimento* (Turin, 1971), pp. 85–100.
Rosand, E., 'Music in the Myth of Venice', *Renaissance Quarterly*, vol. 30, no. 4 (1977), pp. 511–37.
Rossi, V., 'Jacopo d'Albizzotto Guidi e il suo inedito poema su Venezia', *NAV*, vol. 5 (1893), pp. 397–451.
Rowe, J. G. and Stockdale, W. H. (eds.), *'Florilegium Historiale': Essays Presented to Wallace K. Ferguson* (Toronto, 1971).
Rubinstein, N., 'Notes on the Word "Stato" in Florence before Machiavelli', in Rowe and Stockdale (eds.), *'Florilegium Historiale'*, pp. 313–27.

—— (ed.), *Florentine Studies: Politics and Society in Renaissance Florence* (London, 1968).

Ruddock, A. A., 'London Capitalists and the Decline of Southampton in the Early Tudor Period', *EcHR*, 2 ser., vol. 2, no. 1 (1949), pp. 137–51.

Ruggiero, G., *Violence in Early Renaissance Venice* (New Brunswick, N.J., 1980).

Rutenberg, V. I., 'La vie et la lutte des Ciompi de Sienne', *Annales*, vol. 20, no. 1 (1965), pp. 95–109.

—— *Popolo e movimenti popolari nell'Italia del '300 e '400*, trans. G. Borchini (Bologna, 1971).

—— 'Arti e corporazioni', in *Storia d'Italia, vol. 5: Documenti* (Turin, 1973), pp. 615–42.

Ryan, J. A., 'Charity and Charities', in *The Catholic Encyclopedia*, 15 vols. (London, 1907–12), vol. 3, Brow-Clancy, pp. 592–604.

Sagredo, A., *Sulle consorterie delle arti edificative* (Venice, 1856).

Salvemini, G., *Magnati e popolani in Firenze dal 1280 al 1295* (1899, reissued, ed. E. Sestan, Milan, 1966).

Sapori, A., *La crisi delle compagnie mercantili dei Bardi e dei Peruzzi* (Florence, 1926).

—— *Una compagnia di calimala ai primi del '300* (Florence, 1932).

—— *The Italian Merchant in the Middle Ages*, trans. P. A. Kennen (New York, 1970).

Sbriziolo, L., 'Per la stoira delle confraternite veneziane: dalle deliberazioni miste (1310–1476) del Consiglio dei Dieci: Scolae comunes, artigiane e nazionali', *Atti dell'Istituto Veneto di Scienze, Lettere ed Arti*, vol. 126 (*Classe di Scienze Morali e Lettere*) (1967–68), pp. 405–42.

—— 'Per la storia delle confraternite veneziane: dalle deliberazioni miste del Consiglio dei Dieci. Le Scuole dei Battuti', *Miscellanea G.-G. Meersseman*, vol. 2 (Padua, 1970), pp. 715–63.

Schoenbaum, S., *Shakespeare: A Documentary Life* (Oxford, 1975).

Schultheiss, W., 'Der Vertrag der nürnberger Händelsgesellschaft: Bartholomäus Viatis und Martin Peller von 1609 bis 1615', *Scripta Mercaturae*, (1968), part i, pp. 1–20.

Scribner, R. W., 'Civic Unity and the Reformation in Erfurt', *PP*, no. 66 (1975), pp. 29–60.

—— 'Why was there no Reformation in Cologne?', *Bulletin of the Institute of Historical Research*, vol. 49, no. 120 (1976), pp. 217–41.

Sella, D., *Commerci e industrie a Venezia nel sec. 17* (Venice, 1961).

—— 'The Rise and Decline of the Venetian Woollen Industry', in Pullan (ed.), *Crisis and Change*, pp. 88–105.

—— 'The Iron Industry in Italy, 1500–1650', in H. Kellenbenz (ed.), *Schwerpunkte der Eisengewinnung und Eisenverarbeitung in Europa, 1500–1650* (Cologne and Vienna, 1974), pp. 91–105.

—— *Crisis and Continuity: The Economy of Spanish Lombardy in the 17th Century* (Cambridge, Mass., 1979).

Sheedy, A. T., *Bartolus on Social Conditions of the 14th Century* (New York, 1942).

Shennan, J. H., *The Origins of the Modern European State, 1450–1725* (London, 1974).

Simonsfeld, H., *Der Fondaco dei Tedeschi in Venedig*, 2 vols. in 1 (Stuttgart, 1887).

Smith, S. R., 'The Social and Geographical Origins of the London Apprentices, 1630–60', *Guildhall Miscellany*, vol. 4, no. 4 (1973), pp. 195–206.

—— 'Almost Revolutionaries: The London Apprentices during the Civil Wars', *Huntington Library Quarterly*, vol. 42, no. 4 (1979), pp. 313–28.

Stahl, B., *Adel und Volk im Florentiner Dugento* (Cologne, 1965).

Stella, A., 'La crisi economica veneziana della seconda metà del sec.16', *AV*, vol. 58 (1956), pp. 17–69.

Stephens, J. N., 'Heresy in Medieval and Renaissance Florence', *PP*, no. 54 (1972), pp. 25–60.

—— *The Fall of the Florentine Republic, 1512–30* (Oxford, 1983).

Strauss, G., 'Success and Failure in the German Reformation', *PP*, no. 67 (1975), pp. 30–63.

—— *Nuremberg in the 16th Century: City Politics and Life between Middle Ages and Modern Times* (Bloomington, Ind., 1976).

Strayer, J. R., *On the Medieval Origins of the Modern State* (Princeton, N.J., 1970).

Strong, R., *The Cult of Elizabeth* (London, 1977).

Sutherland, N. M., 'Parisian Life in the 16th Century', in W. L. Gundersheimer (ed.), *French Humanism, 1470–1600* (London, 1969), pp. 51–64.

Tabarrini, M. 'Le consorterie nella storia fiorentina del medio evo', in *La vita italiana nel '300* (Milan, 1912), pp. 98–127.

Tacchi-Ventura, P., *Storia della Compagnia di Jesù in Italia*, 2 vols. in 4, (Rome, 1950–51).

Tagliaferri, A., *Struttura e politica sociale in una communità véneta del '500 (Udine)* (Milan, 1969).

Tassini, G., *Feste, spettacoli, divertimenti e piaceri degli antichi veneziani* (Venice, 1890).

Tawney, R. H., *Religion and the Rise of Capitalism* (London, 1938).

Tenenti, A., *Naufrages, corsaires et assurances maritimes à Venise, 1592–1609* (Paris, 1959).

—— *Cristoforo da Canal: la marine vénitienne avant Lépante* (Paris, 1962).

—— *Piracy and the Decline of Venice, 1580–1615*, trans. B. and J. Pullan (London, 1967).

Thomas, K. 'Work and Leisure in Pre-industrial Society', *PP*, no. 29 (1964), pp. 50–66.

Thrupp, S., *The Merchant Class of Medieval London* (Chicago, Ill., 1948).

—— 'The Guilds', in *CEH*, vol. 3, pp. 230–81.

Tierney, B., *Medieval Poor Law: A Sketch of Canonical Theory and its Application in England* (Berkeley and Los Angeles, 1959).

Tramontin, S., 'Lo spirito e le attività, gli sviluppi dell' Oratorio del Divino Amore nella Venezia del '500', *SV*, vol. 14 (1972), pp. 111–36.

—— 'La visita apostolica del 1581 a Venezia', *SV*, vol. 9 (1967), pp. 453–533.

Trevor-Roper, H. R., *Religion, the Reformation and Social Change* (London, 1972).

—— *Princes and Artists: Painting and Ideology at Four Habsburg Courts, 1517–1633* (New York, 1974).

Trexler, R. C., 'Charity and the Defense of Urban Elites in the Italian Communes', in F. C. Jaher (ed.), *The Rich, the Well-born and the Powerful: Elites and Upper Classes in History* (Urbana, Ill., 1973), pp. 64–105.

—— *Public Life in Renaissance Florence* (New York, 1980).

Trinkhaus, C., and Oberman, H. A. (eds.), *The Pursuit of Holiness in Late Medieval and Renaissance Religion* (Leyden, 1974).

Tucci, U., 'The Psychology of the Venetian Merchant in the 16th Century', in Hale (ed.), *Renaissance Venice*, pp. 346–78.

—— 'Bartolomeo Bontempelli', in *Dizionario Biografico degli Italiani* (Rome, 1960 onwards) vol. 12, Bonfadini-Borrello, pp. 426–7.

—— 'Il patrizio veneziano mercante e umanista', in his collected essays, *Mercanti, navi, monete nel '500 veneziano* (Bologna, 1981), pp. 15–42.

Tuccoo-Chala, P., 'Un exemple d'essor urbain: Pau au 16e siècle', *Annales du Midi*, vol. 78, no. 79 (1966), pp. 345–62.

Unwin, G., *Industrial Organisation in the 16th and 17th Centuries* (Oxford, 1904).

—— *The Gilds and Companies of London* (4th edn., London, 1963).

van der Wee, H., *The Antwerp Market and the European Economy*, 3 vols. (The Hague, 1963).

van Houtte, J. A., 'Anvers au 15e et 16e siècles: expansion et apogée', *Annales*, vol. 16, no. 2 (1961), pp. 248–78.

—— 'Déclin et survivance d'Anvers', in *Studi in onore di Amintore Fanfani*, 5 vols. (Milan, 1962), vol. 5, pp. 703–26.

Ventura, A., *Nobiltà e popolo nella società veneta del '400 e '500* (Bari, 1964).

von Ranke, L., *The History of the Popes*, trans. E. Foster, 3 vols. (London, 1866).

Waley, D. P., *The Italian City-Republics* (London, 1969).

Weil, M. S., 'The Devotion of the Forty Hours and Roman Baroque Illusions', *JWCI*, vol. 37 (1974), pp. 218–49.

Weissman, R. F. E., *Ritual Brotherhood in Renaissance Florence, 1200–1600* (New York, 1982).

Westlake, H. F., *The Parish Gilds of Medieval England* (London, 1919).

Williams, G. A., *Medieval London: From Commune to Capital* (London, 1963).

Wilson, C. H., *England's Apprenticeship, 1603–1763* (London, 1965).

—— *The Dutch Republic* (London, 1968).

—— 'Taxation and the Decline of Empires, an Unfashionable Theme', in his *Economic History and the Historian: Collected Essays* (London, 1969), pp. 114–27.

—— *The Transformation of Europe, 1558–1648* (London, 1976).

Wirobisz, A., 'L'attività edilizia a Venezia', *SV*, vol. 7 (1965), pp. 307–43.

Wolff, Ph., *Commerces et marchands de Toulouse, vers 1350–vers 1450* (Paris, 1954).

Woolf, S. J., 'The Problem of Representation in the Post-Renaissance Venetian State', in *Liber Memorialis Antonio Era. Studies Presented to the International Commission for the History of Representative and Parliamentary Institutions*, 26 (UNESCO, Cagliari and Brussels, 1961 and 1963), pp. 65–82.

—— 'Venice and the Terraferma', in Pullan (ed.), *Crisis and Change*, pp. 175–203.

Wootton, D., *Paolo Sarpi: Between Renaissance and Enlightenment* (Cambridge, 1983).

Yates, F. A., *Astraea: The Imperial Theme in the 16th Century* (London, 1975).

Yriarte, C., *La vie d'un patricien de Venise au 16e siècle* (Paris, 1874).

Zagorin, P., *Rebels and Rulers, 1500–1660*, 2 vols. (Cambridge, 1982).

Zampetti, P., *A Dictionary of Venetian Painters*, 3 vols. (Leigh-on-Sea, 1969).

Zanoni, L., *Gli umiliati nei loro rapporti con l'eresia: l'industria della lana ed i comuni nei sec. 12 e 13 sulla scorta di documenti inediti* (Milan, 1911).

Index